# Myanmar
## Transformed?

**ISEAS** YUSOF ISHAK INSTITUTE

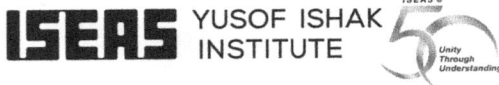

The **ISEAS – Yusof Ishak Institute** (formerly Institute of Southeast Asian Studies) is an autonomous organization established in 1968. It is a regional centre dedicated to the study of socio-political, security, and economic trends and developments in Southeast Asia and its wider geostrategic and economic environment. The Institute's research programmes are grouped under Regional Economic Studies (RES), Regional Strategic and Political Studies (RSPS), and Regional Social and Cultural Studies (RSCS). The Institute is also home to the ASEAN Studies Centre (ASC), the Nalanda-Sriwijaya Centre (NSC) and the Singapore APEC Study Centre.

ISEAS Publishing, an established academic press, has issued more than 2,000 books and journals. It is the largest scholarly publisher of research about Southeast Asia from within the region. ISEAS Publishing works with many other academic and trade publishers and distributors to disseminate important research and analyses from and about Southeast Asia to the rest of the world.

Myanmar Update Series

# Myanmar
## Transformed?

*People, Places and Politics*

**EDITED BY**

**JUSTINE CHAMBERS • GERARD MCCARTHY**
**NICHOLAS FARRELLY • CHIT WIN**

**ISEAS** YUSOF ISHAK
INSTITUTE

First published in Singapore in 2018 by
ISEAS Publishing
30 Heng Mui Keng Terrace
Singapore 119614

*E-mail:* publish@iseas.edu.sg
*Website:* http://bookshop.iseas.edu.sg

*The responsibility for facts and opinions in this publication rests exclusively with the authors and their interpretations do not necessarily reflect the views or the policy of the Institute or its supporters.*

---

### ISEAS Library Cataloguing-in-Publication Data

---

Myanmar Transformed? People, Places and Politics / edited by Justine
    Chambers, Gerard McCarthy, Nicholas Farrelly and Chit Win.
Papers originally presented to the Myanmar Update Conference 2017 held at
    the Australian National University, Canberra, from 17 to 18 February 2017.
    1.     Burma—Politics and government—21st century—Congresses.
    2.     Burma—Social conditions—Congresses.
    3.     Burma—Economic conditions—Congresses.
    I.     Chambers, Justine.
    II.    McCarthy, Gerard.
    III.   Farrelly, Nicholas.
    IV.   Chit Win.
    V.    Australian National University.
    VI.   Myanmar Update Conference (2017 : Canberra, Australia)
DS530.4 B972 2017                 2018

ISBN 978-981-4818-53-7 (soft cover)
ISBN 978-981-4818-54-4 (hard cover)
ISBN 978-981-4818-55-1 (e-book, PDF)

---

*Cover photo:* A candid moment at the opening ceremony of the 21st Century Panglong Conference on 31 August 2016 in Naypyitaw, Myanmar. From left to right: Senior General Min Aung Hlaing, Speaker of the Upper House of Parliament Mahn Win Khaing Than, Vice President Henry Van Thio, State Counsellor Aung San Suu Kyi and President Htin Kyaw.
Photograph by Aung Khant.

Typeset by Maxine McArthur
Printed in Singapore by Markono Print Media Pte Ltd

# CONTENTS

## Part IV Politics

## Part V Epilogue

# LIST OF TABLES

# LIST OF FIGURES

# ACKNOWLEDGEMENTS

The February 2017 Myanmar Update conference at the Australian National University (ANU) brought together academics, researchers and policymakers from Myanmar and abroad for two intensive days of discussion and debate. Commencing with a keynote address by Professor Dr. Aung Tun Thet, Representative of State Counsellor Aung San Suu Kyi, the conference was one of the best attended and thematically expansive conferences of its kind since the Update series began in 1999.

We are immensely grateful for the financial and institutional support the 2017 Myanmar Update conference and this resulting publication received from the Australian National University and its Myanmar Research Centre. The conference convenors, who are also the editors of *Myanmar Transformed?*, are especially thankful for the generous support of the College of Asia and the Pacific and its Department of Political and Social Change, and also to the Australian Government's Department of Foreign Affairs and Trade.

We particularly acknowledge the personal commitment of Professor Michael Wesley, the College Dean, in supporting the ongoing work of our Regional Institutes. The 2017 Update rested heavily on the organising skills of the Regional Institutes team, among whom Samuel Bashfield deserves special mention for his tremendous work. Jean Sum, Olivia Cable and Kerrie Hogan of the Coral Bell School of Asia Pacific Affairs also assisted with crucial logistical and administrative support. Professor Andrew Walker played a key role in the early stages of the conference call for papers, and we acknowledge his efforts. The Menzies Library hosted a superb retrospective about ANU-Myanmar collaboration over the decades, for which we must thank Amy Chan for her enthusiasm and vision.

Thanks are also due to the excellent team at New Mandala, including past and present editors James Giggacher and Liam Gammon as well as associate editor Mish Khan, for helping to promote the conference and podcasting the various panels. James Davies and Amy Doffegnies prepared excellent summaries of the important issues raised at the conference. Special thanks go to the Australian Mon Association for providing hearty and delicious catering throughout the conference, and Yuri Takahashi for running an engaging Burmese language learners session on the afternoon of the first day. The ANU Myanmar Students' Association (ANUMSA) was also instrumental in helping to organise the Burmese language roundtable, supporting the Burmese learners session and coordinating captivating entertainment during the conference dinner. The convenors and editors thank ANUMSA members for their enthusiasm and look forward to the Association's continued flourishing in the years to come.

This edited volume has been a collective effort from start to finish, and has been made possible due to the commitment and cooperation of many people. Special thanks are due to Maxine McArthur, who faithfully and thoughtfully assisted us with copy-editing, indexing and laying out the text of the manuscript. We are grateful for the steadfast backing we have received from the Department of Political and Social Change in providing the staff and resources necessary to ensure the book's high production standards. We also acknowledge the many anonymous colleagues who offered thoughtful and generous reviews of papers. Your support was invaluable in challenging and extending our authors, and the quality of their analysis is testament to your professionalism.

We also thank our contributors who devoted their time and energy to their chapters, especially our Myanmar contributors for whom the publication process was in many cases an entirely new experience. We are delighted that more than half of the chapters in this volume are authored or co-authored by Myanmar scholars and researchers, the largest number of any Myanmar Update publication. Your patience, efforts and collegiality throughout the publication process have alone made this project worthwhile.

Last but not least, we acknowledge Ng Nok Kiong and Rahilah Yusuf at the ISEAS – Yusof Ishak Institute in Singapore for their ongoing support and faith in the Myanmar Update publication series. We look forward to working with our colleagues in Singapore in the future.

# CONTRIBUTORS AND EDITORS

**Ben Belton** is an Assistant Professor of International Development in the Department of Agricultural, Food and Resource Economics, Michigan State University.

**Justine Chambers** is the Associate Director of the Myanmar Research Centre and a doctoral candidate in the Department of Anthropology at the Australian National University.

**Chit Win** gained his PhD in the Department of Political and Social Change at the Australian National University.

**Nicholas Farrelly** is Associate Dean of the College of Asia and the Pacific and was previously Director of the Myanmar Research Centre, both at the Australian National University.

**Giuseppe Gabusi** is a Professor of International Political Economy and Political Economy of East Asia in the Department of Cultures, Politics and Society of the University of Turin, and Head of Program at T.wai, the Torino World Affairs Institute.

**Mike Griffiths** is Director of Research for the Social Policy and Poverty Research Group, and PhD Candidate at the University of Hull.

**Ben Hillman** is Associate Professor and Director of the Policy and Governance Program at Crawford School of Public Policy, Australian National University.

**Khin Sanda Myint** is a freelance researcher and she was an Assistant Lecturer of the Department of International Relations at the University of Yangon.

**Kyaw Zeyar Win** is a researcher and a masters candidate in the Department of International Relations at the Maxwell School of Citizenship and Public Affairs at Syracuse University.

**Lwin Cho Latt** is a Lecturer of the Department of International Relations at the University of Yangon.

**Marlar Aung** is a Lecturer of the Department of International Relations at the University of Yangon.

**Maung Aung Myoe** is a Professor of International Relations at the International University of Japan.

**Gerard McCarthy** is the Associate Director of the Myanmar Research Centre and a doctoral candidate in the Coral Bell School of Asia and Pacific Affairs at the Australian National University.

**Cecile Medail** is a doctoral candidate in the Department of International Political Studies at the University of New South Wales.

**Myat Thida Win** is a masters candidate in the Department of Agricultural, Food, and Resource Economics at Michigan State University.

**Pyae Phyo Maung** is a Yangon-based aid and development consultant specialising in monitoring, evaluation and learning.

**Samuel Pursch** is a research and strategy advisor working on governance and social development in Myanmar and across Southeast Asia.

**Tim Schroeder** is the Head of Program at Covenant Consult, a Yangon-based consultancy firm.

**Si Thura** is the Executive Director of Community Partners International, a US-based non-profit organization that focuses on humanitarian and development work in Southeast Asia.

**Matthew Walton** is an Assistant Professor in Comparative Political Theory at the University of Toronto and was previously the Director of the Programme on Modern Burmese Studies at St Antony's College, University of Oxford.

**Tamas Wells** is a research fellow in the School of Social and Political Sciences at the University of Melbourne.

**Andrea Woodhouse** is a senior social development specialist at the World Bank.

**Michael Woolcock** is lead social scientist with the World Bank's Development Research Group, and a (part-time) Lecturer in Public Policy at Harvard University's Kennedy School of Government.

**Yaw Bawm Mangshang** currently works for the Diplomatic Mission of Finland in Yangon. He earned an MA in Law and Diplomacy from The Fletcher School, Tufts University in 2015.

**Xiaobo Zhang** is Distinguished Chair Professor of Economics at the National School of Development, Peking University in China, and Senior Research Fellow at the International Food Policy Research Institute.

**Matthew Zurstrassen** is a development professional working on social research and justice programs in the Asia Pacific Region and managed research for the World Bank's "Livelihoods and Social Change in Rural Myanmar" study.

# I

# Introduction

# 1

# INTRODUCTION: MYANMAR TRANSFORMED?

## Justine Chambers and Gerard McCarthy

In early February 2016 crowds gathered around televisions in tea shops across Myanmar to watch their new representatives be sworn in to positions in the *Pyithu* and *Amyotha* Parliaments, the lower and upper houses, in the capital Naypyitaw. In a country ruled by soldiers for over five decades, many doubted whether the military would hand legislative and executive power to a government led by Daw Aung San Suu Kyi's National League for Democracy, given its refusal to do so when the party won the elections in 1990. Watching NLD representatives take seats in Myanmar's parliament brought tears of cautious optimism to the eyes of many of these self-proclaimed democrats. Their hopeful sentiment was reinforced a few weeks later when U Htin Kyaw, a close aide of long-time democracy campaigner and opposition leader Aung San Suu Kyi, was made President. Soon after, Suu Kyi herself assumed the newly-created position of "State Counsellor", a role she claimed would place her "above the President" (Marshall and Mclaughlin 2015).

Since the heady months of early 2016, the limits of Myanmar's transformation from military junta to alleged beacon of democratization have become tragically clear. Levels of poverty and household debt remain catastrophic for many households. Meanwhile, on-budget funding for the armed forces, or Tatmadaw, in 2017–18 almost exceeded financing for health, education and welfare *combined*. In contrast to the vibrant political environment and growth in civil society between 2011–15, hopes that the NLD's election would herald a more progressive and inclusive Myanmar have faded rapidly since 2015. Civil liberties have come under repeated attack, with Myanmar declared the "biggest backslider in press freedom" across the globe by the Committee to Protect Journalists as a result of the escalating imprisonment of reporters and social media users during Suu Kyi's tenure. Protests by students in support of education reform have been suppressed, and land disputes remain intractable with little hope for justice or compensation for those dispossessed over decades. Furthermore, the status of religious minorities and progressive activists has become increasingly precarious, as exposed by the blatant assassination of prominent Muslim lawyer and architect of Suu Kyi's "State Counsellor" position U Ko Ni in January 2017.

Nowhere have these dynamics been borne out more tragically and violently than in Rakhine State where the precarious humanitarian, political and security order which had existed since the 2012–13 communal violence has collapsed entirely. Attacks on military outposts by a Rohingya armed group, the Arakan Rohingya Salvation Army (ARSA), in October 2016 and August 2017 prompted successive and escalating waves of what the military termed "clearance operations". Thousands of houses were burnt, driving over 750,000 Rohingya people to neighbouring Bangladesh. At the time of writing in early 2018 authorities continued to restrict access for independent media, human rights monitors and UN-appointed investigators to affected areas of northern Rakhine State. However, refugee testimony, satellite imagery and investigative reports suggesting systematic extrajudicial killings, torture, sexual violence and arson by Myanmar's military and Arakanese militia have led the United Nations to declare this "a textbook example of ethnic cleansing" (Cumming-Bruce 2017). Both the national military and Suu Kyi's government have denied most allegations, labelling ARSA a "terrorist" group whilst reinforcing the message that Rohingya are neither a "national race" nor rightful citizens of Myanmar (see Cheesman 2017).

Images of mass graves and atrocities committed by security personnel against Rohingya have emerged at the same time as protests in Rakhine

State that dramatically exposed the parlous state of relations between Naypyitaw and increasingly assertive Arakanese political elites. Growing resentment towards the NLD's perceived Bamar imperialism, symbolized by the appointment of an NLD chief minister in Rakhine State following the 2015 election, appears to have generated considerable elite and grassroots support from Rakhine people for another militia, the Arakan Army, which is closely linked to Rakhine elites (Davis 2017). Despite the escalating insurgency apparently claiming the lives of hundreds of Tatmadaw soldiers since 2016,[1] far more than the comparatively poorly resourced Rohingya militant group ARSA, the government has been reticent to label the Arakan Army "terrorists". But neither have Naypyitaw officials been willing to include the group in Myanmar's formal peace process. The resulting upsurge in AA attacks since late 2017 targeting security forces in Rakhine and Chin States, combined with the subsequent crackdown of January 2018 when police opened fire on Rakhine protesters, killing eight people before arresting senior Rakhine politicians on charges of treason, threatens to destabilize the region further. As the government in Naypyitaw signals the limits of tolerable dissent, its optimistic plans to repatriate and integrate Rohingya refugees currently in Bangladesh back into Rakhine State are likely to be met with stiff political and military resistance from Arakanese elites.

Beyond Rakhine State, the ethnic and religious fractures which were the topic of the most recent Myanmar Update volume (Cheesman and Farrelly 2016) have become more evident since the 2015 elections. This has been most tragically born out against communities in northern Kachin State. While peace was Aung San Suu Kyi's top priority after taking office in 2016, many ethnic minority community leaders feel betrayed that sustained military campaigns have intensified under her administration. As a result of escalating tensions, in 2016 the United Wa State Army (UWSA) formed its own negotiating "Northern Alliance" with other armed groups including the Kachin Independence Army and Arakan Army after it briefly entered—then dramatically exited—the 21st Century Panglong peace negotiations. Rejecting the demands made by the Northern Alliance partners for "all-inclusion", the Tatmadaw subsequently escalated attacks in Kachin and Shan States. Hundreds of families were forced to join more than 100,000 people already displaced by years of conflict since the breakdown of the 1994 Kachin ceasefire in 2012 (Hedström 2016; Lintner 2017). As trust declines and tensions rise in ethnic states, the path towards long-term peace becomes ever more elusive, compounded by unaddressed insecurity, fear and political grievances.

With the peace process faltering, signatories to the 2015 Nationwide Ceasefire Agreement (NCA) and many ethnic civil society groups fear that prospects for long-promised constitutional reforms and political autonomy are evaporating. For populations in ceasefire areas such as Karen and Mon States, the cessation of hostilities has certainly brought benefits in the form of increased freedom of movement, decreased taxation, access to income opportunities, healthcare and education services and less frequent and severe human rights abuses (see KHRG 2014; South and Joliffe 2015). However, power-sharing mechanisms remain tenuous and informal, with many ethnic armed leaders seeing the increasing intrusion of the Myanmar government and military into ethnic armed organization (EAO)-controlled areas of the country as part of a Bamar state strategy to extend authority and extract natural resources (Brenner 2017; Décobert 2016). The escalating clashes between the Karen National Union (KNU) and the Tatmadaw in early 2018 bodes ill for the viability of current ceasefire arrangements. For many community representatives there is a strong sense that the same dynamics of land grabs and resource extraction without political transformation—which drove a return to conflict in Kachin State—are now occurring in the absence of meaningful moves towards federalism (Sadan 2016; Woods 2011). Yet the substantive political dialogue and constitutional concessions from state officials necessary to breaking the current stalemate remain subject to Tatmadaw veto, reinforcing the limited power of civilian leaders in peacemaking.

Anxieties about the absence of post-conflict institutional reform are interwoven with contentious debates about the boundaries of political community, belonging and citizenship (Farrelly 2014; see Laoutides and Ware 2016; Welsh and Kai-Ping Huang 2016). In a recent volume on citizenship in Myanmar, P'Doh Kweh Htoo Win, the General Secretary of the KNU, emphasizes that even those who have spent their lives fighting the Tatmadaw still see the possibility of a "Myanmar" identity which is predicated on respect for ethnic and religious difference (see South and Lall 2018, pp. 301–3). NLD elites both in Naypyitaw and in ethnic states, however, have taken few meaningful steps to encourage these more inclusive understandings of political community. Instead, the imposition of statues of independence hero General Aung San in Mon and Kayah States against the wishes of local ethnic leaders have only reinforced fears of

"Burmanization".[2] In contrast, when KNU leaders sought to erect a statue of the group's founder Saw Ba U Gyi as part of their celebrations for the Karen New Year in 2017 they were blocked twice by military officials.[3]

The limits of reform as well as the institutional and symbolic contradictions of the peace process partly derive from the ongoing role of the military in governance enshrined in the 2008 Constitution (see Egreteau 2014). Beyond the *real politik* of the tentative power-sharing arrangement, however, informal institutions such as the centrality of "unity" in NLD ideology have also constrained meaningful reform, accountability and effective representation (Walton 2015). Indeed, discord with Tatmadaw officials has been studiously avoided by the NLD to such an extent that moral and even legal culpability for the atrocities in Rakhine State are increasingly attributed by international observers to Suu Kyi and her government rather than the Tatmadaw's Commander in Chief Min Aung Hlaing.

From the perspective of ethnic-minority and progressive members of the NLD, the constraints of "unity" imposed in both parliament and party have placed them on a tight leash. These strictures are especially acute at sub-national level where Naypyitaw Hluttaw parliamentarians and national officials have routinely overruled the concerns expressed by state and regional representatives (see Egreteau 2018). As demonstrated by the controversy over the naming of the Chaungzon Bridge in Mon State, which saw Naypyitaw NLD parliamentarians impose the name "Aung San" against local resistance only to see the party lose a subsequent by-election, the attempt to impose "unity" through top-down decree may only compound growing animosity with and within the ruling party. With ethnic parties across the country merging to present a more "united" front of their own, the stage is set for an increasingly ethno-nationalist electoral politics in many parts of the country ahead of the next elections in 2020.[4]

Growing international condemnation of the civilian government has also begun to complicate the geopolitical "rebalancing" long sought by Myanmar's political elites. Amidst the fall-out from the Tatmadaw's "clearance operations" in Rakhine State old patterns of diplomatic dependence on China and Russia to protect Myanmar officials from scrutiny and indictment have re-emerged (Mathieson 2018). In similar signs of continuity with the past, NLD approaches to thorny issues such as Rohingya repatriation and the peace process have relied on the kind of patronage-based state-business relations typical of the 1990s and

2000s (Turnell 2011). At Suu Kyi's personal solicitation, for instance, in October 2017 some of the most notorious tycoons of the SLORC/SPDC period made financial and in-kind contributions of over US$13 million to the agency charged with constructing model villages and providing livelihoods for Rohingya returnees. Framed as expressions of national "duty" or diplomatic solidarity, it remains to be seen whether and how these domestic and international relational imbalances with powerful actors foreclose the possibility of more equitable and inclusive development for the country as a whole.

Neither the resilient formal role of the military in governance, nor reluctance to challenge the rigid commitment to "unity" preclude the potential for a progressive and inclusive politics. Despite the fractures at the heart of Myanmar's formal political order, the promise of "the political" remains for many activists (see Cheesman 2016). As the contributors to this volume highlight, despite the constraints imposed by the present form of hybrid governance there is considerable scope for civilians to advance visions of reform. Split into three sections that provide grass-roots, spatial and institutional perspectives on reform — People, Places and Politics — the chapters of *Myanmar Transformed?* take stock of the mutations, continuities and fractures at the heart of Myanmar society and politics in recent years. Many of these chapters draw on intensive and immersive research in provincial areas of Myanmar to explore the impacts and prospects for progress opened by political and social liberalization. To ask whether Myanmar has transformed is not simply to question what has and hasn't changed. Beyond an assessment of the progress and pitfalls of transition from junta rule, the authors also assess the scope of action and offer visions of reforms achievable within the context of Myanmar's hybrid civil–military arrangements. In the vexed moment Myanmar's people and leaders now find themselves in, the chapters offer new and alternative ways to understand and improve the lives of ordinary people.

## PEOPLE

Democratic transitions are generally assumed to make governments more responsive to the social demands of median voters, improving accountability and state-led service delivery. Beyond elite-level politics, Myanmar's reforms must therefore be assessed on whether and how they impact the lives of ordinary people. Focusing on social dynamics in rural villages, where seventy per cent of Myanmar's people live, the World Bank team probe Myanmar's social and economic changes by exploring how reforms have altered the "social contract" between citizens and the state. Collating insights from a unique longitudinal qualitative study of villages across the country, they document how interactions with officials have been re-negotiated as villagers gain confidence, calling their newly elected administrators to account through formal mechanisms such as local elections. Especially in land confiscation cases, they show how improved communication with trans-local family and civil society networks via web-enabled smartphones have enabled some villagers to mobilize and even take pre-emptive action against their alienation from land. These mechanisms of accountability have evolved alongside the expansion of government-mediated rural development initiatives, shifting the role of local administrators in sourcing funds from higher tiers of power. Pursch et al. suggest that these dynamics have strengthened expectations of local and Union state officials, including elected representatives, helping to build trust in the state. Yet, there is still much room for improvement, particularly in terms of budget allocation.

Indeed, after decades of neglect of ordinary people by successive regimes, the government may be missing a valuable mechanism to boost state legitimacy. In Chapter 3 Yawbawm Mangshang and Michael Griffiths examine how expanding the scope of state-mediated social protection mechanisms is essential if decades of negative experiences of the state are to be overcome. Focusing on the role that social protection schemes can play in building public trust, and establishing legitimacy based on consent, they argue that welfare provision can bridge the distance between the citizen and the state by demonstrating state commitment to social rather than solely military notions of "security". Their vision is not one of a welfare state developed decades down the line. Rather, they envision more inclusive state-led social protection mechanisms including the expansion of existing schemes, greater government taxation and collaboration with informal sectors of local social protection which are already ubiquitous across Myanmar. While increasing funding for welfare is vital to these goals, state officials and institutions also have an opportunity to generate trust with citizens through acknowledging and partnering with local societal mechanisms of social redistribution that have developed over decades.

Taking societally rooted structures of care seriously is especially important if a sustainable peace is to emerge in Myanmar's restive borderlands. Decades of conflict in many ethnic states has bequeathed complex non-state structures of community-based primary health care often linked to ethnic armed organizations and their aligned civil society networks (Décobert 2016). As Si Thura and Schroeder note in their case-study of health service delivery in Karen State, following the 2012 ceasefire Karen health providers and the Myanmar Ministry of Health and Sport have cultivated relationships of trust essential not just for improving the wellbeing of people in conflict-affected areas but also cultivating more sustainable ceasefire arrangements. Importantly, they note that early efforts in joint training and service delivery in south-eastern Myanmar have been recognised and expanded with high-level commitment from the NLD and MoHS since 2016. Since the Thein Sein-era blueprint for political dialogue remains the basis of peace negotiations (see Su Mon Thazin Aung 2016), more formalized progress in collaborative governance and social service delivery systems across the country can only be advanced once all armed groups have signed the nationwide ceasefire agreement. The goodwill generated by the recognition of non-state expertise and legitimacy since 2014, however, offers a vision of the kind of collaborative approach necessary for a meaningful peace dividend in war-ravaged communities.

## PLACES

Liberalization in Myanmar has brought intensified flows of capital and goods on a scale unseen since the collapse of socialism in 1988. However, as Myanmar has become more integrated into global dynamics of finance and extraction since 2011, the economic and social impacts of deepening marketization have varied significantly across the country. Focusing on rural Myanmar, Myat Thida Win and her co-authors highlight how structural economic shifts have driven extraordinarily rapid agricultural mechanization in recent years. As young and unskilled farm workers have migrated in droves to growing urban centres in search of higher wages, scarcity-driven increases in the price of farm labour have prompted agricultural mechanization at the household level. The resulting uptake of mostly Chinese labour-saving machinery can only be understood in light of new technologies of credit such as hire-purchase arrangements, however. First introduced in Myanmar only in 2013, they now underpin the vast majority of purchases of combine harvesters and four-wheel tractors, and more than a third of two-wheel tractors. These structural changes have not been consistent across the country, though. Indeed, Myat Thida Win et al. reveal substantial variation in mechanization by region and household according to crop-type and degree of household reliance on agriculture as a source of income. What emerges is a picture of agricultural households attempting to manage the risks created by Myanmar's structural economic shifts using the technologies—financial, mechanical and otherwise—now available to them by virtue of the same macro-level reforms.

The paradoxes of Myanmar's social and economic reforms become even more apparent in Myanmar's periphery and in the contestation over resources and their distribution. The political dynamics of extractive industry projects and the associated impacts on community are deeply contentious in the resource-rich areas of Myanmar's ethnic states, where some of the world's longest civil conflicts have been waged since independence in 1948 (Jones 2014; Lintner 1994; Smith 1999). In northern Kachin State, in particular, the question of resources and how they are distributed remains a significant challenge to the peace process (Sadan 2016). One of the most important dimensions of the breakdown of the seventeen-year ceasefire agreement between the Kachin Independence Army (KIA) and the Myanmar government in 2011 was the accommodation between the Myanmar military and Kachin elites around natural resource exploitation, otherwise described as "ceasefire capitalism" (Woods 2011; see also Jones 2016). Few of these dynamics have changed under the NLD government, with deepening grievances regarding exploitation of resources as well as the social dislocation caused by extraction and illicit drugs. This perception has been reinforced after the nomination and election of T Khun Myat as the speaker for the House of Representatives (*Pyithu Hluttaw*) in March 2017 by the NLD. T Khun Myat not only has a history related to the narcotics trade, but he is a former leader of a Kutkai militia that allied with the Tatmadaw in northern Shan State. Indeed, as Gabusi outlines, the legacies of the authoritarian era continue to stall reform in Myanmar and block paths to a more sustainable peace process.

The complexities of natural resource management and the legacies of military rule is similarly exposed in Myanmar's special economic zones. As Pyae Phyo Maung and Tamas Wells note in their chapter, these zones of regulatory exception to promote industrialization have repeatedly been met with stiff opposition from communities sceptical of the promised local economic benefits and fearful of environmental degradation. As freedom of expression has expanded since 2011, special economic zones in Dawei in the country's south, Thilawa, near Yangon, and Kyaukphyu in the country's western conflict-affected Rakhine State have become not just sites of intensified commercial activity and extraction but also places of heightened political contestation. Pyae Phyo Maung and Wells note that campaigns and strategies of public and elite advocacy have forced changes aimed at mitigating the environmentally destructive elements of SEZs as well as securing compensation for land previously expropriated from villagers. Despite these signs of progress, their chapter highlights that groups are constrained by the profound imbalance in resourcing between their own advocacy activities and the SEZ activities led both by companies and by government officials. Indeed, the concessional deals which underpin these special spaces have often proven resilient despite the change in government, creating what one observer colourfully termed "zombie" zones that won't die despite stiff opposition from civil society (see Pyae Phyo Maung and Wells). With international governments and investors placing considerable pressure on the NLD, it remains to be seen whether Suu Kyi's government will be able to provide the robust protections expected by local communities impacted by SEZs.

Perceptions that Myanmar's political representatives are aloof or unresponsive may be compounded by the fact that most decisions about regulating and mediating the consequences of marketization are made by elites ensconced in the capital Naypyitaw. In recent years, Nicholas Farrelly has been on a journey of exploration in Naypyitaw, which has been the heart of national administration since 2005. His chapter explains that the city was carved from scrubland and paddy fields based on the military's commitment to the idea that space is integral to the exercise of power. Naypyitaw tends to be seen by most foreign observers as a bizarre and even lunatic place that apparently defies the ordinary laws of geography, society and culture. As Farrelly notes, however, there has been little serious effort to understand this monumental city beyond its broad boulevards and over-sized infrastructure. Prior to 2011, most people in Myanmar had no notion of the scale of construction and bureaucratic activity outside the historic town of Pyinmana. Yet, as a replacement for Yangon, Naypyitaw has already established its reputation and stature as a burgeoning middle-class city categorically distinct from life in rural or borderland Myanmar. As Farrelly notes, it is little wonder that at moments of domestic and international crisis, the NLD government has made the most of Naypyitaw, the dictator's customized capital, seeking to utilize this spacious alternative to ordinary Myanmar urban or provincial life as a retreat from the harsh scrutiny of voters, troublesome civil society and the international community.

## POLITICS

Over the last five years much has been written on the nature of the country's quasi-civilian governance structures and the influence the military retains over parliament and executive power (Egreteau 2014, 2017; Farrelly and Chit Win 2016; Jones 2014; Slater 2014). In this context, Maung Aung Myoe's chapter takes stock of the tenuous power-sharing arrangement between the civilian administration and the military since the National League for Democracy took power in March 2016. Many of the formal and informal legacies of authoritarian rule—including military control of twenty-five per cent of the parliament and a number of key ministries including the military and Home Affairs—have proven resilient, significantly constraining the ability of the new NLD government to deliver the kind of change expected by everyday people (see also Maung Aung Myoe 2014). Yet, as Maung Aung Myoe demonstrates, the formal dominance of the military over key ministries and its twenty-five per cent representation in parliament have been the source of minimal public tension between Suu Kyi's civilian government and Tatmadaw officials. Only in very rare instances, such as requests to review the qualifications of civilian ministers, has the NLD publicly rebuffed military intrusion into "civilian" affairs. Instead, the NLD government has more or less decided to adopt the Tatmadaw's position as its own default policy in issues related to defence and national security. Such a position not only draws criticism from international observers but has become one of the key sticking points to the peace process and Aung San Suu Kyi's ability to secure a lasting settlement with all EAOs.

The peace process which was initiated under President Thein Sein in 2011 largely remains intact under the NLD (Pederson 2014). However, as demonstrated by Lwin Cho Latt, Ben Hillman and their co-authors, relations between the central government and the country's ethnic armed organizations (EAOs) remain fragile and contested. The lives of people in Myanmar's ethnic states have been wracked by conflict for over six decades (Cheesman and Farrelly 2016). Under brutal military and counterinsurgency campaigns the civilian population of borderlands areas have been exposed to years of instability and egregious human rights violations (Sadan

2016; Smith 1999). These dynamics have sparked mass displacement and migration to neighbouring countries and wreaked incalculable harm on family, community and culture (Hedström 2016; Seng Maw Lahpai 2014). After so many years of conflict, negotiating a peace settlement was always going to be a considerable challenge (Farrelly 2012). But as their chapter explains, the government and the military are increasingly at odds with EAOs around the key notion of which groups get to negotiate the basis of a more federal political system. The transfer of civilian power to Suu Kyi and repeated rounds of negotiations have yet to produce concrete mechanisms capable of resolving these tensions at the heart of the peace process.

Nowhere is the fragility of majority-minority relations more evident than in northern Rakhine State, where since August 2017 state military "clearance operations" have killed an estimated 10,000 people and brutally displaced more than 750,000 people to neighbouring Bangladesh.[5] As Kyaw Zeyar Win's chapter demonstrates, the intractability of the Rohingya situation derives from intense and systematic securitization of the group by successive military governments (see also Schissler 2016; Wells 2016). Following the 1962 coup by Ne Win, Rohingya people were actively positioned as a threat to the territorial integrity and security of the nation state (Cheesman 2017; Thawnghmung 2016). As Kyaw Zeyar Win explains, the negative attitudes towards the Rohingya that are a legacy of military rule have taken on a new degree of ferocity in the more open political environment of contemporary Myanmar. Since liberalization in 2011, anxieties regarding the decline of Buddhism at a time of democratization have taken expression in both print and increasingly accessible social media, often serving to further entrench symbolic depictions of the Rohingya as a threat to ideas of freedom and nation (Brooten and Verbruggen 2017; McCarthy and Menager 2017; Walton and Hayward 2014). In addition to state actors, Kyaw Zeyar Win thus demonstrates that monks, civil society organizations and even everyday people have become agents of securitization, often enlisting social media to shape public opinion and mobilize support against the Rohingya. Indeed, while the UN has said the situation in northern Rakhine state "bears all the hallmarks of genocide" (UNOHCHR 2018), the military campaign against the Rohingya gained widespread grassroots support across Myanmar and has become a rallying call for nationalists against what was largely perceived as a foreign population which poses a threat to the nation state.

In this context, it is no surprise that questions related to identity and citizenship continue to loom large in Myanmar's politics. Where one-third of the of the country's population are non-Burman, issues related to ethnicity remain at the heart of Myanmar's transition (see also South and Lall 2018). Aung San Suu Kyi has expressed firm support for a federal, democratic solution and has unparalleled political authority to deliver it, particularly with the Burman majority. However, as Cecile Medail's chapter shows, without attention to continued differential treatment of ethnic peoples in many parts of the country as well as the privileged position of Burmans with regard to the national "Myanmar" identity, ethnic reconciliation in Myanmar will remain elusive (see also Lall and Hla Hla Win 2012; Walton 2013). Cecile's exploration of Mon people's perceptions of ethnic identity and nationality citizenship provides a telling insight into these dynamics. As she highlights, many Mon people continue to perceive the Myanmar state as dominated by a Bamar majority which seeks to impose its own culture, history and language on ethnic minority peoples. Her chapter also highlights the critical importance of lasting political settlements to ethnic conflicts in border areas through symbolic politics (see also Laoutides and Ware 2016). Indeed, in addition to greater inclusion of non-Burman voices in the political decision-making process, the government of Myanmar will need to open to public discussion the question of what it means to be "Myanmar" and members of all ethnic and religious groups will need to be a part of this process.

## THE MYANMAR UPDATE SERIES AND THIS VOLUME

The chapters in this volume, *Myanmar Transformed?* are based on papers from the Australian National University's Myanmar Update series. The Myanmar Update has been held at ANU bi-annually since its inception in 1990. The main objective of the Update is to inform scholars, government agencies, policy makers, the corporate sector, NGOs, journalists and members of the Australian community about the most significant political, social and economic changes in Myanmar. For many years, the Myanmar Update was one of the few forums for Myanmar and non-Myanmar professionals to come together, discuss and analyse research done on recent developments and issues facing the country. Previous Myanmar Update themes have covered peace and conflict, national reconciliation, state/civil society relations and the role of the military, agriculture and rural development, health and education, economic prospects, and international relations. Since 2011, Myanmar has seen an opening up and many extraordinary social and political changes. However, as the social dynamics explored in this book continue to show, the need for scholarship that addresses emerging issues in Myanmar with a keen eye to practical consequences is more important than ever.

The 2017 Myanmar Update held at the Australian National University on February 15–16 asked participants to consider Myanmar's "transformation" under the new National League for Democracy government. In 2017 Aung San Suu Kyi's special representative, Dr Aung Tun Thet, the President's Economic Advisor and also a member of the President's National Economic and Social Advisory Council, gave the keynote. The majority of the presenters at the conference also hailed from Myanmar institutions, a sign of how far the country has come. Universities, long suppressed in Myanmar, are becoming sites of debate and critical thought, including about Myanmar's civil conflict (Lwin Cho Latt et al., Chapter 10 this volume). A few years earlier it would have been inconceivable to have such senior members of the Myanmar government as well as academics visiting ANU and participating in an academic conference that prides itself on free expression and open debate. We hope this momentum continues and that education reform in Myanmar remains a priority of the NLD government in the years ahead. In 2017, the Myanmar Update grappled with the sense of both "optimism and despair" underpinning Myanmar's difficult political, economic and social changes. In light of the tragic events since mid-2017, identifying as this volume does the enduring legacies of military rule, and how obstacles to a more inclusive and democratic Myanmar can be navigated, is more important than ever.

## Notes

1   Though casualty figures should always be treated skeptically, Myanmar military documents cited by *The New York Times* claim over 300 Tatmadaw soldiers were killed by the Arakan Army in the first half of 2016 alone. See Beech, H. and Saw Nang. "Myanmar Police Gun Down Marchers in Rakhine Ethnic Rally". 17 January 2018.

2   This was most visible in Mon State around the naming of the Chaugzon Bridge in 2017, prompting large-scale protests. More recently the Kayah State government has commissioned a statue to be made of the independence leader

Bojouq Aung San in the capital of Loikaw, at an estimated cost of K150 million (about US$113,000). See Htun Khaing, "NLD's gilded Bogyoke building spree prompts ethnic backlash". *Frontier Myanmar*, 6 March 2018.

3   See Lawi Weng, "Military Blocks 2nd Attempt to Erect Statue of Late Karen Leader". *The Irrawaddy*, 5 February 2018.

4   On mergers in Kachin parties see Nyein Nyein, "Trio of Kachin Parties Agree to Merger". *The Irrawaddy*, 15 January 2018; on Chin parties see Zue Zue, "Chin Political Parties Merge". *The Irrawaddy*, 19 June 2017; on Mon parties see Bo Bo Myint, "Two Mon Parties to Rapidly Implement Merger". *Eleven Myanmar*, 21 January 2018; and on Karen parties see Chan Thar, "Four political parties merge in Kayin State". *The Myanmar Times*, 7 February 2018.

5   This is based on conservative estimates by the medical charity Medicins Sans Frontieres (MSF) in December 2017. See <http://www.abc.net.au/news/2017-12-14/rohingya-death-toll-in-the-thousands-says-msf/9260552> [accessed 9 February 2018].

## References

Brenner, Dave. "Authority in Rebel Groups: Identity, Recognition and the Struggle over Legitimacy". *Contemporary Politics*, 23 (4) (2017): 408–26.

Brooten, Lisa and Verbruggen, Yola. "Producing the News: Repoting on Myanmar's Rohingya Crisis". *Journal of Contemporary Asia*, 47 (3) (2017), 440–60.

Cheesman, Nick. "Myanmar and the Promise of the Political". In *Conflict in Myanmar: War, Politics, Religion*, edited by Nick Cheesman and Nicholas Farrelly. Singapore: ISEAS-Yusof Ishak Institute, 2016.

————. "How in Myanmar 'National Races' Came to Surpass Citizenship and Exclude Rohingya". *Journal of Contemporary Asia*, 47 (3) (2017), 461–83.

Cheesman, Nick and Farrelly, Nicholas eds. *Conflict in Myanmar: War, Politics, Religion*. Singapore: ISEAS-Yusof Ishak Institute, 2016.

Cumming-Bruce, Nick. "Rohingya Crisis in Myanmar Is 'Ethnic Cleansing,' U.N. Rights Chief Says". *New York Times*, 11 September 2017. <https://www.nytimes.com/2017/09/11/world/asia/myanmar-rohingya-ethnic-cleansing.html> [accessed 18 December 2017].

Davis, Anthony. "Myanmar's other Rakhine problem". *Asia Times*, 29 November 2017. <http://www.atimes.com/article/myanmars-rakhine-problem/> [accessed 10 April 2018].

Décobert, Anne. *The Politics of Aid to Burma: A Humanitarian Struggle on the Thai-Burma Border*. New York: Routledge, 2016.

Egreteau, Renaud. "The Continuing Political Salience of the Military in Post-SPDC Myanmar". In *Debating Democratization in Myanmar*, edited by Nick Cheesman, Nicholas Farrelly, and Trevor Wilson. Singapore: ISEAS, 2014.

————. *Caretaking Democratization*. London: Hurst, 2017.

————. "How Myanmar's Ruling Party keeps its Lawmakers Under Control". *Tea Circle*, 1 March 2018. <https://teacircleoxford.com/2018/03/01/how-myanmars-ruling-party-keeps-its-lawmakers-under-control/> [accessed 10 April 2018].

Farrelly, Nicholas. "Ceasing Ceasefire? Kachin Politics Beyond the Stalemates". In *Myanmar's Transition: Openings, Obstacles and Opportunities*, edited by Nick Cheesman, Monique Skidmore, and Trevor Wilson. Singapore: ISEAS, 2012.

————. "Cooperation, Contestation, Conflict: Ethnic Political Interests in Myanmar Today". *South East Asia Research*, 22 (2) (2014): 251–66.

Farrelly, Nicholas and Chit Win. "Inside Myanmar's Turbulent Transformation". *Asia and the Pacific Policy Studies* 3(1) (2016): 38–47.

Hedström, Jenny. "A Feminist Political Economy of Insecurity and Violence in Kachin State". In *Conflict in Myanmar: War, Politics, Religion*, edited by Nick Cheesman and Nicholas Farrelly. Singapore: ISEAS-Yusof Ishak Institute, 2016.

Jones, Lee. "Explaining Myanmar's Regime Transition: The Periphery is Central". *Democratization*, 21 (5) (2014): 780–802.

KHRG. "Truce or Transition? Trends in Human Rights Abuse and Local Response in Southeast Myanmar Since the 2012 Ceasefire". Chiang Mai, Thailand: Karen Human Rights Group, 2014.

Lall, Marie and Hla Hla Win. "Perceptions of the State and Citizenship in Light of the 2010 Myanmar Elections". In *Myanmar's Transition: Openings, Obstacles and Opportunities*, edited by Nick Cheesman, Monique Skidmore, and Trevor Wilson. Singapore: ISEAS, 2012.

Laoutides, Costas and Ware, Anthony. "Reexamining the Centrality of Ethnic Identity to the Kachin Conflict". In *Conflict in Myanmar: War, Politics, Religion*, edited by Nick Cheesman and Nicholas Farrelly. Singapore: ISEAS-Yusof Ishak Institute, 2016.

Lintner, Bertil. *Burma in Revolt: Opium and Insurgency Since 1948*. Boulder: Westview Press, 1994.

————. "Kachin War Explodes Myanmar's Peace Drive". *Asia Times*, 19 January 2017. <http://www.atimes.com/article/kachin-war-explodes-myanmars-peace-drive/> [accessed 3 March 2018].

Marshall, Andrew R.C. and Mclaughlin, Timothy. "Myanmar's Suu Kyi Says will be Above President in New Government". Reuters, 5 November 2015. <https://www.reuters.com/article/us-myanmar-election/myanmars-suu-kyi-says-will-be-above-president-in-new-government-idUSKCN0SU0AR20151105> [accessed 12 April 2018].

Mathieson, David Scott. "How the West won and lost Myanmar". *Asia Times*, 29 March 2018. <http://www.atimes.com/article/west-won-lost-myanmar/ > [accessed 2 April 2018].

Maung Aung Myoe. "The Soldier and the State: The Tatmadaw and Political Liberalization in Myanmar since 2011". *South East Asia Research* 22 (2)(2014): 233–249.

McCarthy, Gerard and Menager, Jacqueline. "Gendered Rumours and the Muslim Scapegoat in Myanmar's Transition". *Journal of Contemporary Asia* 47 (3)(2017): 396–412.

Pederson, Morten B. "Myanmar's Democratic Opening: The Process and Prospect of Reform". In *Debating Democratization in Myanmar*, edited by Nick Cheesman, Nicholas Farrelly, and Trevor Wilson. Singapore: ISEAS, 2014.

Sadan, Mandy, ed. *War and Peace in the Borderlands of Myanmar*. Copenhagen: NIAS Press, 2016.

Schissler, Matt. "On Islamphobes and Holocaust Deniers: Making Sense of Violence, in Myanmar and Elsewhere". In *Conflict in Myanmar: War, Politics, Religion*, edited by Nick Cheesman and Nicholas Farrelly. Singapore: ISEAS-Yusof Ishak Institute, 2016.

Seng Maw Lahpai. "State Terrorism and International Compliance: The Kachin Armed Struggle for Political Self-Determination". In *Debating Democratization in Myanmar*, edited by Nick Cheesman, Nicholas Farrelly, and Trevor Wilson. Singapore: ISEAS, 2014.

Slater, Dan. "The Elements of Surprise: Assessing Burma's Double-Edged détente". *South East Asia Research* 22 (2)(2014: 171–82.

Smith, Martin. *Burma: Insurgency and the Politics of Ethnicity*. London: Zed Books, 1999.

South, Ashley and Joliffe, Kim. "Forced Migration: Typology and Local Agency in Southeast Myanmar". *Contemporary Southeast Asia* 37 (2) (2015): 211–41.

South, Ashley and Lall, Marie. *Citizenship in Myanmar: Ways of Being in and from Burma*. Singapore: ISEAS and Chiang Mai University Press, 2018.

Su Mon Thazin Aung. "The Politics of Policymaking in Transitional Government: A Case Study of the Ethnic Peace Process in Myanmar". In *Conflict in Myanmar: War, Politics, Religion*, edited by Nick Cheesman and Nicholas Farrelly. Singapore: ISEAS-Yusof Ishak Institute, 2016.

Thawnghmung, Ardeth Maung. "The Politics of Indigeneity in Myanmar". *Asian Ethnicity* 17 (4)(2016): 527–47.

Turnell, Sean. "Fundamentals of Myanmar's Macroeconomy: A Political Economy Perspective". *Asian Economic Policy Review* 6 (1)(2011): 136–53.

UNOHCHR. "Myanmar: UN Expert calls for Accountability over Violence in Rakhine State". United Nations Human Rights Office of the High Commissioner, 12 March 2018. <http://www.ohchr.org/EN/NewsEvents/Pages/DisplayNews.aspx?NewsID=22793&LangID=E> [accessed 10 April 2018].

Walton, Matthew J. "The 'Wages of Burman-ness': Ethnicity and Burman Privilege in Contemporary Myanma". *Journal of Contemporary Asia,* 43 (1)(2013): 1–27.

————. "The Disciplining Discourse of Unity in Burmese Politics". *Journal of Burma Studies* 19 (1)(2015): 1–26.

Walton, Matthew J. and Hayward, Susan. *Contesting Buddhist Narratives: Democratization, Nationalism, and Communal Violence in Myanmar.* 71 Policy Studies; Honolulu, HI: East-West Center, 2014.

Wells, Tamas. "Making Sense of Reactions to Communal Violence in Myanmar". In *Conflict in Myanmar: War, Politics, Religion,* edited by Nick Cheesman and Nicholas Farrelly. Singapore: ISEAS-Yusof Ishak Institute, 2016.

Welsh, Bridget and Kai-Ping Huang. "Public Perceptions of a Divided Myanmar: Findings from the 2015 Myanmar Asian Barometer Survey". In *Conflict in Myanmar: War, Politics, Religion,* edited by Nick Cheesman and Nicholas Farrelly. Singapore: ISEAS-Yusof Ishak Institute, 2016.

Woods, Kevin. "Ceasefire Capitalism: Military-Private Partnerships, Resource Concessions and Military-State Building in the Burma-China Borderlands". *Journal of Peasant Studies,* 38 (4)(2011): 747–70.

# II

## People

# 2

# DOCUMENTING SOCIAL AND ECONOMIC TRANSFORMATION IN MYANMAR'S RURAL COMMUNITIES

Samuel Pursch, Andrea Woodhouse, Michael Woolcock and Matthew Zurstrassen[1]

## INTRODUCTION

Myanmar has undergone significant reforms in recent years. A commonly accepted view is that, unlike many of the political shifts experienced elsewhere in the world in the twenty-first century, their impetus came not "from below" but from national elites, prompted by military decisions to open the country to the world and begin to democratize (Pederson 2012, Fink 2014). Much of the literature on Myanmar's transition thus focuses on national dynamics, seeking insights on what has changed, why, and how, by examining shifts among political elites, the business community, and the upper echelons of the Tatmadaw (see Pederson 2012; ICG 2012; Jones 2014). These changes emerged from a variety of elite-led processes, including the drafting of a new constitution in 2008, and accelerated under the Thein Sein-led government starting in 2011. Yet while analysing the motives and strategies of elites is vital for understanding the national impetus behind Myanmar's reforms, it leaves little space for assessing how the transition has played out among the broader populace, particularly in the rural villages where seventy per cent of Myanmar's people live. It also overlooks how the prevailing social institutions at the local level have responded to the various forms and sources of contention (actual and/or potential) inherently accompanying such major changes, and the associated implications for policy and practice in Myanmar.

This paper seeks to contribute to research on Myanmar's social transformation by analysing how governance reforms and changes in the life experiences of people in rural communities are altering the social contract at the village level. The paper argues that the nature and extent of the "social contract" —i.e., the terms on which citizens interact with one another, and the basis on which contending views of citizens' core rights and responsibilities are negotiated with and legitimately upheld by the state—is being re-written in Myanmar. Three areas of change, especially since 2011, have affected how citizens in rural areas interact with the state: village governance, citizens' expectations of the state, and connectivity. Responding to these challenges will require strategies informed by the best available evidence.

We address each of these areas in turn. First, we examine how changes in village governance institutions and structures have reconfigured centers of power and influence at the local level. Next, we examine how an increase in service delivery and the roll-out of national policy reforms have led to changes in what villagers expect of the state. Finally, we trace how villagers' networks beyond their immediate communities are expanding, allowing them to forge new and different connections with others within their townships, across Myanmar, and internationally.[2] We argue that, at the village level, the transition thus far has been effective and (relatively) peaceful because it has provided space for the development of social accountability mechanisms (i.e., ways citizens hold government institutions to account) of sufficient strength to manage what villagers expect of the state and how the state, in turn, responds.

Drawing these three interrelated areas together, we explore the implications for state-society relations at the village level in a context where, we argue, more coherent social accountability mechanisms and procedures are slowly being forged. As important and commendable as this progress is, however, we note that at present this has not been a result of systematic policy planning to encourage bottom-up accountability, but rather because of a perceived greater space for engagement; heightened access to communications tools (i.e., mobile phones), which facilitate more active participation; and the individual leadership abilities of local administrators, staff, and village elites. Integrating and institutionalizing these emerging state-led policy mechanisms with local-level initiatives will be crucial to ensuring that initial achievements are consolidated and expanded, and that potential (or actual) tensions between them are coherently and amicably resolved.

Our findings are grounded in data collected over a four-year period starting in 2012 as part of the World Bank's Qualitative Social and Economic Monitoring (QSEM) research program. QSEM is a large-scale longitudinal panel study on village life in Myanmar, which has tracked fifty-four villages across the country over six research rounds.[3] The study is based on in-depth interviews and focus group discussions held with approximately 1,000 people in each round. Its scale, longevity, and scope make it a unique lens through which to understand how Myanmar's transition is playing out in everyday village life.[4]

The following sections explore these arguments in greater detail. Section 2 briefly reviews the existing literature on Myanmar's social transformation. Section 3 explores how changes in the structure and functions of village governance institutions have led state-society relations to evolve. Section 4 examines changes in citizens' expectations of the state. Section 5 addresses the nature and extent of the steadily expanding economic and social networks of Myanmar's rural citizens. Section 6 considers the interplay between these three vectors of change. Section 7 concludes with preliminary implications for policy and practice.

## PREVIOUS AND ONGOING RESEARCH ON MYANMAR'S SOCIAL TRANSFORMATION

Any study seeking to examine Myanmar's ongoing transition to democracy needs to locate its findings in the scholarly research and policy analysis that has been undertaken since these momentous processes began in earnest in 2011. We thus begin with a brief review of the literature on

Myanmar's governance institutions, economic networks, and citizens' expectations of the state.

The literature explicitly examining Myanmar's state-society relations at the village level is limited. Most studies undertaken during military rule focused on particular aspects of engagement with the state (e.g., Thawnghmung 2003) in a context where access to rural communities was limited. Starting from the 2008 Constitution, the Government of Myanmar has been implementing policies to decentralize what has historically been a heavily centralized structure (UNDP 2014). A growing body of research analyses this decentralization process, including The Asia Foundation's policy research on state/region and township governance (Inada 2014; Nixon 2014) and UNDP's local governance mapping project (UNDP 2015). Most of this work focuses primarily on institutions at the township level and above. Research looking at institutions below the township level is more limited, and includes work by Susanne Kempel on village governance (Kempel 2012, 2014, 2016). The QSEM builds on this by examining how the transition has affected village leadership and decision-making and the implications for rural communities.[5] In recent years there has been an increase in ethnographic and anthropological research.[6] Much of this research has yet to make its way into publications. Exceptions include Thidar Win's (2015) examination of the role of social networks in villages in Mandalay Region and an increasing body of articles on internet forums (such as Tea Circle Oxford; see Whittekind 2015, for example).

The literature on connectivity is more limited. Reports from the International Organization for Migration (IOM) examine how migration is affecting rural communities (IOM 2013), while the recent World Bank study "A Country on the Move" (World Bank 2015a) examines migration patterns in detail. There has been limited academic work to date on the expansion of ICT in Myanmar and its social effects, though a number of journalistic accounts provide some useful context (Mod 2016). We attempt to bring together several strands of applied research (including the effects of migration, improved physical infrastructure, and mobile technology) to show the effects of enhanced and deepened connectivity on community interactions with the state.

A number of studies have examined how communities in Myanmar view and rely on (or actively avoid) state institutions. These include Mike Griffiths' work on community resilience (Griffiths 2016), Gerard McCarthy's research with IGC on non-state social protection (McCarthy

2016), and Helene Kyed's ongoing study into everyday access to justice (Kyed, forthcoming). Similarly, previous Myanmar Update papers have also proven useful in elucidating how land (Wells 2014), access to rural credit (Turnell 2010), and other key issues shape state-society interactions. Much of this work demonstrates the enduring importance of non-state institutions even as formal government services have expanded in recent years. This paper builds on this work, giving particular attention to how this expansion of state-provided services is being received and perceived by people in rural communities, where historically the state has been regarded with deep suspicion or indifference. In this respect, the paper complements Chapter 2 in this volume by Griffiths and Mangshang that focuses on the aims of the government in expanding social protection initiatives, including as an endeavor to strength the political legitimacy of the state (Griffiths and Mangshang 2017).

Building on these foundations, we now consider how data from six rounds of QSEM research enables us to draw initial conclusions about the nature and extent of social change in rural Myanmar since 2012.

## VILLAGE GOVERNANCE

### The role of village government institutions in Myanmar

Village governance institutions in Myanmar play two key functions: they maintain social order and act as interlocutors between community members and external actors (Win 2015). These core functions have changed little since Myanmar's reforms began (Kempel 2013). The QSEM research demonstrates, however, that *how* those functions are carried out and *what factors influence* village institutional actors, have changed significantly since 2012. For example, national reforms have led village tract administrators to grow in stature and influence at the expense of village administrators.[7] Although the current policy framework for local institutions has flaws, we argue that, overall, national reforms have led village institutions to be more responsive to people's needs.

Early research in 2012 found that in the vast majority of villages, villagers themselves perceived village administrators to be the most important actor for managing village affairs, mediating disputes, and representing the village beyond its borders. Village administrators were elected in approximately a quarter of villages. In such villages, for example most QSEM villages in Chin State, villagers reported greater social trust compared to villages where village administrators were selected by township authorities (often on the recommendation of village elders rather than by village consensus), or were long-term incumbents (QSEM 2012). Research across 2012 and 2013 also found that levels of trust between villagers and local leaders were higher in communities where villagers perceived themselves as more distant from the central government (QSEM June 2013), such as in parts of Shan State. In remote areas, the imperative of villagers to act collectively to meet village needs helped to build social bonds (QSEM June 2013).

Other actors played important roles in distinct aspects of village life. Village elders, for example, helped to legitimize village administrator decisions within the village or to balance power. Religious leaders were influential in social and religious affairs and advised village administrators on specific issues. Women, poorer households, and other marginalized groups had limited opportunities to influence village meetings. Across the QSEM panel, no women held local leadership positions in early rounds of research.[8] Despite this, respondents in early rounds of the QSEM research voiced few complaints, perceiving little divergence between their interests and those of village leaders (QSEM 2012).

## A new law results in rapid and consequential changes

The *Ward and Village Tract Administration Law,* passed in 2012, fundamentally changed the village governance institutions that had evolved under military rule. These changes are laid out most clearly in Susanne Kempel and Aung Thun's memo (Kempel 2016), which emphasizes three areas. The first was the decision to empower communities to indirectly elect village tract administrators (VTA) via ten household heads and make the VTA an officially recognized part of the state at the village tract level. VTAs had access to a clerk, were provided with a stipend[9] and were responsible for representing the village tract at the township level. The second was the formalization of the role of village elders to manage local elections. The last change is what was left out: village administrators were not included in the 2012 law (Kempel 2016). Some of the new law's effects on village institutions became rapidly visible following the first VTA elections in late 2012/early 2013; others took root more slowly.[10]

Following these changes, village tract administrators rapidly became the most important center of local power at the expense of village administrators. In QSEM villages in Ayeyarwady in 2013, for example, VTAs took over a range of administrative functions ranging from facilitating land registration to approving SIM card lottery applications. The process of approving land registrations was particularly important, as it enabled the VTA to influence the composition of committees formed to oversee land registration. In Magway, for example, VTAs changed committee memberships to better suit their vision and consolidate power into their hands. There were some regional variations, however. In remote areas of Rakhine, there was little immediate indication that the VTA was becoming more important relative to other institutions, whereas in Shan State, village tract dynamics varied significantly (QSEM, December 2013).

By 2014, power was more generally being consolidated in the position of the VTA at the expense of the village administrator. This was driven by government policy changes, improved pay, and, as new external government and donor assistance began to arrive in more villages, greater responsibility. "I only want to be a village tract administrator. As village administrator, I wouldn't have the right to do village development. As all projects go through the village tract administrator, they steer the projects towards their own village" was how one village leader in Chin State explained the change in influence. Increasingly, though most villagers still identified a village leader as their first point of contact, they perceived that final decision-making power increasingly rested with the VTA (QSEM 2014).

Since the first VTA elections, village administrators reported having less authority to assist villagers, despite receiving a similar number of demands for assistance.[11] Removal of recognition of their role by government meant that their ability to represent their communities was constrained, leading them to feel powerless. This, when compared with the situation of the VTA (with a stipend, specified government role, staff), led them to be less interested in the village administrator role (QSEM 2014). As one village leader from Mandalay Region said, "OK. The village tract administrator gets a salary. But why must I do my work? I do not get anything. I am no longer interested" (QSEM 2014).

The story of the re-balancing of local authority since 2013 is not purely one of VTA ascendance. More recently, VTAs began to report that the responsibilities of being a VTA outweighed the benefits. Although VTAs are the only elected officials within the tract, township, or district, their work remains subject to oversight by township officials of the General Administrative Department (GAD), so in practice their administrative authority is constrained. In more recent rounds of research, for example, some VTAs reported being told by township officials to relinquish their involvement in key committees that oversee the use of development resources and to focus instead on more minor administrative functions (QSEM, forthcoming). Opportunities for personal gain and local hegemony are no longer the clear benefits they once were, making the role less attractive.

As with all experiences of Myanmar's reform period, there are variations—especially between communities close to the political center and those on the periphery. In more central areas, namely across most of Ayeyarwady, Magway, and Mandalay regions, villagers were likely to have more regular interactions with government structures and understand that the Ward and Village Tract Administration Law gave clerks and VTAs greater authority to deal with their issues. They also had more access to people in such positions, and so tended to go directly to them, bypassing and undermining village leaders. This appeared to lead towards the abolition in practice of the village administrator position. In contrast, although remote villages in most states reported still relying on village administrators, it was becoming increasingly difficult for villagers to identify a leader willing to assume this role.

## Local elections in 2013 and 2016: How village politics evolved

The first VTA elections were held in 2013. The QSEM research period that followed showed clearly that the new law had reshaped local competition for power. There was VTA turnover in forty-four per cent of villages visited. Interviews with VTAs and VTA candidates across the QSEM panel indicated that the new elections process had encouraged increased political competition. In fact, a handful of tract elections caused local social tension as new leaders and old sought to gain or retain political power. Respondents perceived the competition to be spurred in part by the potential for private gain (QSEM, December 2013).

This level of electoral competition was, however, temporary. Subsequent local elections, held in late 2015/early 2016 and documented in the sixth round of QSEM research, found a decline in competition for VTA positions. Less interest for incumbents in extending their terms resulted in a high rate of turnover (there was a seventy-five per cent turnover across the QSEM panel compared to forty-four per cent in the 2013 election). Few reports of local campaigning emerged, and unlike in 2013, no villages reported social tension emerging from the election result.

Several factors account for this reduction in interest. Others have identified limitations in the administration of the VTA election process as a key factor (Kyed et al. 2016). However, the QSEM research indicates that the lack of interest instead reflects broader substantive changes in the tasks associated with being a VTA. First, the actual authority enjoyed by VTAs has not lived up to early expectations, and the autonomy of VTAs remains constrained by the administrative authority of township officials. Second, recent reforms have reduced the scope for VTAs to engage in localized authoritarianism. The ability of VTAs to force contributions from villagers has been banned (in practice it remains, but in a greatly reduced fashion), limiting the potential for personal enrichment. Although social pressure to contribute to public goods projects (frequently organized by the VTA and sometimes benefitting them directly) and to local religious institutions remains strong, VTAs reported that they were less able to "make" villagers contribute as in previous years. New sources of development assistance have reduced the controlling role of the VTA or sidelined them to advisory roles. Finally, during the most recent election, villagers and VTAs alike expressed uncertainty about the validity of the election process, assuming that the NLD would at least call new elections, or possibly reform local governance via new legislation. As one respondent in Magway Region commented, "Why hasn't the administrator transferred their tasks yet to someone from the newly elected party?" (QSEM forthcoming).

## All told, some movement toward accountability

The 2015 research round showed that local governance institutions were being pushed to be more responsive to their communities. VTAs across the panel reported that they had been told in regular township meetings to better manage interactions with villagers. In particular, they were informed that the collection of fees from villagers to cover operational costs was no longer allowed.[12] Numerous examples have also been documented of VTAs being scolded by township officials in response to complaints made by community members. This accountability no doubt reflects changes in top-down policy in line with the previous government's emphasis on people-centered development (Nixon 2014).

The research, however, suggests that bottom-up accountability has been as much, if not more, of a driving factor. Perceived changes in the overall environment, reflected in the likes of VTA elections, albeit indirect, and improved information sources documenting successful advocacy pursuits across the country have increased downward accountability, leading villagers to be more willing to lodge complaints (QSEM 2016). Village authorities have reported since 2015 that villagers are more vocal with their demands and more assertive in their dealings with village administrators and VTAs alike. One village administrator in Chin State described this by claiming that "Before, village leaders wielded power. Now the villagers wield power" (QSEM 2014). As their connections beyond the village expand, villagers have also been more willing to question the work of local officials. The QSEM first documented this in 2015, and in 2016 found clear examples of villagers in Chin and Kachin States interacting directly with the township authorities. As ever, there was some divide between the center and periphery; roadblocks to the expansion of VTA authority, such as access challenges or villages circumventing the village tract, were more common in the more remote states than in the central regions (QSEM forthcoming).

## EXPECTATIONS OF THE STATE

Another central issue has been changes in how people interact with the "everyday state"[13] and perceive its role in their lives. The relationship has been shaped by an extended prior period in which the state was coercive but provided few services in return. For example, government regulations determined how villagers used their land (Takashi 2008) and what crops they could grow (Hudson-Rodd 2003), and restrictive laws on freedom of association and expression curtailed local political activity and voicing of grievances (Wells 2014). Villages, in return, received little from the state. Government social spending as a proportion of overall budget expenditure, for example, was one of the lowest in the world (UNDP 2014, World Bank 2015c). People in rural areas expected little from the government and sought to minimize their interactions with state actors, with villages becoming largely self-reliant (Tripartite Core Group 2008).

As part of the transition, policy at the national level emphasized the importance of producing results locally. The previous government's "people-centered development" approach aimed to deliver a "rapid improvement of public services and development with quick wins" (Anon 2014; Nixon 2014). In response, expenditure on health has tripled as a share of the budget, moving from 1.7 per cent of the budget in 2009/10 to 6.4 per cent in 2013/14, while education grew from 7.2 per cent to 12.5 per cent over the same period (World Bank 2015c). This increase in government expenditure has been reflected in the steady increase in government service provision in the QSEM villages. The rollout of these services, combined with the implementation locally of other national policy reforms—particularly land reforms and strengthened information flows—are influencing community expectations of the role of government. In turn, these changing expectations are producing, over time, observable changes in how communities interact with government through greater upwards accountability.

## Increases in government services delivered locally

QSEM research identified a three-fold increase in government-funded services in villages since 2011.[14] In the first three research rounds, each village had, on average, slightly more than one type of government-funded service, consisting mainly of support for primary schools and access to credit (QSEM, December 2013). By late 2013 to mid-2014, each village had on average over three types of service. As one respondent from Shan State noted, "The township administrator asked us to apply for funding. Our village tract received five million *kyat*. We never received anything before this" (QSEM 2014). These increases have since steadied. At the time of writing this paper, villages in the panel received an average of close to four different types of support. This expansion was driven primarily by government funding for local infrastructure, including through a parliament constituency fund, education activities and access to credit.

Approaches to service delivery have also changed. At the outset, government activities at village level were invariably centrally planned and provided limited scope for communities to influence what types of services were delivered or how. Most government services in early rounds centered on education or access to credit, usually in the form of Myanmar Agricultural Development Bank (MADB) loans. Both MADB loans and education services were delivered uniformly across areas.[15] Some villages also received basic school infrastructure projects. Villagers invariably had to contribute financial or in-kind assistance, but their ability to influence the type of support they got was limited.

More recent rounds have found that villagers have limited voice in identifying what types of services they can receive. The QSEM research has yet to identify examples of villages undertaking locally driven, bottom-up planning to identify and articulate their needs. The types of services delivered are invariably centrally designed and rolled out.

The government is, however, providing greater autonomy to villages in how programs are implemented. Two examples from the most recent round of research highlight how this is done. In many QSEM villages in Kachin State and Mandalay Region, a government-funded electrification program allowed approaches to implementation to differ by state or region. Village meetings were also held to discuss locally appropriate mechanisms for targeting and determining household contributions, although in most instances village leaders made final decisions in consultation with the electricity service provider. Similarly, the government's *Mya Sein Yaung* (or Evergreen Village Project), a Department for Rural Development program that provides participating villages with 30 million *kyat* to be distributed as livelihood loans, has enabled villagers themselves to determine criteria for accessing loans, the size of the loans and implementation procedures.

In both cases, adjustments were made to centrally planned programs to provide more space for local voices in decision-making. They reflect much of the ongoing discussion on decentralization in Myanmar. Although national policy directives have emphasized the role of sub-national levels of governance (UNDP 2014), approaches to achieving this have been top-down and ad hoc, with different departments emphasizing different aspects of perceived decentralization. The electrification program reflects a form of fiscal and administrative decentralization to the state/region level, whereas the Evergreen Village Project can be viewed more as administrative decentralization to below the township level. Both examples, however, are consistent with a somewhat minimalist "deconcentration" definition of decentralization, with lower levels of government being provided with increased scope for decision-making within well-defined parameters (Schneider 2003).

## Perceptions of implementation of national reform policies at the local level

As villagers come to expect greater government services, local perceptions of the role of government are also changing based on experience of how national reform policies have been implemented locally. The rollout of such reforms has reinforced perceptions that the transition is not just a national phenomenon, but is also playing out locally in ways that affect people's lives. The research has documented numerous examples of how this is playing out. Changes in the village administration policy framework resulting in more democratic elections of village tract administrators, as discussed in the previous section, is one example. We highlight two other prominent areas here.

The most tangible widespread evidence of the transition being felt locally arose from government policy reforms providing individuals with greater land use rights, including rights to buy, sell, and trade land.[16] In QSEM villages in 2013, there was strong awareness among villagers of the impending rollout of land registration as a result of the *Farmland Law* and the *Vacant, Fallow and Virgin Lands Law*. Villagers expected that local officials would efficiently implement the new policies. In subsequent rounds, land registration had largely occurred, and by mid-2014, eighty per cent of villages in the QSEM panel reported land registration as completed for all individually owned land in their village recognized under the Farmland Law.

In some areas, however, registration was problematic, and villagers have tested the responsiveness of government officials in attempting to overcome these issues. The most prevalent exception stemmed from limitations in the regulatory framework restricting registration for land that was not individually owned, such as communal or shifting cultivation land, or was farmed by individuals but recorded in government records as vacant fallow land. In several QSEM villages, primarily in upland areas, communities have sought to overcome this and begun to transfer communal land management to enable individual households to register land. In upland areas, the primary incentive for this was to reduce the risk of outside interests registering otherwise unregistered land (QSEM, forthcoming).[17] In over a third of villages, there were also reports of administrative barriers to registration, including requests for informal payments or inaccurate registration as officials drew on outdated land records. The research identified numerous instances where villagers, emboldened by their understanding of the new operating environment, pushed back against these administrative barriers. For example, a farmer in Shan State, who was asked to pay 120,000 *kyat* to have the name on the land certificate changed from the previous owner's name, only agreed to pay if the official issued a receipt acknowledging this as an official cost (QSEM 2016).

Villagers also identified perceived changes in the behavior of local officials in implementing their duties and linked these to the national reforms. Research in 2014 identified specific areas where officials were instructed to be more cautious in engaging with communities. As discussed above, respondents in numerous villages claimed village tract administrators received instructions in their regular township meetings that collecting fees from villagers to cover operational costs was no longer permitted now that the government was providing monthly allocations for village tract administration. Similarly, in the same round of research, villagers in Rakhine State and Ayeyarwady Region claimed that fisheries officials were less likely to visit villages to collect licensing fees, as they had been instructed to avoid actions that could generate complaints (QSEM 2015). This combination of actual roll-out of national reforms locally and perceptions among communities, driven in part through emerging norms and networks about how government should act, was changing the balance in the relationship between citizens and the state in rural communities.

## CONNECTIVITY: FROM LOCAL TO GLOBAL

QSEM has documented how the social and economic networks of people living in villages have expanded since the reforms of 2012. Telecommunications access has increased massively; migration networks have improved; road infrastructure has expanded; and access to markets has increased. Together, these have the potential to result in intense social transformation. This section examines the nascent but emerging evidence of this.

Whereas existing research suggests that villages have become much more connected to national and global networks following the transition, such networks already existed before the reforms. Authors such as Wells (2014) and Paung Ku (2010) have documented the building of "bottom-up" civil society networks that existed prior to the transition in parts of the country. Before 2012, these networks most commonly were mobilized as responses to specific issues such as the natural disasters of cyclones Nargis and Giri, and conflicts or concerns relating to the environment, natural resource projects or the like (Paung Ku 2010). Migration networks had also been established throughout the country. Although data on levels, types and destinations of migration has been lacking until recently, sufficient information exists to ascertain that migration was a common livelihood strategy across Myanmar, with significant variations in destination and levels dependent on states or regions (Turnell 2008; World Bank 2015a). Recent analysis suggests, for example, that approximately five per cent of households in Ayeyarwady Region and slightly more in Magway Region had a family member migrating either domestically or abroad in 2010 (World Bank 2015a).

One of the most noticeable changes in connectivity relates to telecommunications. The speed and scale of the rollout of telecommunications access has been documented elsewhere (see Mod 2016). Government of Myanmar figures show that in 2009/10 only four per cent of households owned mobile phones; by April 2014 this figure had risen to thirty-three per cent of households and by April 2015, fully fifty-five per cent of households owned mobile phones (Government of Myanmar 2015). With a government target of connecting ninety per cent of the population by 2019, this number will only continue to rise (ADB 2016).

Expanded mobile coverage is having a significant impact. During fieldwork conducted in mid-2013, villagers reported that, "Previously, there might not even be one landline in a village; one would have to go to a village tract village to find a phone. Now, however, with the cost of mobile phones decreasing, there might be up to ten phones in a village" (QSEM June 2013). The QSEM research has documented the almost immediate impact mobile phone connectivity has had for migration networks (World Bank 2015a).[18] It was assumed that coverage would offer immediate potential for farmers and other livelihood groups through expanded market information. Farmers initially placed greater confidence in information gained through their traditional networks. But patterns of mobile use to inform market choices are emerging (QSEM, forthcoming). Although still nascent, these changes are likely to have important implications on social relations and engagement with the state over time. Others have argued that adoption is likely to be significantly influenced by types of livelihoods and reliance on networks within those livelihoods (Aricat and Ling 2015).

More immediately, there are at least two areas where improved mobile phone connectivity is already having a direct effect on engagement with the state and social relations. First, more recent rounds of research have highlighted how technology and, in particular, social media networks are starting to be used to strengthen or supplement existing communal mechanisms, in particular to respond to community-wide shocks.

Community organizations drew on social media to assist efforts in response to the floods and landslides that affected large parts of Myanmar following Cyclone Komen in mid-2015 (see McCarthy 2018). Affected QSEM villages in Magway Region and Chin State highlighted how they were using Facebook to source donations from networks in Yangon and overseas and keep relatives and friends up to date with recovery efforts. Once immediate needs had been met, in at least one village, the social media group started to support the work of village authorities to raise funds and advocate for a potential move of the village to a new location (World Bank 2015b).

Second, mobile networks have strengthened access to alternative information flows with particular significance in villages facing major external challenges. Wells (2014) explores the increasing role of mobile phone access in strengthening citizen voices in land disputes in Ayeyarwady Region. This work focuses on the importance of expanding mobile phone coverage to strengthen advocacy by linking village advocates to external networks of journalists, members of parliament and technical experts. Our research shows that, in addition, expanded connectivity has played a crucial role in providing villages with alternative sources of information. Villagers have drawn from improved connectivity to access previously inaccessible information about local development issues, using this to mobilize. Examples have included village activists who have drawn on improved information networks to hold awareness-raising meetings in their villages around land confiscation issues close to the Special Economic Zone (SEZ) in Rakhine State, or around land ownership in townships where land is controlled by Myanmar Oil and Gas Enterprises (MOGE) in Magway Region. In Magway Region, villagers received regular updates on advocacy efforts in a neighboring township, hoping that resolution there would provide a pathway for resolving their own issues. Similarly, in several villages, particularly in the uplands, villagers followed news through social media of land confiscation cases being resolved, which generated expectations that their own grievances could be acted on. At times, however, as is discussed in the following section, this access to information can further entrench differences and fuel contestation. While not documented in villages included in the QSEM panel, the most common example of this has been the expansion of anti-Muslim sentiments, amplified and normalized in part by access to digital and social media (see McCarthy 2018, Morrison 2015).

Improved connectivity through migration is also likely to affect pre-existing social networks and power relations. The research has documented an almost doubling of migration rates across villages in each state or region between 2012 and 2015. At the higher end, average rates increased from estimated 10.2 per cent of the population to 16 per cent across villages in Mandalay Region. The lowest migration rates were in Shan State, with increases from 0.8 per cent of the population to 2.6 per cent.[19] Migration patterns varied: migrants from Chin and Rakhine favored international migration, while Ayeyarwady and Magway Regions saw increasing domestic migration to Yangon (QSEM 2016). More extensive research on domestic migration (World Bank 2015a) has yet to identify definitive implications on sending communities as a result of these increases in migration, at least in Ayeyarwady and Magway regions. Our research suggests, however, that the combined impact of households getting richer through remittances, their social networks beyond the village expanding through migration, and demographic change are likely, over time, to have an equally significant influence on local power dynamics and social relations.

Throughout the research, improved connectivity has affected village governance and local power structures. The cases emphasize that improved connectivity can either strengthen the position of existing leaders or provide alternatives and, in the process, generate contestation. The work of the youth group in Chin State supported the village leadership while also enabling emerging leaders to play a role in village affairs. Similarly, in a number of the land confiscation cases documented by QSEM research in the uplands, villagers drew on improved information flows and mobilized around the work of village leaders to pursue their claims. Across several villages in Kachin State, however, this created friction with village tract administrators, who were perceived as being implicitly involved in the transfer of land. The strengthened activist networks in the examples from Magway Region or Rakhine State provided alternative options than those presented by traditional village leaders. To date, the competition generated from these alternative views has not generated social tension, but it does represent a change in village affairs. As one villager from Rakhine State noted after distributing information on the SEZ to villagers, "Twelve months ago the village leader would never have let us hold meetings in this village. Now we can hold meetings, but he will attend and take notes of who came and what we discussed" (QSEM 2016).

## IMPLICATIONS FOR STATE-SOCIETY AND SOCIAL RELATIONS

The preceding sections have examined key areas of social change in communities since the national political transition beginning in 2012. We have argued that the key vectors through which changes in social relations occurs are village governance, citizens' expectations of the state, and the nature and extent of connectivity. However, it is how these three factors combine that most significantly influences social structures in rural Myanmar. In this section, we examine this interplay. One already apparent result of this has been observable shifts in social accountability mechanisms. Another outcome, less apparent but potentially more important, is that the increasing complexity of social relations at the local level will highlight local fault-lines that have previously been glossed over (or just been non-salient politically until now).

### Enhancing social accountability

A platform for community action is emerging that prior to the transition was either off-limits or restricted. This has emerged because of changing community expectations of the state and perceptions that increased voice is permissible, combined with networks that are providing communities with the tools and information to mobilize. If social accountability refers to the ways in which citizens (and civil society) participate directly or indirectly in holding government to account for their actions (Malena 2004), then we argue that the cases we present in this article represent evidence of strengthening social accountability in rural Myanmar.

The most identifiable evidence of enhanced social accountability has arisen from mobilization around land confiscation. Approximately twenty per cent of villages in the QSEM panel faced land confiscation issues, invariably involving large areas of land and multiple households. Most claims are long-standing.[20] The instances documented through the research show that communities take the prevailing political context into consideration in their actions (World Bank 2013). As the political context has changed, so too have community demands.

Across the first three rounds of research in 2012 and 2013, a number of villages reported land confiscation grievances, but the only active efforts to seek redress were in Rakhine State, where villagers requested monetary compensation from pipeline construction and attempted to halt new attempts at confiscation. Since 2013, however, villagers have been significantly more willing to confront land cases, with some success. For example, a military base in Shan State returned land to villagers in 2014. A settlement had been reached to return land confiscated by military business interests in Kachin State and direct negotiations with business interests and government officials were on-going involving land confiscation in Ayeyarwady, Magway and Rakhine. Not all cases in the QSEM panel have been resolved; indeed, several new claims of confiscation emerged during the research period. However, our findings highlight that new opportunities are emerging for communities to seek redress.

The convergence of changes in village institutions, state expectations, and connectivity has driven this increased accountability. Advocacy efforts across all states and regions flowed from an awareness in villages that the national government had acknowledged land confiscation was an issue and that pressure could be placed on local officials to pursue claims. Increased accountability of village leaders, including through the election process, was also a factor. Whereas in the past, village leaders had limited ability to mitigate confiscation efforts and, at times, facilitated confiscation, recent research has documented instances of upwards pressure on village leaders, requiring them to liaise with township officials to seek resolution on behalf of villagers. As one newly elected leader in Rakhine State noted, farmers wanted the question of compensation addressed and, since he owed his position to them, he had an opportunity to help (QSEM 2014). Approaches to pursuing claims also depended on knowledge obtained from other cases. Improved information flows were crucial to this. Similarly, if limited communication channels previously meant that efforts could be blocked or delayed at any level, mobile networks now enable villagers to circumvent or identify alternative advocacy points if and where obstacles emerge.

## Potential implications for social relations

The literature on village-level social relations in Myanmar is limited. Where social relations have been examined, research has tended to emphasize the strong social bonds that exist within villages, as villages rely on communal action to address village needs (Tripartite Core Group 2008). The available literature implicitly assumes that local perspectives are shared by all and actions against the outside are based on local consensus. Studies focusing on bottom-up advocacy such as Wells (2014) and Paung Ku (2010) have, to date, presented a picture of unified community action in opposition to the state. The research presented in this article, however, highlights that the local reality is much more complex than this. Across each of the three drivers we have presented, the evidence shows that there are divergent views and, at times, contestation. An example from one QSEM village in the oil extraction location of Magway Region highlights this contestation across the three drivers. The village falls within an area where MOGE regulates land use and ownership.

Changes in village governance regulations have influenced how villagers and their leaders engage with government. To date, village leaders have sought to avoid confronting MOGE over land ownership claims, instead prioritizing lobbying for greater investment in services, such as school infrastructure. Not everyone in the village agrees, however. Up to early 2015, local activists with township civil society and NLD links used their networks and information on land law to lobby for a more direct approach. In one example, they uploaded photos to Facebook complaining about the quality of construction of the school building funded by MOGE, resulting in the VTA being scolded by township officials, further straining relations between village elites. This level of contestation in decision-making about how external assistance is used and how villages should engage with the government is not unique to this village, but was reflected in several QSEM villages. From an outsiders' perspective, village advocacy efforts against external actors are often perceived as unifying, and indeed in many QSEM villages, villagers did tend to put to one side existing tensions when pursuing grievances against external actors. However, this masked significant underlying contestation. In several land confiscation cases highlighted throughout the research, villagers perceived village tract administrators or village leaders to have helped facilitate such confiscation. Similar local disputes have been documented involving the distribution of development resources from donors, NGOs, or government.

Finally, the case above shows the increasing complexity introduced by improved communication networks, which enable different parties to voice contending views and complain more prominently. The case highlights how different groups can draw on strengthened information flows to further entrench opposing views and, on occasion, escalate disputes. Similar contests exist, for example, in villages around the Special Economic Zone in Rakhine State, where local activists accessing information from civil society networks at the township level often present rather differing views to those presented by village officials and obtained from government meetings.

We would argue that, overall, although local contestation has yet to manifest itself at scale (largely because, for now, local tensions have been put aside while parties focus on external grievances during a period of transition), the rising prevalence of such contestation indicates that once engagement with the state is normalized these tensions have the potential to assume greater prominence. This corresponds with similar trends being documented by others. Maung and Wells, for example, have identified the role of increased connectivity and changes in political dynamics as a challenge for advocacy organizations in mobilizing communities and building consensus in claims relating to Special Economic Zones (see Pyae Phyo Maung and Wells, Chapter 7 this volume). Going forward, forging strategies for anticipating and responding effectively (and equitably) to these tensions must be a priority.

## CONCLUSIONS: IMPLICATIONS FOR POLICY, PRACTICE AND RESEARCH

This paper has explored the implications of Myanmar's transition for people and social institutions at the local level. With seventy per cent of Myanmar's population living in rural villages, understanding how national reforms are being managed locally and how citizens are engaging in and shaping the reform process is crucial. We have sought to provide a first step in this direction by drawing on a unique and extensive dataset to analyse how governance reforms are changing the life experiences of people in rural communities and altering the social contract between citizens and the state.

To date, three changes have most influenced the relationship between the government and communities. First, national reforms in village governance have re-aligned the centers of power and influence at the local level. Second, citizens' expectations of the role of government are changing. This is being driven by an increase in government service delivery, albeit from a low base, combined with changing perceptions of how government officials should act, which in turn is influenced by people's experiences of how transition is manifested in their communities. Third, people's networks beyond their villages have expanded, driven by improvements in telecommunications and local infrastructure and an increase in the movement of people.

An unintended consequence of policy reforms in areas such as telecommunications and nascent decentralization initiatives has been the re-shaping of the social contract between citizens and the state through strengthened mechanisms of social accountability. Communities have both drawn from a perception that transition has led the government to respond more effectively to community needs and, by acting on the perception, have re-enforced and further embedded that accountability. The focus on national transition and citizen engagement with the state has, to date, meant that local contests of authority have remained largely dormant and under-examined.

"Managing" this transition—or, more accurately, the many manifestations of these interacting transformations—requires placing a premium on the legitimacy of the change process, and the mechanisms by which the contests it inevitably generates are addressed. The research identifies a number of areas where government and its partners can work to ensure that the role of communities in Myanmar's transition is further strengthened. These seek to frame "how" Myanmar's transition should be engaged rather than a prescriptive "what" should be done.

A clear, consistent vision for the role of village institutions is required. The government needs to work towards providing villages with some autonomy in decision-making, better defining the scope of authority of village tract administrators and putting in place mechanisms that encourage community participation, transparency and oversight. The broader decentralization agenda would also benefit from a more systematic framework and structured implementation strategy rather than depending on ad hoc initiatives by different government departments. Finally, the research emphasizes the importance of providing timely and accurate information to communities to strengthen the positive role they can play in the transition.

It is also inevitable that how well these transformations are resolved will vary considerably: some places will excel, others will muddle through, and still others will struggle greatly. Continuing to invest in grounded field research will be crucial to documenting this variation and explaining it, as well as offering real time "lessons" to enhance the likelihood that Myanmar's citizens and public officials can learn together how to shape and consolidate their democratic institutions.

## Notes

1   All authors are staff members of, or affiliated with, the World Bank. The views expressed in this paper are those of the authors alone, and should not be attributed to the World Bank, its executive directors, or the countries they represent. We acknowledge the pioneering work of our local research teams, for whom an exercise of this nature, scale, intensity and duration was unprecedented. For helpful comments on earlier drafts of this paper we thank Christina Fink, Gerard McCarthy, Corey Pattison, Caitlin Pierce, Abdoulaye Seck, an anonymous peer reviewer and the conveners of and participants at the 2017 Myanmar Update (held at the Australian National University in February 2017) and the Myanmar Update Forum (held at the University of Yangon in March 2017). Author for correspondence: Andrea Woodhouse (awoodhouse@ worldbank.org).

2   On this later point, while acknowledging that beyond-village networks did exist prior to 2011 (and, indeed, prior to 2008), these networks have expanded, deepened, and strengthened in important ways under the USDP government and since.

3   QSEM is funded by the Livelihoods and Food Security Trust (LIFT) and implemented by a joint team from the World Bank and Enlightened Myanmar Research (EMR). The analytical framework for the research focuses on understanding rural livelihoods, shocks and coping strategies, village governance, social relations and external assistance.

4   The original panel has consisted of nine villages each in three regions (Ayeyarwady, Magway and Mandalay) and three states (Chin, Rakhine and Shan). Villages were purposively selected to ensure representation across a number of variables. A seventh state (Kachin State) was added to the sample for the sixth round of research in early 2015.

5   It should be noted that the QSEM research is conducted also exclusively at the village level. There are a small number of interviews in townships to cross-check information. While there is much discussion within government and by technical experts about the progress of political, financial and administrative decentralization this has not been an area that has attracted a significant degree of interest at the village level over the course of the research.

6   The increased research is, in part, due to an easing of restrictions on research in rural areas.

7   Village tract administrators are official positions under the Ward and Village Tract Administration Law. The VTA represents all villages in a village tract and is important because the VTA acts as the main interlocutor between communities and the state. Prior to the Ward and Village Tract Administration Law, each village was also represented by a village administrator (VA, otherwise known

as a one-hundred household head). Although this position has officially been abolished, most people in any given village are able to identify a village leader who, in practice, continues to perform this role.

8   This includes village tract administrators, village administrators or 10 household heads. The most recent round of research saw a small but noticeable change in this trend, with nine women across two villages each in Mandalay and Magway and one village in Ayeyarwady being elected as 10 household heads (QSEM, forthcoming).

9   Asia Foundation research conducted in 2014 cited VTAs who reported receiving MMK 50,000 per month as support for office expenditure and a further MMK 70,000 as a personal stipend. There is limited wage data on rural Myanmar's civil servants, but in QSEM panel villages in 2016 teachers and rural health workers have been reported to earn between MMK 120,000 and MMK 180,000 per month.

10  It should be noted that electoral accountability remains indirect, through ten household leaders, who are selected via an informal election within each ten-household grouping.

11  Although the role of village administrator was officially abolished after passage of the Ward and Village Tract Administration Law, in all villages in the research panel villagers were able to identify a village leader and there was consensus within that village as to who held that position.

12  Restrictions on the ability of local officials to collect fees were imposed at the same time as the government increased stipends for VTAs and government officials and additional financing was accessible through an increase in development resources at the local level.

13  The idea of the "everyday state" – encounters with staff of government agencies that most citizens (especially those in rural areas) experience most frequently, such as teachers, health workers, police, agricultural extension officers, local officials – comes from Corbridge et al. (2005).

14  Government services are activities funded by the government that are delivered at the village level. Those identified through the research primarily cover village education and health services, local infrastructure and electrification programs and credit services. The research calculates the number of different types of services or programs funded by government in each village. The information is derived from interviews with villagers, including village leaders and updated through each round of research. Through the research approach it is not possible to track the level of funding across government services or per village as information about budgets is, more often than not, not available at the village level.

15  Education services mainly comprised the provision of government teachers, with some villages also receiving funds for basic infrastructure. The approach

to disbursing MADB loans was uniform with the only variation being different loan amounts for paddy growing areas compared to areas where other crops were grown.

16 In March 2012, the government passed two new laws regulating land ownership. For the first time since military rule, the Farmland Law effectively formally acknowledges private interests in agricultural land. The law enables farmers to register land use certificates in their names and freely buy, sell and pawn land. The Vacant, Fallow, Virgin Lands Management Law regulates the use of vacant, fallow or virgin lands, including provisions for leasing such land and enabling farmers to apply to use otherwise unused land (QSEM 2013).

17 It should be noted that in many areas of Myanmar, especially paddy producing areas, an additional driving incentive for registration was to facilitate access to loans and, in particular, Myanmar Agricultural Development Bank (MADB) loans.

18 Mobile phone connectivity is enabling potential migrants to confirm opportunities beforehand, improve safety and facilitating on-going communication through the migration experience.

19 Across each round research teams asked village leaders in each village to estimate the proportion of the population currently migrating. These village averages were subsequently averaged across the villages in each state or region. The research emphasizes significant variations across villages.

20 The claims cover all states and regions in the QSEM panel with the exception of Chin State and Mandalay Region. The land confiscation claims include claims against the military: a village in Shan State that has separate claims against three different military bases bordering the village; claims against business interests with ties to the military: as per several villages in Kachin State and a village in Rakhine State where wives of military officers attempt to seize five hundred acres of communal land; and claims relating to infrastructure investments: such as claims surrounding the gas pipeline in Rakhine State, a railroad built to support a steel factory and oil interests in Magway Region, as per the example above, and land confiscation by a company to build a road in Ayeyarwardy Region. Across a number of these cases, villagers perceive local officials including village administrators or tract administrators and township officials, particularly from the land records department, as playing a facilitating role in the land acquisition process.

# References

Anon. "Union Government to Draw People-Centered Plan to Achieve Goals: President U Thein Sein". *The New Light of Myanmar*, 7 January 2014.

Aricat, Rajiv George and Rich Ling. "Mobile Phone Appropriation and Non-adoption at the Bottom of the Pyramid (BoP): Evidence from the Pre-privatized Telecommunications Era in Myanmar". International Conference on Burma/Myanmar Studies – Burma/Myanmar in Transition: Connectivity, Changes and Challenges, 24–25 July 2015.

Asian Development Bank. "ADB, IFC to Help Extend Mobile Telecom Services across Myanmar". ADB press release, 8 February 2016. < https://www.adb.org/news/adb-ifc-help-extend-mobile-telecom-services-across-myanmar> [accessed 22 November 2016].

Corbridge, Stuart, Glyn Williams, Manoj Srivastava and Rene Veron. *Seeing the State: Governance and Governmentality in India.* New York: Cambridge University Press, 2005.

Economic and Social Commission for Asia and the Pacific. *Statistical Yearbook, 2011.*

Englehart, Neil A. "Is Regime Change Enough for Burma? The Problem of State Capacity". *Political Science Faculty Publications.* Paper 51, 2005.

Faxon, Hilary Oliva. "In the Law and On the Land: Finding the Female Farmer in Myanmar's National Land Use Policy". Masters Dissertation, Graduate School, Cornell University. January 2017.

Fink, Christina. "How Real are Myanmar's Reforms?" *Current History* 113:764, 2014.

Government of Myanmar. "The 2014 Myanmar Population and Housing Census". Myanmar, 2014.

Griffiths, Michael. "Resilience and Community Social Organizations in Rural Myanmar". Social Policy and Poverty Research Group, May 2016.

Griffiths, Mike and Yaw Bawn Mangshang. "Social Protection in Myanmar: A Key Mechanism for Political Legitimacy". Presentation, Myanmar Update, Australian National University, February 2017.

Holliday, I.M. "Myanmar in 2012: Towards a Normal State". *Asian Survey* 53, 2013.

Hudson-Rodd, Nancy and Myo Nyunt. "Control of Land and Life in Burma". Tenure Brief. Wisconsin: Land Tenure Center, No. 3, April 2001.

Inada, Kyosuke. "Catalyzing Subnational Development in Myanmar: Balancing Local Preferences with National and Sector Policy." The Asia Foundation, August 2014. <https://asiafoundation.org/publication/catalyzing-subnational-development-in-myanmar/> [accessed 3 January 2018].

International Organization for Migration (IOM) and Asian Research Center on Migration. "Assessing Potential Changes in the Migration Patterns of Myanmar Migrants and their Impacts on Thailand." December 2013. Report. <https://thailand.iom.int/assessing-potential-changes-migration-patterns-myanmar-migrants-and-their-impacts-thailand> [accessed 3 January 2018].

Kempel, Susanne and Myanmar Development Research. "Village Institutions and Leadership in Myanmar: A View from Below." United Nations Development Program, 2012.

Kempel, Susanne and Aung Thu Nyein. "Local Governance Dynamics in South East Myanmar: An Assessment for Swiss Agency for Development and Cooperation (SDC)." Swiss Agency for Development and Cooperation, 2014.

Kempel, Susanne and Aung Thun. "Ward and Village Tract Administrator Elections 2016: An Overview of the Role, the Laws and the Procedures", January 2016. <http://www.themimu.info/sites/themimu.info/files/documents/Report_Ward_Village_Tract_Administrator_Elections_2016_NPA_Jan2016.pdf> [accessed 22 November 2017].

Kurosaki, Takashi. "Crop Choice, Farm Income, and Political Control in Myanmar". *Journal of the Asia Pacific Economy* 13 (2), March 2008.

Kyed, H.M., A. Pohl Harrison, and G. McCarthy. "Local Democracy in Myanmar: Reflections on Ward and Village Tract Elections in 2016". 2016 <http://pure.diis.dk/ws/files/663836/Myanmar_Elections_WEB.pdf> [accessed 11 July 2017].

McCarthy, Gerard. "Building on What's There: Insights on Social Protection and Public Goods Provision from Central-East Myanmar". International Growth Centre, September, 2016.

McCarthy, Gerard. "Cyber-spaces". In *Routledge Handbook of Contemporary Myanmar,* edited by Simpson, Farrelly & Holliday. Routledge, New York: 2018.

Malena, Carmen, Reiner Forster, and Janmejay Singh. "Social Accountability: An Introduction to the Concept and Emerging Practice". World Bank Social Development Papers. No. 76, December 2004.

Mod, Craig. "The Facebook-Loving Farmers of Myanmar: A Dispatch from an Internet Revolution in Progress". *The Atlantic,* 21 January 2016.

Morrison, Maude. "The New Radicals: Social Media and Communal Violence in Myanmar". Paper presented to SAIS Asia Conference, Johns Hopkins University, 2015.

Nash, Manning. *The Golden Road to Modernity: Village Life in Contemporary Burma.* New York: John Wiley and Sons, 1965.

Nixon, Hamish and Cindy Joelene. "Fiscal Decentralization in Myanmar: Towards a Roadmap for Reform". Subnational Governance in Myanmar Discussion Paper Series No. 5, June 2014.

Oo, Dr Zaw, Dr Aniruddha Bonnerjee, Phoo Pwint Phyu, Giles Dickenson-Jones and Paul Minoletti. "Making Public Sector Finance Work for Children in Myanmar". UNICEF and MDRI-CESD, 2014.

Paung Ku. "Reflections on the Giri Response". November 2010. <http://www.scribd.com/doc/67205436/Paung-ku-reflections-on-giri> [accessed 22 November 2016].

Pederson, Morten B. "Myanmar's Democratic Opening: The Process and Prospect of Reform". In *Debating Democratization in Myanmar*, edited by Nick Cheesman and Nicholas Farrelly. Singapore: The Institute of Southeast Asian Studies, 2014.

QSEM. "Livelihoods and Social Change in Rural Myanmar". QSEM Series. No. 1. World Bank, October 2012.

————— "Livelihoods and Social Change in Rural Myanmar". QSEM Series. No. 2. World Bank, June 2013.

————— "Livelihoods and Social Change in Rural Myanmar". QSEM Series. No. 3. World Bank, December 2013.

————— "Livelihoods and Social Change in Rural Myanmar". QSEM Series. No. 4. World Bank, December 2014.

————— "Livelihoods and Social Change in Rural Myanmar". QSEM Series. No. 5. World Bank, January 2016.

————— "Livelihoods and Social Change in Rural Myanmar". QSEM Series. No. 6. World Bank, forthcoming.

Thawnghmung, Ardeth. "Rural Perceptions of State Legitimacy in Burma/Myanmar". *Journal of Peasant Studies* 30 (2): 1–40, 2003.

The Asia Foundation. "Myanmar 2014: Civic Knowledge and Values in a Changing Society", 2014. < https://asiafoundation.org/resources/pdfs/MyanmarSurvey20141.pdf> [accessed 22 November 2016].

Tripartite Core Group (Government of Myanmar, ASEAN and the United Nations). "Post-Nargis Joint Assessment", 2008. <https://www.gfdrr.org/sites/default/files/GFDRR_Myanmar_Post-Nargis_Joint_Assessment_2008_EN.pdf> [accessed 22 November 2016].

Turnell, Sean. "Recapitalizing Burma's Rural Credit System". In *Ruling Myanmar: From Cyclone Nargis to National Elections*, edited by Nick Cheesman, Monique Skidmore and Trevor Wilson. Singapore: Institute of Southeast Asian Studies, 2010.

Turnell, Sean, Allison Vicary, and Wylie Bradford. "Migrant Worker Remittances and Burma: An Economic Analysis of Survey Results". In *Dictatorship, Disorder and Decline in Myanmar*, edited by Monique Skidmore and Trevor Wilson. Canberra: ANU E-Press, 2008.

UNDP. "The State of Local Governance Trends in Ayeyarwady". UNDP Local Governance Mapping Series, 2014. <http://www.mm.undp.org/content/dam/myanmar/docs/Publications/PovRedu/Local%20Governance%20Mapping/UNDP_MM_LG_Mapping_Ayeyarwady_web.pdf?download> [accessed 22 November 2016].

————— "Women and Local Leadership: Leadership Journeys of Myanmar's Female Village Tract/Ward Administrators". UNDP, 2015.

Wells, Tamas and Kyaw Thu Aung. "Village Networks, Land Law, and Myanmar's Democratization". In *Debating Democratization in Myanmar*, edited by Nick

Cheesman, Nicholas Farrelly and Trevor Wilson. Singapore: Institute of Southeast Asian Studies, 2014.

Win, Thidar Htwe. "A Glance at the Dynamics of the Traditional Social Networks of *Simihtun* Village, *Amarapura* Township, *Mandalay* Region". International Conference on Burma/Myanmar Studies – Burma/Myanmar in Transition: Connectivity, Changes and Challenges, 24–25 July 2015.

Wittekind, Courtney. "An Uncertain 'Progress'". November 2015. <www. teacircleoxford.com/2015/11/07/an-uncertain-progress> [accessed 11 July 2017].

World Bank. "A Country on the Move: Domestic Migration in Two Regions in Myanmar". QSEM Thematic Study. 2015a.

_____ "Myanmar – Post-disaster Needs Assessment of Floods and Landslides: July – September 2015". 2015b.

_____ "Realigning the Union Budget to Myanmar's Development Priorities: Public Expenditure Review". 2015c.

_____ "Social Accountability E-Guide". 2013 <https://saeguide.worldbank.org> Accessed 14 November 2016.

# 3

## SOCIAL PROTECTION IN MYANMAR: A KEY MECHANISM FOR POLITICAL LEGITIMACY?

Yaw Bawm Mangshang and Mike Griffiths

Myanmar is currently undergoing significant political and social reforms, in a context of ethnic and religious diversity, growing inequalities and ongoing armed conflict. Critical to the success of reforms, and to the ongoing peace process, is sustained political legitimacy. Where previous governments have sought legitimacy based on notions of security, the challenge for current and future governments is to build legitimacy on a foundation of equitable pluralism. In such a context, social protection offers a pathway to build public trust, and establish legitimacy based on consent, consistent with social contract theory which obliges mutual benefits and responsibilities between the state and citizens. Although Myanmar has a rich tradition of non-formal social protection and norms of reciprocity, the wider implementation of social protection is still in its infancy. However, the policy direction and implementation approach followed in developing social protection mechanisms are crucial to the success of building public trust and a sustainable peace process. This includes ensuring adequate state funding, potentially through: appropriating mineral revenues; giving sufficient attention to inequalities; identifying and building on existing repositories of social capital; facilitating a more devolved and localized approach to planning and delivery of social protection; and developing more localized approaches to accountability and transparency.

This paper is organized in five sections and is based on existing literature, reports by relevant government departments, development partners, and media as well as personal observation through interactions with ordinary citizens. The first section outlines the key issues of political legitimacy in the Myanmar context, including why political legitimacy is important in the current power structure in Myanmar. The second section considers the "trust deficit" which currently challenges the development of political legitimacy in Myanmar. The third section introduces the general concept of social protection, and the fourth section summarizes historical trends and the current status of social protection in Myanmar. The final section draws on both international evidence and evidence from Myanmar on how social protection acts to build trust and legitimacy and concludes with recommendations on the future direction of social protection in Myanmar, in particular approaches to social protection policy which can contribute to building public trust.

## POLITICAL LEGITIMACY IN MYANMAR: A BRIEF BACKGROUND

Although political legitimacy is an ambiguous concept (Buchanan 2002), consent is widely recognized as a key foundation. Gilley explains that legitimacy is an "endorsement of the state by citizens" (Gilley 2006, p. 502). Although electoral democracy is often considered a key factor in determining consent to state legitimacy, Rothstein (2009) points to outputs as a key determinant of legitimacy:

> Legitimacy turns out to be created, maintained, and destroyed not at the input but at the output side of the political system. Hence, political legitimacy depends at least as much on the quality of government than on the capacity of electoral systems to create effective representation (Rothstein 2009, p. 311).

Creating and maintaining political legitimacy should be "the ultimate goal for any system of governance" (Rothstein 2009, p. 326). Pursuit of political legitimacy is a "never-ending process" (M. Rothschild & Stiglitz 1970; Sun 2015, p. 192) as it can be created and maintained as well as destroyed by the output side of the political system (Rothstein 2009, pp.

313, 325). The performance of service delivery is increasingly recognized as the fundamental for creating and maintaining the political legitimacy of the government (Gilley 2006; Huang, Chang & Chu 2008). Feldmann and Mazepus (2014, p. 3) see legitimacy as a judgment of authority based on public goods it creates or guarantees, as opposed to personal goods. Legitimacy is to some extent conditioned on provision of public goods and services, and thus will dwindle based on performance. Like Ernest Renan's democracy, "Legitimacy has to be re-earned constantly ('le plebiscite de tous les jours') and no system stands still, forever legitimate, without being effective" (J. Rothschild 1977, p. 489). The performance element is perhaps even more significant for non-democratic regimes, where "the performance becomes everything" (Thawnghmung & Myoe 2008, p. 5) and the "achievements and capacities of the regime have to be disproportionately magnified" (Beetham 2013, pp. 234–5). However, the nature of the performance necessary for legitimacy remains contested. What constitutes "grounds for legitimacy" in Myanmar is varied. As Thawnghmung & Myoe (2008, p. 5) explain:

> Different kinds of policies that can be implemented to promote growth [..]
> and the contributions they make with regard to enhancing, or undermining
> a government's legitimacy are varied.

Underpinning "legitimacy by consent" and performance are notions of social contract. Social contract theory hypothesises a pre-political state of nature where there is no law, no government, no security, and no protection of lives and property. To escape this state of nature, people enter into two agreements: (1) *"Pactum Unionis"* and (2) *"Pactum Subjectionis"*. By the first agreement, they looked for protection for their lives and properties. They thus formed a society where mutual respect, peace and harmony are respected. By the second agreement, they altogether pledge to obey an authority and surrender the whole or part of their freedom and rights to an authority (i.e., individual or a group of individuals). In return, the authority guarantees everyone protection of life, property and to a certain extent liberty. Although the early philosophers of social contract theory, Thomas Hobbes, John Locke, Jean Jacques Rousseau and John Rawls, differed in interpreting the condition in the state of nature, they were in agreement that the government has an obligation to uphold the contract. Hobbes placed moral obligation on the government to provide protection for lives and properties while Rousseau and Locke went further, justifying removal of governments which failed to fulfill their obligations (Laskar 2013). John Rawls (2009) views these obligations not as moral duties but as tasks and responsibilities to fellow citizens whose trust and confidence have been sought and with whom a leader is cooperating in running a democratic society. In short, the social contract in modern states entails some form of mutual benefits as well as mutual obligations. Citizens who are party to this contract agreement have implicitly or explicitly accepted responsibilities to participate in voting, paying taxes, and obeying laws. In return, the government is to maintain order/stability, enforce laws, and provide for citizens' wellbeing such as provision of education and healthcare services. This alludes to the earlier point, that different types of "performance" may have different effects on legitimacy.

In Myanmar, successive governments have sought to gain and maintain legitimacy through different means. These can be roughly categorized as: religious/tradition (where legitimacy is derived from notions of entitlement and responsibility vested in religious beliefs, and where a key element of legitimating performance is the patronage and protection of religion and religious traditions) (Adas 1982), security (both personal protection and national sovereignty) and sufficiency (the maintenance of subsistence) (Scott 1977).

Prior to British colonization,[1] in the Burmese kingdoms there was a reciprocal relationship among the king/state, sangha (Buddhist monks and nuns), and the general public. The state protected and supported the sangha and the sangha legitimized the state in return and urged the people to obey the state. The sangha has every interest in the wellbeing of the general public because their livelihood depends on the donations of the people (Ven Rewata Dhamma 1989). According to Buddhist precepts, the legitimacy of the state (or monarch) is assessed based on fulfillment of Ten Duties including generosity and care for the welfare of subjects, honesty and sacrifice for the people.[2] These principles also oblige mutual responsibilities—the king to provide social protection, and in return, the subjects obey the king's authority (Ven Rewata Dhamma 1989). This extended patron-client arrangement arguably underpins much of the process determining what kind of performance is required to generate legitimacy (Scott 1972).

Analysing legitimacy during British colonial rule is problematic, given the context of violent conquest. The legitimacy of colonial rule was frequently challenged, with rebel groups appealing to royal and religious tradition for legitimacy (Maitrii 2011; Thawnghmung & Myoe 2008). The Second World War "brought the consequences of the modern European state system" to Burma (Taylor 1982, pp. 8–9). Following independence in 1948, the emergence of a state (Burma) with central rule of both territory and people (Callahan 2004) was framed by the Panglong agreement (Cheng Guan 2007). According to Taylor (1982), the 1947 Constitution, largely based on its British colonial predecessor, established "a form of truncated federalism which would postpone difficult problems till they could be dealt with over time by the process of democratic multi-party and federalist politics" (p. 9). Despite the ambiguity of Panglong, the notion of national unity has been a key narrative element of successive governments (Cheng Guan 2007), framed since General Ne Win's 1962 coup around a racial and territorial notion of "nation" (Cheesman 2017; Maung 1969).

The military regime led by General Ne Win sought legitimacy by projecting itself as protecting the country from disintegration as a result of "multi-colored insurgencies" and as a promoter of socialist ideals of prosperity and equality through the "Burmese Way to Socialism" (Steinberg 2007; Sun 2015, p. 194). This narrative was continued by the government of SLORC/ SPDC (1988–2010),[3] led by General Than Shwe, whereby without the military in command, the country would disintegrate in the midst of multiple ethnic armed groups who questioned the territorial integrity of the country (Steinberg 2007), perhaps best summarized by the first of the "three national causes" emblazoned on newspapers and billboards across the country—"non-disintegration of the Union" (New Light of Myanmar 2012).

The unity of the country since its independence was—and remains—the key calculus of political legitimacy (Steinberg 2007, p. 114). The process by which the 2008 Constitution was developed and approved did little to enhance the legitimacy of the SPDC in the eyes of the public (Banyan 2014), and the elections of 2010, boycotted by the National League for Democracy (NLD) and several ethnic parties, ushered in a government formed of mainly ex-military leaders of the Union Solidarity and Development Party (USDP). However, the government of President Thein Sein introduced a wide range of political and economic reforms, including rights to assembly, media freedom and the abolition of a range of draconian laws used to punish political activists, which included the freeing of many political prisoners, inluding Aung San Suu Kyi. Following this, the NLD decided to particpate in the 2012 by-elections, and international support swiftly followed, with the lifting of sanctions, billions of dollars of debt relief and visits by foreign leaders including the first ever visit by a sitting US president, Barak Obama, in 2012.

Religion and politics have been intertwined in Myanmar. U Nu declared Buddhism the state religion and advocated to build 60,000 sand pagodas in order to get elected in the post-independence election in 1960 (Steinberg 2016). Since then, Buddhism has been used by successive governments as a mechanism for building legitimacy. The USDP government continued to claim its legitimacy by portraying itself as the protector of national sovereignty, and keeper and promoter of Buddhism. For instance, all publications (magazines, journals, books) were required to include the Three Causes of People. State media also regularly showed images of government officials performing religious rites—a practice which has continued under the NLD-led government.

The post-1990 military government focused on security and infrastructure development to gain legitimacy, while post-2011, the government of President Thein Sein introduced wide-ranging political and economic reforms, with a strong focus on rural poverty alleviation. After the election of the National League for Democracy in 2015, President Htin Kyaw announced four policy priorities: (1) national reconciliation, (2) internal peace, (3) pursuing a constitution toward a federal union, and (4) improving the living standards of the majority of the people.[4] These four priorities reflect the current challenges to political legitimacy: low levels of public trust in government; the legacy (and persistence) of conflict; constitutional arrangements which vest significant amounts of power in unelected officials (in this case, military appointed); and widespread poverty, inequality and lack of (equitable) access to resources.

## LEGITIMACY BY CONSENT AND THE TRUST DEFICIT

The notion of legitimacy by consent is complicated in contemporary Myanmar by the constitution, which vests significant amounts of power in the military and the absence of an adequate framework of religious and ethnic pluralism in a context of ethnic and linguistic diversity (Carnell 1957; Steinberg 2001). The appeal to different performances to build legitimacy illustrates the degree to which views on what constitutes grounds for legitimacy varies considerably among different stakeholders. The existence of dozens of Ethnic Armed Organizations (EAOs) and ongoing civil war in Myanmar, together with repeated demands for a federal structure, is a clear indication that many non-Burman ethnic groups do not give their consent to be ruled by what is perceived to be a Burman-dominated central government (South 2014; Steinberg 2007). In analysing this "trust deficit" it is worth noting that the history of Myanmar as a nation with its current boundaries is recent, and can best be described as an expansion from the centre (Aung-Thwin & Aung-Thwin 2013; Leach 1960) with the somewhat reluctant acquiescence of border areas to central rule (Scott 2009).

The NLD-led government can point to a higher degree of legitimacy based on consent through electoral process by gaining a landslide electoral victory (with the exception of Rakhine State and Shan State) in national polls held in 2015. The NLD also points to a measure of legitimacy gained through persistent opposition and struggle for democracy under the military regime for almost three decades. However, probably the main source of national legitimacy comes from the person of Aung San Suu Kyi, as the leader of the party. As the daughter of General Aung San who led the country to independence from the British colonial rule and recognized as a democracy icon, a winner of the Nobel Peace Prize, and as a Buddhist herself, she commands great influence or moral authority over the majority Buddhist population, and a significant number of non-Buddhist people. Although constitutionally excluded from being president, she exerts leadership through her role as the Chairperson of the NLD, State Councillor, and Foreign Minister. However, the NLD also needs to appeal to ethnic and religious values to sustain some legitimacy, a fact reflected in the under-representation of minorities in Cabinet, the majority of whom are either Burmans or Buddhists.[5] Moreover, the current constitutional arrangements, which vests in the military the legal right to participate in all decision-making processes, potentially constrains the ability to build legitimacy through democratic performance and equitable pluralism, as opposed to security. This illustrates the need for new approaches to cultivating legitimacy.[6] Thus, in the context of continued, considerable military control over government priorities, improving the socio-economic situation of citizens, and especially the strengthening of state-mediated social protection, represents an urgent and powerful approach by which the government can build widespread legitimacy in an inclusive and pluralistic way.

However, building legitimacy through the "performance" of delivering social goods and services is itself contingent on the degree of existing legitimacy required to collect and redistribute revenue (Levi, Sacks &

Tyler 2009). The degree of democratization is automatically associated with changes to the perception of legitimacy leading to increased revenue collection ability (Cheibub 1998), pointing again to the need for other performance indicators to generate "trust".

Myanmar currently has one of the lowest formal taxation bases in the world (Bird & Zolt 2008), and at the same time is considered the most charitable nation in the world (Future World Giving 2016). The widespread practice of donations linked to localized social welfare (Griffiths 2016b; Leehey 2016; McCarthy 2016a) is evidence of the link between performance, trust and legitimacy at local levels. This is illustrated by three different scenarios.

Firstly, evidence points to the widespread existence of village-based welfare organizations[7] in rural areas, which collect and redistribute donations to provide social assistance to the poor, the elderly, children and people with disabilities (Griffiths 2016a). This includes monastic and other non-government schools, which educate up to five per cent of primary school-aged children (Burnett Institute 2014). Drawing on traditions of reciprocity, the scale of welfare provision vastly exceeds central government welfare budgets (ActionAid 2013)

Secondly, volunteer organizations in more urban and peri-urban areas, such as free funeral service organizations (Thawnghmung & Myoe 2008) and organizations to arrange blood donation and fundraising for flood relief (McCarthy 2016a) are thriving. Research by McCarthy (2016a) highlights the degree of people's enthusiasm in contributing income to such organizations, compared to a low degree of willingness to pay taxes (McCarthy 2016b). Localization of legitimacy can be considered "small p politics" as it confers an informal political role to these welfare organizations, possibly at the expense of the legitimacy craved by the official political bodies. This has resulted in considerable attempts by successive governments to co-opt these local networks and organizations into the wider processes of political legitimization.

Thirdly, the growth of civil society in border regions of Myanmar, particularly those not under government control, takes place in a context where non-state actors (in particular, organizations representing the interests of specific ethnic groups) nurture legitimacy not only through appeals to nationalism and security, but through welfare. Networks of organizations, particularly in Kachin State, Shan State, Kayin (Karen) State and Mon State, administer a range of social welfare activities, including education, relief and resettlement and protection (Jolliffe 2014; South 2004, 2008). Recently, political reforms in Myanmar have enabled attempts to use aid as a bridge to trust-building in the peace process, which has then tended to channel aid either through state channels, or through non-governmental organizations co-operating with the state, resulting in decreased funding for Ethnic Armed Organizations (EAOs) (Jolliffe 2014). Of interest here—and a point discussed in the concluding section—is the importance of process and ownership in the ability of welfare performance to establish legitimacy:

> In Myanmar's ceasefire areas, where state presence and legitimacy have never taken hold, deep-set loyalties and hierarchies will not be swept aside through token social services, especially where the government's primary engagements are military operations, and most of its personnel are Burman infantrymen (Jolliffe 2014, p. 8).

Affirming common citizenship through entitlements, common rights and addressing inequalities can then contribute to the process of cultivating government by consent. Arguably, social protection offers an opportunity to implement demonstrable, visible policy to foster public trust in government as an effective agent of equitable redistribution. Such trust is crucial for the development of a stable welfare state which can then provide the "glue" of the wider social contract (Ferguson 2015).

## DEFINING SOCIAL PROTECTION

Provision of social protection is recognized as a vital task of government internationally (Holzmann, Sherburne-Benz, & Tesliuc 2003). It has been linked to economic growth and reducing inequalities (Arjona, Ladaique & Pearson 2003; Barrientos et al. 2003) and is an important source of political legitimacy (Lipset 1959; Scharpf 2002).

Broadly speaking, social protection can be defined as

> All public and private initiatives that provide income or consumption transfers to the poor, protect the vulnerable against livelihood risks, and enhance the social status and rights of the marginalized; with the overall objective of reducing the economic and social vulnerability of poor, vulnerable and marginalized groups (Sabates-Wheeler & Devereux 2007, p. iii).

Social protection is expressed in a variety of ways, depending on its operating framework: the two dominant "trajectories" identified by Devereux and Roelens (2015) refers to "rights-based" social protection, which focuses on "institutionalising social protection in national policy frameworks, underpinned by legislation that endows justiciable claims to social protection entitlements to all citizens or residents, including refugees" and "growth-oriented" social protection, which uses social protection "instrumentally, as a toolkit for achieving poverty reduction and economic growth" (Devereux et al. 2015, p. 7). Social protection may include elements best classified as "safety nets" which include social assistance (including welfare payments), "preventative" measures such as various forms of insurance (including social security) and "springboards"—measures aimed at increasing economic opportunities and social justice (Sabates-Wheeler & Devereux 2007).[8]

Parts of international conventions such as the Universal Declaration of Human Rights, International Rights of the Child and Rights of Persons with Disabilities are potentially addressed through a comprehensive approach to social protection; with the Declaration on Social Justice for a Fair Globalization in 2008, the International Labour Organization (ILO) is mandated to advocate making social security available to all, providing basic income to all in need, and protecting and adapting scope and coverage to manage risk and vulnerability. Promoting employment, social protection, social dialogue and labour rights is agreed to be seen as "inseparable, interrelated and mutually supportive" (ILO 2016, p. xiii), and hence, the right to social security is even enshrined in the constitutions of many European countries (ILO 2016).

Social protection is considered to be a critical element in poverty reduction (Barrientos 2011; Conway & Norton 2002), with the potential to address inequalities (Bambra et al. 2009; Frericks 2011) in times of economic growth—with rising inequality considered a significant constraint on poverty reduction in ASEAN countries (Rigg 2015). In disaster-prone countries, social protection necessarily includes both *ante* and *post* interventions to mitigate the effects of disasters (Davies, Guenther, Leavy, Mitchell & Tanner 2009; Vakis 2006). The role of social protection in building a wider social contract depends to some degree on the nature of the social contract (Hickey 2011). Tilly (1985) and others have warned of the potential dangers of state-led "protection" agendas which use social capital built from delivering protection to the majority to exclude the minority perceived as a threat.

The role of social protection in peace building is under-researched, but a number of case studies illustrate the potential for social protection and welfare policies to be a key component of social and political trust (Barrientos

& Hulme 2009; Raavad 2013). Social protection may thus have the ability to meet the immediate needs of people living in fragile states whilst at the same time supporting peace-building efforts and the demobilization of militias, contributing to improved prospects for national and international security and future growth (Barrientos & Hulme 2009, p. 20).

## SOCIAL PROTECTION IN MYANMAR: A BRIEF BACKGROUND

Given the value of social protection in promoting inclusive growth, protecting citizens from the effects of disasters and building trust and political legitimacy, social protection is indispensable for Myanmar. Crucially for the Myanmar context, social protection may be a critical element of "state building" in post-conflict scenarios (Roberts 2008). Despite an abundance of natural resources and record economic growth (ADB 2016), Myanmar has the lowest levels of human development in the region (UNDP 2017). More than a quarter (25.6 per cent) of Myanmar's population live below the poverty line (UNDP 2011), with per capita gross national income (GNI) estimated to be US$1,270 (ADB 2014). Twenty-three per cent of children under five years are underweight and nineteen per cent of the population has no access to improved drinking water source (ADB 2014). These inequalities undermine poverty reduction achievement as well as trust in the state (Wood 2017).

Additionally, Myanmar is considered extremely vulnerable to the effects of climate change (Kreft, Eckstein & Melchior 2016), with vulnerability rooted in both ecology and politics (Barnett 2006; Rao et al. 2013). Myanmar has faced severe natural disasters with increased frequency in recent years. Social protection in the context of disaster relief is perhaps the most visible expression of social protection, offering substantial opportunities for governments to build trust and strengthen social contracts. This is perhaps most striking in Myanmar, where high levels of altruism are accompanied by low levels of tax contributions, reflecting low levels of public trust in government to deliver protection, especially in times of disaster (McCarthy 2016a). Responses to large-scale disaster such as Cyclone Nargis (Fritz, Blount, Thwin, Thu & Chan 2009; Seekins 2009) and widespread flooding in 2015, however, featured active responses by civil society organizations in response to perceived government indifference, largely dwarfing government-mediated assistance (McCarthy 2018; South, Kempel, Perhult, Carstensen & Sudan 2011). People in Myanmar have relied and continue to rely on one another as a part of their social custom called "thah-yè-nah-yè" in Burmese.[9]

As described earlier, this tradition of social protection at the community level has been recognized as non-formal social protection and its value and ubiquity has been well documented by Leehey (2016) and Griffiths (2016b). However, formal social protection (SP)[10] is something still new to the vast majority of people in Myanmar, as successive governments have failed to implement such programs at the scope and scale of the whole country. In the initial post-independence period, the government developed an ambitious economic and social development plan called "Pyi Daw Tha Programme" that hoped to create a "New Burma" in which all people could enjoy a high standard of living, health and social security and social justice (Lloyd 1954). During this period, among other legislation, the Social Security Act (1954) and laws to protect persons with disabilities were promulgated. However, the effective implementation of these did not last long, as General Ne Win took over the government as "the care taker" in 1958 followed by a coup d'état in 1962, after which he introduced the "Burmese way to Socialism" which, soon proved to be the "Burmese way to Poverty" (Sun 2015, p. 195). This period was associated with the promotion (and brief flourishing) of self-reliance groups (Badgley 1962; Thin, M.M., personal communication September 2016). Post-1988, real investment in the social sector deteriorated.[11]

Arguably, it was not until the initially indifferent response of the Myanmar government to the devastation of the 2008 Cyclone Nargis that discussions on social protection recommenced, against a backdrop of "Responsibility to Protect" (R2P) rhetoric from some UN member states (Barber 2009; McLachlan-Bent & Langmore 2011; Özerdem 2010). The initial clusters formed in the aftermath of Cyclone Nargis were the nucleus for a number of social protection initiatives for women, children and persons with disabilities (Cheesman, Skidmore & Wilson 2010, pp. 323–48). However, the overall scope remained limited, and highly fragmented (Infante Villarroel 2015; Nishino & Koehler 2011).

At a landmark conference held in June 2012, soon after the inauguration of the USDP government, President Thein Sein started the process of developing a national social protection strategy (The Republic of the Union of Myanmar 2014), culminating in the drafting of the Myanmar National Strategic Action Plan for Social Protection. In this document, social protection is defined as policies, legal instruments and programmes for individuals and households that prevent and alleviate economic and social vulnerabilities, promote access to essential services and infrastructure and economic opportunity, and facilitate the ability to better manage and cope with shocks that arise from humanitarian emergencies and/or sudden loss of income (2014, p. 5).

The plan features three types of instruments: first, social assistance (social safety nets) which refers to cash or in-kind transfer, or both; and school feeding and targeted food assistance. Second, social insurance which refers to old-age and disability pensions, and unemployment insurance. Third, legislation and policy reform which includes improving labour regulations and providing skill-building programs. The government aims to allocate 5.41 per cent of GDP to SP programs which are expected to benefit over 36 million citizens by 2024, built around a series of flagship programs summarized in Table 3.1 below. However, the above plan remains aspirational, with little of the required 5.4 per cent of GDP having been allocated.

The Ministry of Social Welfare, Relief and Resettlement (MoSWRR), the lead ministry responsible for implementation of social protection, received only around Myanmar kyat (MMK) 18.24 billion (or 0.09 per cent) of the total government expenditures during the 2016–17 financial year (San San Oo 2016). The ministry has a total of 4,935 staff, the majority of whom are assigned to pre-school education roles.[12] The social pension for senior citizens aged 90 and above will continue but with reduced amount, from the MMK18,000 awarded in 2016, to a planned MMK10,000 per month through 2018. Delivery capacity remains a huge challenge, with the focal ministry having little operational or logistic capacity to undertake this level of program — a common constraint on developing social protection (Barrientos & Hulme 2009, p. 17).

In addition to the Social Protection Plan, the Social Security Law (2012), updating the previous Social Security Act of 1954, aims to provide a range of social and health care benefits through contributions from employers, workers and the government. The new Social Security Law was implemented in 2014, but in a phased manner. As of April 2015, only the existing branches of social security were covered (i.e., medical care and sickness benefits, death, maternity, and work injury).[13] This is a contributory scheme, available to both employed and self-employed workers, operating on a sliding scale of contributions to benefits (Table 3.2). Currently, there are 778,837 enrolled members, although awareness of entitlements and actual claims are well below the actual levels of entitlements.

Table 3.1: Summary of Existing and Planned Social Protection Instruments in Myanmar

| Programs | Beneficiary Criteria | Starting Year | Cost (%) of GDP | Target Beneficiary | Amount in (MMK) | Lead | Program Objective |
|---|---|---|---|---|---|---|---|
| **Cash Allowance** | Pregnant Women | 2015 | 0% | Countrywide | 16,000 per child per month | MSWRR | To support the well-being of all those with disabilities, and to support their access to services that promote all-round development and their best interests, especially during childhood. |
| | Child with disabilities | 2016 | | | 30,000 per adult per month | | |
| | Adult age above 64 | | Estimated (0.98%) when fully operate | 11 million by 2019 | 8,000 per child per month | | The goal is to provide expecting mothers and young children with additional resources they can use to provide for their basic needs, including nutritional needs. |
| | Child age to one | 2017 | Estimated (0.14%) in 2015 and will rise to (0.32%) by 2024 | 2.25 million by 2017 | 15,000 per month per each beneficiary | | |
| | Child age to two | 2018 | | | | | |
| | Children age 3 – 15 | | | | | | |
| **School Feeding** | Start in schools with low net enrolment in highly food-insecure areas. | | Estimated (0.64%) when extended to all schools | 9 million by 2020 | 1 cooked meal per day per child | MOE | To increase enrolment rates, To reduce dropout rates, To regularize attendance, To strengthen the learning capacity of children |

Although not always considered as a part of social protection, consideration of healthcare and education are relevant to social protection particularly with relation to child health and development, maternal health and health of older persons and persons with disability. In contexts such as Myanmar where investments in social protection are low, analysis of appropriations to health and education can be indicative of overall social sector prioritization. Appropriations for health care and education, whilst increasing under the past two governments, remain comparatively low compared to neighbouring Association of South East Asian Nations (ASEAN) countries: 4.33 per cent of government expenditure for health, and 7.5 per cent for education. Even though the expenditure on the sectors has been growing in recent years, the actual value on health expenditure (two per cent of Gross Domestic Product (GDP) in 2011) is still small compared to the neighboring ASEAN states (Oo et al. 2015), and is dwarfed by the sixteen per cent allocated for defence (San San Oo 2016). The inadequacy of public-service, health and education financing is evidenced by high out-of-pocket expenditures for these items, both in the government and rapidly expanding private sector (Griffiths 2015; UNICEF

| No. | Insured Benefits | Contribution Rate | | Total |
|-----|------------------|---------|----------|-------|
|     |                  | Employer | Employee |       |
| 1 | Health & Social care funds | 2% | 2% | 4% |
| 2 | Family Allowance | - | - | - |
| 3 | Work Injury benefits | 1% | 1% | 2% |
| 4 | Family assistance, Invalidity benefit, Superannuation benefit and Survivors' benefit, | 3% | 3% | 6% |
| 5 | Unemployment benefits | 1% | 1% | 2% |
| 6 | Housing plan benefit | - | 25% | |

Table 3.2: Benefits and Contribution Rates under the Social Security Law and Rules (2012)

2012). Reform in both sectors is urgently needed: for example, during 2007–08 to 2011–12 financial years, the expenditure in the Department of Health was dominated by salaries, accounting for more than seventy per cent of total expenditures (UNICEF 2015), which means only about thirty per cent was left for necessary equipment and medicine. The upward trend in real expenditure on healthcare and education reflects a policy of working towards providing universal healthcare and education, but inequalities remain (Wood 2017).

Moves towards free universal education address fiscal issues at two levels: formal and informal payments. Until recently, students in Myanmar had to pay for all textbooks and a school registration fee, as well as significant costs for out-of-school tuition. However, in recent years, much progress has also been made in public education in terms of increased budget. Textbooks have been distributed free of charge since 2011–12 for primary schools, and since 2014–15 for middle schools. Under the Framework of Social and Economic Reform (FSER), School Grant Program for the basic education sector was introduced from 2012–13, which covers basic education (i.e., primary, middle, high school), teachers' training schools, education universities, Sagaing Development University, and monastery education. The amount of grant is based on the number of students (from 1 to 2,500 and above). The government also released a statement ordering that schools should not take any bribe or fee and parents were not to pay any fee. This received wide public praise because it was a great relief for parents given that the school registration fee was a heavy financial burden. A student grant program (needs based) was also introduced with a quota system.[14] However, it is fair to note that the budget increase is disproportionately small compared to what is actually needed. For example, in a middle school with over 200 students in Waingmaw Township, only two students received this grant. The amount of monthly grant is MMK 5,000 for primary school students and MMK 8,000 for middle school students.[15] The NLD government promised to continue to increase expenditures for education, healthcare and social protection and prioritize expenditures in the sectors that give immediate benefits to the public (San San Oo 2016, p. 9). However, promises of increased expenditure and expanded welfare face two significant challenges: firstly, increased revenue requirements in a context of deficits (Nyan Hlaing Lynn 2017) and the lack of administrative capacity to deliver welfare in a transparent and relatively corruption-free manner.

## CONCLUSION: HOW CAN SOCIAL PROTECTION CONTRIBUTE TO LEGITIMACY AND PEACE-BUILDING?

Referring to earlier discussions on legitimacy, there are at least four ways in which social protection can contribute to social trust and political legitimacy in the current Myanmar context. Firstly, relating to the performance of maintaining sufficiency, by ensuring that the basic needs of citizens are met—providing state-managed processes by which vulnerabilities, risks and uncertainties are met. This relates to the "minimal obligations" of the state (Scott 1977). Secondly, where universal social protection and social welfare are provided to citizens[16] on an equal basis, new meanings of national belonging can be framed, essentially providing a narrative for why being part of the "whole" is advantageous. Process is critical to leveraging legitimacy through renewed visions of collective belonging. As Joliffe (2014, pp. 7–8) notes:

> If not carefully sequenced with holistic improvements in the state's relations with the population, as well as with other parties to the conflict, expansion of the state into contested areas risks being viewed as an intrusion into political life, and a threat to local security. While armed hostilities have been curbed so that negotiations can take place, unwelcomed state expansion risks perpetuating tensions on the ground, and undermining the peace process.

Linked to this, thirdly, is the potential for the provision of social protection to frame new iterations of the "protection/security" narrative, where protection is more widely defined as the maintenance of conditions suitable for human thriving, rather than maintenance of territorial integrity or protection against violence. In practice, this begins to address issues such as "ceasefire capitalism" (Woods 2011) where the intersection of state, non-state and commercial interests introduce new risks and threats to rural, mostly ethnic populations. Where the scope of protection is broadened, through inclusion of the social protection narrative, the rights of citizens to "protection" means that the provision of "security" is more than simply protection from violence but requires the protection of the economic and cultural rights of citizens.

Fourthly, dialogue around social protection opens an enabling space for the intersection of "small p" and "big p" politics, which creates the potential for citizenship processes which are not simply defined by relationships between individuals and the state. This is important for three reasons: firstly, where citizenship is only defined by vertical individual-state relationships, where trust levels remain low, there is potential for exclusion of some citizens based on non-engagement with state processes.[17] Secondly, given the extent of non-state actors in providing social protection, and their capacity to generate trust, these organizations and entities offer a space of potential interaction and collaboration between individuals and the state. Thirdly, groups characterizing themselves as "small p" offer substantial potential to enable effective and transparent processes for the actualization of social protection. This does not come without caveats, as we shall discuss shortly. But the potential for a process of social protection which has strong citizen ownership helps contribute to building legitimacy and trust, arguably for both ethnic and central areas with a Burman majority. As explained by South (2004, p. 7):

> Functioning civil society networks are essential for sustained, 'bottom-up' social and political transition in Myanmar, and for conflict resolution at both the national and local levels. It is essential that the country's diverse social and ethnic communities enjoy a sense of ownership in any transitional process, and equip themselves to fill the power vacuum that may emerge, either as a result of abrupt shifts in national politics, or of a more gradual withdrawal of the military from state and local power.

Thus, the potential for social protection to contribute to legitimacy is significant. However, as alluded to earlier, the notion that simply rolling out universal social protection will guarantee legitimacy is misguided. More than simply undertaking social protection, the policy direction and implementation approach are potentially the key variables in achieving greater legitimacy and contributing to peace-building and indeed to the four objectives set out by the president in 2016. The below principles could, when applied to the emerging social protection strategy, maximize the potential for building a strong social contract.

## Ensure adequate funding

The first step to prioritize social protection policy is of course to empower the relevant ministries such as the Ministry of Social Welfare, Relief and Resettlement (MoSWRR), Ministry of Health and Sports (MoHS) and the Ministry of Education (MOE) with substantial budget allocation. Having come into power with a landslide electoral victory, the NLD-led government is in a relatively good position to set priorities in national budget planning (according to Article 221 of the 2008 Constitution).[18] President Htin Kyaw formed the National Budget Commission with twenty-one members, out of which twenty are either NLD members or NLD appointees, according to the Notification (62/2016). Financing social protection is challenging. However, this challenge can be overcome if the government has the political will to be transparent in managing natural resources, especially in the extractive industry.

Myanmar has financial resources to fund social protection if the wealth from natural resources is properly managed and redistributed fairly. According to Myanmar's first Extractive Industries Transparency Initiative (EITI) Report (2015), only forty-five per cent of revenue generated by state-owned enterprises goes into the national budget and the rest is kept in an "other account" held by ministries and state-owned enterprises at a state bank. The report recommended that the government consider counting all revenues from extractives as normal budgetary revenue, and also improving disclosure about the use of "other accounts".[19] One way to introduce the transparency and accountability in natural resources management is by complying with EITI standards. Having applied for EITI membership in 2014, the NLD-led government should speed up securing full EITI membership and utilize all the benefits that come with the membership in managing the natural resources.

## Build on what is already there

The rich resources in social capital, the so-called "moral economy", have been highlighted by Griffiths (2016b) and McCarthy (2016a) and demonstrate that notions and mechanisms of redistribution remain resilient in the majority of rural communities in Myanmar. The concept of "Ku Htu Ku Ta" or self-reliance, also recognized as "informal social protection", is ubiquitous in rural areas. Although most people would reject the argument that self-reliant community organizations are simply a replacement for state provision, traditions of reciprocity are a reservoir for social capital which can potentially be mobilized for wider social protection initiatives. The spirit of self-reliance is an important asset and should continue to be encouraged. In the absence of public trust, it may be best to utilize existing local social organizations (Putnam, Leonardi, & Nanetti 1993). The caveat, initially raised by McCarthy (2016a), is the intertwining of religious values and welfare, which, although effective locally, has the potential to undermine efforts to build equitable plurality of citizenship:

In the context of the 2015 elections, the small p politics of this sort ensured that a formal election processes was lent a distinctly Buddhist nationalist character (McCarthy 2016a, p. 327).

Critics of non-state provision of social protection have also argued that this can "postpone reform of the social service system" (Cammett & MacLean 2011, p. 9) and may create, or sustain inequalities. Some organizations, particularly those drawing on traditional or religious values for legitimacy, may serve to maintain the status quo, and potentially perpetuate inequalities due to gender, disability or ethnicity. However, an approach to social protection which can harness existing social capital for a wider cause surely has promise (Griffiths 2016a, 2017), especially given that the existing role of the state is limited.

## Recognize and accommodate local variation—address inequalities in outcome

One of the challenges of universalized social protection is where to delineate the universal part. Ideally, the universal component focuses more on outcome, rather than simply providing identical entitlements. This is an underpinning principle of addressing inequalities, where structural inequalities may result in differential needs and abilities to use assistance to achieve good outcomes. For example, in contexts of high degrees of inequality of maternal healthcare, the actual outcome derived from the same level of benefit (e.g. cash grant) may be different (Mhatr & Deber 1992). This is highly relevant in debates around inequalities in Myanmar, where—as noted earlier—structural inequalities are perceived as based on ethnicity, religion, gender and political settlements. In this context, legitimacy may be linked to perception of equity in distribution.

To phrase this as a question: in remote areas, or areas with less access to public services and economic opportunities, is legitimacy and public trust built more effectively by receiving an equal/identical entitlement, or by assistance which is adjusted to deliver equitable outcomes? For example: does the provision of a cash grant of $10 to all pregnant women and mothers of young children living in poor and remote regions—the same as would be given in urban areas—build trust more effectively than a program which seeks to address the inequalities in maternal morbidity and child malnutrition through targeted interventions, perhaps of higher value? In essence, this is asking for an approach to social protection which recognizes and addresses inequalities—universal protection, as opposed to identical entitlements.

## Facilitate regionalized approaches to deliver universal protection

Following on from this, if local variation is recognized, it is likely that public trust can be built more effectively by facilitating a regionalized approach to delivering social protection. Several States and Regions developed localized social protection plans under the guidance of the Ministry of Social Welfare, Relief and Resettlement between 2013 and 2016, although only the Chin State plan was ever published (MIID 2014), and that was primarily for child protection. However, the process demonstrated that working with local planning officials, and drawing up plans using localized data, could then be translated into State and Region-level plans which were coherent with National Strategies. As social welfare is important for the government-citizen relationship, the delegation of more responsibility to State and regional governments presents an opportunity to enact policy on a federal basis, which may even include limited powers of localized revenue raising and spending on social protection by State and regional governments. This again tilts towards a pluralist agenda in which the central government facilitates, rather than delivers social protection. The links with peace processes are tangible: negotiating terms of social protection provides potential "first steps" in federal processes and builds links between citizens and government at more localized levels. While it should be noted that decentralization of welfare may be associated with unequal access (Agrawal & Gibson 1999; Cammett & MacLean 2011), in Myanmar such policies would help to open the door to a more inclusive dialogue on welfare, potentially including armed groups.

## Promote localized pathways of accountability

Along with lack of capacity, corruption is a barrier to access to public services, and undermines public trust. For example, it is common to make at least a MMK 50,000 (US$45) "donation" for the processing of a national identity card. Similarly, in legal cases it does not really matter who is right or wrong but rather how much money one is prepared to spend to win. Corruption has eroded public trust in the justice system, and anti-corruption efforts represent a prominent agenda of the current government.

Building localized accountability mechanisms is a crucial element of trust-building in contexts where there is still fear of government and widespread lack of access to justice. This is where a system integrating regionalized implementation together with accountability processes, perhaps facilitated by community social organizations, can strengthen the effectiveness of social protection as a trust-building and legitimizing process. As argued by Joliffe, such mechanisms are essential in contested areas of Myanmar where people should "ideally benefit from the experience and capacities of all service providers, regulate the potential for contestation, and aim to directly address the grievances driving conflict" (Jolliffe 2014, p. 25).

The performance required of social protection delivery to build trust and legitimacy, then, requires contextually aware, inclusive processes, which are already in existence in localized forms across the country. Co-operation with such organizations by the state (rather than co-option of them) within a framework of localized accountability offers significant potential to establish a positive cycle of legitimacy, where increased trust enables greater potential for the revenue generation necessary for enacting wider social protection (Levi et al. 2009). Such reforms could in turn offer the potential to build more sustainable legitimacy.

## Notes

1   The State of Burma (now Myanmar) as a unified territorial entity with central control over territory as well as peoples arguably dates from colonial or post-colonial arrangements onwards. Previous incarnations of states reflected more localized rule, such as kingdoms (Callahan, 2004).
2   Ven Rewata Dhamma (Ven Rewata Dhamma, 1989) cites them as (1) Dana (generosity—the state should give welfare to the people); (2) Sila (high moral character—should never destroy life, lie, steal, and exploit others); (3) Pariccaga (sacrificing for the good of people, prioritizing the interests of the people); (4) Ajjava (honesty and integrity—be sincere in intention and avoid deceiving the public); (5) Maddava (kindness and gentleness); (6) Tapa (austerity of habits—lead a simple life and must not indulge oneself with luxury); (7) Akkodha (freedom from envy, ill-will, enmity); (8) Avihimsa (non-violence—should not harm anyone but promote peace); (9) Khanti (patience, forbearance, tolerance, understanding); (10) Avirodha (non-opposition and non-obstruction—should not oppose the will of the people).
3   The State Law and Order Restoration Council was established post-1988 and was transformed to the State Peace and Development Council in 1997.

4  "Transcript: President U Htin Kyaw's inaugural address", *The Myanmar Times*, 30 March 2016. Available at: <www.mmtimes.com/index.php/national-news/19730-transcript-president-u-htin-kyaw-s-inaugural-address.html > [accessed 2 February 2017].

5  The ministers of Ethnic Affairs and Hotels and Tourism are non-Burmans but are Buddhists. Only Christian Chin Vice-President Henry Van Thio is neither Burman nor Buddhist, an appoint which led Buddhist nationalists to protest the NLD. See Aung Kyaw Min "Nationalists rally against both vice presidents", *The Myanmar Times*, 5 April 2016. Available at: <www.mmtimes.com/index.php/national-news/19820-nationalists-rally-against-both-vice-presidents.html> [accessed 2 February 2017].

6  The degree to which the military is under the command of the elected government is debatable, with six out of the eleven members in the National Defence and Security Council (NDSC), the most powerful decision-making body in the country, appointed by Commander-in-Chief of the Defence Services [Article 201 & 40 (c) of 2008 Constitution]. The constitution does not allow the elected government to appoint the defense minister or Commander-in-Chief of the army and gives no authority to control all armed forces including the army, police, and militias [Articles 20, 232 & 342.] Based on the constitution, twenty-five per cent of both Pyithu Hluttaw (lower house) and Amyotha Hluttaw (upper house) members, and one-third of the total members of the State and Regional Hluttaw are appointed by Commander-in-Chief of the Defence Services [Article (109), 141 (b) & 161 (d)]. Without approval from the military, amending the constitution is impossible within the current constitutional framework as the military has veto power [Article 436 (a)].

7  *Parahitta*, meaning 'for the benefit of the other".

8  Despite the "roll-back" of welfare regimes in many European democracies (Atkinson, 1999; Esping-Andersen, 1996; Therborn & Roebroek, 1986), dominant discourse amongst academics and practitioners presumes its necessity and focuses largely on the form that social protection should take in the twenty-first century (Devereux et al. 2015).

9  "Thah-yè" means good affairs (eg., wedding, religious ceremony) while "nah-yè" refers to bad affairs (eg., sickness, funeral).

10 A formal social protection system refers to government-funded programs. Non-government funded programs are recognized as an informal social protection system, which is ubiquitous in Myanmar as studied by Leehey (2016). This paper focuses on the first type of system.

11 Illustrated by a drop in government expenditure on education from three per cent in 1972 to about 0.5 percent in 2000 (OECD 2016).

12 Ministry of Social Welfare, Relief and Resettlement, <www.mswrr.gov.mm/index.php/main/about> [accessed 1 February 2017].

13  "Building Resilience, Equity and Opportunity in Myanmar: The Role of Social
    Protection, Strengthening Social Security Provision in Myanmar", World
    Bank Group (Social Protection & Labour), Note 7. Available at: <https://
    openknowledge.worldbank.org/handle/10986/22325> [accessed 2 February
    2018].
14  Interview with the headmaster of a middle school in Waingmaw Township,
    Kachin State, Myanmar (15 November 2016).
15  Ibid.
16  One could argue for provision based on residency, rather than citizenship,
    given the conflicted notions of citizenship currently present in Myanmar. This
    points to potential mechanisms for addressing conflict in areas where citizenship
    rights are disputed, but where the fulfilment of both basic needs, and fostering
    of trust, is likely to be an essential element of long-term solutions.
17  For example: many citizens do not possess identity cards, for a variety of
    reasons. Conditioning social protection on the participation in citizenship
    processes such as possession of an NRC card potentially excludes both those
    who would wish to obtain one, but are unable, and those who do not trust
    government processes sufficiently to attempt to apply for one.
18  Article 221 says "The Union Government shall draft the Union Budget Bill
    based on the annual Union budget, after coordinating with the Financial
    Commission, and submit it for approval to the Pyidaungsu Hluttaw in accord
    with the provisions of the Constitution."
19  For more information on the beneficiaries of oil and gas industry, *Global Witness*,
    October 2014; of the jade industry, *Global Witness*, October, 2015; and of the
    forest industry, EIA report, 2015.

# References

ActionAid. "Public Sector Service Reform." Yangon, Myanmar, 2013.

Adas, Michael. "Bandits, Monks, and Pretender Kings: Patterns of Peasant Resistance and Protest in Colonial Burma, 1826-1941." *Power and Protest in the Countryside* 75 (1982): 105.

ADB. <www.adb.org/publications/basic-statistics-2016 >

ADB. ""What's the Fastest Growing Country in Asia? Surprise! It's Myanmar"." News release, 2016 <http://www.adb.org/news/features/whats-fastest-growing-country-asia-surprise-its-myanmar> [accessed 31 October 2017].

Agrawal, Arun, and Clark C. Gibson. "Enchantment and Disenchantment: The Role of Community in Natural Resource Conservation." *World Development* 27, no. 4 (1999): 629–49.

Alagappa, Muthiah. *Political Legitimacy in Southeast Asia: The Quest for Moral Authority*. Stanford University Press, 1995.

Arjona, Roman, Maxime Ladaique, and Mark Pearson. "Growth, Inequality and Social Protection." *Canadian Public Policy/Analyse de Politiques* (2003): S119–S39.

Atkinson, Anthony Barnes. *The Economic Consequences of Rolling Back the Welfare State*. MIT Press, 1999.

Aung-Thwin, Michael, and Maitrii Aung-Thwin. *A History of Myanmar since Ancient Times: Traditions and Transformations*. Reaktion Books, 2013.

Badgley, John. "Burma's Military Government: A Political Analysis." *Asian Survey* (1962): 24–31.

Bambra, Clare, Dan Pope, Viren Swami, Debbi Stanistreet, A. Roskam, Anton Kunst, and Alex Scott-Samuel. "Gender, Health Inequalities and Welfare State Regimes: A Cross-National Study of 13 European Countries." *Journal of Epidemiology and Community Health* 63, no. 1 (2009): 38–44.

Barber, Rebecca. "The Responsibility to Protect the Survivors of Natural Disaster: Cyclone Nargis, a Case Study." *Journal of Conflict & Security Law* 14, no. 1 (2009): 3–34.

Barnett, Jon. *Climate Change, Insecurity and Injustice*. Cambridge Massachusetts: MIT Press, 2006.

Barrientos, Armando. "Social Protection and Poverty." *International Journal of Social Welfare* 20, no. 3 (2011): 240–49.

Barrientos, Armando, Monica Ferreira, Mark Gorman, Amanda Heslop, Helena Legido-Quigley, Peter Lloyd-Sherlock, V. Moller, João Saboia, and MLTW Vianna. "Non-Contributory Pensions and Poverty Prevention: A Comparative Study of Brazil and South Africa." London: Help Age International, DFID (UK), 2003.

Barrientos, Armando, and David Hulme. "Social Protection for the Poor and Poorest in Developing Countries: Reflections on a Quiet Revolution: Commentary." *Oxford Development Studies* 37, no. 4 (2009): 439–56.

Beetham, David. *The Legitimation of Power*. Palgrave Macmillan, 2013.

Bird, Richard M., and Eric M. Zolt. "Tax Policy in Emerging Countries." *Environment and Planning C: Government and Policy* 26, no. 1 (2008): 73-86.

Buchanan, Allen. "Political Legitimacy and Democracy." *Ethics* 112, no. 4 (2002): 689–719.

Burnett Institute. "Monastic Schools in Myanmar a Baseline Assessment." 2014.

Callahan, Mary Patricia. *Making Enemies: War and State Building in Burma*. NUS Press, 2004.

Cammett, Melani Claire, and Lauren M. MacLean. "Introduction: The Political Consequences of Non-State Social Welfare in the Global South." *Studies in Comparative International Development* 46, no. 1 (2011): 1–21.

Carnell, Francis G. "Ethnic and Cultural Pluralism in Burma, Thailand and Malaya." 1957.

Cheesman, Nick, Monique Skidmore, and Trevor Wilson. *Ruling Myanmar: From Cyclone Nargis to National Elections*. Institute of Southeast Asian Studies, 2010.

Cheibub, José Antonio. "Political Regimes and the Extractive Capacity of Governments: Taxation in Democracies and Dictatorships." *World Politics* 50, no. 3 (1998): 349–76.

Cheng Guan, Ang. "Political Legitimacy in Myanmar: The Ethnic Minority Dimension." *Asian Security* 3, no. 2 (2007): 121–40.

Conway, Tim, and Andy Norton. "Nets, Ropes, Ladders and Trampolines: The Place of Social Protection within Current Debates on Poverty Reduction." *Development Policy Review* 20, no. 5 (2002): 533–40.

Davies, Mark, Bruce Guenther, Jennifer Leavy, Tom Mitchell, and Thomas Tanner. "Climate Change Adaptation, Disaster Risk Reduction and Social Protection: Complementary Roles in Agriculture and Rural Growth?". *IDS Working Papers* 2009, no. 320 (2009): 1–37.

Devereux, Stephen, Keetie Roelen, and Martina Ulrichs. "Where Next for Social Protection?". (2015).

DSW. "Myanmar National Social Protection Strategic Plan." <http://www.social-protection.org/gimi/gess/RessourcePDF.action?ressource.ressourceId=50377 > 2015.

Economist, The. "What's Wrong with Myanmar's Constitution?" 2014.

Esping-Andersen, Gøsta. "After the Golden Age? Welfare State Dilemmas in a Global Economy." *Welfare States in Transition: National Adaptations in Global Economies*, edited by Gøsta Esping-Andersen, UNSRID, 1996.

Feldmann, Magnus, and Honorata Mazepus. "Social Contract and Legitimacy: The Case of Putin's Russia." (2014).

Ferguson, James. *Give a Man a Fish: Reflections on the New Politics of Distribution.* Duke University Press, 2015.

Frericks, Patricia. "Marketising Social Protection in Europe: Two Distinct Paths and Their Impact on Social Inequalities." *International Journal of Sociology and Social Policy* 31, no. 5/6 (2011): 319–34.

Fritz, Hermann M., Christopher D. Blount, Swe Thwin, Moe Kyaw Thu, and Nyein Chan. "Cyclone Nargis Storm Surge in Myanmar." *Nature Geoscience* 2, no. 7 (2009): 448–49.

Future World Giving. "2016 World Giving Index Shows Myanmar Is Most Generous Nation." <https://futureworldgiving.org/2016/10/25/2016-world-giving-index-shows-myanmar-is-most-generous-nation/ > [accessed 31 October 2017].

Gilley, Bruce. "The Meaning and Measure of State Legitimacy: Results for 72 Countries." *European Journal of Political Research* 45, no. 3 (2006): 499–525.

Griffiths, M. "Community Based Social Protection and Maternal and Child Cash Transfers." *Bulletin of the Social Policy & Poverty Research Group* 1, no. 10 (1st October 2016).

————. "Community Social Protection Organizations in Rural Myanmar." *Bulletin of the Social Policy & Poverty Research Group* 2, no. 3 (2016).

————. "Dimensions of Poverty, Vulnerability and Social Protection in Rural Communities in Myanmar." *Department of Rural Development, Government of Myanmar,* 2015.

————. "Emerging Co-Dependent Networks: Precarity and Community Social Organizations in Rural Myanmar." *Journal of Contemporary Asia* (2017).

Hickey, Sam. "The Politics of Social Protection: What Do We Get from a 'Social Contract'approach?". *Canadian Journal of Development Studies/Revue canadienne d'études du développement* 32, no. 4 (2011): 426–38.

Holzmann, Robert, Lynne Sherburne-Benz, and Emil Tesliuc. *Social Risk Management: The World Bank's Approach to Social Protection in a Globalizing World.* Washington DC: World Bank, 2003.

Huang, Min-hua, Yu-tzung Chang, and Yun-han Chu. "Identifying Sources of Democratic Legitimacy: A Multilevel Analysis." *Electoral Studies* 27, no. 1 (2008): 45–62.

ILO. "The Right to Social Security in the Constitutions of the World: Broadening the Moral and Legal Space for Social Justice.". ILO: ILO, 2016.

Infante Villarroel, Alba Mariana. "Inventory of Social Protection Programs in Myanmar." *World Bank, Washington: Social Protection Discussion Paper Series,* 2015.

Jolliffe, Kim. *Ethnic Conflict and Social Services in Myanmar's Contested Regions*. Asia Foundation Yangon, 2014.

Kreft, Sönke, David Eckstein, and Inga Melchior. *Global Climate Risk Index 2017: Who Suffers Most from Extreme Weather Events? Weather-Related Loss Events in 2015 and 1996 to 2015*. Germanwatch Nord-Süd Initiative eV, 2016.

Laskar, Manzoor Elahi. "Summary of Social Contract Theory by Hobbes, Locke and Rousseau." (2013).

Leach, Edmund R. "The Frontiers of "Burma"." *Comparative Studies in Society and History* 3, no. 1 (1960): 49-68.

Leehey, J. "Community-Based Social Protection in the Dry Zone." Myanmar: HelpAge International, 2016.

Levi, Margaret, Audrey Sacks, and Tom Tyler. "Conceptualizing Legitimacy, Measuring Legitimating Beliefs." *American Behavioral Scientist* 53, no. 3 (2009): 354–75.

Lipset, Seymour Martin. "Some Social Requisites of Democracy: Economic Development and Political Legitimacy." *American Political Science Review* 53, no. 1 (1959): 69–105.

Lloyd, John. "Planning a Welfare State in Burma." *Int'l Lab. Rev.* 70 (1954): 117.

Maitrii, Aung-Thwin. "The Return of the Galon King: History, Law, and Rebellion in Colonial Burma." Athens, Ohio and Singapore: Ohio University Press and NUS Press, 2011.

Maung, U Maung. *Burma and General Ne Win*. Asia Publishing House, 1969.

McCarthy, Gerard. "Buddhist Welfare and the Limits of Big 'P'politics in Provincial Myanmar." *Conflict in Myanmar: War, Politics, Religion* (2016): 313.

———. "Building on What's There: Insights on Social Protection and Public Goods Provision from Central-East Myanmar." International Growth Centre, 2016.

———. "Meta-Frames and Buddhist Revivalism: Social Action, Moral Citizenship and the Refraction of Extremism into Local Life in Provincial Myanmar." In *International Conference on Burma Myanmar Studies*. Chiangmai, Thailand, 2015.

McLachlan-Bent, Ashley, and John Langmore. "A Crime against Humanity? Implications and Prospects of the Responsibility to Protect in the Wake of Cyclone Nargis." *Global Responsibility to protect* 3, no. 1 (2011): 37–60.

Mhatr, Sharmila L, and Raisa B. Deber. "From Equal Access to Health Care to Equitable Access to Health: A Review of Canadian Provincial Health Commissions and Reports." *International Journal of Health Services* 22, no. 4 (1992): 645–68.

Ministry of Planning and Finance. "Fiscal Year: Summary of Estimated Revenue and Expenditure of Myanmar Government." Edited by Ministry of Planning and Finance, 2016.

New Light of Myanmar. *New Light of Myanmar*, 2012.

Nishino, Yoshimi, and Gabriele Koehler. "Social Protection in Myanmar: Making the Case for Holistic Policy Reform." *IDS Working Papers* 2011, no. 386 (2011): 1–27.

Nyan Hlaing Lynn. "Deficit Rises, Social Spending Deferred in 2017-18 Budget Proposal." *Frontier*, 1st February 2017.

OECD. "Structural Policy Country Notes: Myanmar." <www.oecd.org/site/seao/ Myanmar.pdf>.

Oo, Zaw, Cindy Joelene, Paul Minoletti, Phoo Pwint Phyu, Kyi Pyar Chit Saw, Ngu Wah Win, Ian Porter, Mari Oye, and Andrea Smurra. "Fiscal Management in Myanmar." 2015.

Özerdem, Alpaslan. "The 'Responsibility to Protect' in Natural Disasters: Another Excuse for Interventionism? Nargis Cyclone, Myanmar." *Conflict, Security & Development* 10, no. 5 (2010): 693–713.

Putnam, Robert D., Robert Leonardi, and Raffaella Y Nanetti. "Making Democracy Work: Civic Institutions in Modern Italy." Princeton: Princeton University Press, 1993.

Raavad, AJ. "Social Welfare Policy – a Panacea for Peace? A Political Economy Analysis of the Role of Social Welfare Policy in Nepal's Conflict and Peace-Building Process." London School of Economics, 2013.

Rao, Madhu, Saw Htun, Steven G. Platt, Robert Tizard, Colin Poole, Than Myint, and James E.M. Watson. "Biodiversity Conservation in a Changing Climate: A Review of Threats and Implications for Conservation Planning in Myanmar." *Ambio* 42, no. 7 (2013): 789–804.

Rawls, John. *A Theory of Justice*. Harvard University Press, 2009.

Rigg, Jonathan. *Challenging Southeast Asian Development: The Shadows of Success*. Routledge, 2015.

Roberts, David. "Post-Conflict Statebuilding and State Legitimacy: From Negative to Positive Peace?" *Development and Change* 39, no. 4 (2008): 537–55.

Rothschild, Joseph. "Observations on Political Legitimacy in Contemporary Europe." *Political Science Quarterly* 92, no. 3 (1977): 487–501.

Rothschild, Michael, and Joseph E. Stiglitz. "Increasing Risk: I. A Definition." *Journal of Economic theory* 2, no. 3 (1970): 225–43.

Rothstein, Bo. "Creating Political Legitimacy: Electoral Democracy Versus Quality of Government." *American Behavioral Scientist* 53, no. 3 (2009): 311–30.

Sabates-Wheeler, Rachel, and Stephen Devereux. "Social Protection for Transformation." *IDS bulletin* 38, no. 3 (2007): 23–28.

Scharpf, Fritz W. "The European Social Model." *JCMS: Journal of Common Market Studies* 40, no. 4 (2002): 645–70.

Scott, James C. *The Art of Not Being Governed: An Anarchist History of Upland Southeast Asia*. Yale University Press, 2014.

_____. *The Moral Economy of the Peasant: Rebellion and Subsistence in Southeast Asia*. Yale University Press, 1977.

_____. "Patron-Client Politics and Political Change in Southeast Asia." *American Political Science Review* 66, no. 1 (1972): 91–113.

Seekins, Donald M. "State, Society and Natural Disaster: Cyclone Nargis in Myanmar (Burma)." *Asian Journal of Social Science* 37, no. 5 (2009): 717–37.

South, Ashley. "Armed Groups and Ethnic Legitimacy." *Myanmar Times*, 23 June 2014.

_____. *Civil Society in Burma: The Development of Democracy Amidst Conflict*. Institute of Southeast Asian Studies, 2008.

_____. "Political Transition in Myanmar: A New Model for Democratization." *Contemporary Southeast Asia* (2004): 233–55.

South, Ashley, Susanne Kempel, Malin Perhult, Nils Carstensen, and South Sudan Sudan. "Myanmar-Surviving the Storm: Self-Protection and Survival in the Delta." Local to Global Protection, website <*www. local 2global. info*> 2011. Accessed 31 October 2017.

Steinberg, D. "Burma's Modern History: What If…." *Irrawaddy*, 2016.

Steinberg, David I. *Burma: The State of Myanmar*. Georgetown University Press, 2001.

_____. "Legitimacy in Burma/Myanmar: Concepts and Implications." *Myanmar: State, Society and Ethnicity*, 109–42, 2007.

Sun, Tsai-wei. "Envisioning Burma: Legitimacy, Leadership, and Political Reform." In *Asian Leadership in Policy and Governance*, 189–211. Emerald Group Publishing Limited, 2015.

Taylor, Robert H. "Perceptions of Ethnicity in the Politics of Burma." *Southeast Asian Journal of Social Science* (1982): 7–22.

Thawnghmung, Ardeth Maung, and Maung Aung Myoe. "Myanmar in 2007: A Turning Point in the 'Roadmap'?". *Asian Survey* 48, no. 1 (2008): 13–19.

Therborn, Göran, and Joop Roebroek. "The Irreversible Welfare State: Its Recent Maturation, Its Encounter with the Economic Crisis, and Its Future Prospects." *International Journal of Health Services* 16, no. 3 (1986): 319–38.

Tilly, Charles. "War Making and State Making as Organized Crime." *Violence: A reader* (1985): 35–60.

UNDP. "Integrated Household Living Conditions Survey in Myanmar (2009–2010)." 2011.

_____. "International Human Development Indicators." <http://hdr.undp.org/en/countries>.

UNICEF. "Child Focused Local Social Plan, Chin State." <http://www.mmiid.org/sites/default/files/Chin%20State%20Local%20Social%20Plan%20%28Vol.%20II%29-%20English.pdf > 2014.

_____. "Situation Analysis of Children in Myanmar (Sitan)." Yangon: UNICEF, 2012.

_____ "Snapshot of Social Sector Public Budget Allocations and Spending in Myanmar." 2015.

Vakis, Renos. "Complementing Natural Disasters Management: The Role of Social Protection." *Washington, DC: The World Bank Social Protection Paper* 543, 2006.

Ven Rewata Dhamma. "Buddhism, Human Rights and Justice in Burma." New York: Church Center for the UN, 1989.

Wood, D. "Policy Dialogue Brings Income Inequality to the Forefront of Development Discussions." *Mizzima*, 19 June 2017.

Woods, Kevin. "Ceasefire Capitalism: Military–Private Partnerships, Resource Concessions and Military–State Building in the Burma–China Borderlands." *Journal of Peasant Studies* 38, no. 4 (2011): 747–70.

# 4

## HEALTH SERVICE DELIVERY AND PEACEBUILDING IN SOUTHEAST MYANMAR

Si Thura and Tim Schroeder

Myanmar has been experiencing internal armed conflict between successive Bamar-led governments and Ethnic Armed Organizations (EAO) for nearly seven decades. By the time of independence from the British Empire in 1948, ethnicity had become a defining category of political orientation in Burma and years of ethnic tensions led to violence across the country (Smith 1991). Since the outbreak of armed conflict between the Karen National Union (KNU) and the newly independent government of Burma in January 1949 on the outskirts of Yangon and across the country, the country has seen more than six decades of civil conflict.

Years of counterinsurgency strategies by the Myanmar Army (Tatmadaw), especially through its "four cuts" strategy—*Pya Lay Pya*—had severe negative consequences on local populations living in conflict-affected areas of Myanmar's ethnic states. Adopted in 1968, the doctrine was to sever insurgents from their key inputs: funding, food, intelligence and recruits (ICG 2000, p. 17). Communities suffered both from brutal repression and severe human rights abuses by the Tatmadaw, and also from systematic structural discrimination and political repression. The military's approach to civilians and ethnic minority people in particular was reflected in minimal spending on social services and development in general during the authoritarian period (see Mangshang & Griffiths, Chapter 3 this volume).

In response to the dire needs of conflict-affected communities, EAOs and their aligned civil society networks established their own structures for community-based primary health care service provision. A coalition of four EAO health departments and three local non-governmental health organizations in southeast Myanmar collectively known as Ethnic Health Organizations (EHOs) emerged parallel to the government health system run by the Myanmar Ministry of Health and Sports (MoHS). A range of basic health services such as for the treatment of common diseases, war-injury management, reproductive and child health care services, community health education, and water and sanitation programmes have developed over time. Due to the shifting zones of armed conflict and governance, rural parts of southeast Myanmar in particular play host to a mosaic of stationary clinics and mobile teams operated by these EHOs, supported by funding from international aid donors (Davis and Jolliffe 2016, p. 10).

The conflict situation in southeast Myanmar changed in 2011 and 2012, when bilateral ceasefires were signed between Thein Sein's government and the majority of EAOs in southeast Myanmar. These ceasefires have greatly contributed to increased stability and security throughout the region. The agreement with the Karen National Union (KNU) has temporarily stopped the longest-running armed conflict in the world. Though far from being a post-conflict environment, the more-or-less stable ceasefires have tremendously improved the situation of conflict-affected populations — with important reservations. With the signing of the National Ceasefire Agreement (NCA) in October 2015, though non-inclusive and often regarded as controversial, the peace process reached a preliminary goal (see Lwin Cho Latt et al., Chapter 10 this volume). In particular, the NCA commits key stakeholders to conduct and engage in a political dialogue to address underlying grievances. Despite these positive developments, conflict-affected communities continue to have poor access to health services, lack livelihood opportunities and frequently experience human rights violations (Davis and Jolliffe 2016).

Significantly, ceasefires and the emerging peace process have allowed for increased engagement between EHOs and the MoHS, which has mostly been facilitated through the assistance of international aid organizations.

Whilst there had not been any relationship between these health service providers and systems in the past, the cooperation and coordination increased significantly after the 2012 ceasefire with both actors willing to further engage with each other. While the cooperation between the different systems is a growing issue of interest, mechanisms of political control will become increasingly blurred. Ambiguities may compound as the two systems cooperate and coordinate closely to achieve greater universality of health care, a key commitment made by both the Karen National Union and the National League for Democracy government. In a context where health services have long been tied to contested control over territory, there are deep challenges between health services and political legitimacy. The MoHS and EHOs' commitment and ability to move towards more universal health coverage (UHC), as outlined under Myanmar's National Health Plan 2017–2021 (NHP), also depends on the progression of national peace negotiations, a process over which neither have direct influence (see Maung Aung Myoe, Chapter 9 this volume).

Health convergence efforts in southeast Myanmar have so far had little tangible impact on elite-level conflict negotiations. However, informed by our in-depth experience with ethnic health organizations and the politics of ceasefires in southeast Myanmar, we argue that coordination and cooperation efforts in the health sector since 2012 have contributed to building trust and confidence at different societal levels. Informed by a World Health Organization (WHO) framework linking health collaborations to peacebuilding processes, in this article we show how such collaborations are an essential foundation for a sustainable peace which tangibly improves the wellbeing of populations in conflict-affected areas.[1]

The article proceeds by briefly reviewing the armed ethnic conflict in southeast Myanmar and the still incomplete peace process. It then outlines the health situation in conflict-affected areas, exploring the progress and impacts of health-focused collaborations between Myanmar health workers and ethnic health organizations in recent years. We conclude with a discussion of implemented health activities, their impact in building trust in the post-conflict context of southeast Myanmar and the challenges that remain.

## CONFLICT SITUATION IN SOUTHEAST MYANMAR

Southeast Myanmar has experienced armed conflict since the country's independence in 1948 between EAOs and successive Bamar-led military governments, with severe humanitarian impacts on local Karen, Mon, Shan, Karenni and other ethnic populations, with many of them surviving as IDPs or as refugees at the Thai-Myanmar Border. For decades, larger EAOs were able to control large parts of southeast Myanmar, exercising varying degrees of local governance, including health service provision to local communities. According to South (2017, p. 2), many conflict-affected communities have long regarded the administrative and political leadership provided by EAOs as equally and often as more legitimate than those of the Myanmar state. The state is still perceived by many ethnic communities as dominated by elements of the Bama majority.

The most influential EAO across southeast Myanmar is the Karen National Union (KNU), which has substantial influence across Karen communities. The organization was founded in 1947 by Karen lawyers, politicians and military commanders, who had been prominent figures in Burma's self-government and security apparatus under the British colonial system. For the next fifty years, the KNU was able to operate as a de facto government across many parts of southeast Myanmar, where many Karen populations can be found. Especially since the 1994 mutiny of Buddhist soldiers who formed the Democratic Karen Buddhist Army (DKBA), however, the Karen National Liberation Army and the Karen National Defense Organization have been fighting a defensive battle, losing control of much of their territory including their headquarters to coordinated Myanmar Army and DKBA attacks. Within a few years, the DKBA had overtaken the KNU as the most powerful Karen non-state actor in some parts of southeast Myanmar. The KNU thus lost many of its once exclusively controlled areas, although the organization still exerts great influence over contested areas through its administrative system (South 2011, pp. 8–10). The organization was further weakened by various breakaway factions during the late 1990s and in 2007, through the creation of the KNU/KNLA Peace Council, led by the aging KNLA 7th Brigade commander.

With the peace process, which emerged in late 2011, and the transformation of the DKBA majority into a Border Guard Force under Myanmar Army control, the KNU saw itself re-emerging as the leading organization of the Karen national movement and a major stakeholder in the Myanmar peace process. The organization signed a bilateral ceasefire agreement with the Myanmar government on 12 January 2012, after a series of negotiations between the conflict parties. Bi-lateral ceasefire agreements such as this have been important steps in peace making and have improved the situation of conflict-affected populations in southeast Myanmar (Myanmar Peace Support Initiative 2014).

The NCA of 2015, though only signed by eight EAOs, has opened the way for a political dialogue process on a national level as well as ceasefire monitoring through the Joint Monitoring Committees formed at state/ regional and local levels. While these have been positive steps in the peace process, challenges such as ceasefire demarcations and a mechanism to determine Interim Arrangements (IAs) during the period between ceasefires and a negotiated political settlement have so far not been addressed. The lack of demarcations and interim arrangements mechanisms have thus enabled the expansion and penetration of government administration and services, as well as state-driven development into contested areas without a joint agreement, leading in some contexts to skirmishes between conflict actors (Jolliffe 2014, pp. 27–8).

Chapter 6 of the NCA acknowledges EAOs' authority in the fields of education, health, natural resource management and security, and allows for international assistance in these fields with the joint agreement of the government and EAOs. However, unlike political dialogue and ceasefire monitoring arrangements, there is no adequate mechanism for implementing IAs. Government ministries such as the MoHS, the Ministry of Education (MoE) and others have very limited involvement in the peace process and have mostly refrained from implementing activities in partnership with EAOs. This raises questions regarding whether EAO governance administrations, and related economic activities, will continue in parallel with the government, or whether the government and its business and development partners will expand into EAO areas, thereby contesting or displacing the authority and agency of armed groups and related civil society partners. Though international support to EAO service delivery systems is permitted as part of the 2015 NCA, there is no explicit avenue for international support, other than for refugee and IDPs (South 2018). The current absence of mechanisms to negotiate Interim Arrangements suggests that conflict actors were reluctant to adopt a one-size-fits-all approach to governance in negotiating the initial ceasefire. Rather, the

Myanmar government and each EAO determine the most appropriate arrangements for coordinating programmes and projects on the basis of the conditions and issues in their particular area. The health sector provides a useful prism into increased cooperation and coordination between state and non-state service delivery regimes following ceasefires.

## HEALTH IN CONFLICT-AFFECTED AREAS OF SOUTHEAST MYANMAR

Myanmar's health sector has received very low levels of public spending over many decades. In 2011–12 for example, only 1.3 per cent of total government expenditure was allocated to the health sector, equivalent to around US$2 per capita. Combined with the country's political isolation, poor economic performance and ethnic armed conflict, these limited resources have translated into very low levels of basic health services, resulting in one of the highest out-of-pocket expenditures for health in the world (at almost eighty per cent in 2011–12). All key areas of the country's health system display fundamental weaknesses, including chronic shortage of essential drugs and supplies, especially in facilities at township level and below, as well as poor health infrastructure in terms of both coverage and condition. Health information is incomplete and questionable, with major gaps in data from the community level and from hard-to-reach and conflict-affected areas. There is a severe shortage of trained medical and paramedical staff. Pre-service training is inadequate and in-service training, which is mainly provided through projects, is poorly coordinated. Transport is inadequate to ensure effective service delivery, supportive supervision and timely referral.

These fundamental weaknesses are further compounded in southeast Myanmar where the effects of armed conflict on security and governance situation, health infrastructure, and the relationship between EAOs, ethnic communities and the government, all have deep implications for the strengthening of health care systems in conflict-affected areas (Davis and Jolliffe 2016, p. 7). Decades of armed conflict as well as government repression and neglect have led to considerable inequalities in access to health services with severe negative consequences on the mental and physical health of communities. Ethnic communities also continue to face language and cultural barriers in accessing government health services, as health staff are often unable to speak local languages. In this context, communities living in EAO-administrated and mixed administrated areas have depended for decades on health service networks provided by EHOs and their associated networks.

Before the 2012 ceasefire agreement and the NCA in 2015, staff of various ethnic health organizations worked under severe security conditions, as they were regarded as unlawful associations aligned with armed groups. There were incidents in which EHO medics and health workers were arrested while attending to patients, with some killed during periods of active conflict. In addition, some MoHS staff regarded EHOs as disreputable health providers or *"quacks"*. Consequently, there was no direct communication or coordination between EHOs and MoHS on any level throughout much of the authoritarian period (Davis and Jolliffe 2016, pp. 4–6).

Research from ceasefire areas of southeast Myanmar in 2013 show that vulnerable populations in conflict-affected areas were less likely to experience human rights violations following the signing of ceasefires (Parmar P. K. et al. 2015). However, access to health services was still severely constrained, and the risk of disease and death remains substantially higher in these areas than the country as a whole. Mortality rates among infants (94.2)[2] and children under five (141.9)[3] were substantially higher than official statistics for the country as a whole. Traditional birth attendants continued to be the main primary service providers, with seventy-three per cent of the women interviewed responding that their last babies were delivered by traditional birth attendants within the last two years. Only 16.4 per cent of the women interviewed received four or more antenatal care visits as recommended by WHO. The survey also found that 54.1 per cent of women respondents had an unmet need for contraception whilst malaria is still the leading cause of death (17.7 per cent of deaths in all age groups). In addition to health and disease, the survey also reveals that 3.5 per cent of respondents experienced forced labour in the twelve months prior to the survey, and nearly eight per cent experienced destruction or seizure of food, livestock, or crops, and impunity for human rights abuses by uniformed personnel, an unacceptably common occurrence in a post-conflict context. It also highlights that household exposure to one or more human rights violations was associated with malnutrition in children, demonstrating the negative impact that insecurity can have on health outcomes.

In the context of wide-spread conflict-induced vulnerability, the provision of social services, including health services, is an important part of some EAO's governance efforts and represents a core element of their relationships with communities. Naturally, these efforts have also become entwined with the desire for self-determination and autonomy held by EAOs (Jolliffe 2014, pp. 6–7). EHOs in southeast Myanmar comprise four formal EAO health departments and three ethnic Community Based Organizations (CBO), affiliated with EAOs to serve populations residing in their administrated areas. These EHOs have been working cohesively throughout times of active conflict and have formed a parallel health system, providing often life-saving health and nutrition services. Rooted in their communities, a majority of their staff live and work in their home villages and have developed a unique understanding of local communities and their needs. In addition to providing basic preventive and curative services for the most common communicable diseases (particularly diarrhea, malaria, and respiratory infections), EHOs also provide basic reproductive health care, child health services, health education campaigns, control of disease outbreaks, relief during acute emergencies, and water and sanitation projects (Health Information System Working Group 2015, pp. 10–13). A short description of these various health providers in the context of southeast Myanmar is found in Table 4.1 below.

Table 4.1 A short description of the prominent EHOs in southeast Myanmar

| Karen Department of Health and Welfare (KDHW) | The Karen Department of Health and Welfare (KDHW) was established as a line department of the KNU in 1956 with the mission to provide primary health care to all people living in Karen areas throughout the southeast. From the 1990s onwards and under immense pressure from Myanmar Army offensives the department has worked together with the BPHWT, MTC, BMA, and other relief groups to develop a mobile health clinic model. This had been done with the assistance of INGOs based in Thailand with the purpose of reaching conflict-affected populations throughout southeast Myanmar. Today, KDHW serves a target population of around 190,000 people through sixty-one clinics, employing over 700 health workers throughout southeast Myanmar (Davis and Jolliffe 2016, p. 14). |
| Karenni Mobile Health Committee (KnMHC) | Provides health services through twenty mobile teams in Karenni State. Health programmes include curative and preventive health services, reproductive and child health, environmental health, health training, and health information programmes. |

| | |
|---|---|
| Backpack Health Worker Team (BPHWT) | This team was founded by Dr. Cynthia Maung and other ethnic health leaders in 1998 with the objective of providing health services for displaced persons in conflict areas in southeast Myanmar. The concept of the mobile health team was to train villagers to provide health services to the people in their own communities. When villages were displaced, the medics would be displaced with them, and were able to provide medical services during flight and relocation. BPHWT has more 1,352 staff, excluding traditional birth attendants, and operates over 100 mobile teams across thirty-two townships of southeast Myanmar, targeting a population of 213,341. The 100 teams include thirty-seven stationary primary health care clinics in areas with more stability and security. |
| Burma Medical Association (BMA) | The Burma Medical Association was founded in 1991 by a group of health professionals from Burma. It is an independent non-profit organization and has been the leading body for policy development and capacity building related to the provision of quality health care services in ethnic areas of Myanmar. In southeast Myanmar, BMA supports 166 reproductive and child health workers, 131 community health workers, and 549 traditional birth attendants at thirty-nine BMA-supported clinics and supports specialized health programmes for EHO clinics. |
| Mon National Health Committee (MNHC) | A non-profit health organization founded in 1992 that serves communities along the Thai-Myanmar border, deep inside Mon state and some areas of Karen State and Tenassarim Region. MNHC is the main provider of primary health care to internally displaced persons (IDPs) living along the Thai-Burma border in Mon State and also operates an additional thirty-three clinics deeper inside Mon State. Annually, MNHC provides health care to approximately 20,000 patients, with a target population of over 60,000 IDPs. |
| The Shan State Development Foundation (SSDF) | The foundation was founded in 2012 by uniting the Shan State Health Committee, the Shan Education Committee and the Shan Relief and Development Committee. The organization provides emergency relief assistance, health treatment, education, and community development programmes. The SSDF is mandated by the Restoration Council of Shan State to engage with other EHO, CSOs, INGOs and donors to implement social projects in its controlled area. It operates a clinic in each of the five Shan IDP camps in RCSS territory along the Thai-Myanmar border (Health Information System Working Group 2015, p. 11). |
| Mae Tao Clinic (MTC) | The clinic is a community-based organization, founded in February 1989, and operates along the Thai-Myanmar border to provide primary health care services for the Burmese community displaced by civil war. Initially established to provide basic health services, over time it has become a comprehensive health service provider and training facility. To respond to different types of community needs, MTC also operates other development programmes including education, women's empowerment, and child protection. |

## PROGRESS IN THE CONVERGENCE JOURNEY (2012–17)

In the context of negotiations of ceasefires, Interim Arrangements and political transformation, a major point of contention remains the degree of convergence envisioned as occurring between the Myanmar government health system and ethnic health organizations.

The term "convergence" is a vague term, as it has different meanings to different actors. A leader of KDHW defines it as "the systematic, long-term alignment of government, ethnic and community-based health services and at the same time, to promote collaboration and coordination between EHOs, MoH and INGOs through inclusive and broad consultations". Other senior staff from KDHW elaborated that "the term convergence does not mean that we (EHOs) will be integrated into the government health system but maintaining our own identities (cultures, customs and language), delivering the same services as MoHS health facilities in the government-controlled areas".[4] According to a leader from BMA, the desired convergence health system by EHOs has to be a devolved health system decentralized to the state level which recognizes and accredits EHOs' health workforce and the larger community-based approach focused on local norms and culture on which it is based.[5] In such a devolved health system, resources from the national budget would be distributed to each state and regional government, who would then have sole discretion to manage and allocate their budget.

Within the Myanmar Ministry of Health and Sport (MoHS), awareness of "health convergence" was very limited until late 2014. EHOs' health workers and health facilities were perceived as parallel service providers or competitors and sometimes, as gate keepers, which halted expansion of MoHS services into the conflict-affected areas. Although there were a few sympathetic MoHS staff who worked in the areas which were partially covered by EHOs health services, the lack of clear guidelines and policies in dealing with EHOs meant few were willing to risk establishing direct relationships with EHOs.

Envisioning more engagement with MoHS, key EHOs established an alliance named Health Convergence Core Group (HCCG)[6] in 2012 for policy dialogue in health-related matters. HCCG formulated a framework of the various steps in engagement with MoHS. The HCCG rocket ship model (see Fig. 4.1 below) explains that engagement with MoHS by EHOs will be contingent upon the progress of the national political dialogue process. A pragmatic approach for collaboration and coordination among MoHS and EHOs was thus developed in which each party would not be able to collaborate or coordinate without the approval of their respective political leadership body. This step-by-step approach enabled EHOs to keep their existing role as health authorities in EAOs' areas and create room for flexibility to revert back to earlier modes if needed. The notion of complete convergence, defined as the integration of estranged health systems from ethnic-controlled areas, is envisioned as occurring only after attainment of a Federal Union.

Following this framework, cooperation and coordination activities between the MoH and EHO slowly started at the end of 2012, gradually increasing dialogue and building trust and confidence between different organizations, community members and service providers. The MoHS in particular accelerated its efforts of collaboration to ensure access to malaria services nationwide, including EAO-controlled areas, as drug resistant malaria was emerging as a major threat to the country. In this situation, MoHS sought to develop strategic implementation with EHOs through a discussion around the crisis. A range of EHOs were invited to attend along with a NGO named Community Partners International (CPI), which had previously worked cohesively with the EHOs network, including KDHW, of which one of the co-authors is executive director. During these initial discussions, CPI described its malaria work with EHOs in hard-to-reach and conflict-affected areas. MoHS senior staff expressed their interest to better understand the malaria situation in EHOs' catchment areas and articulated the importance of malaria data consolidation for a nationwide malaria control planning and implementation programme. Community Partners International facilitated the communication between EHOs and the Infectious Diseases Control Unit of the MoHS. EHOs initially resisted the collaboration due to security concerns and limited trust. In particular, reflecting on past experience, it was feared that sharing malaria data would reveal the geographic location of EHOs health clinics, with potential negative consequences for EHO staff safety and security, as they had been targeted during counterinsurgency activities in the past.

In 2013, CPI started the implementation of a malaria project supported by the multi-donor-trust-fund 3MDG, which brought together four EHOs and two faith-based ethnic organizations to work together within the Myanmar Artemisinin Resistance Containment framework. The project required all partners to utilize the same training curriculum, standard malaria treatment protocols, standard data collection tools and consolidation of data at MoHS. After a series of consultations, EHOs agreed to share malaria data but utilized their respective administrative boundaries and indigenous villages names.[7] CPI involvement had been crucial, as the organization had worked together with EHOs for a number of years and could therefore act as a connector and facilitator between MoHS and EHOs.

Though MoHS staff at central level were starting to slowly develop a relationship with EHOs during the initial years of project implementation, township-level MoHS staff were mostly reluctant to engage with EHOs on a regular basis out of fear of being punished for engaging with an unlawful organization. In 2014, however, the Deputy Minister of MoHS held a meeting with senior staff from KNU and KDHW, which can be considered as a breakthrough for enhanced communication and coordination between EHOs and MoHS (Davis and Jolliffe 2016, pp. 27–8). Later in 2014, a senior staff member from KDHW was invited to join the regular coordination meetings for malaria held in Nay Pyi Taw. Until late 2014, most of the bilateral discussions were centered on collaborative activities for malaria between EHOs and MoHS. One of the positive results of this engagement at policy level has been the ongoing participation of three EHOs during quarterly Technical Strategy Group meetings (Malarial, TB, HIV/Aids), which are regularly held at MoHS in Nay Pyi Taw.

Other collaborations gradually began to develop from these initial openings. The International Rescue Committee (IRC), for instance, began discussions with the University of Community Health in Magway for provision of a public health course for EHOs health workers, facilitated through Thammasat University (Thailand). A series of Auxiliary Midwives (AMW) Training conducted by Backpack Health Worker Team and Karen State Public Health Department, in which local volunteers from EHOs areas were trained according to the AMW curriculum of MoHS, was another turning-point in progress towards "convergence".

Coordination and cooperation continued during 2015 with high-level malaria policy discussions in Washington D.C. jointly organized by CSIS and the University of Maryland. The event was attended by the Deputy Minister of MoH, other government senior officials from MoHS, MoFA, representatives from EHOs (Karen, Kayah, Shan), members of parliaments, representatives from political parties and other CSOs members (Swiss Agency for Development and Cooperation 2016). A joint statement was announced by the meeting attendants, mentioning that regardless of any political change in November 2015, all key participants acknowledged the coordination was critical in fighting against drug-resistant malaria and expressed their commitment to malaria elimination.

Following the election of the NLD government in November 2015, another key milestone in convergence was the establishment of a health policy advisory group intended to develop a roadmap for health reforms across Myanmar. Founded by Dr. Tin Myo Win,[8] Chairman of the NLD National Health Network (NHN), since April 2016 the group has organized a series of workshops, inviting international and local public health professionals to craft a roadmap towards Universal Health Coverage (UHC) in accordance with the NLD manifesto. A consultation meeting with key leaders from different EHOs (including KDHW) was organized by the group in Yangon, offering a mechanism for EHOs to raise their voices to policy makers within the NLD. In these discussions representatives of EHOs emphasized their role as service providers in conflict-affected areas, the need for regular communication, and a mechanism for accreditation of EHOs health workers. Echoing these discussions, the NHN subsequently released a report named "Program of Health Reforms: A Roadmap towards Universal Health Coverage in Myanmar (2016–2030)" in March 2016, which described EHOs as important stakeholders for promoting health service access in conflict-affected areas (National Health Network 2016).

The momentum of these initial interactions with Myanmar's newly elected government was sustained through several dialogues on HIV, TB and immunization activities organized between EHOs and MoHS staff. For instance, MoHS senior staff visited Hpa-an and Maesot (Thailand) to meet with senior leaders of KDHW and other EHOs. The Maternal and Reproductive Health Division (MRH) of MoHS also provided training courses for EHOs on emergency obstetric care so that EHOs could train their workers in alignment with MoHS nationwide standards.[9]

Similar progress has been made in immunization. Earlier discussions during 2014 had raised the possibility of a coordinated campaign of vaccination in EAO and contested areas. However, redlines from both sides (MoHS and KDHW) prevented the campaign from occurring. For example, MoHS suggested that their vaccination team would go to the KDHW catchment areas to provide injections to the children. KDHW refused, saying they had qualified health workers to provide the shots. Since 2016, however, MoHS staff have provided basic immunization training to KDHW medics in order for them to administer injections. The opening ceremony of the scheme has received high-level support from all sides, being attended by the Chief Minister of Karen State and the Chairperson of KNU. The successful advance of collaboration between KDHW and MoHS is enabled by the trust built between the two institutions through iterative cycles of practical discussion and implementation as well as a change in the attitude of the MoHS once the NLD formed government.

Despite these positive developments, ceasefires remain heavily contested and militarized as conflict parties continue to struggle over populations and territory. The expansion of social service delivery by the government, including MoHS and other government departments, during the last five years without substantial consultation and agreement into contested areas has further exacerbated fears among some EAOs that the government will manipulate ceasefires to expand its territorial and administrative control rather than negotiate a political settlement (Davis and Jolliffe 2016, p. 12). In addition, ethnic leaders remain concerned that progressing health convergence without progress in the political dialogue process may be detrimental to long-term ethnic reconciliation.

The described joint efforts in policy, training and service delivery initiatives between the MoHS and EHOs have nevertheless contributed to increased trust and confidence among the conflict protagonists. Whilst empathy and compromise have certainly emerged between actors in the two systems, these developments have been weakly institutionalized, usually depending on concerted engagement with specific individuals within the MoHS (Davis and Jolliffe 2016, p. 38). Indeed, in some cases, MoHS staffs have been openly hostile to EHO staff. Given the consistently high turnover of MoHS staff, which was a key characteristic of many government departments under successive Bamar-led military governments, future progress in convergence is not assured. Decades of armed conflict and military governance have also denied MoHS staff, which are predominantly ethnic Bamar, access to information and understanding of the concerns and aspirations of ethnic nationalities. Respect, appreciation and recognition by MoHS staff of EHO staff will be essential in further creating trust and confidence building. Walton's (2017) argument about the Union Peace Conferences is also true for engagement between MoHS and EHOs:

> There can be no personal transformation where, as has been the case among military and political leadership for decades, prominent individuals believe that their job is merely to lecture, instruct, and admonish, rather than listen and learn through participating in a mutually transformative discussion.

In order to increase meaningful contact between the MoHS and EHOs it is thus important to have a structured and institutionalized process rather than ad hoc encounters based on personal relationships. A clearer MoHS policy regarding convergence with EHOs, for example regarding Interim Arrangements in particular, may be useful. While the Myanmar government has started promoting a more people-centered approach to service delivery at the local level, citizen–state relationships are still characterized by top-down relations, limited real dialogue and absence of clear accountability and oversight structures. As a result, effective "check and balance" mechanisms are absent, eroding trust between citizens and the state. The framework for township-level coordination envisioned in the MoHSs National Health Plan 2017–2021 may provide an opportunity for increased communication and cooperation, as well as transparency and accountability, essential to continued progress on convergence.

## EFFORTS ON ACHIEVEMENT OF UNIVERSAL HEALTH CARE AT THE NATIONAL LEVEL

Since forming government in March 2016, the NLD-led government has committed to improving access to and quality of health services throughout the country as part of its reform agenda. In particular, it has expressed its commitment to move towards achievement of Universal Health Care (UHC). UHC is defined as all people having access to most essential health services without experiencing financial hardship and has become a global health priority. It is one of the Sustainable Development Goals agreed by all UN Member States to be achieved by 2030. In December 2016, MoHS released the National Health Plan 2017–2021, which describes the first phase in the country's move towards UHC and envisions a wide scope for collaboration between EHOs and Myanmar government health workers.

The development of the NHP, initiated by Dr. Myint Htwe, the Minister of MoHS in September 2016, was a uniquely inclusive process in the context of Myanmar, as the committee for developing the NHP included government officials as well as representatives from civil society and EHOs.[10] Four major workshops were conducted, in which representatives from EHOs were invited. KDHW participated actively in the process of NHP development and additionally organized parallel consultation meetings among Karen EHOs and representatives from NCA signatories and provided collective inputs from different EHOs.

Figure 4.1

**Health Convergence Core Group (HCCG)**
Primary Health Care Convergence Model for Burma/Myanmar
March 2014

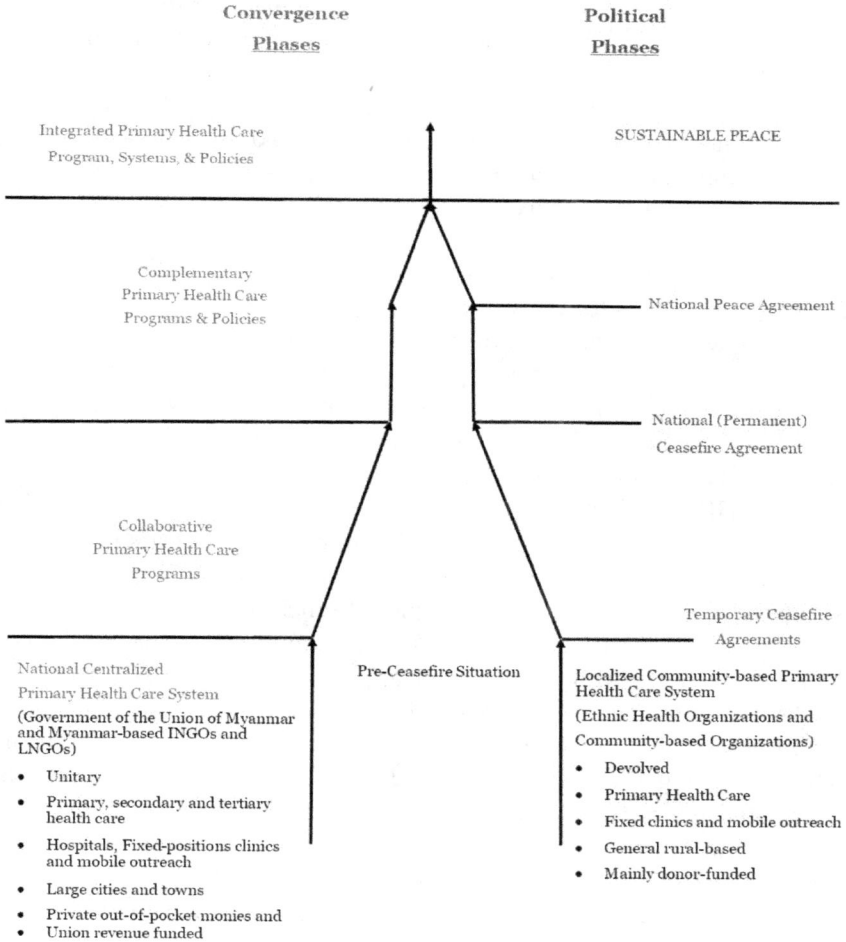

Convergence
Phases

Political
Phases

Integrated Primary Health Care
Program, Systems, & Policies

SUSTAINABLE PEACE

Complementary
Primary Health Care
Programs & Policies

National Peace Agreement

National (Permanent)
Ceasefire Agreement

Collaborative
Primary Health Care
Programs

Temporary Ceasefire
Agreements

Pre-Ceasefire Situation

National Centralized
Primary Health Care System

(Government of the Union of Myanmar
and Myanmar-based INGOs and
LNGOs)

- Unitary
- Primary, secondary and tertiary
  health care
- Hospitals, Fixed-positions clinics
  and mobile outreach
- Large cities and towns
- Private out-of-pocket monies and
  Union revenue funded

Localized Community-based Primary
Health Care System

(Ethnic Health Organizations and
Community-based Organizations)

- Devolved
- Primary Health Care
- Fixed clinics and mobile outreach
- General rural-based
- Mainly donor-funded

The developed framework focuses on addressing health system issues in prioritized geographic areas to provide basic health services package to the whole population in Myanmar by 2021. The plan also underlines that MoHS will not be able to achieve UHC alone, but only in partnership with other health care providers such as EHOs, NGOs and GP clinics at large. The NHP endorses a possible way of proper recognition of the EHOs health workforce through clinical standardization training for different tiers of the EHOs health system. It also suggests the development of a compatible accreditation mechanism of education programmes in EHOs areas (MoHS 2016). Furthermore, the NHP plans to recognize EHOs health facilities as health service access points for conflict-affected areas and to set up a common data platform for different types of health care providers. To ensure quality health services, an accreditation system of health facilities would be developed, which would also accredit EHOs health facilities. To promote accountability of health service providers, NHP intends to explore possibilities for meaningful participation of representatives from civil societies and EHOs at different administrative levels.

Finally, the plan proposes to pilot a new financing model for different health providers, thereby ensuring sustainability, which may also enable EHOs to receive funds from the national budget, regardless of the attainment of a more federal structure of government.

The NHP is the first national-level document which recognizes EHOs as health care providers in the context of Myanmar. KDHW leaders said they were pleased with the process and delighted by the NLD government's recognition of their role and willingness to include them in the journey towards UHC.[11] KDHW senior leaders made a commitment that they would cooperate with the MoHS for further implementation of NHP.

As part of the NHP, the MoHS will introduce the Inclusive Township Health Plans that will be prepared by multi-stakeholder Township Health Working Groups, including EHOs. These working groups will be crucial in order to coordinate health service delivery and promote equity in access to health. They will also be important in bringing together government township medical staff and EHO staff, as well as local governance administrators from both sides and increase cooperation and coordination, as the two systems' catchment areas are intertwined and frequently overlap. The government township's capacity and willingness to implement the Inclusive Township Health Plan will be crucial and would be severely hampered by centralized decision-making and unwillingness

**Figure 4.2: Framework of National Health Plan (2017–2021)**
*Ministry of Health and Sports 2016, p. 8*

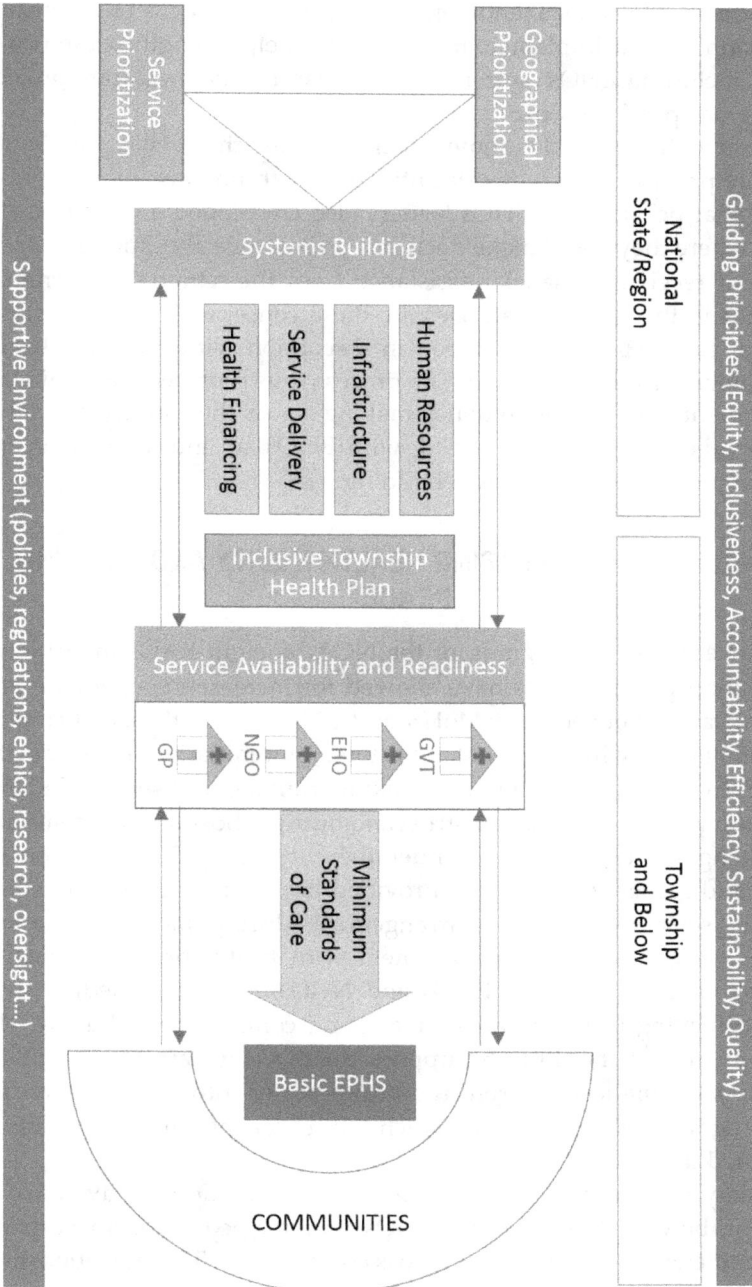

to include all relevant stakeholders in the process. A focus on township-level planning and implementation will also help strengthen the health system, including EHOs' systems, rather than running separate projects focusing on specific diseases.

However, there are also some criticisms from other EHOs. Firstly, the plan only provides a framework until 2021, with no guarantee of policy beyond that point. Some EHOs leaders also envisioned a federal health system where they could make decisions on resource allocation in health, instead of receiving financial assistance from the national government budget as in the current plan. Despite these concerns, it is important to note that the NHP was developed in discussion with non-state health care providers for the first time. The process thus represents a significant development in consultative policy making across the country as well as a major milestone in trust-building with EHOs, an indicator of further potential progress in social peacebuilding.

## CONCLUSION—INCREASING HEALTH EQUITY AND BUILDING PEACE

Bilateral ceasefires, the signing of the NCA by eight EAOs in 2015 and the resulting peace process have allowed for increased cooperation and communication between the MoHS and EHOs in southeast Myanmar, often facilitated by international aid actors. Joint initiatives have enabled collaborative approaches to policy making, training and service delivery to develop where previously mistrust and outright hostility was common. The willingness of the MoHS under the current NLD government to engage and recognize EHOs has provided hope for future effective and politically sensitive health care arrangements during the interim period. The NHP promotes active engagement with health providers outside the public sector, including EHOs and NGOs and acknowledges their role in achieving UHC in hard-to-reach and conflict-affected areas. The NLD-government should fully support MoHS's engagement with EHOs and take valuable lessons from the health sector into consideration for other programmes and projects which fall under Interim Arrangements as outlined in the NCA.

In many respects, international organizations and donors have acted as connectors between the MoHS and EHOs, bringing people together around health and enabling cooperation across conflict lines. These relationships are still in their initial stage and need continued support through careful action aimed at creating a space for dialogue, fostering mutual respect and building trust between the conflict actors. Development partners should champion the MoHS's NHP and encourage the ministry to maintain its ongoing effort to include EHOs in health sector reforms. Given the complex situation, development partners also need to be observant of conflict sensitivity in contested areas and fully recognize EHOs' governance and service delivery mandate.

The NHP presents an unprecedented opportunity for EHOs to cooperate with MoHS for accreditation of health workers, sustainability of their operations, and delivery of quality health services in their catchment areas. Other EHOs which have less coordination with MoHS should also contemplate the vision of health sector collaboration contained within the NHP and discuss how they can play a role in delivering quality health services in their catchment areas, regardless of direct coordination with MoHS or not. Such progress relies on respective EAOs creating an enabling environment for their EHOs to cooperate with MoHS, and the Ministry institutionalizing an inclusive and consultative approach which relies heavily on key individuals at present. Developing more formalized mechanisms to implement the NHP in partnership with the EHOs is essential.

At present, more formalized changes to governance and social service delivery systems can only be resolved once all armed groups have signed the nation-wide ceasefire agreement and formal discussions commence (see Lwin Cho Latt et al., Chapter 10 this volume). In the interim period, it is therefore essential that communities in conflict areas have their basic needs met and are empowered to engage in processes which will determine the future of their wellbeing and livelihoods. In recognition of the state's contested authority in these areas, both state and EAOs need to engage in coordination and collaboration on local development and public service delivery, as outlined under IAs in the NCA. South (2018) advocates the importance of engaging with pre-existing structures, authorities and institutions of "hybrid governance" which deliver public goods/services in areas of limited statehood. International aid actors must therefore engage not only with the institutions and interest of the Myanmar state, but also encourage and enable it to more expansively include EAOs and "hybrid" service delivery systems such as EHOs in central government planning and service delivery. For its part, the Myanmar government needs to be cognizant that despite risks, attempting to ensure equitable social service delivery in conflict-affected areas in partnership with EHOs can advance rather than erode the course of national reconciliation. Building trust and confidence, and encouraging communication and collaboration will take time, however, and expectations thus need to be realistic. The health convergence process in Myanmar will be a long-term process, evolving at local and elite levels alongside the national political dialogue process. Increased collaboration and coordination at the local level, especially at township level, will ensure improved health service delivery can provide the foundation for confidence building and a more sustainable peace.

## Notes

1    The framework titled *"Health as a Bridge for Peace" (HBP)* sought to link human rights principles to health ethics, combining conflict-sensitive approaches, peace-building concepts and practices into health sector development. Available at: http://www.who.int/hac/techguidance/hbp/about/en/ (accessed 24 January 2018).

2    Infant mortality rate is the number of deaths of children under one year of age per 1000 live births.

3    Under five mortality rate (probability of dying by age 5 per 1000 live births).

4    Interview with Dr. Marta (Senior Consultant of KDHW, former EC member of KNU).

5    Interview with Saw Nay Htoo (Director of BMA).

6    HCCG is composed of EHOs from Chin, Karen, Karenni, Mon and Shan and CBOs affiliated with EAOs such as BPHWT, MTC and BMA.

7    Government administration and EAOs use different names for the same village in some circumstances.

8    Dr. Tin Myo Win is now chairman of National Peace Commission.

9    This training course plan was facilitated by three organizations (IRC, CPI and JEPHIGO).

10   Directive of the Minister of MoHS, issued in September 2016.

11   KNU Health Policy has commitment to UHC as a goal.

## References

Davis, B. and Jolliffe, K. "Achieving Health Equity in Contested Areas of Southeast Myanmar". The Asia Foundation, 2016. Available at <https://asiafoundation.org/publication/achieving-health-equity-contested-areas-southeast-myanmar/> [accessed 24 January 2018].

Health Convergence Core Group. "A Federal, Devolved Health System for Burma/ Myanmar — A Policy Paper," Health Convergence Group, 2014. Available at: <http://hiswg.org/?p=3578> [accessed 2 February 2018].

Health Information System Working Group. "The Long Road to Recovery – Ethnic and Community-Based Health Organizations Leading the Way To Better Health in Eastern Burma." 2015. Available at: < http://hiswg.org/wp-content/ uploads/2015/02/The-Long-Road-to-Recovery-2015_Eng-1.pdf> [accessed 2 February 2018].

International Crisis Group. "Burma/Myanmar: How Strong is the Military Regime?" International Crisis Group, 2000. Available at: <https://d2071andvip0wj. cloudfront.net/11-burma-myanmar-how-strong-is-the-military-regime.pdf>. [accessed 2 February 2018].

Jolliffe, K. "Ethnic Conflict and Social Services in Myanmar's Contested Regions". The Asia Foundation, 2014. Available at: <https://asiafoundation.org/resources/ pdfs/MMEthnicConflictandSocialServices.pdf> [accessed 2 February 2018].

Ministry of Health and Sports, The Republic of the Union Of Myanmar. *Myanmar National Health Plan (2017–2021)*. 2016.

Myanmar Peace Support Initiative. "Lessons Learned from MPSI's Work Supporting the Peace Process in Myanmar, March 2012 to March 2014". Yangon: Myanmar Peace Support Initiative, 2014.

National Health Network. "Program of Health Reforms: A Roadmap Towards Universal Health Coverage in Myanmar (2016–2030)". March 2016.

Parmar, P. K., Barina, C., Low, S., Kyaw Thura Tun, Otterness, C., Mhote, P., Saw Nay Htoo, Saw Win Kyaw, Nai Aye Lwin, Maung, C.,  Naw Merry Moo, Eh Kalu Shwe Oo, Reh, D., Nai Chay Mon, Singh, N., Goyal, R. and Richards, A. "Health and Human Rights in Eastern Myanmar after the Political Transition: A Population-Based Assessment Using Multistaged Household Cluster Sampling". *PLoS One* 10 (5), 2015. Available at: <https://www.ncbi.nlm.nih.gov/pmc/articles/ PMC4430217/> [accessed 24 January 2018].

South, A. *Burma's Longest War, Anatomy of the Karen Conflict*. Amsterdam: Burma Center Netherlands, 2011.

_____ . "'Hybrid Governance' and the Politics of Legitimacy in the Myanmar Peace Process". *Journal of Contemporary Asia*, 48(1) (2018): 50–66.

_____ . *The Politics of Peace in Myanmar: Ethnicity, Conflict and Building Legitimate State in Burma*. Copenhagen: NIAS Press, 2018.

Swiss Agency for Development and Cooperation. "Midterm Evaluation Report for Primary Health Care Project in Myanmar". December 2016.

Walton, M. "Political Communication and Transformative Citizenship in Myanmar (Part II)," *Tea Circle*, 7 September 2017. Available at: <https://teacircleoxford. com/2017/09/07/political-communication-and-transformative-citizenship-in-myanmar-part-ii/> [accessed 24 January 2018].

# III

# Places

# 5

## MYANMAR'S RURAL REVOLUTION: MECHANIZATION AND STRUCTURAL TRANSFORMATION

Myat Thida Win, Ben Belton and Xiaobo Zhang

Development economists see structural transformation—the process by which labour leaves the rural agricultural sector for the more productive urban industrial and service sectors—as fundamental to economic development. As progressively more labour relocates from rural to urban zones the former are transformed from labour surplus to labour deficit areas, and a "turning point" is reached when rural wages begin to catch up with urban ones (Lewis 1954). Recent evidence of this pattern can be found in many Asian countries such as Bangladesh and China (Zhang et al. 2011; Zhang et al. 2014). Agricultural mechanization, the process by which capital in the form of machinery is substituted for labour in agriculture, is viewed by agricultural economists as a labour-saving response to labour scarcity and rising rural wages (Binswanger 1986; Takahashi and Otsuka 2009). Binswanger (1986, p. 32) notes that "mechanization is profitable and contributes most to growth where land is abundant, where labor is scarce relative to land and where labor is moving rapidly off the land". As such, agricultural mechanization can be read as a symptom of structural transformation that helps to maintain the viability of farming in the face of labour shortages and rising production costs (Zhang et al. 2017).

In contrast to this model of development, in which economic and social transformation along the rural-urban axis is predictable and linear in form, recent work by development geographers highlights processes of agrarian transition that are far more complex, partial and varied than the mainstream economics literature would suggest (e.g. Rigg & Vandergeest 2012). For instance, Rigg et al. (2016, p. 118) observe that—contrary to the expectations of most commentators—smallholders in East and Southeast Asia "have persisted in the face of rapid and profound social and economic transformation". But they do so in a variety of new hybrid forms that reflect the conjuncture of variations in physical geography, mobility, markets, and government policies.

These debates have particular resonance for Myanmar as it emerges from five decades of isolation and becomes more deeply integrated into the regional and global economy. Three processes central to structural transformation have emerged post-2011. First, the economy is growing rapidly. GDP growth is forecast to reach 8.3 per cent in 2017, making Myanmar the fastest-growing major economy in the region (ADB 2016). Second, Myanmar is experiencing high levels of migration. For example, fourteen to twenty-six per cent of households in six townships in Chin State, Magway and Ayeyarwady had at least one migrant (Pritchard et al. 2017). International migration flows are well-established and relatively well-documented (e.g. Pearson and Kusakabe 2012), but internal rural-urban migration has increased significantly since 2011 (World Bank & LIFT 2016). Third, rural outmigration is driving wage increases in migrant sending areas. For example average inflation-adjusted wage rates for casual labour in four rural townships close to Yangon increased by forty per cent from 2011 to 2016, apparently in response to a migration-induced tightening of the labour market (Win and Thinzar 2016).

According to Dawe (2015), the two most important factors in determining the rate of agricultural mechanization are the level of wages and the land/labour ratio, with higher wages and land/labour ratios promoting the adoption of labour-saving machinery. The confluence of rapid urban growth, rural outmigration, and rising rural wages noted above thus suggest that rapid mechanization is likely to occur in at least some areas of Myanmar.

However, this transformation is not widely recognized to have taken place to date. For example, a major study of farm production economics conducted by the World Bank in 2013–14 in Ayeyarwady, Bago, Sagaing, and Shan State found very low rates of mechanization. For instance, levels of combine harvester use in rice cultivation stood at just one per cent. The report's authors argued that a combination of low wages in rural areas, excess agricultural labour, poor infrastructure, a lack of service providers, a poor regulatory environment, and lack of access to long-term capital by farmers were preventing investments in agricultural machinery (World Bank 2016). Recent media reports present a similar view. For example, a story in the *Myanmar Times* reports on the failure of farming to mechanize in the face of high rates of outmigration from the Ayeyarwady Delta (Myanmar Times 2016). The article states that "private market sellers and rental services remain underdeveloped", and that combine harvester services are used by just fifteen per cent of farmers in Ayeyarwady, and remain too expensive "for the vast majority who own small plots".

This chapter addresses, empirically, the disconnect between evidence of a dynamic and rapidly transforming economy, and the low levels of agricultural mechanization widely reported. It also seeks to account for regional differences in observed patterns of mechanization. We use a mix of quantitative data and qualitative observations from our own surveys to analyze the current state of agricultural mechanization in four townships close to Yangon and provide insights from scoping in other areas of the country. Historical data from the national Integrated Household Living Conditions Assessment (IHLCA) survey of 2005 and 2010 is also drawn upon for comparative purposes.

Contrary to the findings of the World Bank (2016) we find ample evidence that extremely rapid agricultural mechanization has begun in the main area studied in Lower Myanmar. Our survey data shows that these changes occurred concurrently with greater labour mobility, high levels of outmigration, and rapidly rising wages. This confluence of events supports the inference that structural transformation is under way, at least in the main area studied. A particularly notable observed characteristic of agricultural mechanization is the emergence of machine rental services markets, which has made the adoption of agricultural machinery close to scale neutral at the point of use.[1] This finding belies the perception that mechanization is only possible with, or must result in, concentration of agricultural landholdings, lending support to the position that processes of agrarian transformation can occur in ways that are highly unpredictable and contextually specific.

Similarly, we find that agricultural machinery dealerships have increasingly spread beyond the country's traditional agricultural heartlands to penetrate more peripheral areas of the country, but this process has been far from uniform. Place-based spatial variations in uptake of different types of machinery are identified, linked to differences in physical connectivity, agro-ecology, crop choice, and the economic logic of different forms of farming (i.e. commercial and subsistence). The question of whether mechanization has contributed to rural differentiation, deagrarianization and shifts in the balance of gender relations is important, but cannot be answered with the data available, and remains an important topic for future research.

The paper is organized as follows. Section 2 presents data and methods. Section 3 provides a historical overview. Section 4 analyzes the current characteristics of mechanization in Myanmar from both demand and supply sides. Section 5 examines drivers of mechanization. Section 6 evaluates place based determinants of geographical variation in the extent and form of mechanization. Section 7 concludes.

## 2. DATA AND METHODS

This chapter paper draws on four sources of data. (1) Historical data taken from datasets of the nationally representative IHLCA surveys for 2005 and 2010. (2) Information on agricultural machinery ownership and use from a structured survey of 1,100 households in Ayeyarwady and Yangon regions—the Myanmar Aquaculture-Agriculture Survey (MAAS)—completed by the authors in early 2016. (3) An enterprise survey of twenty-seven agricultural machinery supply businesses in Yangon (the Yangon Mechanization Cluster Survey), completed in mid-2016. (4) Rapid qualitative scoping assessments conducted in Ayeyarwady, Yangon, Mandalay, Magway and Sagaing regions, and Mon State from 2016 to early 2017. Surveys 2, 3 and 4 were conducted by a collaborative research team comprised of the Centre for Economic and Social Development (CESD), International Food Policy Research Institute (IFPRI), and Michigan State University (MSU). Details of the three structured surveys are outlined in sequence below.

The IHLCA datasets were used to estimate levels of ownership and use of agricultural machinery among farm households by geographical zone in 2005 and 2010. IHLCA is a nationally representative household survey for Myanmar of 18,660 households, conducted under the auspices of the Ministry of National Planning and Economic Development and the United Nations Development Programme. The survey instrument contained a detailed list of agricultural assets owned and used, including all the main categories of agricultural machinery (IHLCA, 2011).

The MAAS was fielded in May 2016 to fulfil a variety of purposes, including generating a baseline of information on farm yields, size, tenure status, management practices and profitability, and evaluating patterns of migration, and the ownership and utilization of agricultural machinery. A two-stage sampling strategy was followed. For the first stage, forty village tracts from four townships (Kayan and Twantay, Maubin and Nyaungdon) were selected purposively based on an assessment of the farming systems present in each. All the selected village tracts fell within approximately a sixty-kilometre radius of Yangon. For second-stage sampling, enumeration areas (EAs) were selected from these village tracts by probability proportional to size, using the national population census of 2014 as the sampling frame. This procedure yielded a sample of seventy-eight EAs. A census of households was conducted in every selected EA to serve as the final sample frame for randomized selection of respondent households. Eight farm and seven non-farm households were selected for interview in each EA. Respondents from 1,102 households, representing a total population of 37,390 households, were interviewed. Although the results of the survey provide insights into areas in close proximity to Yangon, they are not necessarily representative of more remote agricultural areas.

To supplement household-level data, the Yangon Mechanization Cluster Survey was conducted in July 2016 to generate a picture of the supply side of Myanmar's agricultural machinery market. Machinery supply businesses (machinery dealerships) were surveyed in a commercial area in western Yangon, located close to the main road and river routes leading to the country's agricultural heartland, the Ayeyarwady Delta. Pre-survey scoping interviews indicated that most of the machinery supply dealerships in Yangon are located in this area, which is by far the largest "cluster" of agricultural machinery supply businesses in Myanmar, and which houses branches of most of the country's major suppliers. The survey thus captured information on a large share of national agricultural machinery sales. A census of businesses in the cluster was conducted prior to survey rollout.

A total of thirty businesses selling agricultural machinery and twenty-seven shops selling spare parts for agricultural machines were listed. All agricultural machinery suppliers and spare parts shops in the cluster were selected for survey. Three machinery suppliers and five spare parts shops declined to participate, giving a total sample size of forty-nine businesses. This chapter presents survey findings on the twenty-seven agricultural machinery supply businesses.

## 3. HISTORICAL OVERVIEW

Comparison of IHLCA data for 2005 and 2010 shows that agricultural machine use increased only incrementally over this period, from a very low base. For example, the share of farm households using four-wheel tractors increased four percentage points (from eight to twelve per cent). Similarly, use of two-wheel tractors (power tillers) increased three percentage points (from four to seven per cent of households), while use of mechanical threshers rose two percentage points (from four to six per cent). By 2010, overall rates of agricultural machine use remained very limited, with just eight per cent of farm households nationally making use of the most common type of machine, the two-wheel tractor (Figure 5.1).

Mechanization was farthest advanced in the main rice-growing agricultural "core" regions of Lower Myanmar (Ayeyarwady, Yangon, Bago)—the agro-ecological zone where our own MAAS survey was implemented; among households with large landholdings; and among those double cropping paddy (i.e. with access to irrigation). However, even here, overall rates of machine use were very low. Machine use was almost non-existent in Rakhine and Chin States (isolated and predominantly upland areas on Myanmar's western periphery), and were very limited among households with small landholdings and those growing a single non-paddy crop.

These patterns are consistent with the common perception of Myanmar's rural economy and agricultural sector as static, traditional and lacking in dynamism. Little change took place over the five-year period between surveys, and the adoption of agricultural machinery was the

Figure 5.1: Share of agricultural households (per cent) using machinery, by area of country and type of machinery, 2010
(Source: IHLCA, 2010)

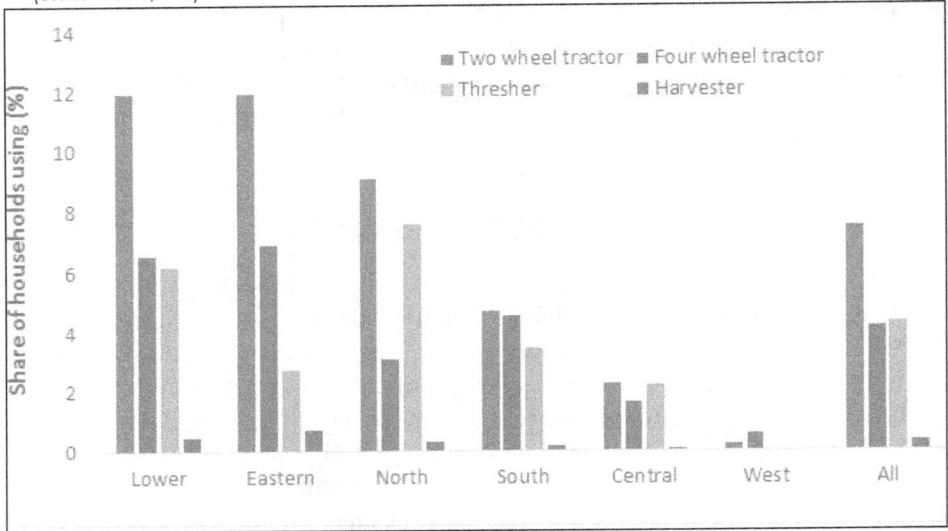

exclusive preserve of the uppermost stratum of farmers. Rental markets for agricultural machinery also remained poorly developed in 2010. With the exception of threshers and combine harvesters, users of all types of agricultural machinery were more likely to own than to rent them. Lack of access to rental services accounts in part for the concentration of machine use among a small segment of large farms.

## 4. THE SCALE AND DYNAMICS OF RECENT MECHANIZATION

In contrast to the historical picture painted by IHLCA data, our own surveys implemented in 2016 reveal that rapid and widespread mechanization took place in the intervening years in surveyed townships in the Ayeyarwady Delta and some other areas of the country. Evidence of the current extent of agricultural mechanization and its recent dynamics is presented in the following sub-sections.

### 4.1 Changes in machine ownership

Compared to data from IHLCA 2010, results from MAAS indicate that a dramatic change in agricultural machinery use had taken place in the four townships surveyed by 2016. Machinery had almost completely replaced animal traction in agriculture in the areas surveyed by this time. Ninety-four per cent of households reported using machinery for land preparation in 2015–16, while only fourteen per cent of farm households continued to use draft animals for this purpose. Sixty-eight per cent of farm households used two-wheel tractors for land preparation, and seventeen per cent used four-wheel tractors. The use of draft animals for transporting inputs or crops all but disappeared, while forty per cent of households used machines for this task (Figure 5.2).

Widespread mechanization of harvesting and threshing also occurred. Half of all sampled paddy farming households reported using a combine harvester for this purpose, and thirty-eight per cent used mechanical threshers to separate manually harvested paddy from paddy straw. This means that close to ninety per cent of paddy produced in the area of Lower Myanmar surveyed underwent mechanized harvesting and/or threshing. The enormity of this shift is apparent when one considers that only 0.5 per cent and six per cent of households in Lower Myanmar made use of either a combine or thresher, respectively, in 2010 (Figure 5.1).

**Figure 5.2. Machinery and Draft Animal Use in Paddy Cultivation, 2015–16**
(Source, Own survey: MAAS 2016)

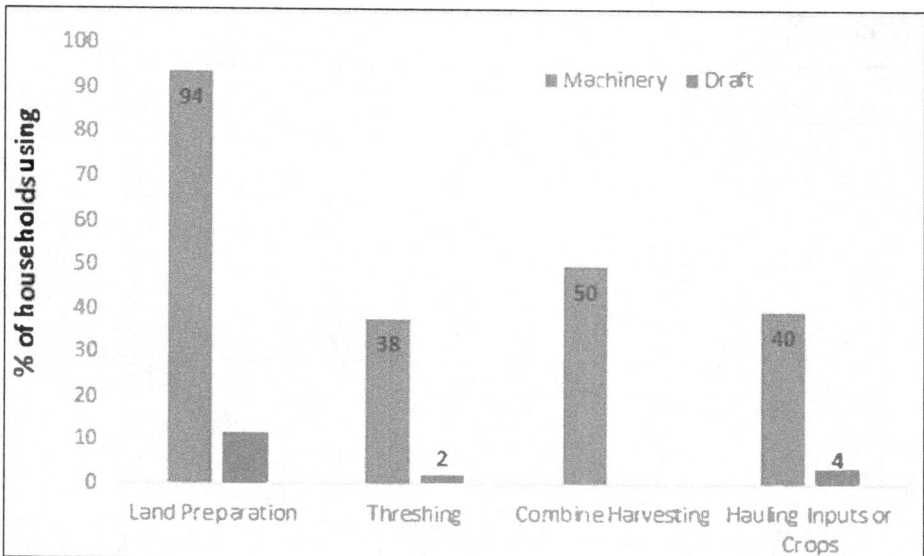

Changes in machine use have occurred in step with rapid increases in ownership of agricultural machinery, and changes in the composition of that machinery. This is illustrated in Figure 5.3, which presents data on the (population weighted) number of machines of different types purchased by households in surveyed village tracts in each year from 1990 to 2015. Very limited adoption of surface-water pumps began in the early 1990s, followed by two-wheel tractors in the mid-1990s. Purchases of mechanical threshers and four-wheel tractors began almost a decade later, after 2000. Combine harvester purchases are a very recent phenomenon, occurring only from 2013. Sales of water pumps, two-wheel tractors and threshers all grew very slowly until the late 2000s, whereupon they increased rapidly, accelerating particularly quickly from 2010 onwards. This trend is consistent with the sequential pattern of mechanization observed in many countries, in which stationary "power intensive" operations such as pumping water and threshing are mechanized first, followed by mobile "control intensive" operations such as harvesting (Pingali 2007, p. 2008).

Examining the total value of machines purchased over time reveals an even more dramatic change. Figure 5.4 depicts the rate of mechanization in terms of the total value (adjusted to 2015 prices) of different types of machinery purchased in the survey area from 2000 to 2015. Similar to the

**Figure 5.3. Cumulative Purchases of Selected Machinery (1990–2015).**
Source: MAAS (2016)

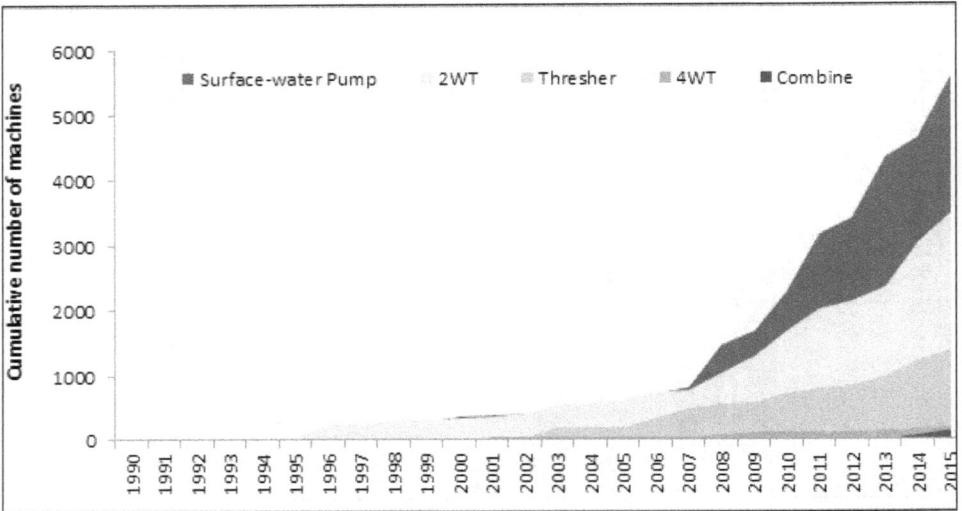

pattern illustrated in Figure 5.3, expenditure on machinery grew slowly from a low base in 2000, and was initially comprised mainly of two-wheel tractors and water pumps. The total value of sales began to increase more rapidly after 2009–10 as the purchase value of threshers and four-wheel tractors rose, and then more than tripled in the space of just two years from 2013 to 2015.

Four-wheel tractors and combine harvesters alone contributed about half of the total value of machinery purchases in 2015. The contribution of four-wheel tractors to the total value of purchased machinery was low prior to 2013, even though the total number of four-wheel tractor units purchased changed little before and after 2013, suggesting that expensive high-performance imported four-wheel tractors were increasingly purchased after 2013.

## 4.2 Changes in machine supply

Our survey of agricultural machinery dealerships in Yangon provides evidence of similar patterns in the volume and composition of machinery sales. The product assortment offered by suppliers has diversified over time. Sales were initially comprised primarily of small machines (water pumps, engines and two-wheel tractors). Numbers of suppliers stocking these grew quickly from 2005, and more than two-thirds of businesses

**Figure 5.4. Total Real Purchase Value of Selected Machinery (2000–15).**
Source: MAAS (2016)

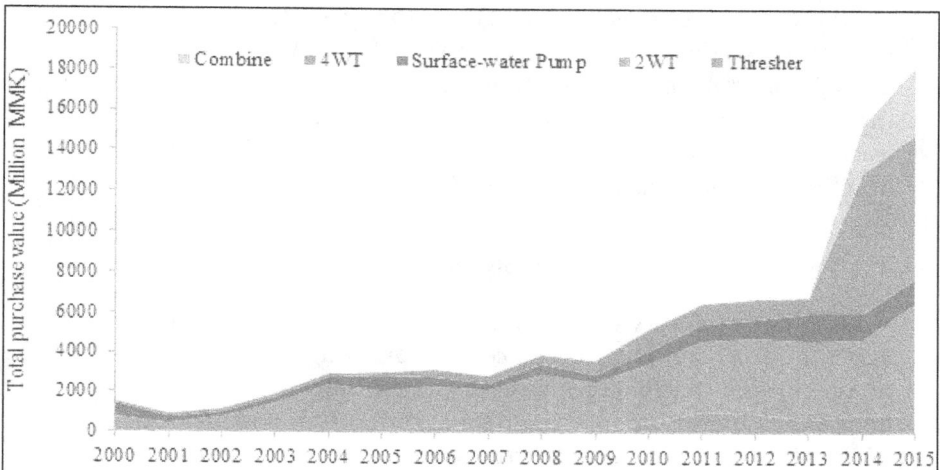

surveyed stocked them in 2016, reflecting high levels of demand and widespread use. The number of dealerships stocking four-wheel tractors increased sharply from 2009, followed by combine harvesters, which were first sold in 2012, and grew rapidly thereafter, with both types of machine sold by around forty per cent of dealers in 2016.

Five of the machinery dealerships surveyed began to stock mechanical rice planters in 2016, suggesting the possibility of a further shift toward an even more specialized labour-saving technology. However, few sales of these machines had been made at the time of the survey, and their uptake is likely to be slower than that of other types of machinery because of technical and organizational complexities in preparing rice seedlings for use with them.

Growth in the volume of sales made by machine supply businesses between 2012 and 2016 parallels the upsurge in machine ownership evident in Figures 5.3 and 5.4. The total number of units sold (all types of machinery) increased by 592 per cent over this period, from 18,283 to 126,572 (Table 5.1).[2] Sales of four-wheel tractors and combine harvesters increased particularly quickly after 2014. Annual combine harvester sales grew nearly 6,000 per cent in four years (from 40 to 2,372), with ninety per cent of this growth taking place in 2015 and 2016 (Table 5.1). Sales of four-wheel tractors increased almost 1,100 per cent between 2012 and 2016 (from 275 to 3,200). The average number of sales staff employed by surveyed dealerships grew forty-three per cent between 2013 and 2016, reflecting the increasing volume of sales made.

Large machines have already begun to replace smaller ones. Sales of threshers dwindled by seventy-nine per cent from a high of 220 in 2014 to 46 in 2016, while annual growth in sales of reapers peaked in 2015 after three years of brisk growth and fell by eight per cent thereafter. Four-wheel tractors also appear to have eaten into sales of two-wheel tractors, sales of which plateaued from 2014 to 2015.

## 4.3 The machine services rental market

A machine rental services market has developed in step with increasing agricultural machinery sales since 2010. Although sales and ownership of agricultural machinery increased dramatically after 2010, most farm households access this equipment through short-term rentals. The growth of rental services has played a critical role in facilitating farmer access to these items. As expected, ownership of agricultural machinery is most common among farmers with large landholdings, while smaller farmers are more likely to access machinery by renting. Use of rental services is most common for the most expensive machinery (combine harvesters and four-wheel tractors). The emergence of rental service markets has driven sales of these machines, as renting out machinery provides revenue that enables owners to pay off outstanding hire purchase loans and quickly recoup their investments.

The rental services market for large machines is dominated by larger farmers and other rural entrepreneurs who buy machines principally to rent out to others. Combine harvester owners often offer rental services in both the local vicinity and more distant areas of the country to take advantage of regional differences in the timing of harvesting seasons. After providing services in nearby villages, combine owners from the Delta transport their machines to other rice farming regions, such as Shwebo in Central Dry Zone, using rented trucks. Similarly, combine owners from the Dry Zone provide rental services to the Delta during their local off-seasons. Rentals

**Table 5.1: Annual sales by surveyed machinery dealerships in Yangon (2012–16)**

|  | Year |  |  |  |  |
|---|---|---|---|---|---|
| **Item** | 2012 | 2013 | 2014 | 2015 | 2016 |
| Two wheel tractor & accessories | 9598 | 11715 | 14912 | 14872 | 20684 |
| Engine, dynamo & water pump | 8105 | 11547 | 62806 | 59103 | 99026 |
| Four wheel tractor | 275 | 420 | 870 | 1662 | 3200 |
| Combine | 0 | 40 | 237 | 955 | 2372 |
| Reaper | 305 | 335 | 860 | 1351 | 1244 |
| Thresher | 0 | 30 | 220 | 167 | 46 |
| Total | 18283 | 24087 | 79905 | 78110 | |

of smaller machines (two-wheel tractors, threshers etc.) are provided principally by farm households with medium or large landholdings, within the immediate vicinity of their villages. The machine rental services market is dominated by this vibrant informal private sector. Although the government's Agricultural Mechanization Department (AMD) offers some machinery rental services, none of the households surveyed in MAAS reported making use of them. The provision of machine rental services by formal businesses (e.g. machinery dealerships) is also very limited.

Recall data on the share of farm households owning, renting or borrowing machinery used for land preparation and harvesting at three five-year intervals (2006, 2011, and 2016) is presented in Figure 5.5. The percentage of households using some type of machinery for land preparation rose steadily from thirty-six per cent in 2006 to seventy-two per cent in 2011, reaching ninety-seven per cent in 2016. In all three years, approximately half of these households reported owning the machine used, while the other half rented in. The share of households using machines for harvesting changed little from 2006 to 2011 (increased from five to ten per cent), but jumped steeply to fifty-seven per cent in 2016. Rentals accounted for ninety-three per cent of all machines use for harvesting in 2016.

## 4.4 Mechanization and Farm Size

Agricultural mechanization is commonly perceived not to be scale neutral because machines are "lumpy" inputs that require high levels of initial capital investment and "reach their lowest cost of operation per unit at relatively large areas", thus favoring adoption by large farms (van Zyl et al. 1995, p. 3). This leads Pingali (2007, p. 2790) to state, with reference to Southeast Asia, that "in the absence of land consolidation and the re-design of the rice land to form large contiguous fields, the prospects for large-scale adoption of the harvester-combines are limited."

Evidence from MAAS contradicts this characterization. In surveyed village tracts, farm size and adoption of agricultural machinery are, at best weakly correlated. Figure 5.6 presents data on the share of farm households using machinery for land preparation and harvesting in paddy cultivation during the twelve months preceding the survey, by farm size. Farms are divided into three categories (<5 acres, 5–10 acres, and >10 acres). The three categories correspond approximately to small, medium and large farms in the Myanmar context. The share of households using two-wheel tractors and four-wheel tractors for land preparation varies very little among farm size categories. Use of combine harvesters varies somewhat more, ranging from fifty per cent on farms sized <5 acres to sixty-one per cent on farms of >10 acres, but the difference is small.

The highest rental rates occur among households with small farms. For instance, more than ninety-five per cent of farms under five acres that

**Figure 5.5. Use of Machinery for Land Preparation and Harvesting In Paddy Cultivation, by Source of Machinery, 2006–16.**
Source: MAAS (2016)

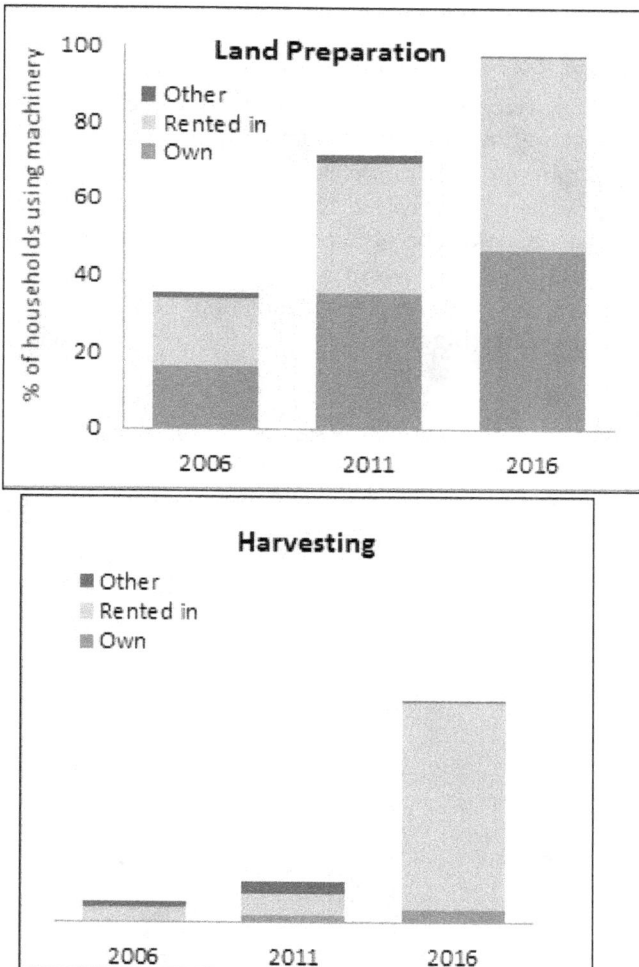

made use of combine harvesters in 2015–16 rented these in, as compared with seventy-four per cent of farms operating >10 acres of land. The rapid growth of competitive machinery rental markets has allowed smallholders to enjoy many of the benefits obtained from mechanization by larger farmers (e.g. reduced labour costs, timely completion of activities). Accelerated social differentiation and land consolidation (as might be expected if only large farms were able to utilize these technologies), thus appears unlikely to occur as a result of the introduction of machinery. These results also demonstrate that land consolidation is not a necessary precondition for the widespread adoption of agricultural machinery. However, although our scoping experience and surveys indicate that the rental market is flourishing in the Delta and some parts of Dry Zone, it may remain less well-developed in remoter areas where infrastructure is poor. It is probable, though we have yet to test this empirically, that farm size and machine use are more closely correlated in those areas.

Myanmar's experience in this respect is similar to that of other Asian countries. For instance, the adoption of two-wheel tractors, made possible by a thriving rental market, is very widespread in Bangladesh, where just three per cent of households own such a machine, but eighty per cent of farmland is tilled with them (Biggs et al. 2011). Moreover, average farm

**Figure 5.6. Share of Households Using Machinery for Land Preparation and Harvesting in Paddy Cultivation, by Farm Size Group (2015/16).**
Source: MAAS (2016)

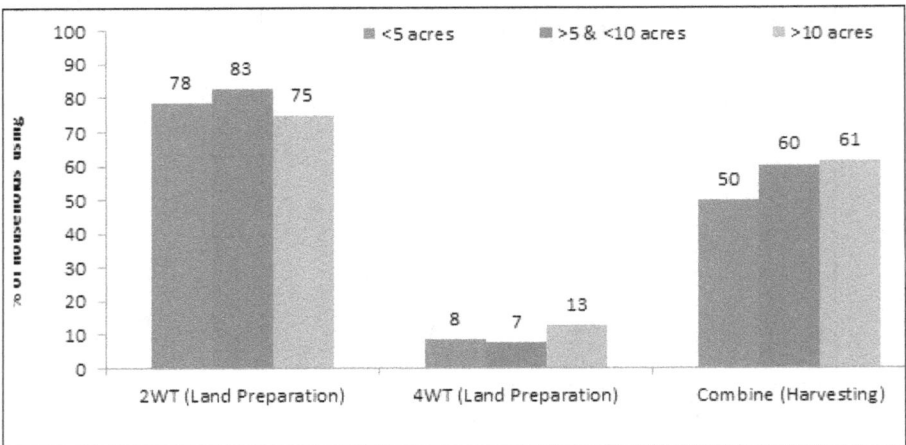

sizes in Bangladesh are around an order of magnitude smaller than in Myanmar, and are continuing to decline. Similarly, Zhang et al. (2017) find that despite small landholdings and a high degree of land fragmentation, farmers in China have outsourced activities such as harvesting to specialized mechanization service providers, who travel throughout the country to harvest crops at very competitive prices.

## 5. DRIVERS OF MECHANIZATION

This sub-section elaborates on the characteristics of two key drivers of mechanization. First, from the demand side, changes in the Myanmar labour market are linked to migration and increasing mobility. Second, from the supply side, changes in access to formal financial services have made it easier for buyers to purchase agricultural machinery.

### 5.1 Migration, land and the changing labour market

In addition to data on mechanization, MAAS collected information on migration, wage rates and landholdings. Migration flows follow a similar timeline to the adoption of agricultural machinery. Eighty per cent of current migrants left their households after 2010 (Figure 5.7). Migration increased rapidly but steadily from 2011 until 2014, after which it accelerated further. These shifts coincide with the relaxation of restrictions on freedom of movement imposed under military rule, and rapid urban growth post-2011.

The role of urban growth in stimulating migration is reflected in the fact that a large majority (seventy per cent) of migrants from the four townships surveyed engaged in manufacturing work, with most of the remainder working in services, or as skilled labour in trades (Htoo and Htun 2016). Ninety per cent of migrants from surveyed households were reported to work in urban areas. The most important of these was nearby Yangon, which was the destination of sixty-one per cent of all migrants. Unlike in other areas of the country such as Mon State, where international migration (particularly to Thailand) is very common, only eight per cent of migrants from the locations surveyed worked abroad.[3] In addition to permanent migrants, forty-four per cent of all individuals working a monthly salaried job resided at home but commuted regularly to nearby urban areas, representing a further reduction in the rural workforce (Htoo and Htun 2016).

Sixteen per cent of households surveyed in the four townships close to Yangon had at least one long-term migrant at the time of interview. Although this share seems modest, average age at first migration is twenty-one, meaning that migrants are disproportionately concentrated among the most productive, economically active segment of the labour force, and their departure results in a large reduction in the availability of rural workers. The gender balance of migrants in surveyed townships was approximately equal (fifty-five per cent male, forty-five per cent female). As men and women participate in harvesting (the most labour-intensive agricultural activity) in roughly equal numbers, the gender implications of mechanization are not immediately clear, but deeper analysis is warranted.

The question of whether systemic or idiosyncratic "push factors" have contributed to this migration boom also warrants consideration. Rates of landlessness were high in the communities surveyed, with well over half of all households (fifty-eight per cent) having no agricultural land.

**Figure 5.7: Cumulative share of migrants by year and destination**
*(Source: Htoo & Htun 2016)*

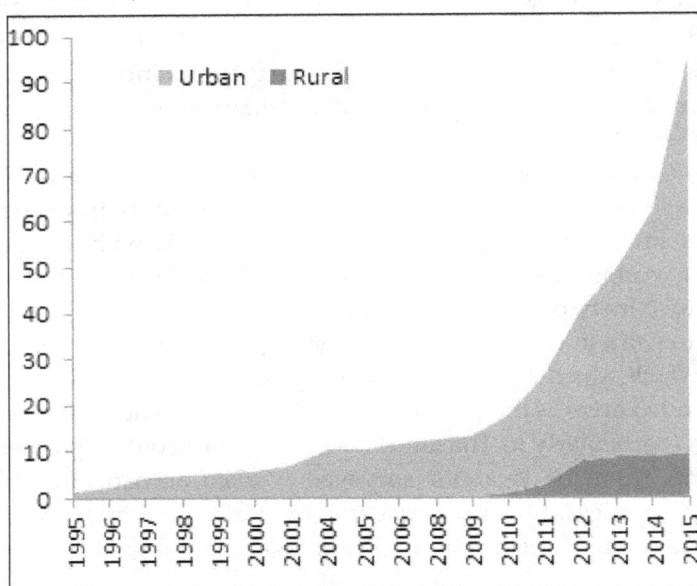

Moreover, although the mean area of agricultural land cultivated is 10.2 acres, farmland is highly unevenly distributed: the third of households with the smallest agricultural landholdings own just three per cent of the total area of farmland, while the third of households with the largest agricultural landholdings own sixty-nine per cent. It is probable that landless households and agricultural producers with very small landholdings struggle to reproduce themselves, providing a strong incentive to migrate in search of alternative opportunities. However, migration rates were not found to differ widely across categories of households with different resource endowments and livelihood strategies (e.g. landed/landless, farm/non-farm).

Moreover, high levels of landlessness and small agricultural holdings do not appear to be a recent, nor recently intensified, phenomenon. Although the area surveyed has experienced high levels of land confiscation in the past, with approximately ten per cent of households reporting having lost land due to confiscation or appropriation by the state or private entities within the past thirty years, few households had lost any land for this reason since 2006. The rate of loss of land due to indebtedness has also changed little recently. Cyclone Nargis is known to have displaced large numbers of households from Ayeyarwady region, but this happened in 2008, two years before migration began to gather pace, and the cyclone did not severely damage villages in the townships surveyed.

The movement of labour to urban areas has brought about a tightening of the rural labour market in the areas surveyed. The real (inflation adjusted) agricultural wage rate increased moderately from 2011 to 2013, by eight per cent (MMK4,2607 to MMK 2,820), before jumping by a further thirty-two per cent to MMK 3,718 in 2016. Although it is not possible to establish causality on the basis of this trend alone, there is a strong correlation between the timing and characteristics of rural-urban migration, increasing rural wage rates, and the adoption of agricultural machinery, all of which accelerated most rapidly at precisely the same time. This confluence of events supports the interpretation that structural transformation is beginning to take hold in this area of Myanmar.

## 5.2 The emergence of formal financial services

On the supply side, the advent of customer finance provided by private banks has played a pivotal role in the growth of machinery sales and the emergence of machine service rental markets. Two forms of customer finance are available: (1) Hire purchase financing offered by machinery dealerships using their own working capital; (2) Hire purchase financing provided by banks and other commercial financial institutions. In both cases, customers make an initial down payment on the item they intend to buy. In the case of direct financing by dealerships, the remainder of the balance is repaid by the customer to the dealership, in installments with interest, over a fixed period (usually twelve months). In the case of hire purchase arrangements made through banks, the bank usually pays the loan balance to the machinery dealership and the customer repays the loan to the bank, with interest, over a fixed period (again, usually twelve months). Interest rates are capped at thirteen per cent per year, in line with national financial regulations. The uptake of these services has been remarkable. Banks first offered hire purchase arrangements in 2013, but by 2016 these loans accounted for the majority of purchases of combine harvesters (seventy-seven per cent) and four-wheel tractors (sixty-eight per cent), and one third (thirty-five per cent) of purchases of two-wheel tractors (Figure 5.8).

The success of these schemes stems from their removal of credit constraints to both machinery dealerships and their customers. Banking regulations mean that machinery dealerships are only able to borrow from banks up to the value of their fixed assets, making it difficult for them to extend large volumes of customer credit, particularly in the case of large machines which cost from $13,000 to $31,000 on average, depending on brand and country of origin. This is reflected in Figure 5.8, which shows that direct hire purchase financing from machinery suppliers accounted from just five and two per cent of four-wheel tractor and combine harvester sales in 2016. Hire purchase arrangements have also improved the ease with which customers can access machinery, as the ability to obtain finance from a bank removes the need to save the entire cost of a machine before making a purchase, or to borrow from informal at lenders at rates of interest averaging five per cent per month (sixty per cent per year).

The emergence of formal financing for machinery purchases has been possible in part due to the Farmland Law, instituted in 2012, which made agricultural land use rights transferrable. All land in Myanmar is the property of the state (Union), with households granted use rights that allow land to be used for specific purposes. Prior to 2012, agricultural land use rights were not legally transferrable from one individual to another.

The new law means that loan applicants can now use agricultural land use certificates ("Form 7") as guarantees for bank loans.[5] This pattern is consistent with Pingali's observation (2007, p. 2801) that "formal land titles empower small farmers further by providing them the collateral necessary for acquiring credit for the purchase of machinery."

## 6. GEOGRAPHY AND SPATIAL VARIATION

Data presented above on the adoption of agricultural machinery and its links to economic transformation are specific to four townships located close to Myanmar's largest and most economically dynamic city, raising the question of whether this case is a localized geographical anomaly, or indicative of more pervasive structural change at the national level. The Yangon Mechanization Cluster Survey provides evidence of a generalized tendency, but one that is proceeding at different intensities in different

**Figure 5.8: Share of 2016 machinery sales by source of finance and machine type**
Source: Mechanization Cluster Survey (2016)

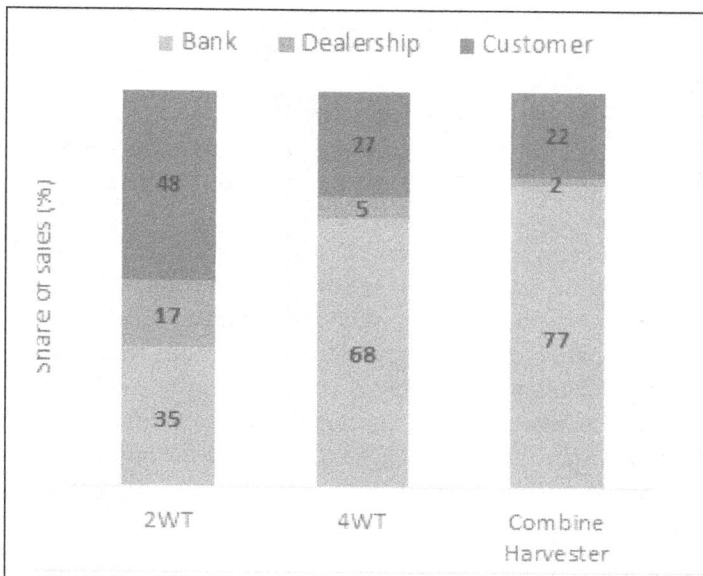

locations. This pattern reflects the influence of a variety of factors discussed below.

Machinery dealerships surveyed in Yangon were asked for the location and date of establishment of other branches that they operated. These data are summarized in Figure 5.9, for the years 2010, 2013 and 2016. Before 2011, sales outlets were highly concentrated in Yangon, Mandalay, Bago and Ayeyarwady. Yangon and Mandalay cities are Myanmar's two largest commercial centers, while rural Ayeyarwady, Bago, and Yangon are part of Myanmar's "rice bowl", providing the majority of the country's paddy. Together these four regions form a "core" agricultural corridor, running through the center of the country along the course of the Ayeyarwady River. The businesses surveyed in Yangon operated a total of fifty-seven branches in 2010, of which eighty-nine per cent were located in these four "core" regions. From 2011 to 2013 the number of branches operated by surveyed businesses grew thirty per cent, to seventy. Most of this growth occurred in the southern part of the core zone, in rice-growing areas close to Yangon. From 2013 to 2016, branch numbers increased by a further twenty-nine per cent. Growth in Lower Myanmar continued during this period, but was also accompanied by the establishment of branches in the northern part of the core corridor (Mandalay), as well as in the agriculturally "intermediate" regions of Magway and Sagaing, and the "peripheral" states of Shan, Mon and Tanintharyi. Geographical concentration of machinery businesses decreased as a result, with seventy-seven per cent of branches located in the original core regions in 2016.

This pattern of spatial development can be interpreted in two ways: (1) On the supply side, machinery suppliers may have sought to open new branches in hinterland areas in order to extend their customer base as markets in the country's agricultural heartland have matured. (2) On the demand side, labour shortages and wage rate increases that first occurred in the agricultural zone surrounding Yangon may have spread to remoter and less dynamic rural areas, as mechanization has followed labour shortages and rising wages. However, striking as these changes are, observations made in the field during scoping research indicate a greater degree of complexity and variability than suggested by these narratives alone.

First, certain crops and farming environments lend themselves more readily to particular types of mechanization than others. As seen in Figure 5.9, mechanization was initially concentrated in Lower Myanmar, where virtually all crop farmers produce monsoon paddy. Farmers in this zone

Figure 5.9: Number and location of machinery suppliers, 2010, 2013, and 2016.

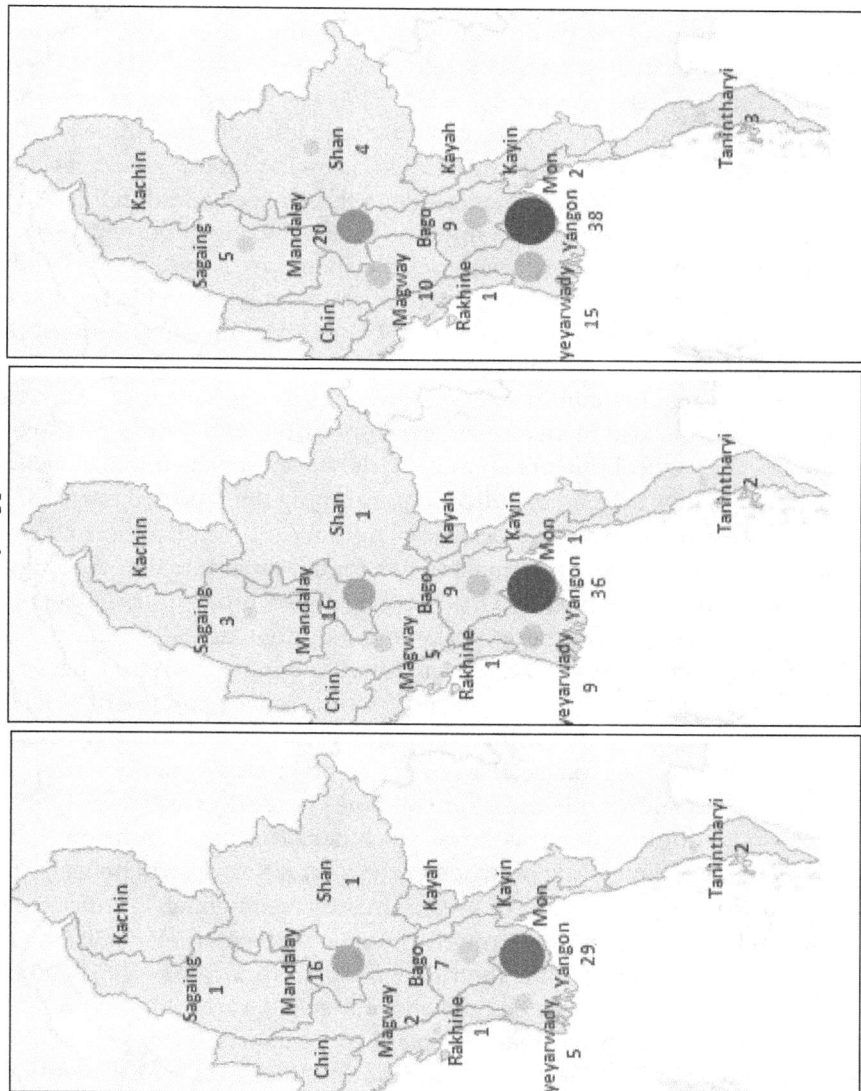

**2010 (left panel):**

Kachin

Sagaing 1

Shan 1

Mandalay 16

Chin

Magway 2

Bago 7

Kayah

Rakhine 1

Kayin

Mon

Yeyarvady 5

Yangon 29

Tanintharyi 2

**2013 (middle panel):**

Kachin

Sagaing 3

Shan 1

Mandalay 16

Chin

Magway 5

Bago 9

Kayah

Rakhine 1

Kayin

Mon

Yeyarvady 9

Yangon 36

Mon 1

Tanintharyi 2

**2016 (right panel):**

Kachin

Sagaing 5

Shan 4

Mandalay 20

Chin

Magway 10

Bago 9

Kayah

Rakhine 1

Kayin

Mon 2

Yeyarvady 15

Yangon 38

Tanintharyi 3

rapidly adopted two-wheel tractors (which quickly replaced draft animals for land preparation) and combine harvesters. Adoption of four-wheel tractors proceeded more slowly here because large machines are not well suited to operation on wet soils. In addition, the homogeneity of rice-based farming systems in the Delta means that rental service providers have a large customer base to work with, leading to the widespread provision and adoption of their services.

In contrast, mechanization in the Dry Zone has preceded at a somewhat slower pace (and with different characteristics), despite increases in domestic and international outmigration, growing labour shortages and rising real wages of a similar magnitude to those experienced in the Delta. Oilseeds (mainly peanut and sesame) and pulses (mostly importantly green gram, pigeon pea and chick pea) are the main crops cultivated. Paddy cultivation occurs in a scattered pattern in about half of the villages, and is concentrated particularly in a small number of townships with large-scale dam irrigation. The predominance of non-rice crops, which are grown on dry soils, means that adoption of four-wheel tractors has preceded more rapidly than the use of two-wheel tractors in the Dry Zone. However, although four-wheel tractors are now widely used for the initial plowing of hard soils, they are poorly suited to performing the repeated harrowing that the oilseed crops require prior to planting. As a result, almost all Dry Zone farmers continue use animal traction for this latter function. Adoption of combine harvesters in the Dry Zone has been rapid in irrigated rice growing pockets where there are large contiguous areas of paddy, but slower in areas where paddy farms are fewer and more dispersed, because operation in the latter areas does not offer sufficient economies of scale to rental service providers. Furthermore, harvesting of pulses and oilseeds has yet to be mechanized at all, as the open pollinated varieties currently grown are not sufficiently erect for combines to work effectively.

Second, adoption of agricultural machinery can occur in response to different logics, depending on whether the orientation of farm households is predominantly subsistence or predominantly commercial. Production of paddy in Lower Myanmar is strongly oriented to the market. For example, seventy-five per cent of the monsoon paddy produced by households in MAAS survey areas is sold, and the share sold varies little with farm size. Most farms in these areas also plant a (commercial) dry season crop of green gram or paddy. In mechanizing, these farmers seek not only to minimize production costs, but to reduce risk (e.g. delayed harvest due to labour shortages resulting in crop damage), and minimize the fallow period between crops.

In contrast, in Mon State, paddy is a more subsistence-oriented crop, with only half of rice producers selling any paddy, and the marketed surplus averages only thirty per cent. In addition, few farms plant a dry season crop of any kind (CESD, IFPRI & MSU 2016). Levels of migration in Mon are much higher than in surveyed townships around Yangon, with almost half of the households in the state having at least one migrant member, ninety-five per cent of whom work in Thailand. Remittances in Mon account for a similar share of household income as agriculture (twenty-two versus twenty-four per cent, respectively) (CESD, IFPRI & MSU 2016), and arguably subsidize farming livelihoods to a large extent. Mechanization was already fairly advanced in Mon State in 2015, with fifty-eight per cent of households using a machine for land preparation, and fifty-seven per cent using a machine for threshing. However, given the context in which it occurs, the logic of mechanization in Mon State appears to have less to do with maximization of returns subject to constraints (as it is in Lower Myanmar), than with assisting an aging population of farmers, who are unable or unwilling to migrate to find higher paying jobs abroad, to stay on the land.

## 7. CONCLUSIONS

Our research reveals extremely rapid agricultural mechanization occurring in four townships close to Yangon. Following decades of stagnation, economic reforms and accompanying urban growth since 2011 appear to have given rise to the beginnings of a structural transformation, in which labour is moving from agriculture to urban industrial and service sectors. In surprisingly short order this shift has led to rural labour shortages and rising wage rates, and a corresponding jump in the use of machinery for land preparation, harvesting and threshing. Of particular note is the finding that the concurrent rise of rental markets for mechanization services has enabled farmers with small and large landholdings alike to access machines, making adoption virtually scale neutral at the point of use, thereby supporting the viability of smallholder agricultural production in the face of rising labour costs. Increasing access to formal financial services and the introduction of transferrable land use rights have also contributed to accelerated sales and the use of agricultural machinery, especially from 2013 onwards. In these respects, the patterns of mechanization observed correspond well with the dynamics predicted by conventional economic theory.

However (as indicated in the preceding section), despite the pervasive influence of these "fundamentals", the form, pace and depth of mechanization reflect regional geographical variations that include the extent and nature of migration and labour shortages, physical accessibility, logics of production (subsistence versus market), and crop choice (in large part a function of differing agro-ecologies). These findings underline that, despite commonalities in their underlying drivers, contemporary processes of agrarian transition are marked by place-specific diversity, unevenness, and spatial complexity, with often unpredictable outcomes (Rigg and Vandergeest 2012). This chapter demonstrates, along with other research in this volume on Special Economic Zones (Maung and Wells, Chapter 7) and on Myanmar's periphery (Gabusi, Chapter 6), that the variable of place is pivotal to understanding the local impacts of Myanmar's economic and political transformations.

Two important questions for future research remain unanswered. First, is whether the advantages gained by producers able to access agricultural mechanization services are contributing to geographical differentiation in farm competitiveness. This may occur if rental services are concentrated in areas with large numbers of potential users that offer economies of scale to machine services providers (e.g. major rice growing regions in Lower Myanmar and the command areas of large irrigation schemes in the Dry Zone that are well served by combine harvester rentals), but do not reach areas where crop production is more scattered (such as parts of the Dry Zone where rainfed paddy cultivation is dispersed widely). It is also possible that similar patterns of inequality in access to services may emerge at a smaller scale within villages that receive machine rental services, for farms with plots that are difficult for machines to access (e.g. in low lying or waterlogged areas, or those that are particularly uneven, or distant from access roads).

Second, although mechanization evidently offers significant benefits to most farmers, its effects on landless households (who in most parts of Myanmar represent a large part of the rural population, including many of its poorest members) remain unclear. Further analysis is required to determine whether rising rural wage rates, out-migration and emerging opportunities in the rural non-farm economy off-set or exceed any reductions in income caused by the loss of casual work for agricultural wage labourers. Such research would help us understand in more depth the varied and contingent impacts of Myanmar's mechanization revolution, and has an important role to play in guiding agricultural, rural development and social policies implemented by Myanmar's new government.

Note: This research was made possible by the generous support of the United States Agency for International Development (USAID) funded "Food Security Policy Project" (Associate Award No. AID-482-LA-14-00003), and financial assistance from the Livelihoods and Food Security Trust Fund (LIFT) Grant Support Agreement Number: R1.4/029/2014 for the project "Agrifood Value Chain Development in Myanmar: Implications for Livelihoods of the Rural Poor". The contents are the responsibility of the authors and should not be taken to reflect the views of either organization.

## Notes

1   A "scale neutral" agricultural technology is one which for which farm size does not pose a barrier to adoption.
2   This figure excludes sales made by branches outside the cluster. Sales volumes for 2016 are extrapolated, based on sales made during the first six months of 2016. Key informants confirmed that sales during the first and second half of the year are usually similar.
3   Others migrated to regions outside Yangon and Ayeyarwady (21 per cent), elsewhere in Yangon and Ayeyarwady (5 per cent), and 'other locations' (5 per cent).
4   MMK = Myanmar Kyat. USD 1 was valued at approximately MMK1200 in 2016.
5   Form 7 replaced the previous land titling document, "Form 105", which was assigned to parcels of land already registered on cadastral maps of agricultural land. The system of creating cadastral maps and associated agricultural land use categories dates from the British colonial period. An informal market in sales and, to a much lesser extent, rentals of land already existed in the townships surveyed prior to this change, so the main effect of the law in these locations appears to have been to strengthen pre-existing formal tenure, rather than to incorporate "new" land (e.g. land accessed under customary tenure rules) into new sets of tenure arrangements.

## References

Asian Development Bank. *Asian Development Outlook 2016: Asia's Potential Growth.* Manilla: Asian Development Bank, 2016.

Binswanger, H. 1986. "Agricultural Mechanization: A Comparative Historical Perspective". *World Bank Economic Observer* 1 (1986): 27–56.

CESD, IFPRI & MSU. *Rural Livelihoods in Mon State: Evidence from a Representative Household Survey.* Food Security Policy Project Research Report #7. August 2016. East Lansing: Michigan State University, 2016.

Dawe, D. "Agricultural Transformation of Middle-income Asian Economies: Diversification, Farm Size and Mechanization". ESA Working Paper No. 15-04. Rome: Food and Agriculture Organization, 2015.

Gabusi, G. "Change and Continuity: Capacity, Co-ordination, and Natural Resources in Myanmar's Periphery". In *Transforming Myanmar*, edited by G. McCarthy, J. Chambers, C. Win, and N. Farrelly. Singapore: Institute of Southeast Asian Studies, 2018.

Htoo, K., and A.M. Htun. *Rural-Urban Migration around Yangon City, Myanmar.* Food Security Policy Project Research Highlights #5. Michigan State University, 2016. <http://fsg.afre.msu.edu/fsp/burma/Research_highlight_5.pdf > [accessed 15 November 2017].

IHLCA. *Integrated Household Living Conditions Survey in Myanmar (2009-2010): Poverty Profile.* Yangon: Ministry of National Planning And Economic Development, United Nations Development Programme, United Nations Children's Fund, Swedish International Development Cooperation Agency, 2011.

Lewis, W. A. "Economic Development with Unlimited Supplies of Labor". *The Manchester School* 22 (2, 1954): 139–91.

Maung, P. P. and Wells, T. 2018. "Advocacy Organizations and Special Economic Zones in Myanmar". In *Transforming Myanmar*, edited by G. McCarthy, J. Chambers, C. Win, and N. Farrelly. Singapore: Institute of Southeast Asian Studies, 2018.

Myanmar Times. As Labourers Leave Myanmar Delta, Farmers Struggle to Mechanise. *Myanmar Times*, 06 December 2016. <http://www.mmtimes.com/ index.php/business/24067-as-labourers-leave-myanmar-delta-farmers-struggle-to-mechanise.html> [accessed 15 November 2017].

Pearson, R., and Kusakabe, K. *Thailand's Hidden Workforce: Burmese Migrant Women Factory Workers.* London and New York: Zed Books, 2012.

Pingali, P. "Agricultural Mechanization: Adoption Patterns and Economic Impact". In *Handbook of Agricultural Economics* Vol. 3, edited by R. Evenson and P. Pingali, pp. 780–800. Amsterdam: Elsevier, 2007.

Pritchard, B., M. Dibley, A. Rammohan, Z. S. Htin, S. M. Nay, T. Thwin, M. Pan Hmone, K. Htet, M. Vicol, A. M. Aung, K.K. Linn, J. Hall. *Livelihoods and Food Security in Rural Myanmar: Survey Findings*. University of Sydney, 2017.

Rigg, J., A. Salamanca, E.C. Thompson. "The Puzzle of East and Southeast Asia's Persistent Smallholder". *Journal of Rural Studies* 43 (2016): 118–33.

Rigg, J. and P. Vandergeest. *Revisiting Rural Places: Pathways to Poverty and Prosperity in Southeast Asia*. Singapore: NIS Press, 2012.

Takahashi, K., and K. Otsuka. "The Increasing Importance of Nonfarm Income and the Changing Use of Labor and Capital in Rice Farming: The Case of Central Luzon, 1979–2003". *Agricultural Economics* 40 (2009): 231–42.

van Zyl, J., H. Biswanger, C. Thirtle. *The Relationship between Farm Size and Efficiency in South African Agriculture*. Policy Research Working Paper 1548. Washington D.C.: World Bank, 1995.

Win, M.T. and A. M. Thinzar. *Agricultural Mechanization and Structural Transformation in Myanmar's Ayeyarwady Delta*. Food Security Policy Project Research Highlights #2. Michigan State University, 2016. < http://fsg.afre.msu.edu/fsp/burma/Research_highlight_2.pdf> [accessed 15 November 2017].

World Bank. *Myanmar: Analysis of Farm Production Economics*. Washington D.C.: World Bank, 2016.

World Bank and LIFT. *A Country on the Move: Domestic Migration in Two Regions of Myanmar*. Yangon: World Bank, 2016.

Zhang, X., S. Rashid, K. Ahmad, A. Ahmed. "Escalation of Real Wages in Bangladesh: Is it the Beginning of Structural Transformation?" *World Development* 64 (2014): 273–85.

Zhang, X., J. Yang, T. Reardon. "Mechanization Outsourcing Clusters and Division of Labor in Chinese Agriculture". *China Economic Review* 43 (2017): 184–95.

Zhang, X., J. Yang, S. Wang. "China has Reached the Lewis Turning Point". *American Journal of Agricultural Economics* 22 (2011): 542–54.

# 6

## CHANGE AND CONTINUITY: CAPACITY, CO-ORDINATION, AND NATURAL RESOURCES IN MYANMAR'S PERIPHERY

Giuseppe Gabusi

Over the past few years, the Republic of the Union of Myanmar has undertaken a three-pronged transition strategy with regard to politics, the economy, and internal security (Farrelly and Gabusi 2015). The first transition is undoubtedly of a political nature. In 2011, following the adoption of a new constitution three years earlier, the military junta, which had long led the country in the form of the SPDC (State Peace and Development Council), orchestrated a top-down power transition towards a new semi-civilian government led by President Thein Sein. In November 2015, Nobel Peace Prize laureate Aung San Suu Kyi and her tightly controlled party, the National League for Democracy (NLD), won the first democratic general elections in two generations. In March 2016, with the election of NLD loyalist Htin Kyaw as president, Aung San Suu Kyi assumed the roles of Minister of Foreign Affairs, Minister of the President's Office, and State Counsellor, *de facto* becoming the undisputed civilian leader of the country.

The second transition concerns the economy. With new liberalization measures,[1] by opening up to trade and foreign direct investment (FDI), and following the suspension or end of international sanctions, Myanmar intends to definitively abandon the socialist autarchy of the past, which had been a weighty burden of General Ne Win's 1962 coup. With an average year-on-year growth rate of more than eight per cent between 2013 and 2016, Myanmar now belongs to the World Bank's group of lower-middle-income countries. Between 2011 and 2014, exports, concentrated in the primary sector, grew at an average rate of eleven per cent, and in fiscal year 2015–16 Myanmar received FDI totalling a record-high 9.4 billion US dollars. However, tied with Cambodia, the country still has the lowest level of GDP per capita in the ASEAN countries at 1,275 current US dollars.[2] Poverty is concentrated in the countryside (where seventy-six per cent of the country's poor reside) and in border areas, only one-third of the population has access to electricity, and fifty-seven per cent of the labour force is still employed in the informal economy (Danish Trade Union Council for International Development Cooperation 2016). According to the UNDP Human Development Index, Myanmar ranks 145th, still among the low human development countries.[3]

Finally, a transition is underway from a state of belligerency to a national ceasefire between the military (the Tatmadaw) and the ethnic armed organizations (EAOs), which could — despite significant challenges — lead to an "eternal peace"[4] (Lun Min Mang 2016). Of the eighteen EAOs active in the country, eight signed the Nationwide Ceasefire Agreement (NCA) in October 2015, some have signed a separate agreement at the Union or State level, and four (including the Kachin Independence Army, KIA) are still recognized as combatants.[5] At the end of August 2016, the government convened the "21st century Panglong Conference" aimed at resolving all ongoing domestic conflicts (Nyein Nyein 2016), a prospect that seems very unlikely for the foreseeable future. In May 2017, a new session of the Conference marked an important development as the government and the armed forces seemed to be ready to agree on a federal structure for the state, provided the EAOs give up their demands for secession (Lwin Cho Latt 2017).

These transitions are intertwined, as each one affects the others, revealing a complex reform path whose eventual success should not be taken for granted. Moreover, in this process, sweeping changes are taking place alongside some elements of continuity, which creates multiple challenges for the country (Ditlevsen 2014). To start with, the Tatmadaw considers itself to be the guardian of political order in the country.[6] A further element of institutional continuity is the centralization of power. Not only is Aung San Suu Kyi in firm control of her party, but at the periphery she has installed NLD-only regional governments without consideration for the concerns of ethnic parties, many of which have continued to view her with suspicion as she is a member of the Bamar majority, the very people who have historically dominated the minorities, including through the actions of the Tatmadaw. Perhaps the role of the military in business endeavours best exemplifies the mixture of change and continuity in Myanmar's economy. The military still controls two conglomerates, the Union of Myanmar Economic Holdings Ltd. (UMEHL) and the Myanmar Economic Corporation (MEC), whose revenues have often represented an off-budget lifeline for the Tatmadaw (Rieffel 2015).[7] The military's economic interests are so pervasive that even in the private sector many businesses are owned and managed by former military people, members of their families, or cronies in general (Lall 2016, pp. 135–6; see also Aung Hla Tun 2016). Moreover, many ethnic minorities still feel disenfranchised, and the legal and illegal exploitation of natural resources (like timber, jade, and gems) continues unabated, thus perpetuating historical dynamics of environmental depletion and social inequalities. However, new initiatives like the establishment of business-friendly Special Economic Zones open up political spaces for discussion and contention, which were unthinkable in pre-2011 Myanmar (see Maung and Wells', Chapter 7 this volume). In security terms, the presence as "guests" at the 21st Century Panglong Conference of seven EAOs (including the powerful United Wa Army) united under the umbrella of the Northern Alliance, which opposes the NCA, shows how elements of continuity in Myanmar can be an obstacle to change. The lack of trust between the EAOs and the central government runs deep,[8] which diminishes the chances of obtaining clear, definitive results in the near future. It is mostly a political issue, as combatant EAOs would like to start a political dialogue before signing a ceasefire, and not vice-versa (Interview 9, 2016). They also suspect that the Tatmadaw does not really wish for an inclusive ceasefire because keeping an armed conflict with some EAOs allows them to both exert pressure and force them to the bargaining table and justify the military's ongoing role in national politics. From this perspective, the Tatmadaw needs these conflicts to justify its role in politics, and there is a widespread fear that an alliance between the NLD and the armed forces will be established in order for them to manipulate the EAOs for their respective political goals. Finally, there is also an economic dimension to the conflict, which is mainly linked to the exploitation of natural resources, as so often happens in developing countries (see, for instance, UNEP 2009). On the one hand, the military is still engaged in land-grabbing activities, without any respect for the land use rights of local communities, which exacerbates conflicts with the local population. On the other hand, profits from the extraction of mineral resources are mainly sent to central state coffers, which reduces the benefits for the local government. These dynamics of economy and violence in fact best explain the challenges that Myanmar faces in its periphery, and they require proper analysis.

## THE POLITICAL ECONOMY OF VIOLENCE

In fragile states like Myanmar,[9] where minorities often show little or no loyalty to the central state, "the structures of government tend to reinforce rather than mitigate dynamics of conflict and violence" (Bates 2008, pp. 129–30). Since state structures and actions are not accepted as legitimate and are therefore contested, conflict can be regarded as "the emergence of an alternative system of profit, power and even protection", rather than the "breakdown" of a well-established and functioning institutional framework (Keen 2000, p. 22, quoted in Ganson and Wennmann 2016, p. 110). In such a fragile setting, any economic activity runs the risk of being trapped in a power fight that potentially leads to new conflicts, as "a defining feature of fragile environments is the lack of institutions with the legitimacy or capability to manage acute socio-political tensions, such as the accumulation of unfulfilled expectations and small grievances that create a growing sense of imbalance between winners and losers from an investment" (Ganson and Wennmann 2016, p. 119). In fact, how resources are distributed, winners and losers generated, and conflicts (eventually) resolved depends on the political settlement of a community (Knight 1992). Not only is the political settlement here limited to formal laws and regulations, but it also includes "the informal rules, shared understandings and rooted habits that shape political interaction and conduct, and that are at the heart of every political system" (OECD 2011, p. 31).

Thus, state-building is first and foremost a social process built around the destruction of old power relationships and in search of a new political equilibrium among different individual and collective actors[10] (Ganson and Wennman 2016, p. 154, which also refers to OECD 2011 and Tilly 1993). In other words, in order to analyze state-building dynamics, we have to look at the often conflictual interactions of different stakeholders in society: "The outbreak, the continuation, the end, and the consequences of violent conflict are closely interrelated with how people behave, make choices, and interact with their immediate surroundings, and how all these factors may shape the lives and livelihoods of those exposed to conflict and violence" (Justino et al. 2013, p. 5, quoted in Ganson and Wennmann 2016, p. 168).

Over-reliance on extractive industries projects can fragment communities and power relations within them, as they usually involve strong capital investment in search of high return coupled with human resources that often come from the outside.[11] In response, local people would claim that "their rights to participate in, influence, and share control over development initiatives, decisions, and resources are ignored", and their grievances often produce "ongoing conflict that is detrimental to all stakeholders' interest" (EIR 2003, p. 18). For central governments, state-building in fragile states often means tightening their grip on the local economy instead of involving the people whose lives are affected by capital investment in the creation of a larger political space (Ganson and Wennmann 2016, p. 208). In other words, "authentic state-building (...) arises from the emergence of sufficient social consensus" (ibid., p. 210). This "local approach" to conflict management requires horizontal co-operation among different stakeholders, as well as vertical co-ordination:

> Party interests related to conflict and its management play out differently at the various levels of a fragile socio-political system. It is therefore often necessary to create vertical linkages – that is, relationships and channels of communication between different levels – in order to manage manifestations of conflict that present locally but can only be managed at a regional, national or international level (ibid., pp. 185–6).

This co-ordination problem presents a capacity dimension related to a framework of general rules that the state is able to adopt and implement beyond relationships of a personal nature. The distinction between "open access orders", based on relationships among "impersonal categories of individuals", and "limited access orders/natural states" (the authors use the terms interchangeably), revolving around "personal relationship among powerful individuals" (North, Wallis and Weingast 2009, p. 2) can be a useful tool to analyse the political economy of violence in Myanmar. Limited access orders/natural states define states where non-contestable institutions are captured by an elite that controls access to power, which is usually restricted to selected actors, somehow and to different degrees related to the same elite through patron–clients arrangements. In other words, at the core of the distinction, there is the difference between "rights" and "privileges". Douglass North and his co-authors argue that the depth and width of the political space allowed by the state to other social organizations classify natural states as either fragile (no space for actors other than the state itself), basic (some support for organizations connected to the state's institutional framework), and mature (support for "a wide range of elite organizations outside the immediate control of the state") (ibid., p. 21).[12] As "limited access orders"/extractive institutions tend to be dominated by special interests, they create a vicious circle of political repression and economic stagnation, while "open access orders"/inclusive institutions would tend to create broad coalitions pursuing a virtuous circle of political openness and economic growth (see also Depice and Vallely 2014).[13] For now, political power and economic activities in Myanmar are very intertwined, as has been the case since as far back as Ne Win's coup in 1962 (Brown 2013). As President Thein Sein stated in September 2013, "without political stability economic development cannot be realized and without socioeconomic development political stability cannot be achieved, because politics and economy are interrelated" (quoted in Ditlevsen 2014a, p. 388).

Not surprisingly, Myanmar's case is not unique in this respect. Rather, it is similar to what normally happens in natural states. As a solution to the fundamental problem of controlling violence in social communities, this type of state limits access to privileges to "members of the dominant coalition". Thus, "elites create credible incentives to cooperate rather than fight among themselves", and "the political system ... manipulates rents that then secure political order" (North, Wallis and Weingast 2009, p. 18). If, for any reason, during the transition from a basic to a mature natural state a new political order is not in line with old rents (for instance, because the would-be losers are more powerful than the newcomers, or because the state has not developed flexible enough mechanisms of institutional adaption), the transition could also backpedal from a mature to a basic and even a fragile state (ibid., p. 51). Therefore, building state capacity is central as institutions create the conditions for a peaceful adjustment to the new political space where new political actors have to confront entrenched rent-seekers. In Myanmar's case, the capacity issue presents two integrated dimensions, in line with Ganson and Wennmann's analysis on local conflicts:

> Vertically, the government's actions will have to solve coordination problems with ethnic states and regions – indeed, the holding of ceasefire and peace agreements is necessary for Myanmar not to slide back into a fragile state condition. Horizontally, the military has to decide whether it wants to maintain its economic privileges … or cooperate in a national economic project set to bring benefits to all (Gabusi 2015, p. 74).

As we have said before, extractive industry projects play a crucial rule in these power-and-wealth dynamics. The reason is that they have a significant impact on the social communities living on the territory chosen for the capital investment. For a start, they require control of land, obtained through either legal means such as authorizations or licences—which, in turn, might require political leverage to secure—or illegal means, for example through violent land-grabbing. It is true that in Myanmar the legal process has underpinned the vast bulk of land grabs, but this has not prevented violence from occurring between authorities and communities, since the extractive nature of Myanmar's institutions (in Acemoglu and Robinson's terms) exclude residents' voices from the same legal process. As a result, procedures might be legal, but they might well be perceived as illegitimate. Secondly, extractive industries deprive residents of resources they have been living on, leading them to question both the political legitimacy of the investment ("Who authorized it?") and its economic benefits ("Who is profiting from it?"). This socio-political tension is evident in Myanmar's periphery, where a decades-long history of ethnic insurgencies, military intervention, centralized political control, and widespread outside exploitation has fuelled the logic of the political economy of violence. In fact, "what can be seen is a strategic struggle for control of these resource-rich border regions, an area over which the state has never had control" (Wai Moe 2014, p. 278). The situation in Kachin State demonstrates the dilemmas of change and continuity in contemporary Myanmar.

## CHANGE AND CONTINUITY IN KACHIN STATE

In colonial times, the territory now known as Kachin State, which is located in northeastern Myanmar and shares a long and porous border with the Chinese province of Yunnan, was designated a restricted zone by the British—a "buffer zone" between India and China. Isolated, disconnected, and dissociated by the forces of modernity and imperialism, the Kachin people were granted autonomy under the new constitution of an independent Myanmar in 1948—an "appropriate" concession since this region had never been included in the political system of pre-colonial Burmese kingdoms (Sadan 2014, p. 286). After 1948, together with the gradual diffusion of the Christian faith, Kachin ethno-nationalism grew as a modern political identity: "It built upon the dislocations and disruptions to traditional economic and social systems that colonial rule and wider changes in the geopolitics of the region had brought upon a society that increasingly referred to itself as 'Kachin'" (ibid., p. 287). The promise of autonomy by the central state was not fulfilled, and in 1961 the Kachin Independent Organization (KIO) was founded, and was soon followed by the Kachin Independence Army (KIA). Hostilities with the Tatmadaw continued for decades, and it was only in 1994 that a ceasefire agreement was signed. The KIO kept control of a large swathe of territory around the city of Laiza, and the ceasefire allowed the KIO people to profit greatly from logging, jade mining, and trade with China. In addition, the military was able to strengthen its presence on the territory by devoting itself to the exploitation of natural resources, often with Chinese capital, in a process of military state-building that has been dubbed "ceasefire capitalism": "In this way a military regime appropriates (trans)national capital networks to form military-private partnerships to solidify *de jure* sovereignty into *de facto* territorial control" (Wood 2011, p. 749).

The economic incentive to engage in profitable business was such that the Tatmadaw did not balk at working with ethnic leaders, who "negotiated ceasefires in return for lucrative resource concessions, impunity and new lives in capital cities", thus "blurring the lines between battlefield enemy and business partner" (ibid., p. 753) (see also Lall 2016, p. 96; Keenan 2013). Beyond jade[14] (Global Witness 2015) and gold (KDNG 2007) mining, the military was particularly involved in deforestation, land confiscation, and the creation of rubber plantations (KDNG 2010; 2015), thereby forcing out peasants and setting up a partnership with Chinese companies that sometimes also involved Kachin officials (Wai Moe 2014, p. 264). The logging trade also became a remarkable source of revenue for many Kachin-Chinese middlemen, at least until 2006, when the Burmese and Chinese governments clamped down on the business. Subsequently, the trade has continued on a lesser scale, but its patron–client framework has changed, since with the consolidation of a ceasefire Chinese traders were able to contact regional military commanders directly, "squeezing out" intermediation services offered by the Kachin people who had found a way to access resources and escape economic marginalization (Woods 2011, pp. 757–8). Consequently, "people here did not get anything, while the government got a lot of advantages—they grabbed land, and they made big projects" (Interview 7, 2016). Undoubtedly, these changing dynamics in the political economy of areas occupied by the KIO played a role in bringing an end to the ceasefire, and fighting resumed in June 2011.[15] Furthermore, since the ceasefire capitalism approach in the long run seems to favour the military over the EAOs (Ruzza 2015), the KIO might have realized that war would be the only way to halt the decline of the KIO's grip on its territory. However, the opening up of the economy to the outside world, which Myanmar has experienced since 2011, might well contribute to reinforcing entrenched dynamics of the political economy of violence, with just more business opportunities available for long-established economic actors in the region. In a sense, change (vis-à-vis the attitude to global capital) could just superficially mask continuity (regarding the recipients of economic benefits). In North, Wallis and Weingast's (2009) framework, this is clearly a case where the persistence of entrenched privileges impedes the transition from a "limited access order" to an "open access order".

In times like these, institutions come to the fore, and the question is whether they are flexible enough to respond to old social grievances and old economic pressures while enlarging the political space to accommodate a new dominant coalition. Or would they just replicate old political economy patterns under different names? In fact, as highlighted in the previous paragraph, if institutions are not able to manage the socio-political tensions created by a sense of injustice and an imbalance between winners and losers, government structures will strengthen the dynamics of violence and resistance (Ganson and Wennmann 2016). A crucial test in Myanmar was the first reasonably free general election held in November 2015. In Kachin State, the NLD secured an absolute majority of seats in both the Pyithu Hluttaw (Lower House) and the Amyotha Hluttaw (Upper House).[16] This result was in line with a nationwide trend of the NLD emerging victorious over ethnic parties.[17] In the Lower House, the military-affiliated USDP (Union Solidarity and Development Party) won three seats, while the Lisu National Development Party (LNDP) obtained two seats, and the Kachin State Democracy Party (KSDP) just one. With regard to the Upper House, the National Unity Party (NUP) sent one representative to Naypyidaw, while an independent candidate won the only other seat spared by the NLD landslide victory. In truth, ethnic parties informally campaigned for the NLD and its leader, as they probably thought that only the charismatic figure of Aung San Suu Kyi could successfully confront the military, the long-standing enemy of the KIO: An NGO activist confirmed that "people voted NLD for change, not because they like it" (Interview 2, 2016). For many the elections were really a referendum on her, a national and international heroine, who, as the daughter of General Aung San, the founding father of an independent Myanmar, is viewed as having "royal" blood (Interview 1). By contrast, the military encouraged fragmentation: "the army went to KIO places like Laiza to tell them to form new parties — they were playing many games. Some KIO officers then suggested to vote for NLD, as KIO policy was to vote for change" (Interview 5, 2016).

However, the election results of the Kachin State Hluttaw show a more fragmented picture of the political space. While the NLD won twenty-two seats and the USDP seven, four ethnic parties each sent a single representative to the Hluttaw in Myitkyina — the KSDP, the LNDP, the Shan Nationalities League for Democracy, and the Unity and Democracy Party of Kachin State. The National Unity Party, however, which had had ten elected members in the Hluttaw before 2015, did not manage to win a single seat. In other words, the fragmentation of ethnic parties put them at a disadvantage, as Myanmar's first-past-the-post electoral system clearly favoured the NLD. Reducing fragmentation will be crucial for ethnic parties in the 2020 elections, as clearly expressed by a senior leader of the KDSP: "I don't like power alliances. We are trying to reconstruct one party, to form just one party" (Interview 1, 2016).

Without any consideration for the substantial support that ethnic parties have enjoyed in Myanmar's periphery, the NLD took note of its majority and installed a NLD government in all thirteen states and regions[18] (Interview 5, 2016). In fact, the relationship between the NLD and the ethnic armies has always been difficult: "The NLD never showed up when Kachin parties were inviting all parties to discuss the situation. The NLD is too centralized" (Interview 2, 2016). An official from the WMR, the Kachin National Consultative Assembly,[19] confirms this scepticism towards the NLD: "We are worried by the NLD. We are expecting the NLD to implement federalism and full democracy, but we have fears. [After all,] Aung San was not our leader" (Interview 3, 2016). It comes as no surprise that, to many Kachin people, Suu Kyi's definition of the military as "my father's military" sounded like a sinister omen (BBC News 2013). A KDSP Member of the Kachin State Hluttaw was even more explicit:

> Aung San Suu Kyi talks much about human rights. It is not enough, she should talk about ethnic rights. She neither recognizes nor knows the ethnic people.... The whole Cabinet is from the NLD.... Is this the federal view of Aung San Suu Kyi and the NLD? She doesn't understand the real situation of our ethnic party. She is a politician just for the Burmese. It would not be difficult for her to give positions to other parties.... There is no need to have permissions from the military (Interview 5, 2016).

No less crystalline are voices from the Technical Advisory Team (which used to be a KIO liaison office):

> Can Aung San Suu Kyi lay down the right path? Without changing the 2008 Constitution? No way! ... We are still under military rule, so the NLD cannot overcome the 2008 Constitution. We do not expect too much from Aung San Suu Kyi: We don't have doubts about her – she is really committed, but the 2008 Constitution is a big barrier.... It is not real change, but it looks like change (Interview 9, 2016).

If we combine this attitude with the traditional mistrust of the military, the fear of being squeezed between the two major political actors becomes clear: "The Tatmadaw needs these conflicts to justify its role in politics.... EAOs will be used by the NLD and the military for their political aims and interests" (Interview 4, 2016). To avoid being perceived as an external actor in Kachin's social sphere, an NGO activist encouraged the NLD to be more inclusive: "I say to the NLD: You have to practise democracy, not just talk about democracy. How is the NLD talking to other stakeholders [outside the party]?" (Interview 12, 2016). If—as Ganson and Wennmann (2016) assert—a state-building process requires the destruction of old power relationships in order to achieve a new equilibrium, simply adding a new unitary actor (the NLD) to the old one (the Tatmadaw) would hardly incorporate into the political system those social forces that do not identify themselves with the central government.

Acknowledging and supporting pluralism are in fact the essence of federalism, which appears to be another key issue in resolving Myanmar's conflicts and enlarging the political space: "This negotiation process is not a game; it is to share a political space with all the others" (Interview 9, 2016). According to a senior leader of the KSDP, "Federalism—as unity in diversity—would be the only medicine to heal the wounds of civil war. For us, genuine federalism means symmetrical and fair power sharing, tax sharing, and resource sharing" (Interview 1, 2016). In the same tone, an official from the WMR states: "We want genuine federalism, as Kachin must decide what kind of future it wants" (Interview 3, 2016). Between the centre and the periphery, talk about federalism is no longer taboo, but "the discussion is about what federalism is about. Ethnic people must be satisfied. They must enjoy equal rights. They must not be seen as second-class citizens. More ethnic rights will lead to more peace, and not vice-versa. The [Kachin] State government must keep its revenue in the state" (ibid.). This is not the case today: "In Kachin, ninety-five per cent of fiscal resources of the state have to go to Naypyidaw, while only five per cent of the resources stay here" (Interview 2, 2016). Furthermore, in some cases even material resources are not physically marketed in Kachin State: "The best jade goes to Naypyidaw and cannot be sold in Kachin—only polished jade stays in Kachin" (Interview 8, 2016).

However, apart from the idea of resource sharing, there seems to be a strategic ambiguity about the meaning of "genuine federalism"—an ambiguity that increases the mistrust between the centre and the periphery: "There will be a federal constitution only if each state has its own constitution. We don't want the constitution from Naypyidaw; we want it from the Kachin people, from Kachin State" (Interview 3, 2016). An NGO activist appears to confirm the bottom-up approach to the term "federalism" with the following words: "We want a division of power. We want self-determination! Every state should have a prime minister elected by the people" (Interview 14, 2016). Finally, for some, it looks like federalism also includes the right to secede, which is what was originally envisaged in the Panglong Agreement: "The KIO changed from independence to federalism in 1975, but the Thailand-based Kachin National Organisation (KNO) still thinks of independence. People are confused.... The government is suspicious. 'Do they say self-determination, or do they mean independence?' Our situation is worse than before" (ibid., 2016).

Advocating a voice in the political space is the consequential action emerging from the sense of neglect that is pervasive among the Kachin people, as is evident in the following statements: "The central government ignores Kachin State. Kachin State is being ignored" (Interview 2, 2016); "We feel oppressed. We haven't felt the fruit of post-war independence"

(Interview 7, 2016); and "National reconciliation is living together in equality" (Interview 14, 2016). Acknowledging diversity in the military would also address the concerns coming from Kachin: "All positions, even top positions, in the military should be open to anybody, and not only to Bamar people" (Interview 1, 2016) (see also Taylor 2017). However, once again, political recognition would be the pre-condition to any sustainable peace: "To incorporate the EAOs in the military, you should also reduce the number of Tatmadaw troops.... [W]hy should we disarm before having any rights?" (Interview 14, 2016). The resentment also has a large economic dimension, as local people feel discriminated against in a general context of deprivation:

> People resent the Bamar migration from lower Burma. Kachin people here can earn 6,000 kyats per day, while Bamar people accept to work for 4,000 kyats per day — in fact, they would earn 1,500–2,000 kyats per day if they stayed in lower Burma. Hundreds of people come freely from lower Burma, while we have to report to the immigration office when we go outside Myitkyina. Outside Kachin State, I am a guest. (Interview 2, 2016)

Not only migrant labour but also non-Kachin capital seems to reduce the economic space available to the locals: "Business people from lower Myanmar got our land, and they based their business here", often in partnership with Chinese companies (Interview 7, 2016).

One of the main concerns of Kachin activists is to ensure that growth and development would benefit society at large, and not just the military and its business partners — thus moving away from a state based on privileges to one in which all individuals are considered equal (North, Wallis and Weingast 2009):

> We need to push the government to implement free market economy in the country. National resources belong to the people, not to the government or the businesses. People have to benefit from [the exploitation of] natural resources. We want to invite foreign investment to cooperate with local investment and to give jobs to local people. Every family here should get a sort of income. We should get money from the mines, put it in other sectors such as construction and infrastructure and also save funds for other states. (Interview 1, 2016)

These words are echoed by the Kachin Minister of Finance and Planning, an NLD appointee: "The State should control natural resources. Only then can we welcome investment in the hotel industry, tourism, and factories to manufacture and export" (Interview 13, 2016).

One of the most common features of the exploitation of natural resources characterizing the political economy of violence is land-grabbing, and in this respect Kachin State follows a trend:

> In some villages residents living there for sixty years have seen their land taken away by Chinese bosses who work with the government and with the Tatmadaw. They started to build banana farms, but there are rumours that they will be converted into industrial plants in the future. Bananas are then exported to China, but there are side effects... They use pesticides, spread by local labour for 10,000 kyats per day... they don't wear masks, and this causes health problems.... They leave plastic trash in the fields.... Companies do intensive farming in one area for five years and then shift to another area. They exploit the soil. The environment is completely destroyed, and the neighbouring farms cannot even farm because streams and ground water have been contaminated. (Interview 6, 2016)

For Kachin activists, real household needs and aspirations need to be addressed: "Land ought not to be given to cronies through occupation or confiscation, by the military, their cronies or friendly businessmen. Land should be given to small farmers in order to diversify the economy" (Interview 3, 2016). The military involvement in these activities is also clearly a destabilizing factor in the region: "The Army has to protect its resources in Kachin: [To this end,] it pushes away the KIO, creating many internally displaced persons [IDPs]" (Interview 8, 2016). The land-grabbing issue is much debated within Myanmar, but increased public awareness (a sign of change) co-exists with a tension between the centre and the periphery (an element of continuity with the past). For example, with regard to civil society consultation when the National Land Use Bill was being drafted, "even though the process has become more transparent, the decision is still made in Naypyidaw, not even at the state level" (Interview 12, 2016).

In truth, the NLD Kachin government seems to be perfectly aware of the need to put its house in order (Interview 11, 2016) with respect to resource exploitation:

> Control of natural resources is key.... If the Union government plays a role in the control of natural resources, the State government has to monitor: We are doing a survey on the resource business, listing all companies, collecting all facts, and distinguishing legal from illegal activities.... There are 311 companies working with permission from the government, and there are several hundred other companies... At this rate of exploitation, all resources will soon be gone. We have to limit [the exploitation] and make use of

resources just for our needs... The military and the Union government should work together to preserve Kachin's resources. (Interview 13, 2016)

But for this commitment to be turned into reality effectively, adequate institutional capacity would be needed, in line with North, Wallis and Weingast's (2009) framework. The weakness of Myanmar's institutions of bureaucratic implementation and oversight thus adds scepticism to mistrust. In the words of an NGO activist,

> NLD candidates at the state level are just normal people. They are not qualified, and they are not reliable, technically. But we can help them to build this capacity.... Aung San Suu Kyi is a bit far from the ground. She is a national leader, but she has just started to work without knowing the ground.... She doesn't have a lot of information from the domestic environment. (Interview 12, 2016)

Even the central government points out that the states and regions cannot operate autonomously in an effective way: "One of the ministers said that whilst the principle of decentralization was permissible in principle, the state governments don't have the capacity to deliver services yet, and that even the central government doesn't have the necessary capacity at present. Therefore, decentralization needs to be balanced" (Lall 2016, p. 106).

Thus, we reach the same crucial point we started from, namely the institutional capacity to absorb new political, economic, and societal actors without disrupting the entire system (Ganson and Wennmann 2016). Adaption is not an easy task: "We believe technical assistance is crucial— money is not the main thing. The budget is OK, but there are challenges in terms of co-ordination and co-operation" (Interview 12, 2016).

## CONCLUSION

This paper looked at the issue of change and continuity in Myanmar from the perspective of its periphery. In particular, the analysis focused on Kachin State, since the territory's ongoing conflicts between the Tatmadaw and the KIA and abundance of natural resources allow us to apply a political economy of violence framework to our research. In Kachin State, (mainly "macro") elements of change co-exist with (mainly "micro") aspects of continuity. On the one hand, the NLD has emerged as the new political actor formally in charge, but its centralized vision of power is raising suspicions about the party's willingness to address ethnic concerns. On the other hand, at the point of intersection between economic activities and violence, the military still seems to be pulling the strings, often in partnership with labour and capital from outside Kachin State, which causes resentment and frustration among the local population. Moreover, one of the main political legacies of the 1990s ceasefires has been the creation of new business ventures between the Tatmadaw and some members of the KIO. This activity caused political fracturing in the organization and ultimately led to the resumption of war (Brenner 2015), the "commercialisation of insurgency" (Woods 2016), and military-led state-building that incorporated activities—once regarded as illegal—into the legal economy (Jones 2016). In other words, old political economy patterns seem to be alive and well, with even more available opportunities created for the traditional economic actors by the relative opening up of the market to a new flow of foreign investment. As the sense of neglect persists, which is evident in many interviews I conducted, institutions need to address these grievances. This requires a local, bottom-up approach to conflict management (Ganson and Wennmann 2016), as well as the transformation of the country into a "mature natural state" where privileges[20] are not restricted to the dominant coalition alone (North, Wallis and Weingast 2009). Horizontally, that would mean incorporating local stakeholders into the new political space created by the transition. To begin with, for example, the Kachin State government should be able to offer "voice", in Hirschman's (1970) sense, to ethnic representatives, as well as societal organizations and local entrepreneurs. The military also ought to be part of the process, as it has to decide whether it wants to hold onto economic privileges or contribute to the overall welfare of the population. Horizontal co-operation should then be accompanied by vertical co-ordination, as many seemingly intractable problems in Myanmar's periphery derive from the absence of fair revenue-sharing and resource-sharing processes between the state and regional governments and the Union government. Clearly, this co-ordination would also contribute to creating trust. The Kachin State government is well aware of the path to be taken in this direction, but its goodwill has to be matched by similar steps taken by the Union government and the Tatmadaw. The NLD landslide victory at both levels should facilitate the dialogue, but the party probably needs to have a truly multi-ethnic composition in order to be accepted as a fully legitimated actor in the periphery. For instance, what if after mapping the system of exploitation of natural resources in Kachin State, the State government found itself incapable of changing the system to include new economic and societal actors and move forward to a more sustainable and inclusive development pattern?

The only way for both the local and the central state to overcome potential losers' plausible resistance to change and to slowly but steadily move away from the logic of a political economy of violence is to adopt flexible mechanisms of institutional adaptation ready to accommodate old and new actors in a new and more inclusive political space. In countries in transition, all actors have to recognize that political space is contested between "groups strong enough to demand that others respect their interests, rights, and property—not just stability or administrative improvements", and reforms are successful "when distinctions between state and society, public and private, are not just abstractions but accepted boundaries drawn, redrawn, and defended by actively contending groups" (Johnston 2005, p. 217). Building institutional capacity is crucial to accommodate change. In this regard, the admirable efforts of the NLD government to collect facts and information before taking decisions could be combined with the transfer of knowledge offered by external experience on crucial aspects of democratic state-building, like constitutionalism and federalism. This would at least help to mitigate the strategic ambiguity around the meaning of "federalism". In my interviews, I found that different agents have different understandings of the word "federalism" and different expectations on its actual implementation. Indeed, there seems to be a conceptual thinness which should be addressed through more detailed public discussion, that donors could support by sharing, disseminating and debating different historical experiences of state-building. This would empower the elite and the people of Myanmar with more substantial knowledge to make their own decisions about the future path of their country.[21] Time for action is running out, however. For example, in a context of growing expectations, the business community had waited for months to hear the government's new economic policies, and then reacted with frustration when in July 2016 Aung San Suu Kyi announced twelve fundamental objectives that the government wanted to pursue. The document does not outline any specific strategy to obtain a set of general goals like greater liberalization (with the privatization of some state-owned enterprises), greater efficiency in tax collection and public spending, more transparency and less bureaucracy, environmental sustainability, infrastructure investment, and a balance between industrial growth and an increase in agricultural productivity. Nor does the document indicate economic priorities, which is necessary in a country that has challenging structural problems. The gap between high expectations and poor results could once again create social discontent and expose Myanmar's continuing fragility, thereby missing a golden opportunity to put the country on a firm path towards sustainable development.

## Notes

1   In fact, some liberalization policies were already implemented in the 1990s.
2   World Bank data available at: <http://data.worldbank.org/indicator/NY.GDP. PCAP.CD>.
3   UNDP data available at: < http://hdr.undp.org/en/countries/profiles/MMR>.
4   The phrase has often been met with ironic comments: "It doesn't sound good. To have eternal peace, you have to die" (Interview 5, 2016).
5   Data from the Myanmar Peace Monitor website (http://mmpeacemonitor.org/).
6   Notoriously, twenty-five per cent of MPs are nominated by the military, which is also in charge of the Ministries of Defense, Internal Affairs, and Border Affairs. Moreover, in the case of declaring an emergency, the legislative, executive, and judicial powers are transferred to the Chief of Staff. Since constitutional amendments can be approved with a majority of three-quarters of the votes in parliament, the Tatdmadaw has veto power on any change to the constitution.
7   For now, most European and US companies are not interested in co-operating with the MEC because the risk to their reputation is too high (Mahtani 2016).
8   "Village leaders don't trust the government because in the past the government in Yangon did not implement the Panglong Agreement. We simply don't trust each other" (An official from WMR, the Kachin National Consultative Assembly, Interview 3, 2016).
9   The very conditions that define fragility are "social division, legacies of grievance, weak institutions, lack of trust in government, pressing socio-economic challenges, or the presence of spoilers content to exploit or tolerate conflict to meet their narrowly defined interests" (Ganson and Wennmann 2016, p. 183). As we have seen in the previous paragraphs, all these weaknesses are present to a high degree in Myanmar.
10  Actually, Ganson and Wennmann's criticism of the liberal approach to conflict management (like in NGCA 2013) begins with this very observation.
11  This element is of the utmost importance when the community consists mostly of indigenous people and has been historically closed to contacts from the outside.

12 Daron Acemoglu and James A. Robinson (2012) make a similar argument when they correlate nations' success with inclusive political and economic institutions and nations' failure with extractive institutions.

13 I have argued elsewhere (Gabusi 2015) that Myanmar is now a basic natural state in the process of possibly becoming a mature natural state, which would be characterized by a condition of separation between political and economic interests. One of the conditions to an open access order envisaged by North, Wallis and Weingast (2009, p. 26) is the "consolidated political control of the military", which is not currently being met in Myanmar.

14 In fact, the "ceasefire gave the mining of jade to the central government" (Interview 2, 2016). According to art. 37 of the Constitution, jade and all resources are owned and managed by the Union.

15 Technically, hostilities broke out "when the army moved in troops to protect three dams under construction near the Chinese border", and the KIA "suspected that the army was bringing more troops than had been agreed upon" (Wai Moe 2014, p. 265).

16 All electoral data come from IFES and MIMUM 2016.

17 The only exceptions were the Shan Nationalities League for Democracy (SNLD) and the Arakan National Party (ANP) in Rakhine State.

18 According to the 2008 Constitution, the president nominates Region and State Chief Ministers and appoints them after Region or State Hluttaw approval.

19 The WMR represents all the Kachin people, no matter where they are. It was founded in October 2002 to give voice to the Kachins: 267 representatives were then sent to Laiza from all of Myanmar's regions and from all over the world.

20 It is worth recalling here that for North, Wallis and Weingast (2009), privileges turn into rights only in open access orders, where the military is controlled by civilians.

21 On the possible contributions of international aid to conflict mitigation and (possibly) resolution, see, for example, Kivimäki and Pasch (2009).

## References

Acemoglu, Daron, and James A. Robinson. *Why Nations Fail. The Origins of Power, Prosperity and Poverty*. London: Profile Books, 2012.

Aung Hla Tun. "Suu Kyi's Party Accepts Crony Donations in Reform-era Myanmar". Reuters, 17 January 2013. Available at: <http://www.reuters.com/article/us-myanmar-suukyi-idUSBRE90G0C820130117> [accessed 7 November 2016].

Bates, Robert. H. *When Things Fell Apart. State Failure in Late-Century Africa*. Cambridge: Cambridge University Press, 2008.

BBC News. "Aung San Suu Kyi Tells of Fondness for Burma Army". 27 January 2013. Available at: <http://www.bbc.com/news/world-asia-pacific-21224307> [accessed 5 November 2016].

Brenner, David. "Ashes of Co-optation: From Armed Group Fragmentation to the Rebuilding of Popular Insurgency in Myanmar". *Conflict, Security & Development* 15, no. 4 (2015): 337–58.

Brown, Ian. *Burma's Economy in the Twentieth Century*. Cambridge: Cambridge University Press, 2013.

Danish Trade Union Council for International Development Cooperation. *Labour Market Profile Myanmar 2016*. Copenhagen, 2016. Available at: <http://www.ulandssekretariatet.dk/sites/default/files/uploads/public/PDF/LMP/lmp_myanmar_2016.pdf> [accessed 9 August 2017].

Depice, David and Tom Vallely. *Choosing Survival. Finding a Way to Overcome Current Economic and Political Quagmires in Myanmar*. Cambridge, Mass: ASH Center for Democratic Governance and Innovation, 2014. Available at: <http://ash.harvard.edu/files/choosing_survival.pdf> [accessed 8 February 2017].

Ditlevsen, Marie. "Economic Fundamentals, Ongoing Challenges". In *Burma/Myanmar: Where Now?* edited by M. Gravers and F. Ytzen. Copenhagen: Nordic Institute of Asian Studies, 2014.

_____. "Development Challenges and Environmental Issues". In *Burma/Myanmar: Where Now?* edited by M. Gravers and F. Ytzen. Copenhagen: Nordic Institute of Asian Studies, 2014a.

Extractive Industries Review (EIR). *Striking a Better Balance: The World Bank Group and Extractive Industries* – Volume I. Washington, DC: EIR, 2003.

Farrelly, Nicholas, and Giuseppe Gabusi. "Explaining Myanmar's Tentative Renaissance". *European Journal of East Asian Studies* 14, no. 1 (2015): 7–14.

Gabusi, Giuseppe. "State, Market and Social Order: Myanmar's Political Economy Challenges". *European Journal of East Asian Studies* 14, no. 1 (2015): 52–75.

Ganson, Brian, and Achim Wennmann. *Business Conflict in Fragile States. the Case for Pragmatic Solutions*. London and Abingdon: The International Institute for Strategic Studies and Routledge, 2016.

Global Witness. *Jade: Myanmar's "Big State Secret"*. London: Global Witness, 2015.

Hirschman, Albert O. *Exit, Voice and Loyalty. Responses to Decline in Firms, Organizations, and States*. Cambridge, MA: Harvard University Press, 1970.

International Foundation for Electoral Systems (IFES) and Myanmar Information Management Unit (MIMU). *Myanmar Election Maps 2010–2015*. Arlington, VA and Yangon: IFES and MIMU, 2016.

Jones, Lee. "Understanding Myanmar's Ceasefires. Geopolitics, Political Economy and State-Building". In *War and Peace in the Borderlands of Myanmar. The Kachin Ceasefires, 1994-2011*, edited by M. Sadan. Copenhagen: Nordic Institute of Asian Studies, 2016.

Johnston, Michael. *Syndromes of Corruption: Wealth, Power and Democracy*. Cambridge: Cambridge University Press, 2005.

Justino, Patricia, Tilman Brück, and Philip Verwimp. "Micro-Level Dynamics of Conflict, Violence, and Development: A New Analytical Framework". In *A Micro-Level Perspective on the Dynamics of Conflict, Violence, and Development*, edited by P. Justino, T. Brück and P. Verwimp. Oxford: Oxford University Press, 2013.

Kachin Development Networking Group (KDNG). *Valley of Darkness. Gold Mining and Militarization in Burma's Hugawng Valley*. Chiang Mai: KDNG, 2007.

_____. *Tyrants, Tycoons and Tigers. Yuzana Company Ravages Burma's Hugawng Valley*. Chiang Mai: KDNG, 2010.

_____. *Kachin State Natural Resources Development Discussion Paper*. Chiang Mai: KDNG, 2015.

Keen, David. "Incentives and Disincentives for Violence". In *Greed and Grievance: Economic Agendas in Civil Wars*, edited by M. Berdal and D. Malone. New York: International Peace Academy, 2000.

Keenan, Paul. "Business Opportunities and Armed Ethnic Groups". Briefing Paper No. 17. Yangon: Burma Centre for Ethnic Studies, 2013.

Kivimäki, Timo, and Paul Pasch. *The Dynamics of Conflict in the Multiethnic Union of Myanmar. PCIA Country Conflict-Analysis Study*. Berlin: FES, 2009.

Knight, Jack. *Institutions and Social Conflict*. Cambridge: Cambridge University Press, 1992.

Lall, Marie. *Understanding Reform in Myanmar: People and Society in the Wake of Military Rule*. London: Hurst & Company, 2016.

Lun Ming Mang. "NLD Leader Outlines Plans for Expanded Peace Process". *Myanmar Times*, 5 January 2016. Available at: <http://www.mmtimes.com/index.php/national-news/yangon/18318-nld-leader-outlines-plans-for-expanded-peace-process.html> [accessed 5 November 2016].

Lwin Cho Latt. "Myanmar Stumbling Over Non-secession". *East Asia Forum*, 30 June 2017. Available at: <http://www.eastasiaforum.org/2017/06/30/myanmar-stumbling-over-non-secession/> [accessed 9 August 2017].

Mahtani, Shibani. "Myanmar's Vast Conglomerate Goes Public". *The Wall Street Journal*, 10 June 2016. Available at: <http://www.wsj.com/articles/myanmar-militarys-vast-conglomerate-goes-public-1465554913> [accessed 5 November 2016].

Myanmar Now. "NLD Government Announces 13 New Chief Ministers; Angers Rakhine Party". 28 March 2016. Available at: < http://www.myanmar-now.org/news/i/?id=0bf27037-c8d7-4f63-8021-b04cf2a76be3>. [accessed 8 November 2016].

Network of Global Agenda Councils (NGAC). *Natural Riches? Perspectives on Responsible Natural Resource Management in Conflict-Affected Countries*. Geneva: World Economic Forum, 2013.

North, Douglass C., John Joseph Wallis, and Barry R. Weingast. *Violence and Social Orders. A Conceptual Framework for Interpreting Recorded Human History*. Cambridge: Cambridge University Press, 2009.

Nyein Nyein. "21st Century Panglong Conference Kicks off in Naypyidaw". *The Irrawaddy*, 31 August 2016. Available at: <http://www.irrawaddy.com/news/burma/21st-century-panglong-conference-kicks-off-in-naypyidaw.html> [accessed 5 November 2016].

Organisation for Economic Co-operation and Development (OECD). *Supporting Statebuilding in Situations of Conflict and Fragility: Policy Guidance*. Paris: OECD, 2011.

Rieffel, Lex. "Policy Options for Improving the Performance of the State Economic Enterprise Sector in Myanmar". Singapore: ISEAS Working Paper no. 1/2015. Available at: <https://www.iseas.edu.sg/images/pdf/ISEAS_Working_Paper_2015_No.%201_Policy_Options_for_Improving_the_Performance_of_the_State_Economic_Enterprise_Sector_in_Myanmar.pdf> [accessed 5 November 2016].

Ruzza, Stefano. "There Are Two Sides to Every COIN: Of Economic and Military Means in Myanmar's Comprehensive Approach to Illiberal Peacebuilding". *European Journal of East Asian Studies* 14, no. 1 (2015): 76–97.

Sadan, Mandy. "Religion, Identity and Separatism – the Case of the Kachin". In *Burma/Myanmar: Where Now?* edited by M. Gravers and F. Ytzen. Copenhagen: Nordic Institute of Asian Studies, 2014.

Taylor, Robert, "Myanmar's Military and the Dilemma of Federalism". ISEAS Perspective 7 (2017). Available at: <https://www.iseas.edu.sg/images/pdf/ISEAS_Perspective_2017_7.pdf> [accessed 8 February 2017].

Tilly, Charles. *Coercion, Capital and European States, A.D. 990-1990*. Oxford: Blackwell, 1993.

United Nations Environment Programme (UNEP). *From Conflict to Peacebuilding: The Role of Natural Resources and the Environment*. Geneva: UNEP, 2009.

Wai Moe. "The Struggle for Peace in Northern Myanmar". In *Burma/Myanmar: Where Now?* edited by M. Gravers and F. Ytzen. Copenhagen: Nordic Institute of Asian Studies, 2014.

Woods, Kevin. "Ceasefire Capitalism: Military-Private Partnerships, Resource Concessions and Military-State Building in the Burma-China Borderland". *The Journal of Peasant Studies* 38, no. 4 (2011): 747–70.

_____. "The Commercialisation of Counterinsurgency. Battlefield Enemies, Business Bedfellows in Kachin State, Burma". In *War and Peace in the Borderlands of Myanmar. The Kachin Ceasefires, 1994–2011*, edited by M. Sadan. Copenhagen: Nordic Institute of Asian Studies, 2016: .

## Interviews in Kachin State, May 2016

Interview 1 with a senior leader of the Kachin State Democratic Party (KDSP)
Interview 2 with an NGO activist (education)
Interview 3 with officials from the WMR – Kachin National Consultative Assembly
Interview 4 with an official from a Kachin education institute
Interview 5 with a KDSP member of the Kachin State *Hluttaw*
Interview 6 with NGO activists (legal support)
Interview 7 with businessmen from a pressure group advocating peace and reconciliation
Interview 8 with NGO activists (environment and natural resources)
Interview 9 with officials from TAT (Technical Advisory Team)
Interview 10 with an official from the Maina Kachin Baptist Church IDP Camp
Interview 11 with the Kachin State Minister of Natural Resources
Interview 12 with NGO activists (human rights and political and social awareness)
Interview 13 with the NGO Kachin State Minister of Planning and Finance
Interview 14 with an NGO activist (women's rights)

# 7

## ADVOCACY ORGANIZATIONS AND SPECIAL ECONOMIC ZONES IN MYANMAR

Pyae Phyo Maung and Tamas Wells

The Myanmar government announced in January 2012 that, due to environmental concerns, they had cancelled plans for the construction of a coal-fired power plant in Dawei, in the south of the country. The proposed power plant was to produce 4,000 MW, making it one of the largest coal-fired power plants in the region. It was also part of larger plans for a deep-sea port and Special Economic Zone (SEZ) in Dawei—a project led by Thailand's largest building contractor, Italian-Thai Development. In the lead-up to the cancellation of the coal-fired power plant, there had been significant mobilization of local citizens in Dawei in opposition to it, involving distribution of information about the power plant, use of local media, and protests. Local activist groups had also established transnational links including with advocacy organizations in Thailand and in Europe.

This incident, which was early in the period of the Thein Sein government, highlighted the unique place of Special Economic Zones at the intersection between, on one hand, economic liberalization, and on the other hand, political liberalization in Myanmar. The shift away from authoritarian military governance to the Union Solidarity and Development

Party (USDP) government under U Thein Sein, and then to the National League for Democracy (NLD) government after the 2015 elections, facilitated increased flows of investment into development projects such as the planned Dawei development project. Yet on the other hand, the end of direct rule by the State Peace and Development Council (SPDC) also ushered in greater freedoms and opportunities for citizens to network, mobilize and oppose development projects when the projects diverged from their hopes or visions.

The SPDC government under General Than Shwe sought to control citizens and local organizations largely through coercion and the threat of crackdown. The operation of social or political organizations during these periods thus depended often on *avoidance* of, rather than engagement with, the state (Fink 2001). This legacy of military rule remains, to some degree, in the relations between communities, government and companies in SEZs. Yet there have also been striking changes since 2011 in the forms of contentious politics in Myanmar. Many advocacy organizations are seeking to *engage* the state and businesses through formal institutions and through forging new direct relationships with policymakers. However, the shift away from the overt coercive power of the military, and the emergence of new opportunities for advocacy has not necessarily meant that citizens can have greater power over decision-making that affects them.

The dynamics of politics have changed since the period of military rule, and new challenges have emerged for advocacy groups and communities. In particular, the transitions from military government under the SPDC to the USDP government under U Thein Sein, and then from the USDP government to the NLD government, have not brought an even shift toward more responsive and liberal governance. As will be described further in this chapter, some advocacy organization leaders felt that the NLD government in fact created a more restrictive environment for "civil society" groups than that under the military-aligned USDP. Further, the liberalization of the economy and the increase in foreign investment has not meant that the economic interests of Myanmar's military elites have been sidelined. In fact, through what Jones (2014) describes as "politico-military-business nexuses" military elites retain significant economic influence. For example, the military-owned Union of Myanmar Economic Holdings Limited has joined with Chinese investors in plans for a multi-billion dollar oil refinery near Dawei (Thiha 2016).

The incident of protests against the coal-fired power plant in Dawei in 2012 demonstrated how SEZs in Myanmar are sites of "special" economic conditions, but also of intensive citizen responses to perceived problems, especially related to land rights and environmental concerns. The particular intensity of economic activity in Special Economic Zones can therefore stimulate special forms of political activity through citizen mobilization. In some senses, these spaces are also "special political zones".

On one hand, several valuable studies have explored SEZs as "enclaves" (Ferguson 2006; Sidaway 2007) with unique political dynamics, detached from the "development" of the nation state. Our emphasis here though is on how these "special political zones" are also illustrative of emerging shifts in the wider political environment in Myanmar. SEZs are a valuable focus of inquiry in understanding the ways advocacy organizations are responding to Myanmar's rapid economic changes, and how advocacy organizations themselves are transforming. In his analysis of Dawei's SEZ project, Soe Lin Aung (2014, 1) suggests that "we can see, in Dawei, something of the emergent in Burma's political present."

This chapter examines the work of advocacy organizations on issues related to the Special Economic Zone in Dawei, and also Thilawa SEZ, near Yangon. We outline the actions advocacy organizations have taken in addressing the accountability of Special Economic Zone projects to local communities. We then examine the impacts of these efforts—on both advocacy organizations themselves, and on the planning and implementation of SEZ projects. Finally, we trace out the particular enabling and constraining factors that advocacy organizations face in their resistance to Special Economic Zone projects. In answering these questions, we draw on our own field research from mid-2016 which involved interviews with members of advocacy organizations, a review of organization documents, and local media reports.

## SPECIAL ECONOMIC ZONES

Special Economic Zones have become a popular model in Asia for stimulating economic growth. Prefigured historically by treaty ports and colonial concessions, they are areas of intensive infrastructure development, which rely on the ability to circumvent the challenging taxation and policy environments of emerging economies. China adopted the SEZ model with Shenzhen in 1980, which has been cited as a success (Chen 1993, Liang

1999). Subsequently Thailand took on the model of industrial parks, the most prominent of which is Map Ta Phut, which was established in 1990 and is one of the largest petrochemical hubs in the world. In the 2000s, India established hundreds of special economic zones around the country. These SEZ projects have also been associated with protest and opposition, though varying in form in different places.

The phenomenon of Special Economic Zones has received considerable scholarly attention, though most prominently from an economic perspective (Litwack and Qian 1998; Wang 2013; Farole and Akinci 2011; Aung Min and Kudo 2012). Political (Ong 2006; Sidaway 2007; Soe Lin Aung 2016; Thabchumpon et al. 2012) and cultural (Bach 2011) perspectives on SEZs are emerging, including specific investigation issues of land confiscation in SEZs (Levien 2012; Loewen 2012). Loewen (2012) in particular examines the Dawei SEZ in Myanmar and argues that "land grabbing" needs to be considered not so much through the lens of *who* confiscates land but the underlying relationship between state and capital. There remain, however, few empirical studies, especially in Myanmar, mapping community and activist responses to Special Economic Zones, and their impacts. This chapter seeks to address this gap by focusing on the strategies that advocacy groups took in responding to special economic zone projects, the impact of these actions, and advocacy group perceptions of the opportunities and constraints that they face in Myanmar's transition.

Against the background of SEZ development in other countries in the region, the State Peace and Development Committee adopted the Special Economic Zone model for Myanmar in the 2000s. Plans emerged for several new Special Economic Zones (SEZs) in the country—in Dawei in the country's south, Thilawa, near Yangon, and Kyaukphyu in the country's western conflict-affected Rakhine State.[1] Dawei initially became a focal point for Thai investment, with the Italian Thai Development Corporation taking the lead role. Despite plans being in place since 2008, the Dawei development project has faced a series of setbacks in securing investment. There have been a number of false starts for the project, with optimistic announcements by project implementers followed by periods of inactivity. One NLD adviser described the Dawei SEZ project as like a "zombie—it keeps on coming back!" (Marks and Chou 2017, p. 1). In contrast, the Thilawa SEZ attracted significant Japanese investment through the Japan International Cooperation Agency (JICA) and the zone became operational in 2015.

The cases of Dawei and Thilawa SEZs have seen local communities face land confiscation on a large scale, livelihood insecurity related to land loss, and human rights violations as a result of business activity. The situation has been compounded by corruption in government systems at the local and union levels, a weakness in the legal protection framework that was unable to protect rights, and low awareness among the local community regarding their own rights and potential impacts of the SEZ projects.

## THE ADVOCACY STRATEGIES OF LOCAL ORGANIZATIONS

In response to the issues that community members were facing in both Dawei and Thilawa, a number of new local advocacy groups and networks emerged. These groups took a range of different forms in Dawei—from specialized media groups (Dawei Watch Group) and legal networks (Dawei Lawyers Network), to groups with a more generic focus on rights issues such as Dawei Development Association. Despite the variation in form and scope of work, these groups often had overlapping membership and worked together in tackling common issues related to the Dawei SEZ.

Meanwhile in Thilawa, local village leaders formed a network to take action against issues of land rights and compensation. Community members joined with local and international NGOs to form the Thilawa Social Development Group (TSDG). Amidst new emerging opportunities and constraints in Myanmar, these groups engaged primarily in three types of advocacy activities: informing and mobilizing affected communities; direct appeals to government policy makers, companies and investors; and wider public campaigning.

### Informing communities

Making information accessible to communities was a common strategy used by the advocacy groups in Dawei and Thilawa. It involved, for example, distributing pamphlets or conducting meetings informing communities about the SEZs' potential impacts. Advocacy groups shared information about the scale of SEZ projects, their potential impacts, community rights, investment standards and legal frameworks (at both national and international level). Activists claimed that affected communities received only selective information about the SEZ projects from companies or government, and that information about certain adverse impacts or company responsibilities was often excluded. The hope from advocacy groups was that if community members were informed about the projects—and the underlying economic and legal frameworks—then they may be able to engage with government and private sector actors from a stronger, albeit still unequal, bargaining position.

## Appeals to policymakers, companies and investors

Along with a strategy of informing affected communities about the projects, local advocacy groups also sought to collect evidence related to the impacts of SEZ projects and make direct appeals to policy makers, companies and investors. In engaging with the key stakeholders in government or private sector, advocacy organizations used formal institutional mechanisms (such as complaints mechanisms) and also informal communication channels.

In Dawei, local advocacy groups conducted research on archaeological sites that were in a village in the SEZ area. This mapping of archaeological sites was then used as an advocacy tool to inform the local government. Evidence was also used to directly advocate to foreign governments, especially the Thai government, who supported the investment projects. For example, the Dawei Development Association collected evidence about the impact of the deep seaport project and sent an appeal letter to the prime minister in Thailand. The most provocative public action may have been in the Dawei SEZ project where, after companies had confiscated land from one community, community members collectively obstructed the road-link construction route and successfully asked the company for compensation. In this sense, community groups and activists at times attempted to bypass government policy makers and appeal to companies directly.

In late 2013 in the Thilawa area, eighty-one households were evicted from their land by the Yangon Region government (Yen Saning 2014). Community members claimed that they had not been informed about the project, had been threatened by the government, and that they had received neither compensation, nor appropriate relocation. In June 2014 the Thilawa Social Development Group (TSDG) supported the submission of a formal complaint to the Japan International Cooperation Agency (JICA), who had a ten per cent stake in the Thilawa SEZ project (Yen Saning 2014). Advocacy group representatives also travelled to Japan and appealed directly to the Japanese government about the issues, and indirectly through the Japanese media. The resulting JICA investigation admitted some shortcomings of the government yet was broadly positive that the process of land acquisition had met international standards. Representatives of the TSDG, and some international organizations, including Japanese NGO Mekong Watch, subsequently criticized the report for overlooking the complex challenges, especially related to livelihoods and sanitation, that relocated residents faced (Yen Saning 2014).

The point here is that along with local mobilization of communities, advocacy groups in SEZs increasingly used both formal institutional mechanisms (such as the JICA complaints process) and informal approaches (such as the road blockade) to make appeals to decision-makers in the Myanmar government, implementing companies and investors. These may sound like obvious campaign strategies yet in Myanmar this represented a significant shift from the SPDC era. During the rule of the SPDC there were virtually no formal government or company complaints mechanisms for local communities to access related to development projects, and informal approaches were heavily constrained by the lack of free media and broader freedoms of speech and association.

## Public campaigns

Advocacy organizations also engaged in public campaigning to gain support from the citizens more broadly and pressure government or companies into responding. A local advocacy network from Thilawa area organized a press conference presenting SEZ-related social injustice issues to the Myanmar media. The aim of these press conferences was to gain wider public attention regarding the issues faced by the community.

In Dawei, an advocacy group collaborated with a local journal and produced weekly supplements covering the information about SEZs and their impacts. Local advocacy groups in Dawei also collectively organized a beach-cleaning event at Maungmakan beach where activists distributed pamphlets to the public about the negative impacts of the proposed 4,000 MW coal-fired power plant. Meanwhile, in Thilawa area, local groups organized a highly visual public advocacy campaign where the community's goals and issues were printed on large vinyl sheets and posted along roads.

While in these examples activists sought to build public awareness of the issues related to SEZ projects, on the whole, advocacy groups did not engage in highly provocative demonstrations or protests. Aside from the example of the road blockage, local groups most often found ways to publicly challenge government and companies while maintaining a tone that was broadly cooperative, rather than one which threatened the legitimacy of the USDP government, or more recently the NLD government. In his analysis of SEZ-related campaigns in Dawei during the Thein Sein period, Soe Lin Aung (2014, p. 1) similarly suggests the politics of local groups was "not in the register of a confrontational, insurrectionary popular politics". It was "a popular politics based not on a rejection or evasion of the state apparatus, but rather one that appeals to it, that demands something from it, that sees the state as a ground of *possibility* rather than a *site of rejection*" (Soe Lin Aung 2014, p. 1). This tone of advocacy—in making public appeals rather to the state rather than rejecting it—may in part be a legacy of military rule. There is a degree of uncertainty amongst activists as they sense the possibilities associated with political liberalization yet also continue to perceive a threat of government crackdowns and arrests. Despite greater freedoms of speech and association under the USDP and then NLD governments, activists were still wary of their vulnerability.

Overall advocacy organizations in Thilawa and Dawei Special Economic Zones developed a wide repertoire of advocacy strategies including informing affected communities, appealing to power holders and public campaigning. As we unpack later in this chapter, these were employed in a fluid way based on calculations about political opportunities and constraints. At times of widespread public anger about, for example, land confiscations or plans for the coal-fired power plant, advocacy groups sensed the opportunities for public campaigning. At other times, assessing the opportunities of making appeals to policy makers through more formal institutions, advocacy groups focused more on evidence gathering.

## IMPACT OF ADVOCACY ORGANIZATION STRATEGIES

Through implementing these actions, there were impacts both on the planning and implementation of SEZ projects and also impacts within advocacy groups and local communities themselves.

### Changes in planning and implementation of SEZs

At the wider community level, the efforts exerted by the advocacy groups contributed to changes in planning and implementation both from government and investors. In Dawei area, research about archaeological sites within the SEZ area was used to advocate to government and the area was granted status as a natural heritage zone, protecting it from any SEZ-related plans. As stated in the introduction, the campaign against the potential impact of the coal-fired power plant no doubt contributed to the government's subsequent cancellation of the plans, though it should be noted that the Myanmar government continues to develop plans for coal-fired power plants elsewhere in the southeast of the country (Hintharnee 2017). In addition, advocacy efforts about specific land confiscation cases resulted in many people receiving more compensation for their land. The community-led blockage to the road link development in Dawei resulted in the company providing compensation for the confiscated land.

In Thilawa, the various advocacy strategies contributed to a decision by the companies involved to provide greater compensation and support for relocation of the houses to the newer place, including construction of a village water system and connecting electricity. In addition, after the Japan advocacy trip, during which time advocacy groups used JICA's formal "Objection Mechanism", JICA launched a livelihood security program called Income Restoration Program (IRP) targeting income generation opportunities among relocated villagers.

Although the changes happened at this level, it is difficult to attribute changes to advocacy groups alone. There was involvement of multiple actors (donors, local and international supporters) and multiple factors (including the government and investors' willingness to change the situation). For example, in the case of the cancellation of the coal power plant in Dawei, it is important to acknowledge other actors' roles such as that of the media, in contributing to wider public attention about the issue, and international networks, like Earth Rights International, for supporting campaign strategies of local groups. Thai non-government organizations created advocacy channels targeting the Thai prime minister, and national-level civil society strengthening organizations like Paung Ku provided mentoring and funding to help local advocacy group actions. While recognizing the importance of others' contributions, it needs to be acknowledged that local advocacy groups were taking higher risks and took an active lead in campaigning on these local problems. The efforts exerted by the local advocacy organizations were crucial in the eventual changes in the policy and implementation of SEZ projects.

## Changes for advocacy groups themselves

In Dawei and Thilawa there were some external impacts from advocacy. Yet behind this, there was a deeper transformation of advocacy organizations themselves. Advocacy groups sought out new ideas, funding, strategies and networks, and often became more professionalized. In some cases, it also led activists to reflect that they were more disconnected from affected communities themselves.

At the individual capacity level, members of groups expressed increased awareness of technical skills. Through learning opportunities such as training, exposure trips, exchange visits and mentoring provided by the local and international supporters, CSO members' individual knowledge on subject matters such as human rights, land rights, investment policies and legal frameworks increased in both Thilawa and Dawei areas. Group members said that they had more confidence in making direct dialogue vis-à-vis investment issues with the government and the investment companies.

Advocacy group networks also expanded. Activists became more connected with donors, media, legal experts, academics, government, members of parliament and company representatives—from the local level to the regional, union levels and the international level. Further, because of their ability to make formal and direct dialogue with the government and the investors, the advocacy groups were recognized by both government and companies as stakeholders essential to the projects. For example, the local government in Dawei created five observer positions at the local parliament for Dawei Development Association members to provide input into laws. In Thilawa, the representatives from advocacy groups were invited to attend the regular multi-stakeholder meetings organized by the Thilawa SEZ management committee in order to directly voice their concerns.

In his analysis of civil society in Cambodia, Norman (2014) portrays this shift toward greater professionalization in advocacy organizations negatively. He argues that through the integration of "civil society organizations" into the agenda of "good governance", Western donor agencies are reducing advocacy groups to holding technical watchdog roles within a neoliberal framework of governance. Local organizations, Norman (2014) suggests, have moved from "shouting to counting" and thereby lost their more emancipatory agendas within a neoliberal framework.

Yet the evidence from Dawei and Thilawa suggests that while there may be similar professionalization and integration of advocacy groups into technical roles in governance, this is not necessarily a shift brought about solely by Western donor agencies. If applied to Myanmar's SEZs, Norman's (2014) notion of moving from "shouting to counting" may underestimate the agency and strategic calculations of local organizations. The shift toward widening skills and networks was also a result of activists seeking new opportunities that different strategies might be able to offer in the context of nascent political liberalization. Intermediary advocacy organizations in Myanmar, such as Paung Ku, also acted in some ways to shield local organizations from the direct pressures of donors. The movement toward "counting" and quantifiable evidence may thus be a self-protection mechanism for activists due to the legacy of military rule and fear of government backlash against communities or activists who opposed SEZ projects.

For some advocacy organizations members, however, greater professionalization — through acquiring new ideas, skills and networks — led to a feeling of disconnection from local communities who were affected by SEZs. As the leaders of advocacy groups became more involved in activism they developed wider linkages and worked at higher (union and regional) levels of policy advocacy. These activists also started to engage with wider social issues affecting the whole country, rather than just their local area. As they broadened their experiences, they also began to develop ideas that at times diverged from the communities affected by SEZ projects. In an interview in 2016, one activist leader from Dawei said that "because of better engagement with like-minded actors playing at regional and national level" they had tended to "connect, talk and work with them [regional and national actors] more" and had become "disconnected" from the Dawei community.

In this sense, while the professionalization of advocacy groups in SEZs has provided a new repertoire of strategies to achieve advocacy goals, the new ideas and networks they acquired through engaging in advocacy meant that some activists felt less connected to the communities that they were striving to represent.

# EMERGING OPPORTUNITIES AND CONSTRAINTS FOR LOCAL ADVOCACY GROUPS

## Emerging opportunities for advocacy groups

As we have noted, local advocacy organizations did not work alone. Political liberalization during the Thein Sein period allowed their networks to extend to national and international organizations, media, legal specialists, government counterparts and parliamentarians. Through these networks advocacy groups could mobilize resources and develop wider connections to communities and policy makers. For both Dawei and Thilawa areas, working together with national and international partners has been a major new opportunity for the success of their actions.

In particular, advocacy groups from both Dawei and Thilawa area expressed the crucial roles of intermediary NGOs in providing hands-on support and nurturing them since their formation. The connections they made, the technical skills they received, and the experience they learned from others were sought out through training opportunities, connecting with media and other organizations, and exposure trips to meet with experienced advocacy organizations. For example, one local intermediary organization organized an exposure trip for Thilawa advocacy groups to learn how the compensation system works in Dawei SEZ and how advocacy groups use different advocacy strategies to address SEZ-related issues. Advocacy groups working on Special Economic Zone issues have been at the forefront of these new forms of networking and campaigning in Myanmar.

Another opportunity created by economic liberalization and growing international investment is the presence of formal accountability mechanisms. Many international investors have internal quality control standards and principles to maintain the quality of the investment to be more socially responsible. In the case of JICA, their internal standards, including objection mechanisms, favours advocacy groups to use formal channels. For example, Myanmar's membership of the Extractive Industry Transparency Initiative (EITI) allows advocacy groups to become a legitimate party in consultation (along with other two formal parties: government and the company) and provides new formal check and balance mechanisms. Where under the military regime, communities and local organizations most often attempted to avoid government interaction, local organizations are, at least in certain parts of the country, now better able to use formal institutions to engage directly with government and businesses, albeit with no guarantee of shifting government or company practice. Wider cross-sectoral and international networks, and access to formal mechanisms of government and private sector accountability, have brought significant new opportunities for advocacy groups, and these have been used extensively in Dawei and Thilawa.

## Constraints for advocacy groups

The state of flux after the end of direct military rule has on the one hand opened up possibilities for communities and advocacy groups to network in new ways and collectively voice concerns about development projects that affect them. Yet the state of flux in both the political and economic environment has also presented new constraints for advocacy groups. These constraints have been related to the growing diversity of reactions to SEZ projects amongst community members, an imbalance of resources for negotiation, and a hardening of government attitudes toward local advocacy organizations.

One constraint was related to diverging responses among community members. A rhetorically powerful claim that advocacy groups working on SEZ projects could make was that they represented affected communities. However, over the years of the campaigns—from 2012 to 2016—community members did not always maintain consistent positions related to key issues such as compensation. In both Thilawa and Dawei areas, community members at times were divided over the best strategy. For example, in the case of Dawei, while some community members only wanted to get their land back—which most advocacy groups were also advocating for—many other community members wanted to receive compensation. Similarly, in Thilawa, while advocacy leaders—along with some members of community—aimed to get gain higher compensation amounts for their lost lands, some community members were in fact satisfied with the lower compensation fare proposed by the company. As some community members agreed to and received compensation they became less active in the campaign and activists reflected that this took momentum away from their advocacy actions. During the period of military rule, the experience of neglect or intimidation at the hands of government meant that communities may have been more likely to be unified in their opposition. Yet the new era of compensation and negotiation in economic development projects makes the work of advocacy groups more complex by diluting their central claim of "representing" the voices of affected communities. With no unified community voice, such claims by advocacy groups are more tenuous.

In addition to this challenge of diverging responses within communities, there was also an issue of imbalance in resources between investors and developers on one hand, and local advocacy groups and communities on the other. As described earlier, advocacy groups working in SEZs now have access to new financial and technical resources to support their efforts. However, the new engagement of corporations and investors such as JICA has also led to greater sophistication in development projects. Under the SPDC, the government often engaged in development or infrastructure projects in a heavy-handed manner and neglected the rights of affected communities. Yet at the same time, these projects were also limited in their scope and influence due to a dearth of funding and technical skills within government. It was deeply challenging for government actors to gain the active support of local communities for their projects.

In the new era of international investment and SEZ development, the financial and technical skills employed in development and infrastructure projects has increased. Companies have sophisticated strategies to undermine community opposition to projects, and solidarity within advocacy groups. Financial incentives and technical expertise is used to convince communities of the benefits of projects. In Dawei, companies were in some cases successful in convincing local community members that the SEZ project would bring employment opportunities for local people. While some Dawei community members continued to resist the SEZ project, other community members expected new jobs and significant compensation for their land from the company. In some cases, investors recruited members of the community as lobbyists. For example, in Thilawa, the investor recruited a group of people from the local community and formed a new local organization which fully supports the company's actions.

The resources that companies could mobilize in their efforts to "sell" the benefits of the SEZ were far superior to those of local advocacy groups, and the imbalance of resources between local groups and development project decision-makers may in fact now be greater than during the SPDC era. This led to difficulties for advocacy groups in sustaining their campaigns. While advocacy group access to external financial and technical resources has grown, there is no guarantee of its continuation. Some advocacy group leaders expressed concerns about the shifting priorities of local and international funding agencies. Reflecting in 2016 on the opening up of the government and especially the victory of the more internationally acceptable NLD government, one activist said that donors may become more interested in "institution-building of the government" resulting in "less interest towards civil society strengthening". Further challenging the sustainability of advocacy groups was the livelihood insecurity of individual activists. The long-term nature of the advocacy process led some advocacy group members, some of whom worked voluntarily, to gradually lose motivation due to personal challenges and the extremely long timeframes of the project development. The new political and economic environment surrounding SEZs in Myanmar gave advocacy groups new opportunities, yet many activists remained concerned about the sustainability of their work.

A final challenge for advocacy organizations is the NLD government's perception of local advocacy groups. Advocacy organization members reported that the National League for Democracy government is, to some extent, paying attention to their demands and actions. For example, the State Counsellor expressed formal recognition of "civil society" groups in Myanmar's peace process and democratic transformation at the opening speech of the 21st Century Panglong Conference in September 2016. In addition, at State and Divisional levels the local government has expressed willingness to support the action of "civil society" organizations. For instance, advocacy groups reported that the Dawei Chief Minister has a close relationship with some Dawei activist leaders. However, while activists were able to take advantage of these opportunities for engagement, on the whole advocacy organization members reported that the overall space for civic actions had in fact narrowed from the period of the Thein Sein government to the new NLD government.

Advocacy organization members reported that during the Thein Sein period of government, members of parliament from the USDP had shown a willingness to interact more with "civil society" groups. As it was widely perceived as military-backed, and therefore less credible in terms of civic representativeness, the Thein Sein government was seen by activists to have made more efforts to develop its credibility amongst citizens. With the new NLD government, activists feel that interaction between government and "civil society" groups is not being prioritized.

In addition, advocacy organizations also have a concern regarding the NLD government's relationship with international governments and welcoming international investors. For example, community group leaders from Thilawa were worried about growing ties between the Japanese and Myanmar governments which they thought could result in the current SEZ project being expanded and investment scaled up. The second stage of the Thilawa SEZ project in particular could present communities with similar problems of land confiscation and dispossession as seen elsewhere in the country. Faced with these concerns, several activists were sceptical about the NLD government's efforts to develop more robust protection mechanisms for local communities.

## CONCLUSION

Special Economic Zone projects in Myanmar are sites of both intensive economic development and mobilization by advocacy organizations in response to those changes. Advocacy organizations use an increasingly wide repertoire of strategies in seeking to protect local land rights and the environment—these strategies include informing affected communities, making appeals to policy makers and engaging in public campaigning. Through these efforts local advocacy organizations have contributed to significant policy shifts—including the cancellation of the coal-fired power plant in Dawei. Advocacy organizations themselves have also developed significantly in their levels of knowledge of policy and legal processes and their ability to engage directly with policy makers.

The success of local advocacy groups has been in part due to a unique new set of opportunities—the ability to connect with, and receive resources from, national and international aid organizations, and the liberalizing of political culture more broadly since 2011. Growing international investment has also provided new formal institutions for advocacy to SEZ projects through for example, JICA's complaint mechanisms. Some activists also perceive that as they have professionalized, their connections to, and solidarity with, local communities may have been challenged.

However, advocacy groups also point to significant constraints in the new political and economic environment in Myanmar, and SEZs in particular. In the long term, groups are constrained by the profound imbalance in resourcing between their own advocacy activities and the SEZ activities led by companies and government. Maintaining momentum in advocacy campaigns in the face of activists' own livelihood challenges, company pressure, and incentives for communities is challenging. Special Economic Zones in Dawei and Thilawa are sites of intensive investment and infrastructure development, and also sites of unique actions by local advocacy organizations and communities. Our argument in this chapter has been that through analysis of the shifting context of advocacy in SEZs we may glimpse the emerging dynamics of political interactions in Myanmar more broadly.

## Notes

1  In order to coordinate the development of these Zones, the previous governments set up SEZ committees. These bodies remained outside the responsibility of one particular ministry and became powerful in determining plans and implementation of SEZ projects. However, under the SEZ law, these committees expired at the conclusion of the Thein Sein administration, to be re-formed under the new President Htin Kyaw. The aim of the committee will be to plan and manage projects along with fixing rates for fees, tax, capital and exemptions. In this sense, the SEZ Central Management Committee could have considerable influence in determining levels of accountability in the development of the Dawei, Thilawa and Kyaukphyu SEZs. Whilst the new SEZ committee is not yet officially functioning, business on the Thilawa SEZ in particular is proceeding. During the Thein Sein administration, these committees were also not joined up to other planning processes at region/state level (e.g. the state economic development plans which are the responsibility of region/state government).

## References

Aung Min and Toshihiro Kudo. "Newly Emerging Industrial Development Nodes in Myanmar: Ports, Roads, Industrial Zones along Economic Corridors." *Emerging Economic Corridors in the Mekong Region*, edited by I. Masami, BRC Research Paper 8, 2012.

Bach, J. "Modernity and the Urban Imagination in Economic Zones". *Theory, Culture & Society*, 28, no. 5 (2011): 98–122.

Chen, J. "Social Cost-Benefit Analysis of China's Shenzhen Special Economic Zone. *Development Policy Review*, 11, no. 3 (1993): 261–72.

Earthrights International (ERI). "Analysis of the Affected Communities' Rights and Remedies under Myanmar Law and JICA's Guidelines: A Briefer on the Thilawa Special Economic Zone." Yangon: ERI. 2015.

Farole, Thomas, and Gokhan Akinci, eds. *Special Economic Zones: Progress, Emerging Challenges, and Future Directions*. World Bank Publications, 2011.

Ferguson, J. *Global Shadows: Africa in the Neoliberal World Order*. Duke University Press, 2006.

Fink, Christina. *Living Silence: Burma under Military Rule*. Zed Books, 2001.

Hintharnee. "CSOs Oppose Karen State Coal-fired Power Plant." *The Irrawaddy*, 22 June 2017.

Jones, L. "The Political Economy of Myanmar's Transition." *Journal of Contemporary Asia*, 44, no. 1 (2014): 144–70.

Levien, Michael. "The Land Question: Special Economic Zones and the Political Economy of Dispossession in India". *The Journal of Peasant Studies, 39*, no. 3–4 (2012): 933–69.

Liang, Z. "Foreign Investment, Economic Growth, and Temporary Migration: The Case of Shenzhen Special Economic Zone, China." *Development and Society*, 28, no. 1 (1999): 115–37.

Litwack, John and Yinqyi Qian. "Balanced or Unbalanced Development: Special Economic Zones as Catalysts for Transition". *Journal of Comparative Economics*, 26, no. 1 (1998): 117–41.

Loewen, Elizabeth M.R. *States, Capital, and Enclosures: Thailand, Myanmar, and the Dawei Special Economic Zone*. Erasmus University, 2012.

Norman, David J. "From Shouting to Counting: Civil Society and Good Governance Reform in Cambodia". *The Pacific Review*, 27, no. 2 (2014): 241–64.

Ong, Aihwa. *Neoliberalism as Exception: Mutations in Citizenship and Sovereignty*. Durham: Duke University Press, 2006.

Sekine, Yukari. "Environmental Governance and Development Policy in Southeast Asia", at Graduate School of Global Studies Workshop, Sophia University, Tokyo, Japan on 10 January 2015.

Sidaway, J.D. "Enclave Space: A New Metageography of Development?" *Area* 39, 3 (2007): 331–9.

Soe Lin Aung. "The Thick and Thin of the Zone", LIMN 2016. <http://limn.it/the-thick-and-thin-of-the-zone/> [accessed 6 January 2017].

Soe Lin Aung. "Power after the Imperium: Territory, Population, and Migrant Labour in the Borderlands of Burma/Myanmar". Presentation at Columbia University Dept. of Anthropology, March 2014.

Thabchumpon, Naruemon, Carl Middleton, and Zaw Aung. "Development, Democracy, and Human Security in Myanmar: A Case Study of the Dawei Special Economic Zone." International Conference on International Relations and Development (ICIRD), Chiangmai University, 2012.

Thiha. "The Fight for Resources in Myanmar's Deep South." Consult Myanmar. 30 May 2016. <https://consult-myanmar.com/2016/05/30/the-fight-for-resources-in-myanmars-deep-south/> [accessed 25 August 2017].

Wang, Jin. "The Economic Impact of Special Economic Zones: Evidence from Chinese Municipalities". *Journal of Development Economics* 101 (2013): 133–47.

Yen Sanaing. "Residents Group Slams Report on Thilawa Evictees." *The Irrawaddy*, 17 November 2014. < https://www.irrawaddy.com/news/burma/residents-group-slams-report-thilawa-evictees.html> [accessed 12 January 2017].

# 8

# EXPLAINING NAYPYITAW UNDER THE NATIONAL LEAGUE FOR DEMOCRACY

Nicholas Farrelly

Naypyitaw, the capital of Myanmar since 2005, was carved from scrubland and paddy fields with the founding idea that space is integral to the exercise of power. Its creation in the geographical centre of the country signalled a retreat from the colonial legacies found on almost every street in the old capital, Yangon. The decision to invest so heavily in a new place to govern the country was made by senior military men, isolated from both their own people and much of the rest of the world. It is only natural that the creation of this new and gargantuan city has baffled many observers, some of whom are still unprepared to consider the rationality, determination and imagination encapsulated by the new national monument. Naypyitaw tends to be classified as a "surreal" and even lunatic place, that apparently defies the ordinary laws of geography, society and culture (for instance, see Richmond et al. 2014, p. 156). There has been little serious effort to understand the city beyond its broad boulevards and other infrastructure (for exceptions see Dulyapak 2009, 2011; Seekins 2009b; also Farrelly 2018).

The infrastructure still tends to get the attention. When visitors arrive in Naypyitaw they are immediately struck by the distances between facilities and the vast network of roadways that are designed to tie the city together. Happy snaps taken on the ceremonial motorway leading to the legislative complex and presidential palace fill the Facebook pages and Twitter feeds of visitors. They often gush about how few cars use the roads and how the over-sized avenues take up too much space. The same astonishment tends to follow a visit to any of the official buildings. The legislative compound, a place that many Myanmar and foreign visitors get to see up close, is a good example. Encompassing thirty-one large buildings, a symbolic nod to the thirty-one Theravada Buddhist planes of existence, the legislature is so spread out that people tend to take a buggy, car or bus between the different parts of the complex. Only a few of the buildings are linked together by covered walkways. On a hot day it is impossible to get between the other buildings without breaking a sweat. The conclusion of most of those who work at the site is that the complex is probably not optimized for legislative activity.

The legislative complex, like much of Naypyitaw, has only been in use since 2011. When it was originally constructed its final purpose, in terms of the relationship between constitutional requirements and architectural priorities, was unclear. Even the way that the legislature functions has evolved rapidly and not without some false starts since the first group of elected and appointed legislators arrived in the city at the start of 2011. Most of that initial cohort were from the Union Solidarity and Development Party, which had emerged from the civilian organization that supported the former military dictatorship (for context, see Taylor 2012). In November 2010 it won a popular vote that was neither free nor fair (for details see Turnell 2011; Lidauer 2012). But, before long, the legislature was welcoming a cohort of National League for Democracy representatives who won their seats at the April 2012 by-election. That group included Aung San Suu Kyi, who took her seat in the Union Assembly representing Kawhmu, one of the Yangon Region townships. Now, the same facilities are adjusting to the next stage in this political re-arrangement, with the election of a majority of National League for Democracy legislators who started their work in 2016. They currently control many of the key levers of power in Naypyitaw, including the presidency, both of the national-level legislatures, and the newly created position of State Counsellor, which is Aung San Suu Kyi's compromise with a constitutional bar on taking the presidency for herself. She is also Foreign Minister. This profound re-shaping of

Myanmar politics is remarkable, in so many respects. In this chapter I will focus on the development of Naypyitaw and its relationship to the NLD's concessions to the military's way of politics.

## MAKING NAYPYITAW WORK

Naypyitaw, even today, is a work in progress: still under construction. It is a city of timber, concrete, marble; street lights, roundabouts, flagpoles. The buzz and hammer of new work shows no sign of easing up. Given the scale of the city, there is no shortage of space for new projects and installations. It will forever be a question of will and resources. After years of effort some neighbourhoods are increasingly taking on a mature feel, particularly once they have adjusted to prevailing economic, social and political trends, including, for instance, the arrival of the NLD. The key market zones—particularly Myoma and Thapyagone—already have an air of settled prosperity. With this physical environment now in place, the hard work of serving as the national capital is well underway.

Over the past decade, Naypyitaw has grown to become the primary node for doing Myanmar's political business. It is home to government ministries, the place of residence for senior officials, the headquarters of the armed forces, and the key site for the renegotiation of institutional priorities, including through the peace process and in terms of the crisis in northern Rakhine State. The Constitutional Court, Union Election Commission, public service agencies, national sporting facilities and key cultural endowments, are all located in the city. It is only natural that from the Defence Services Museum to the sporting hubs built for the 2013 Southeast Asian Games, right through to the newly opened war heroes' memorial and the lavish jade emporium, there is ongoing debate and discussion about what these sites should mean, and how they might fit into Myanmar's political and cultural future.

For a time, there was serious consideration among NLD leaders about abandoning the city. It was, they sought to remind the people, custom-built to serve the needs of the former military dictatorship. However, since taking power in 2016, the NLD has become increasingly comfortable with the opportunities that the city offers. With regular criticism from the international community for the government's handling of the 2017 Rakhine State crisis, Naypyitaw provides a protective bubble for elected leaders and their bureaucratic support staff. Under these conditions there are advantages for a government in Naypyitaw which can control access to its precincts, block out potential protesters and curate any interactions with foreign delegations.

There are other, more abstract, reasons why Naypyitaw works for the NLD's vision of political business. The reality for those who built the city and who now make it work is that Naypyitaw fits a specific vision of Myanmar's past. The country has, from this perspective, enjoyed historical strength when it is ruled from the centre. Within a modest drive of Naypyitaw, across central Myanmar, are the ruins of former capitals— places like Sri Ksetra, Amarapura and Bagan—each their own monument to Myanmar's strength and culture. The cherished idea is that Naypyitaw, encapsulated by the city's occasional translation as "abode of kings", returns to an old pattern of central leadership of what is an otherwise fragmented realm. Given the country's recent history of inter-ethnic conflict (see Cheesman and Farrelly 2016), the Bamar majority have sought to impose certain visions of unity on the rest of the peoples. Naypyitaw is a monument to this nation-shaping agenda. The iconography that dominates much of Naypyitaw, especially at key political sites, is distinctively and directly tied to such claims to political and cultural continuity.

It also matters that the former capital of Yangon gained its status under the British colonial government that ruled from 1824 to 1948. This dented national pride and has meant that Yangon is forever, in certain minds, deemed a reflection of weakness, subjugation and decline (for context see Salem-Gervais and Metro 2012). Inevitably, given its status as the country's commercial hub, Yangon itself has been vernacularized and re-spatialized over the past seven decades (see Than Than Nwe 1998; Roberts 2016; Menager 2014; Peleggi 2005). The old British names for neighbourhoods, streets and locations have been long removed, and a whole new culture of post-colonial economic and political life has emerged. For example, the old Scott Market became Bogyoke Aung San Zay, General Aung San Market. And the city's official English language name was changed from Rangoon to Yangon, just as Burma was forced, in official usage, into the frame of Myanmar (for a note on such usage, see Cheesman, Skidmore and Wilson 2010, p. xv).

All of these changes are part of a decades-long effort to restore pride in Myanmar's national project and, with it, the rejuvenation of its independent status. Even before the creation of Naypyitaw, under all post-1948 governments, the ardent defence of local traditions has been a common element of post-colonial politics. People are still encouraged to wear what is usually described as "traditional" dress. For men, this often takes the form of a *longyi*, a style of Myanmar skirt, and a shirt or jacket, while women generally choose from more ornate sarong and blouse combinations. In Naypyitaw, such dress is standard across government agencies, at public functions and, most strikingly, at legislative sessions and other major political events. It is only among today's teenagers that these clothes are going out of fashion; many young people now shop at Naypyitaw's handful of western-style shopping malls.

In a country of great cultural diversity there is not, however, any single way to be "Myanmar", and Naypyitaw similarly seeks to reflect the great variety of cultural formats. Across the country, this diversity has caused great tension and, on a regular basis, sparked conflict, such as the long wars between the central government and the Karen, Shan and Kachin (see South 2008, 2013; also Meehan 2011). The demographic dominance of the Bamar population, who are around two-thirds of Myanmar's people, makes it difficult for other groups to get the status they claim (Chambers 2015). This is where the creation of Naypyitaw as a re-centering mechanism needs to be taken into account (see, for adjacent points, the argument in Jones 2014a). It has sought to demarcate a set of spaces that reflect an ideology of contrasting parts: national unity, cultural difference and over-arching belonging. It is only the groups excluded from Naypyitaw, the most notable being Muslims, which are also disenfranchised by broader political and cultural forces. The absence of any planned sites for Islamic worship in the new areas of Naypyitaw, especially in a country with a significant Muslim minority, points to the limits on inclusion under current ideology.

## RE-CENTERING POWER

With the elected NLD government now defining the national agenda from Naypyitaw, it can be easy to forget that the big recent shifts to the new city's political system started under what was a closely supervised style of authoritarian rule. In the beginning, access to Naypyitaw was heavily regulated, and few foreigners were invited to see the city for themselves. The closest that many people got was the airfield where some commercial flights would land to drop off, or pick up, top officials and military leaders on their journeys around the country. Yet, slowly and surely, the city became more open to outside scrutiny. Foreign diplomats increasingly transacted their business in the city, though most struggled to get any sense of its scope. Upon arrival in the hotel zone or guest house precincts where visitors would stay, they would be ferried to meetings in distant compounds where the ministries and other agencies had been transplanted. Familiar faces from Yangon were now captured by the peculiarities of life in Naypyitaw. In those years, the military, in the habit of remaining aloof from most interaction with foreigners, was still hard to get to know. Its own headquarters, built in the far northeastern corner of the city, were off-limits beyond one or two buildings that were used to receive official delegations.

Then, in May 2008, Cyclone Nargis slammed into the Ayeryawaddy delta leaving around 140,000 people dead, and millions of acres of farmland destroyed. Yangon suffered some damage but the might of the storm was felt at its catastrophic worst in low-lying villages and towns across the delta region. Floodwaters rose rapidly, with the tidal surge, making escape impossible for many people, especially children. It took weeks for a full assessment of the damage, during which time the military government dragged its feet, seemingly unable to comprehend the scale of the disaster. The world watched and waited, pleading for access to help survivors and avert any further humanitarian calamity. The tension was palpable with the stubborn generals looking to protect their own positions at the expense of their long-suffering people (see Selth 2008; Seekins 2009b). Eventually, a deal was made to bring in foreign assistance under the auspices of the Association of Southeast Asian Nations. This helped to save face for the military leadership but much more importantly it served to deliver the needed aid and assistance to millions of people in the disaster-hit delta.

In the wake of the disaster, Myanmar civil society and community groups began to organise their own responses (Seekins 2009b). Trucks and boats laden with supplies gingerly made their way down in to the delta to offer food, water, medical care and other assistance and supplies. The government, at all levels, started to turn a blind eye to these mobilizations, quietly thankful that civilians were prepared to make the best of a terrible situation. These groups, many of which had no political aspirations, were motivated by the charitable sentiment so important to Myanmar society in its Buddhist, Christian and Muslim interpretations (for a keen analysis of the cultural context see McCarthy 2016). People came together to help provide the immediate relief that was required. This was followed by the major investments of the international community, including the reconstruction of the local agricultural and fishing economies. Across the delta there are still many signs of these initiatives.

All these years later, it is still difficult to understand why, two weeks after Cyclone Nargis hit, the government went ahead with its referendum to endorse the 2008 Constitution. This was not a democratic process, but it was the culmination of a carefully guided Constitution Convention that had begun back in 2003. That constitution enshrined the primacy of the armed forces and was widely condemned by dissenting views in Myanmar and abroad. Its endorsement so soon after the disaster of Cyclone Nargis has still not been forgotten. Yet the confluence of these events also encouraged the senior military leadership to think differently about their country and its standing. Cyclone Nargis revealed profound national weaknesses, not only in disaster response but in the overall strength of the economy and society. The poverty of the response was a direct reflection of the country's lacklustre economic performance. A military that had long presented itself as the defender of the nation was completely ill-equipped to help its own people.

At the highest levels there was, in the wake of Cyclone Nargis, a growing awareness that Myanmar could not continue on the same path. Myanmar was quickly falling well behind its Southeast Asian peers such as Thailand and Indonesia in terms of social, political, economic and cultural advancement. While the armed forces had robustly consolidated their position, and faced no immediate threat from the democratic opposition or ethnic armed groups, they needed to make hard decisions about the next chapters in the national story (Jones 2014b). What happened next will be the subject of ongoing assessment for generations to come, and it is a story that has already introduced completely new dimensions to the analysis of Myanmar affairs. Decisions were made in Naypyitaw, the new exemplary centre, where the leadership was confronted by the need to find a better way of governing the country. The direct dictatorial model, which had been in place in different forms since 1962, had reached the end of its useful life. But what would come next?

This is the phase, from 2010 onwards, when Myanmar, and thus Naypyitaw, shifted from an isolated authoritarian system to a gradually more open society, where a level of political competition became acceptable to the military leadership. The general election of November 2010 saw scores of political parties vie for seats in Naypyitaw's pristine legislative chambers (Lidauer 2012). That election was dominated by the Union Solidarity and Development Party, which won a strong majority of the seats at the national level, and in the fourteen state and region legislatures.

While other parties including ethnic political vehicles contested the vote they struggled to match the USDP for national reach and campaign resources. The vote was also, in many areas, manipulated to the advantage of USDP candidates. With no external monitoring of the process, and little transparency in aspects of its conduct, it was impossible to claim that the USDP win reflected the people's will (Lall and Hla Hla Win 2012). The NLD boycotted the poll and Aung San Suu Kyi remained under house arrest. But there were further important changes to come.

## A SITE FOR REFORM

Aung San Suu Kyi was released from what proved to be her final period of detention a week after the 2010 poll, by which time the military was confident that it would control, through its proxy USDP, the levers of power for the next five years. From this point onwards, Myanmar began to move quickly, with fresh international attention to the political changes rapidly building momentum (Taylor 2012; Holliday 2013; Jones 2014a). The government that was formed by President Thein Sein in early 2011 was a hybrid of civilian and military personnel. The president himself had been the fourth ranking officer in the former military regime. His first cabinet was filled with appointees who had similar backgrounds, and former military officers took key positions on the presidential staff. In the legislature, Khin Aung Myint, a former head of the Psychological Warfare Directorate who later became the military government's Minister of Culture, became the first speaker of the upper house while Thura Shwe Mann, another retired general, took the reins of the lower house. Khin Aung Myint had the responsibility as first speaker of the joint houses, known as the Union Assembly, to launch Myanmar's legislative experiment. He did so cautiously, aware that the processes and practices of the new system would require sustained efforts to develop (for further discussion of these early years see Chit Win 2016; Farrelly and Chit Win 2018).

Whatever the problems of this democratic system, the combined efforts of the executive and legislative powers encouraged the rest of the world to pay more attention. It helped that Aung San Suu Kyi and her NLD were able to rebuild their public profile. While inclined to voice scepticism about the quality of the so-called "transition" they also learned to welcome the opportunities for fresh interaction with the newly civilianized powerbrokers. The entire system received a big bump when, in April 2012, the NLD contested by-elections for seats that had been vacated by senior members of the new executive. These were seats that had, in most cases, been won by military figures at the 2010 election who then went on to take roles close to the new president. For the first time since 1990, people in Myanmar were able to vote on who they wanted to lead the country. Under these circumstances it would have proved inconvenient, and probably dangerous, if the NLD had done badly. That outcome was not in the interests of the USDP or President Thein Sein. The NLD, as such, won almost all of the available seats and, before long, sent its first delegation of elected representatives to Naypyitaw. This victory had an immediate impact on the reputation of the legislature, and helped to ensure that the nascent culture of democratic representation began to look more credible.

In Naypyitaw, the NLD team found a legislative system still struggling. The staff of the legislatures had only been in their positions for a few years, and there were constant grumbles about resourcing. It took time to build up the teams to support consistent legislative activity. Key staff often moved in with the senior figures. Khin Aung Myint and Thura Shwe Mann, as the two most obvious examples, brought senior staff from their former lives to assist with legislative work. However, their enthusiasm for professionalizing legislative practice was on show whenever they travelled abroad. From 2012 both of the speakers and their teams began to make regular international trips, many of which allowed them to get a close look at the culture and history of more established democratic systems. The two speakers would, in those days, often proudly tell visitors to Naypyitaw that their legislative innovations had been inspired by what they had seen around the world. Nonetheless, the early years of Naypyitaw legislative practice were hard work for all involved and required a great deal of patience. Representatives—whether from the USDP, NLD, the ethnic parties or the military—were forced to survive with relatively little external assistance. They were not provided with office space, nor was there any allocation for personal staff. In the early years, their salary of $300 per month was also deemed inadequate given their responsibilities.

During this exuberant phase of Naypyitaw's development, a great deal of change occurred quickly. In 2012, the system of pre-publication censorship that had been in place in various forms since the 1960s was finally abolished. This greatly liberalized the media landscape and led to a boom in privately owned journal and newspaper publication (Brooten 2016; Kean 2018). Many publishers sought to push the envelope, hoping to produce the type of journalism that would garner audiences and make money, while also contributing to the country's tentative democratic awakening. With a relatively small cohort of established journalists, many publications went on a hiring binge, looking to employ graduates from donor-backed journalism training programs. Among the publications that emerged during this period, many struggled for long-term readership and found that the deregulated media market was quickly flooded with competitor publications. In parallel, the internet landscape, which had always been subjected to strict government controls, went through its own series of major reforms. These included the abolition of blocks to stop access to sensitive political content, the rapid reduction in the cost of internet access, especially through smartphones, and the creation of new platforms for Burmese vernacular internet use. Facebook made early and very successful adjustments to meet these changed market conditions. It quickly grew to become the de-facto interface for Myanmar internet experiences (for further discussion, see McCarthy 2018).

The level of international attention to Myanmar matters also spiked. This was helped by an increase in foreign visitors, with unprecedented flows of tourists galloping through the airport in Yangon. They were joined by waves of government officials, businessmen, journalists and development workers, all keen to leave their mark on what was increasingly described as "Asia's last frontier" (e.g. Kent 2012; Parker 2016). Myanmar began to host major international events, including investment promotion conferences. In 2013, it hosted the World Economic Forum in Naypyitaw, which was attended by senior figures from around the world. There were speeches by President Thein Sein and Aung San Suu Kyi. In the same year, Naypyitaw was home to the Southeast Asia Games (see Creak 2014), a regional initiative that required the construction of facilities for dozens of different sports, including athletics, swimming, BMX riding and *sepak takraw* (caneball), which people in Myanmar call *chinlone*. The Mount Pleasant Cycling Field, also known as the Naypyitaw Cycling Venue, as an example, has a warmup area, media area, VIP stand, and facilities for medical, security and administrative personnel. It was only used once for such serious competition. Then, in 2014, Myanmar was, for the first time, the host of the ASEAN Summit. While much of the attention focused on the arrival of world leaders in November, Myanmar's ASEAN responsibilities actually required the hosting of over 400 related meetings over the course of the year. A new hotel zone was built in Naypyitaw for this purpose, and a second conference centre was also constructed. Given that US President Barack Obama attended, the triumphant summit event was widely considered a great success.

Throughout this busy period, Myanmar's internal politics remained centred on activities in Naypyitaw (see Farrelly and Chit Win 2018). By 2015, preparations for the next general election were taking up most of the extra energy. A tussle for control of the USDP leadership in August 2015 saw the purge of Thura Shwe Mann from his senior party positions. This destabilized the ruling group in the lead-up to the vote. The vote was also defined by the heavy foreign presence and interests. In certain Myanmar government agencies, most notably the Union Election Commission, the number of foreign technical staff swelled. And then the election itself was closely monitored by an array of foreign observer missions. Naypyitaw, once off-limits to foreign visitors, now welcomed them in a dizzying round of delegations, meetings and conferences. It became impossible for many individual officials to both do their job and keep the flow of conversation with visitors going. The victory by the NLD in the November 2015 general election has, however, led to some important shifts in how Naypyitaw functions.

## NLD ON TOP?

It is this current phase of Naypyitaw's development that will need the most attention in the years ahead. For now, a preliminary assessment is the best available. Since the NLD government took power it has been forced to adjust its own ideas about the city and its future. For a long period, the NLD leadership had in mind that it would be best to move the capital back to Yangon. That policy was formulated at a time when few people understood Naypyitaw's vastness, or the immense expense that accompanied its construction. Few could foresee that while it was designed as a dictator's paradise, it would play a key role in the creation of a nascent democratic culture. For the NLD, part of the frustration with the city was its distance from the other population centres, and particularly from the commercial bustle of Yangon. Even before taking government, the NLD had suggested that it might move aspects of government business, in the form of representative offices for key government agencies, back to Yangon.

Naypyitaw remains the central part of the NLD's over-arching conundrum about what it should do with the legacies of military rule. Abandoning Naypyitaw, or even greatly reducing its role in national affairs, would be a costly decision. Any further upheaval to official practice would prove disruptive to the physical and human infrastructure of government that is now well-established in Naypyitaw. It was built to be the "abode of kings", a place where the military would be safe from its many enemies, but where older traditions of rule would also have their chance to blossom. The anti-colonial ideology that motivated Naypyitaw's construction may not have earlier figured so centrally in the concerns of the NLD, yet it now finds itself at home in the new city. Under these conditions, they will need to convince the Myanmar people that the new city is worth the country's continued investment at a time when there are pressing budgetary needs in many other areas. Health, education, peace building and livelihood development will all be areas where the NLD government seeks to make its mark. But Naypyitaw, as it is currently working, and whether people appreciate it or not, is crucial in all these efforts.

The further problem for the NLD is the criticism that has emerged since the 2017 crisis in northern Rakhine State and the exodus of almost 700,000 Rohingya to Bangladesh. The NLD, from its Naypyitaw base, has struggled to respond. As the NLD has found, the "969" movement which morphed into the Committee for the Protection of Race and Religion, commonly known by its Myanmar acronym, "Ma Ba Tha", has offered sustained opposition to those seeking to better integrate Muslims into Myanmar society (for a subtle analysis, see Walton and Hayward 2014; also Walton and Jerryson 2016). The group draws its strength from monasteries where threats to Buddhism have become a rallying-cry for young, activist monks. Their most famous advocate is Wirathu, a monk from Mandalay imprisoned by the former military government for his anti-Muslim agitation. In recent years, he has spearheaded moves to challenge the status of Muslims in Myanmar (Coclanis 2013). He is incensed that the Rohingya, a persecuted Muslim minority from northern Rakhine State, might be entitled to the same rights and obligations as other people, and much of the violence in recent times can be traced to this style of preaching. Excluding the Rohingya as "Bengali" interlopers has proved a popular political ploy. This activism has made it difficult for moderate views to build support. Instead, the fault line between Muslims and Buddhists has deepened (for thoughtful consideration see Chambers 2017).

For its part, in the lead-up to the 2015 election the NLD decided to avoid endorsing any Muslim candidates. The decision was prompted by fears that Ma Ba Tha would vilify the party for being too cosy with

Muslims. Such vilification occurred anyway, in claims that Aung San Suu Kyi is secretly a Muslim and that the NLD is working for the Islamization of the country. NLD spokespeople parried away these claims, relying on the common sense of the people at large. In the end, the election campaign saw increasingly absurd efforts by Buddhist nationalists to present the vote as a referendum on Muslim presence in the country.

In this effort they failed profoundly. The vote was shaped, more than any other factor, as a referendum on decades of military rule. For that reason the NLD carried the weight of popular support but also won an important argument about the future of the country. Their political mandate was forged in opposition to a military government that appropriated national resources for its own purposes. Vanity projects—temples, bridges, dams and factories—came to define their investment in infrastructure to increase military pride. Among these varied efforts the standout was Naypyitaw, a city now home, perhaps ironically, to the NLD government.

What the development of a more open political culture has encouraged, in this sense, is the creation of new ideas about the city itself. These ideas are made legible in a context where the military's stranglehold has been loosened and people are eagerly embracing the chance to have their say about the country's future. Naypyitaw was never endorsed by a people's vote. Nor was the change of the country's official name to Myanmar or the English language re-designation of Rangoon as Yangon. These are decisions that were made behind closed doors by a senior clique who built their reputations on implacable resilience in the face of dissent. They wanted to build something new. Naypyitaw has, through all this effort, became the symbolic home for a vision of the Myanmar state which the NLD has even needed to embrace.

## ADJUSTING TO THE NEW

It usually takes time for people to adjust to something new. In the case of Naypyitaw the first decade of the city's development came with the inevitable dismissal of the agenda and ambition represented by the new city. Many commentators remain baffled by its existence, development and role. The idea that a new city can be created, from scratch, and with little outside scrutiny, defies many of our notions about how things happen in the 21st century. However, the emphasis on concrete and steel, gardens and fences, has caused some analysts to lose their sense of perspective.

Everything starts somewhere. It is just that we rarely have the chance to see these processes up close, especially when they are the product of decisions made, in secret, by military rulers keen to guard their own lives and legacies against opposition forces. The genesis and evolution of Naypyitaw is worthy of considered attention, especially during a time when Myanmar, under the NLD, confronts a mind-boggling set of political and economic challenges.

Naypyitaw is, first and foremost, a monument to the ideas and ambitions that have proved so important during Myanmar's history, particularly those that have dominated since the military first seized power in 1962. There are royalist, anti-colonial, socialist and democratic strands to the resulting ideology, all fused to the uncompromising demand for unity amongst Myanmar's "national races" (see Cheesman 2017). Though democracy is the more recent addition, Naypyitaw inherits many of the ideologies that went into the design of former capitals, including the key site of Bagan from which so much of the country's architectural endowment is inspired. As a monument to what the military leadership deemed was most valued in Myanmar society it offers lessons in forms of belonging, and exclusion, and in the variety of ways that spaces can be manipulated to serve grand political or cultural purposes.

Lived experiences in Naypyitaw also need to be considered in this discussion. The people of the city come from all corners of the country, and many of them have sought new economic and social opportunities as it has grown (for a fuller reflection on the nascent "Naypyitawrians" see Farrelly 2016). There are also the residents of the three townships around which "new" Naypyitaw was built: Lewe, Pyinmana and Tatkone. In the case of Pyinmana, a bustling trading town situated on the old north-south trunk route between Yangon and Mandalay, life has been transformed by the economic activity that goes with Naypyitaw's continued development. Pyinmana, it should also be noted, is home to a significant Muslim minority.

Naypyitaw is now the base for almost half of Myanmar's government officials, including most of the senior ranks (from Deputy Director through to Director-General). They live in scattered apartment complexes and suburbs of standardized bungalows, testament to the regulation of life that accompanied its pioneering generation. Shopping precincts, recreational facilities and service hubs have emerged to cater to the population's diverse needs. Restaurants, karaoke venues and bustling beer stations are all key locations for the creation of capital city lifestyles. The city's religious sites, one of which is an almost identical replica of Yangon's much more famous Shwedagon Pagoda, are increasingly busy places when the weather is good. The fact that the first group of Naypyitaw-born babies are now at school is a further sign that whatever its beginnings, Naypyitaw is taking on a life of its own.

And yet life for Naypyitawrians is not without elements of contestation. People in other parts of Myanmar voice their frustration with the over-sized investment in the city's infrastructure when their own villages and towns struggle with reliable electricity or passable roads. How these tensions are handled by the government is a major question for the years and decades ahead. Naypyitaw was built to symbolize the possibilities of Myanmar's modernity: straight roads; clean, manicured public spaces; pride in the unifying mission. For critics it has not yet filled its mandate as an exemplary centre from where a story of political and social harmony can be made real for people who have long suffered through the machinations of authoritarian fancy. Under the NLD there is an expectation that Naypyitaw should now deliver for the people who elected its government. The early evidence, especially after 2017's Rakhine State crisis, is that such delivery will be much more difficult than most democratic activists had ever imagined.

## References

Brooten, Lisa. "Burmese Media in Transition". *International Journal of Communication* 10 (2016): 182–99.

Chambers, Justine. "Minorities and the Vote". *New Mandala*, 5 November 2015.

_____. "Unpicking an (A)moral Anthropological Stance: Ongoing Violence in Myanmar". *The Familiar Strange*, 30 November 2017.

Cheesman, Nick. "How in Myanmar 'National Races' Came to Surpass Citizenship and Exclude Rohingya". *Journal of Contemporary Asia* 47, no. 3 (2017): 461–83.

Cheesman, Nick, Monique Skidmore, and Trevor Wilson, eds. *Ruling Myanmar: From Cyclone Nargis to National Elections*. Singapore: Institute of Southeast Asian Studies Press, 2010.

Cheesman, N. and N. Farrelly, eds. (2016). *Conflict in Myanmar: War, Politics, Religion*. Singapore: Institute of Southeast Asian Studies Press.

Chit Win. "The Hluttaw and Conflicts in Myanmar". In *Conflict in Myanmar: War, Politics, Religion*, edited by Nick Cheesman and Nicholas Farrelly. Singapore: Institute of Southeast Asian Studies Press, 2016.

Coclanis, Peter A. "Terror in Burma: Buddhists vs. Muslims". *World Affairs* (2013): 25–33.

Creak, Simon. "National Restoration, Regional Prestige: The Southeast Asian Games in Myanmar". *The Journal of Asian Studies* 73, no. 4 (2014): 853–77.

Dulyapak Preecharushh. *Naypyidaw: The New Capital of Burma*. Bangkok: White Lotus Press, 2009.

————. "Myanmar's New Capital City of Naypyidaw". *Engineering Earth* 2011: 1021–44.

Eleven. "Ministry Aims to Boost Nay Pyi Taw Tourism". *Eleven*, 29 March 2015.

Farrelly, Nicholas. "Who are the 'Naypyitawrians'?" *The Myanmar Times*, 29 February 2016.

————. "The Capital". In *Routledge Handbook of Contemporary Myanmar*, edited by Adam Simpson, Nicholas Farrelly and Ian Holliday. London: Routledge, 2018.

Farrelly, Nicholas, and Chit Win. "Disciplining Democracy: Explaining the Rhythms of Myanmar's First Hluttaw, 2011–2016". In *Public Policy in the 'Asian Century'*, edited by Sara Bice, Avery Poole and Helen Sullivan. London: Palgrave Macmillan, 2018.

Holliday, Ian. "Myanmar in 2012: Towards a Normal State". *Asian Survey* 53, no. 1 (2013): 93–100.

Jones, Lee. "Explaining Myanmar's Regime Transition: The Periphery is Central". *Democratization* 21, no. 5 (2014a): 780–802.

————. "The Political Economy of Myanmar's Transition". *Journal of Contemporary Asia* 44, no. 1 (2014b): 144–70.

Kean, Thomas. "Public Discourse". In *Routledge Handbook of Contemporary Myanmar*, edited by Adam Simpson, Nicholas Farrelly and Ian Holliday. London: Routledge, 2018.

Kent, Justin. "Myanmar, The Last Frontier?" *Forbes*, 9 November 2012.

Lall, Marie and Hla Hla Win. "Perceptions of the State and Citizenship in Light of the 2010 Myanmar Elections". In *Myanmar's Transition: Openings, Obstacles and Opportunities*, edited by Nick Cheesman, Monique Skidmore and Trevor Wilson. Singapore: Institute of Southeast Asian Studies Press, 2012.

Lidauer, Michael. "Democratic Dawn? Civil Society and Elections in Myanmar 2010–2012". *Journal of Current Southeast Asian Affairs* 31, no. 2 (2012): 87–114.

McCarthy, Gerard. "Cyberspaces". In *Routledge Handbook of Contemporary Myanmar*, edited by Adam Simpson, Nicholas Farrelly and Ian Holliday. London: Routledge, 2018.

————. "Buddhist Welfare and the Limits of Big 'P' Politics in Provincial Myanmar". In *Conflict in Myanmar: War, Politics, Religion*, edited by Nick Cheesman and Nicholas Farrelly. Singapore: Institute of Southeast Asian Studies Press, 2016.

Menager, Jacqueline. "Law Fuckers, Cultural Forgers and the Business of Youth Entitlement in Yangon, Myanmar". *South East Asia Research* 22, no. 2 (2014): 201–12.

Meehan, Patrick. "Drugs, Insurgency and State-building in Burma: Why the Drugs Trade is Central to Burma's Changing Political Order". *Journal of Southeast Asian Studies* 42, no. 3 (2011): 376–404.

Parker, Edward. "Myanmar's Opening: Doing business in Asia's Final Frontier". *The Diplomat*, 18 November 2016.

Peleggi, Maurizio. "Consuming Colonial Nostalgia: The Monumentalisation of Historic Hotels in Urban South-East Asia". *Asia Pacific Viewpoint* 46, no. 3 (2005): 255–65.

Richmond, Simon, et al. *Myanmar (Burma)*, 12th edition. Melbourne: Lonely Planet Publications, 2014.

Roberts, Jayde Lin. *Mapping Chinese Rangoon: Place and Nation among the Sino-Burmese*. Seattle: University of Washington Press, 2016.

Salem-Gervais, Nicolas, and Rosalie Metro. "A Textbook Case of Nation-Building: The Evolution of History Curricula in Myanmar". *Journal of Burma Studies* 16, no. 1 (2012): 27–78.

South, Ashley. *Ethnic Politics in Burma: States of Conflict*. London: Routledge, 2008.
_____. *Mon Nationalism and Civil War in Burma: The Golden Sheldrake*. London: Routledge, 2013.

Seekins, Donald M. "State, Society and Natural Disaster: Cyclone Nargis in Myanmar (Burma)". *Asian Journal of Social Science* 37 (2009a): 717–37.
_____. "'Runaway Chickens' and Myanmar Identity: Relocating Burma's Capital". *City* 13, no. 1 (2009b): 63–70.

Selth, Andrew. "Even Paranoids Have Enemies: Cyclone Nargis and Myanmar's Fears of Invasion". *Contemporary Southeast Asia* 30, no. 3 (2008): 379–402.

Taylor, Robert H. "Myanmar: From Army Rule to Constitutional Rule?" *Asian Affairs* 43, no. 2 (2012): 221–36.

Than Than Nwe. "Yangon: The Emergence of a New Spatial Order in Myanmar's Capital City". *Sojourn: Journal of Social Issues in Southeast Asia* (1998): 86–113.

Turnell, Sean. "Myanmar in 2010: Doors Open, Doors Close". *Asian Survey* 51, no. 1 (2011): 148–54.

Walton, Matthew J., and Susan Hayward. "Contesting Buddhist Narratives: Democratization, Nationalism, and Communal Violence in Myanmar." *Policy Studies* 71 (2014).

Walton, Matthew J., and Michael Jerryson. "The Authorization of Religio-political Discourse: Monks and Buddhist Activism in Contemporary Myanmar and Beyond". *Politics and Religion* 9, no. 4 (2016): 794–814.

# IV

## Politics

# 9

## PARTNERSHIP IN POLITICS: THE TATMADAW AND THE NLD IN MYANMAR SINCE 2016

Maung Aung Myoe

The year 2016 was a milestone in the political history of Myanmar as it gave birth to a popularly elected civilian government for the first time since the military takeover of the state in March 1962. In the elections held on 8 November 2015, it was clear within a few hours that the National League for Democracy (NLD) had won a landslide victory. When the result was finalized, the NLD won 57.20 per cent of valid votes (12.79 million) for the Pyithu Hluttaw (House of Representatives) and 78.95 per cent of contested seats (323 seats). Similarly, for the Amyotha Hluttaw (House of Nationalities), the party won 57.68 per cent (13.10 million) of the valid votes and 80.36 per cent of contested seats (168 seats). The 2008 Constitution is essentially designed by the military to require partnership with civilian politicians, allocating twenty-five per cent of the seats in both houses to military members and allowing the military to nominate a vice-presidential candidate along with ministers for Defence, Home Affairs and Border Affairs.[1] In a mix of parliamentary and presidential systems, the NLD's nominee Htin Kyaw became the president and the Tatmadaw's nominees, ex-general Myint Swe, and the other NLD nominee, Henry Van Thio, became vice-presidents. In this constitutional setting and with the results of the 2015 election, the NLD has become a ruling partner for the Tatmadaw.

In his inaugural address, President Htin Kyaw pledged that his government would "implement four policies: national reconciliation; internal peace; the emergence of a constitution that will produce a democratic, federal union; and the improvement of the quality of life of the majority of the people". At the same time, he cautiously stated: "I am responsible for the emergence of a constitution that will be in accord with the democratic norms suited to our country. I am also aware that I need to be patient in realizing this political objective, for which the people have long aspired" (GNLM 2016, p. 1). [2]

In order to streamline the cabinet size, the NLD government initially reduced the numbers in the ministry from twenty-eight to twenty-one, yet it created the Ministry of Ethnic Affairs, and the number of ministers was reduced from thirty-two to eighteen with no deputy ministers. At that point in time, Aung San Suu Kyi herself held four ministerial portfolios. The list of ministers included three ministers for the portfolios of Defence, Home Affairs and Border Affairs, seconded by the Commander-in-Chief of the Defence Service. After much controversy, Aung San Suu Kyi was made State Counsellor on 6 April 2016. An additional ministry was created for her, in parallel with the president, and Kyaw Tint Swe, a retired diplomat, was appointed as its minister on 17 May 2016, making a total of twenty-two ministries. The first deputy minister appointment was for the Ministry of Foreign Affairs on 5 April 2016. It was later followed by the appointment of a deputy minister for the Ministry of Agriculture, Livestock and Irrigation on 2 May 2016 and three deputy ministers at Defence, Home Affairs, and Border Affairs, which are under the influence of the Tatmadaw. As of the end of 2017, the Myanmar government has twenty-four ministers, one minister-level office holder — the Attorney General — and fourteen deputy ministers. [3] The appointment of some ministers drew public criticism as they held questionable qualifications.

Nearly three months after the elections, the first regular session of the second Pyithu Hluttaw was convened on 1 February 2016. [4] Within a year, during three regular sessions, the Hluttaw passed nineteen bills, out of which only five are new and the other fourteen are either amendments or repeals of earlier legislation.

There are criticisms of the NLD government's failure to deliver campaign promises and to meet public expectations. For instance, at this stage there has been no discussion of amending the constitution, as promised during the election campaign. Another area of criticism regards freedom of expression and the media. Under the NLD government, restrictions were imposed on the media reporting from the Hluttaw and there is no longer direct access to the chambers. Moreover, charges against individuals with section 66(D) of the Telecommunication Law have increased during the NLD administration; ninety-five out of the total of 106 charges made between November 2015 and November 2017 are during the NLD administration (Shoon Naing 2017).[5]

In this context, this paper focuses on three areas of political process and development in Myanmar, which are directly related to the management of national defence and security, since the NLD came to power on 31 March 2016. They are (1) civil-military relations, (2) the peace process, and (3) foreign relations. Since the NLD administration only took government in March 2016, this is an interim assessment. However, it is argued that the Tatmadaw has so far carefully managed to retain its political influence over security-related issues and the NLD administration has increasingly endorsed the Tatmadaw's policy guidance. At this stage, there is little evidence to suggest that the NLD government has embarked on any major transformation in the country's political structure.

## CIVIL-MILITARY RELATIONS

One of the key issues that the NLD government promised to review and address is civil-military relations. The pattern of civil-military relations outlined in the 2008 Constitution provides the military considerable privileges or prerogatives as well as leverage over civilians. There is also almost no meaningful civilian oversight over the military or in national security issues more broadly. While civil-military relations have been stable, they have not been without occasional tensions.

When NLD leaders realized that they were going to form a government in the aftermath of the November 2015 elections, they reached out to the Tatmadaw leadership. Before the transfer of power, Aung San Suu Kyi met Commander-in-Chief Min Aung Hlaing three times. After their first encounter on 2 December 2015, he commented that the meeting had produced "good results". The Commander in Chief's office later issued a statement stating, "in line with the desires of the people, they agreed to cooperate on peace, the rule of law, reconciliation and the development of the country" (Fuller 2015).[6] However, little was reported on their second and third meetings on 25 January and 17 February 2016 respectively. Speculation focused on their potential discussion of power-sharing, presidential nominations including possible amendment or suspension of the constitutional provision that barred the NLD leader from the presidency, as well as the appointment of chief ministers in some states such as Kachin, Shan and Rakhine (Ei Ei Toe Lwin 2016; Ei Ei Toe Lwin & Htoo Thant 2016).[7] The meetings appeared to clarify areas of cooperation and mutual interest.

At the same time, the Tatmadaw leadership gave out mixed messages through public statements such as persistently warning of the dangers of foreign interference, including those of "mixed-blood people", in the internal affairs of the country.[8] The other message was targeted towards disloyal or "treacherous acts" of unspecified individuals towards the Tatmadaw and the country. In this regard, on 23 February 2016, at the Myanmar Army Officer's Training School (Bahtoo), Min Aung Hlaing remarked: "Tatmadaw had to save the nation from disintegration resulting from treacherous armed struggle during the early post-independence period, while making a lot of sacrifices. The result of this treacherous misconduct is the conflicts that the country still has to deal with until this day. History shows the generation of gross political confusion by the acts of disloyalty to the nation, the allegiance to foreign countries, and the betrayal of the Tatmadaw. The Constitution stipulates some provisions to prevent recursion of such political disorders" (Myawaddy 2016, pp. 1, 16–17).[9]

Moreover, in February 2016, the Tatmadaw published its very first Defence White Paper. The content of this 99-page document provides a general overview of Myanmar's perception of national, regional and international security challenges, a basic outline of national defense policy, the objectives and structure of the armed forces, and the Tatmadaw's "legitimate and firm stance" on safeguarding the "independence, sovereignty and national interests" of Myanmar. Citing its spirit as "guardian of the state," the Tatmadaw laid out key priorities in its missions. However, what is significant is the timing of the release of the paper. The timing appeared to suggest that amidst the country's unprecedented transition from decades-long, military-backed rule to an administration run by the NLD, the Tatmadaw wanted to signal that it remained the institution controlling security policy. At that time, its release could be a signal to the incoming NLD-led government that the Tatmadaw intended to remain at the heart of the country's political and security life—and that it was willing and capable of playing a leading role in governing the country. In addition, the paper sent a strong message that it was the Tatmadaw that defined the security of the nation and was responsible for its defence.

Since the start of the tenure of the NLD-controlled Hluttaw in March 2016 there have been five notable occasions of friction in civil-military relations. The first issue came about when the Hluttaw nominated vice-presidential candidates.[10] The second issue was related to the appointment of members for the "Constitutional Tribunal" on 29 March 2016 when Tatmadaw representatives in the parliament requested the re-submission of fuller bio-data of two nominees.[11] A week later, the "State Counsellor Bill" stirred up another major issue in civil-military relations in both houses of the Pyidaungsu Hluttaw. The bill was hotly debated by members of parliament and opposition was overwhelmed by NLD lawmakers. The situation led Brigadier General Maung Maung to remark that the passage of the bill constituted "democratic bullying by the majority" or the "tyranny of majority".[12] Hostilities between civilian and military parliamentarians also occurred when a motion was submitted by a member of the Pyithu Hluttaw from Rakhine state to reorganize the "Rakhine State Advisory Commission", headed by Kofi Annan and staffed by two other foreign citizens, so that it could comprise only local experts. While Tatmadaw representatives supported this motion, it was voted down by the powerful NLD block.[13] Finally, there were differences of opinion with regard to the voting on an emergency motion "urging the Hluttaw to express concern over sovereignty, stability and peace process due to attacks of four armed groups in Shan State that led to the losses of lives and property". The motion was proposed by a USDP member of the Pyithu Hluttaw on 2 December 2016 and supported by the other military delegates. The Minister for Defence explained the situation from a broad historical and political perspective and urged the Pyithu Hluttaw to brand these armed groups as terrorist organizations. However, when voting took place, the motion received only 141 votes in support, with 244 against and seven in abstention, and so it was not approved; it was just put on record.

In the midst of frictions between the NLD's Hluttaw representatives and the military delegates, at the 71st anniversary of Armed Forces Day on 27 March 2016, the Commander-in-Chief reminded the country of the constitutionally guaranteed leading political role of the Tatmadaw and outlined broadly the position of the Tatmadaw in the emerging political context. He said:

> The two main hindrances to democratization are lack of abiding by the rule of law, regulations and the presence of insurgencies. These problems could lead to a chaotic democracy. If we want a multi-party democracy to take root in our country, there must be proper discipline and adherence to the law. We will have to work with our maximum capacity both physically and mentally with unity and loyalty to the country if we love our motherland and want to witness its development. The Tatmadaw will cooperate to serve the interests of the country and the people. Shouldering the national political duty by the Tatmadaw is only to safeguard and act in the national interest, the interest of the people and the state. Not of party politics.

The Tatmadaw's position was clear: it will safeguard the constitution and protect the interests of the state and the people. At this time, there were some speculations that the Tatmadaw may be thinking of mounting a military coup based on comments made by the Commander-in-Chief in a speech at the National Defence College (NDC) on 26 November 2016 with reference to "the state of emergency" clause prescribed in the 2008 Constitution (Callahan 2016).[14] It was selectively quoted in official newspapers but was published in full, both in Myanmar and English languages, in the military-owned *Myawady* newspaper. The scoop of the coverage was the Commander-in-Chief's reference to "Emergency Provisions" in the 2008 Constitution, which was amplified by some private papers to generate rumours of an impending "military coup". In practice, the speech was a routine exercise in guidance for NDC trainees. The reference was, perhaps, to address the current state of affairs in Rakhine and Shan states, yet it could also be a gentle reminder of the importance and the role of the National Defence and Security Council (NDSC) in such situations.

Similarly, during his trip to Europe, to attend a European Union Military Committee (EUMC) meeting in Brussels in November 2016, the Commander-in-Chief made a reference to the emergency provision in his speech but noted that the constitution stipulates that not only could the military not easily seize power and remain in power for too long, but it also requires the military to act in accordance with the president's approval. If the Commander-in-Chief is serious about the threat of a military takeover, he would have referred to Article 40(C) of the 2008 Constitution which states: "If there arises a state of emergency that could cause the disintegration of the Union, disintegration of national solidarity and loss of sovereign power or attempts therefore by wrongful forcible means such as insurgency or violence, the Commander-in-Chief of the Defence Services has the right to take over and exercise State sovereign power in accord with the provisions of this Constitution." According to this article, the Commander-in-Chief does not need to consult anyone and he alone can decide.[15] Yet, so far, there is no evidence to indicate that the Tatmadaw is thinking of and preparing for a coup.

The NLD's attempt to reshape the pattern of civil-military relations could be seen in its signature campaign for constitutional amendments in 2014, which ran from 27 May to 19 July. The campaign was clearly aimed at ending the military's veto on constitutional amendments by changing Article 436; to lower the threshold for approval for amendment as a starting point for other structural changes in the constitution. The NLD managed to gather about five million signatures. The issue of constitutional amendment was a policy platform upon which the NLD and its leaders campaigned during the 2015 elections. Yet once the NLD came to power, the issue of constitutional amendment appeared to be shelved. While the party leadership is still morally committed to changing the constitution, the NLD itself has also found it useful for advancing the party's interests. For example, thanks to the 2008 Constitution, the NLD appointed chief ministers from among its ranks in Shan and Rakhine states where the local assemblies were controlled by non-NLD members. Finally, during a press conference on 10 June 2016, the Speaker of the Pyithu Hluttaw, Win Myint, said that the constitutional amendments would not sought until the peace process was completed. In other words, the NLD is, for the time being, prepared to accept the current pattern of civil-military relations enshrined in the constitution.

In the meantime, on 28 November 2016, when the security situation in northern parts of Rakhine State deteriorated, the Union Solidarity and Development Party (USDP) and twelve other political parties held a meeting and signed a joint declaration calling the government to hold a National Defence and Security Council (NDSC) meeting. The NDSC is a powerful body of eleven members where the Tatmadaw holds a majority.[16] The joint declaration noted that the NDSC should hold a meeting on the situation in conflict-wracked Rakhine State because the country's territorial sovereignty is at stake. It also said that "renewed fighting between ethnic armed groups and the Myanmar army in northern Shan state, the recent explosions of three handmade bombs in a Yangon supermarket, rising crime throughout the country, and the stalled national peace process had created a general crisis which forced the military to take action" (Mizzima 2016; Kyaw Thu, Win Naung Toe and Win Ko Ko Latt 2016).[17] This call was criticized by some people as promoting the military role in managing national security and prolonging military dominance in politics. Then again on 14 January 2017, the USDP and fourteen other political parties asked the government to hold a NDSC meeting to tackle security challenges facing Myanmar.

Nevertheless, in order to minimize the Tatmadaw's political role and influence, the NLD government has so far avoided calling a NDSC meeting. The meeting held on 14 October 2016 to discuss the security situation in border areas was not an NDSC meeting.[18] On 9 February 2017, *The Irrawaddy* (English Version) reported that there was an unpublicized meeting between Min Aung Hlaing and Aung San Suu Kyi on 4 February during which the former reportedly asked the latter to convene a NDSC meeting as soon as possible (The Irrawaddy 2017).[19] The appointment of Thaung Tun as National Security Advisor on 10 January 2017 could be considered as another indication to undermine the NDSC. Despite the serious deterioration of the security situation in Rakhine state since August 2017, there has still been no NDSC meeting.

## PEACE PROCESS AND NATIONAL RECONCILIATION

The peace process and national reconciliation were major policy platforms upon which the NLD government engineered its campaign slogans and promises and formed a top priority of its governing agenda. From the start of its administration, the NLD has devoted its energy, time, and resources to the peace process. Before coming to power, the NLD leaders, particularly Aung San Suu Kyi, held cautious, even negative, views of the Nationwide Ceasefire Agreement (NCA), negotiated between the USDP government and Ethnic Armed Organizations (EAOs). At one stage, she told EAOs that they should not be in a hurry to sign the document (Whtut 2015; Mizzima 2015).[20] She also rebuffed the NCA signing ceremony in October 2015 and the NLD refused to ink the document; reasons which were explained by an NLD member of the Pyithu Hluttaw on 7 December 2015 when the document was ratified:

Our NLD Chairperson didn't sign this NCA. The main reason behind not signing this agreement is its failure to cover the entire nation and it is in the nature of partial coverage only. And another reason is it can likely create misunderstanding among signatory organizations and non-signatory organizations and the last reason is the government may likely exert pressure on non-signatory armed organizations. (Nay Thar 2015)[21]

Nevertheless, eight EAOs signed the NCA on 15 October 2015. However, once they came to power, the NLD endorsed the NCA and continued to follow the line of the Tatmadaw on the peace process. For instance, at a Joint Monitoring Meeting at the Union level held on 27 April 2016 soon after taking office, Aung San Suu Kyi highlighted the importance of the ceasefire agreement. She said: "A ceasefire is the first step to peace. After having a ceasefire, we can step forward and obtain eternal peace. The ceasefire must represent the peace process" (Kyemon 2016c, p. 1).[22] On 12 February 2017, in her Union Day address, she also urged non-signatory EAOs to sign the NCA.

The NLD administration also created two new ministries to deal with ethnic minority issues and the peace process: Ministry of Ethnic Affairs and Ministry of State Counsellor. The Thein Sein-era Myanmar Peace Centre was also transformed into the National Reconciliation and Peace Centre (NRPC). During her briefing, on 16 May 2016, to coordinate matters relating to the establishment of the NRPC and preparations for the 21st Century Panglong Conference, the State Counsellor said: "concerning national reconciliation and internal peace, what counts is for all participants to discuss on the basis of what they can give rather than what they would like to take (Kyemon 2016d, p. 1)."[23] In terms of guidance, she went on to say that discussions at the conference were to be based on the NCA but with flexibility and that the agenda for the conference should be in line with the framework for political dialogue. She also advised that the CSO Forum had to be organized by CSOs themselves, and suggestions and recommendations made by the CSO Forum are to be taken into account, and the discussions should not include too many people (Kyemon 2016d, p. 3).[24] In short, the NLD government has largely followed the USDP's approach to peace negotiation. Having said that, the NLD government did fine-tune the process without compromising or undermining the key principles of the peace negotiation, adding a *Peace Talk with Youths* in Naypyitaw on 1 January 2017, a *Peace Dialogue* in Pinglong on 12 February 2017, and commencing plans for an ethnicity-based forum in

Pha-An, a region-based forum in Thanintharyi Region, and a CSO forum in Naypyitaw. Furthermore, with pomp and splendor, the 21st Century Panglong Peace Conference was held in August 2016.

Meanwhile, under the umbrella of the United Nationalities Federal Council (UNFC), EAOs, including both signatories and non-signatories to the NCA, met in Mai Ja Yang in late July 2016, along with CSOs and political parties, to discuss their common position at the 21st Century Panglong Conference.[25] The Tatmadaw voiced its disapproval of the meeting. At the press conference on 20 July 2016, Tatmadaw Spokesman Lt. General Mya Tun Oo told the press that the military would not prevent it from happening although it did not want it to happen. The Tatmadaw also objected to another meeting of similar format to be held in Chiang Mai in July 2017; at the request of the Tatmadaw, the Thai Army ordered its cancellation (Mathieson 2017).[26] The Mai Ja Yang conference came up with a common position of EAOs to present at the 21st Century Conference (Lun Min Mang 2016).[27] One of the most significant aspects of the common position was the issue of "federal armed forces".[28]

At the 21st Century Panglong conference, eighty-two papers were presented by various groups, including ten from the Tatmadaw and seventeen from EAOs. Several suggestions and recommendations were made to improve the peace process and for lasting settlement of armed conflicts in Myanmar. However, the legacy and historical baggage of the 20th century "Panglong" loomed large over the proceedings and the political commentary which followed.[29]

**Table 9.1 Groups and papers at the 21st Century Panglong Conference**

|   | Groups/Papers | Papers | Seats |
|---|---|---|---|
| 1 | Tatmadaw | 10 | 150 |
| 2 | Political Parties | 28 | 150 |
| 3 | Government | 3 | 75 |
| 4 | Hluttaws | 3 | 75 |
| 5 | Ethnic Minorities | 13 | 50 |
| 6 | Ethnic Armed Organizations | 17 | 150 |
| 7 | Special Invitees | 8 | 50 |
|   | **TOTAL** | 82 | 700 |

Here, the writer would like to present the views and positions of some stakeholders in the peace process. The UDSP government's peace overture is based on six key elements: no surrender of arms, equality in negotiation, political dialogue, all-inclusiveness, constitutional amendment, and democratic federal union. Thein Sein also intended to introduce a new political culture of compromise and consensus into Myanmar society. Since the USDP government and the Tatmadaw worked closely and shared similar views, the latter supported the former's policy and there was a significant level of coordination between the two institutions. Now, the NLD is in power. Although the NLD government follows its predecessor's position in general terms there are some differences in style and emphasis; it also needs cooperation from the Tatmadaw in order to make progress in the peace process.

At the 21st Century Panglong conference, the EAOs focused on the creation of a federal union for Myanmar with new division of territorial states. They also discussed the issue of a "federal union army" with rotation of Commander-in-Chief among different nationalities. On the third day of the 21st Century Panglong conference, the common positions of the EAOs were presented as following:

(1) All armed forces must be under the control of civilian administration.

(2) The Union army [Federal Army] must be under the administration of defense ministry, and defense minister must be a civilian.

(3) The military commander-in-chief, deputy commander-in-chief and chiefs of army, navy and air force branches must be representative of different ethnic minorities.

(4) Police and security forces must be under the control of the Ministry of Home Affairs.

(5) There must be only one Union army in the country.

(6) A military leadership council must be formed with equal representatives of the states in order manage the Union army.

(7) All levels of the Union army must be formed with equal ethnic representation from the states.

(8) The total size of the Union army and state security forces must not exceed 0.5 percent of the total population of the Union.

(9) All states have the right to form a security force, and security forces must be under the control of state government. Union government has the right to enlist the use of state security forces in the event of a state of emergency.

(10) The government must establish a Union-wide police force as well as separate state police forces.[30]

Another point which they emphasized is that the disarmament, demobilization and reintegration (DDR) processes should be developed in conjunction with the security sector reform (SSR) process. There was also demand for a much broader representation of non-Bamar nationalities in national and regional politics. Moreover, the EAOs expressed their desire for a greater share of the natural resources in their respective regions. In making these requests, the EAOs demanded significant changes to the existing constitution which included civil-military relations, removing the military's privilege in national affairs and ultimately placing it under civilian control.

Since the Tatmadaw is the most important stakeholder, if not the veto-player as some analysts believe, in the peace process, it is important to know its position. There are several key positions taken by the Tatmadaw. First, the peace process should be within the framework of the 2008 Constitution. At the 21ˢᵗ Century Panglong Conference, Tatmadaw representatives argued that the 2008 Constitution is in fact federal in nature. They also indicated that the Tatmadaw is in favour of keeping present territorial division of states and regions. Second, it is argued that the present Tatmadaw is the "Union Armed Forces" (*Pyidaungsu Tatmadaw*) and there is no need for so-called "federal union armed forces". Third, it is generally stated that the DDR process should come first and SSR could follow later. Fourth, they emphasized that any negotiation with the non-signatories of the NCA should be based on the NCA principles.

The Tatmadaw laid down and announced six principles for the peace process. They are: (a) genuine desire to make a lasting peace; (b) keeping promises and commitment to peace agreements; (c) refrain from taking unfair advantage from the peace agreement; (d) avoid placing a heavy burden on local people; (e) strict adherence to existing laws; and (f) cooperation in democratic reform process based on the 2008 State Constitution, our three main national causes, and the essence of democracy. At the 21ˢᵗ Century Panglong conference, Min Aung Hlaing told the audience that "we should have a dialogue for peace without being too ethnocentric". At the Armed Forces Day parade on 27 March 2015, the Commander-in-Chief also said:

> In implementation of ceasefire and peace processes, DDR for security reconciliation is essential. As examples, paying no heed to security reconciliation processes, many countries gave priority to a ceasefire, resulting in subsequent problems which are still left unresolved till now, and

it is also found that the systematic implementation of security reconciliation processes brought peace to many countries. So, it is compulsory for the implementation of security reconciliation processes in the ceasefire and peace process. I'd like to say that integration of national solidarity, national reconciliation and making peace will be carried out without fail as Tatmadaw is the Union Defence Services formed by ethnic people of the Union (GNLM 2015).[31]

In line with this view, the Senior General recently stated that the participation of EAOs in the future peace conference should be based on the NCA.

Meanwhile, the NLD government has more or less endorsed the Tatmadaw's position and asked all remaining EAOs to sign the NCA before their participation in political dialogue. In addition, it also appears that the NLD government agreed with the Tatmadaw's stand on three EAOs, namely the Myanmar National Democratic Alliance Army (MNDAA, otherwise known as Kokang Army), the Ta'ang National Liberation Army (TNLA) and the Arakan Army (AA). In following the Tatmadaw, the NLD has also refused to invite them for negotiations as they launched attacks against civilian targets and military outposts in northern Shan State alongside the Kachin Independence Army (KIA), under the banner of the "Northern Alliance" in November 2016. On 10 November 2016, the alliance launched attacks at the 105-mile trade zone in Kutkai Township, killing three civilians and five members of government security forces, with eighteen civilians and eleven members of the security forces injured. The armed conflict further escalated and the Tatmadaw launched counterinsurgency operations against the "Northern Alliance". By deploying airpower and artillery support, the government security forces captured KIA's outposts one after another, driving significant numbers of Internally Displaced Persons across the Chinese border. Since it keeps silent on the Tatmadaw's military activities in Northern Myanmar, in Shan and Kachin states, it is generally assumed that the NLD government takes the same position as the Tatmadaw and it is the Tatmadaw that has been shaping and framing the peace process and national reconciliation. In other words, it is safe to assume that, as far as the peace process is concerned, the NLD has endorsed the Tatmadaw's policy as its default approach.

## FOREIGN RELATIONS

Since it came to power the NLD government has maintained a pragmatic, yet delicate, and balanced relationship among major powers. However, the NLD government has found it increasingly difficult to manage international pressure on humanitarian issues, such as the Rohingya crisis.

When the NLD issued the manifesto for national elections in 2015, it provided the following statement on foreign policy:

> (1) To pursue an active and independent foreign policy, and to establish friendly and close political relations. With regard to international matters that may arise firmly on the side of genuine democratic values. (2) To identify and cooperate with other countries on joint economic enterprises of mutual benefit. In particular, to work together for the benefit of the region on issues relating to regional organizations and programmes. (3) To have close and strong relations with the UN, the World Bank, the International Monetary Fund, and other such organizations. (4) To give particular emphasis to the role of civil society organisations in communicating with the international community (NLD 2015, p. 8).[32]

In her interview with the *Washington Post* on 19 November 2015, about ten days after the election results became clear, Aung San Suu Kyi confirmed that her government would follow a non-aligned foreign policy (Weymouth 2015).[33] Just one week after the inauguration of the NLD government, on 7 April 2016, the state-owned *Myanmar Alin* newspaper, now controlled by the NLD's Minister for Information, carried an editorial on Myanmar foreign policy, which was entitled "Myanmar's Foreign Policy has become Dynamic", and said that "the essence of Myanmar foreign policy, persistently practiced from the time of the liberation from the colonial yoke to the present, is maintaining friendly relations with countries all over the world" (Myanma Alin 2016, p. 2).[34] Furthermore, the editorial also claimed that "Myanmar's foreign policy, based on friendship with all, will not only continue to be consistent with the changing world politics but also, besides enhancing national interests, serves the world peace, development, and prosperity as it enters into the 21st century" (ibid).[35]

In her Myanmar New Years message as the Minister for Foreign Affairs on 18 April 2016, Aung San Suu Kyi briefly explained Myanmar's foreign policy in somewhat vague and ambiguous terms. She stated: "Ever since the attainment of independence, our country has maintained good relations with other countries all over the world. This is something that our country can be very proud of. Since regaining independence in January 1948, our country, despite being a small and amidst war-torn damaged country, has always won international respect" (Kyemon 2016a, pp. 1, 3).[36] Her briefing to the diplomatic community in the country on Myanmar's foreign policy on 22 April 2016 was also short on details and missing key principles, objectives, goals and strategies that Myanmar will pursue. Instead, it provided insight on the approach to diplomacy that Myanmar's foreign policy would embrace, including neutralism, universal friendship and human rights. She stated:

> Since we became independent in 1948, we have adopted a policy of neutrality and universal friendship. We are one of the first signatories to the United Nations charter and to the United Nations' Charter on [Universal Declaration of] Human Rights, which means we always pay emphasis on the need of international cooperation and on the need to respect human beings as required because friendship and peace are dependent on security and happiness of all people in the world. This has always been our aim — that our country should be the grounds for fostering better relations not just between our neighbors and ourselves, but between us and the rest of the world and between all other countries as well.[37]

What is not clear in her statement is to what extent the NLD government believes in the collective security of the UN and the centrality of international regimes in interstate relations. In addition she explained:

> We are not a very big or very powerful country. But we hope that we will be able to lead the world when it comes to approaching all the problems that beset our globe with sincerity, with goodwill towards all, and with a genuine desire to work hard to achieve the kind of situation of which all human beings dream, which we very seldom manage to achieve. It is always good to have goals, even if these goals seem sometimes unattainable, I think it is a basic necessity that we should aim high.[38]

The rest of the briefing focused on what she called "a new approach" to people-centered diplomacy. The briefing was hailed in editorials in state-owned newspapers on 23 April 2016. In *Kyemon Daily* under the title of "International Relations based on Friendship among People", it praised the briefing that "such a clear official explanation on Myanmar foreign policy was rarely heard in the past" (Kyemon 2016b, p. 2).[39] "We are witnessing a change from government-to-government relations that we used to see in the past to people-based relations", the paper claimed (ibid.). It further waxed lyrical on the "people-based diplomacy" by saying that "in reality, friendly relations among countries all over the world is a necessity for peace to prevail among people on the globe and this kind of universal friendship could be possible only with the people-centered relations" (ibid.).

However, many others privately critiqued the rhetorical shift of focus from government-to-government relations to people-centered relations as ambiguous and unclear. It could just simply be in line with the NLD's overall slogan of "Together with the People" or something to do with an emphasis on "consular affairs" in its conduct of diplomacy towards other states. Overall, the NLD's foreign policy statements indicate that a key objective is to put Myanmar back on the international stage and on the world map. It is also about Myanmar's foreign policy, under the guidance of Aung San Suu Kyi, becoming more independent and active on the international stage.

The first foreign dignitary to be received by the newly inaugurated President and Minister for Foreign Affairs was Chinese foreign minister Wang Yi on 5 April 2016. It was believed by some observers that the visit was purposely allowed to happen to illustrate the NLD government's pragmatic approach to relations with China. In the view of the Chinese foreign ministry, the visit, at the invitation of the Myanmar foreign minister, "showcase[d] the importance attached by the two sides to further developing bilateral ties" and it "demonstrate[d] their resolve and confidence in fostering bilateral relations".[40] Wang stated that "the China-Myanmar 'paukphaw friendship' goes beyond differences in social institutions . . . and the changes in Myanmar's inner affairs will not alter China's Myanmar policy" (Xinhua 2016).[41] In addition, Wang reportedly told his counterpart that "on the basis of respecting Myanmar's sovereignty and territorial integrity, China stands ready to play a conducive role in Myanmar's national reconciliation in accordance with Myanmar's needs and willingness" (ibid).[42] In a friendly diplomatic gesture, Aung San Suu Kyi replied: "As the new Myanmar government aspires to promote national reconciliation and achieve stability and development, the substantial assistance from China in various aspects means a great deal for our country" (ibid).[43]

A month later, on 6 June 2016, both President Htin Kyaw and State Counsellor cum Foreign Minister Aung San Suu Kyi together journeyed to Laos, chair of ASEAN, as their first foreign trip. This was the least controversial overseas trip by the NLD government and, so far, is the only strip on which both the president and the State Counsellor travelled together. President Htin Kyaw went to Russia in May 2016 for a Russia-ASEAN summit, to Mongolia in July for the 11th ASEM Summit, and to Vietnam in October for the 8th CLMV Summit and 7th ACMECS Summit. For bilateral state visits, he journeyed to India in August 2016 and to Cambodia in February 2017.

The de facto head of government, State Counsellor Aung San Suu Kyi's first destination for a bilateral visit was to Thailand in June 2016, where the most significant number of Myanmar labour migrants live. This trip was closely followed by her visit to China in mid-August. Her trip to China was thought to be a pragmatic choice of destination as China plays an instrumental role in Myanmar's stability and security. Her earlier critical tone regarding China was replaced by a pragmatic outlook in her dealings with the giant neighbour. She was cordially received by Chinese leadership and graciously extended special treatment. When the Chinese side raised the issue of the resumption of the Myit-Sone hydropower dam project, she simply replied that the matter was under review by a special committee and she would follow the committee's recommendations. September 2016 was the busiest month for the State Counsellor as it saw her travel extensively, first to Laos for the 28th and 29th ASEAN summits and related summits, then to the United Kingdom and the United States, and finally to the UN to attend the General Assembly. As a gesture of support for the NLD government, the US announced the lifting of sanctions and removed significant barriers to doing business in Myanmar. Then in the middle of October, the State Counsellor went to India for the BIMSTEC summit where she also had separate bilateral meetings with the presidents of Sri Lanka and China. She visited Japan in early November where she secured Yen 40 billion in development aid and reciprocated a visit to Singapore a month later.

Within nine months after coming to power, foreign ministers from China, Italy, Canada, The United States, Thailand, Turkey, Luxenberg, and the Netherlands came to Myanmar to meet their counterpart. In January 2017, foreign ministers from Ukraine and Czech Republic and the Foreign Secretary of the United Kingdom visited the country. Visits by the Singaporean prime minister in June 2016, the Laotian president in August, and the Thai deputy prime minister in February 2017 showcased the importance of neighbouring countries in Myanmar's external relations.

However, the NLD's foreign policy agenda has been significantly impacted by the crisis in northern Rakhine state. Despite opposition from

Rakhine and military members of the Hluttaw, in August 2016 the NLD government sought to internationalize the Rohingya issue by forming an advisory commission led by former UN Secretary General Kofi Annan "to propose concrete measures for improving the welfare of all people in Rakhine State" and "to provide recommendations to the Government of Myanmar to secure peace and prosperity in Rakhine State".[44] The security situation deteriorated rapidly, however, and in early October 2016, the western border area of northern Rakhine state saw armed attacks on security outposts run by the police carried out by a group of Rohingya extremists, the Aarakan Rohingya Salvation Army (ARSA).[45] The situation prompted a counterinsurgency operation by Myanmar's military forces and there were accusations about gross violation of human rights against Rohingya people. The situation in Rakhine State deteriorated rapidly after the Kofi Annan Commission delivered its final report on August 25 2017. Coordinated attacks on police outposts took the lives of more than twelve state security officers, provoking far more extensive "clearance operations" by the Tatmadaw (Kyemon 2017, pp. 1, 8).[46]

At the time of writing, more than 750,000 people have reportedly fled the violence, and the United Nations has declared this to be "ethnic cleansing". The situation in Rakhine State has been further amplified as a result of mounting international pressure on the NLD government to investigate claims of mass graves and crimes against humanity. Accusations leveled against the NLD government are not merely by activists and international media outlets but also by UN representatives and the UN Human Rights Council.

This situation has had a significant impact on Myanmar's foreign relations. Following the initial October 2016 attacks, the UN Human Rights Council called for a fact-finding mission to Myanmar to investigate alleged human rights violations in northern Rakhine state. Some ASEAN countries, particularly Malaysia and Indonesia, responded by pressing the Myanmar government to address the issue more fully. The Malaysian government requested an informal ASEAN foreign minister retreat be held to discuss the matter. The subsequent meeting, chaired by the Laotian foreign minister, was convened in Yangon at the invitation of the Myanmar government. Open and frank discussions were held during which the Myanmar government agreed to give humanitarian access, most importantly the delivery of food, to Indonesia and Malaysia.

By early 2017, the UN—the Office of the UN High Commissioner for Human Rights—released a report on the Rohingya issue, which resulted in immense pressure on the NLD government and the State Counsellor. In August, when the Tatmadaw launched counter-terrorism operations in northern Rakhine state, in response to the series of attacks against security outposts and civilians, the UNSC, some international organizations, and several countries criticized the State Counsellor for the military's alleged excessive use of force and violation of Rohingya's rights. The Rakhine crisis triggered a UN General Assembly resolution, put forward by the Organisation of Islamic Cooperation (OIC) and adopted by a vote of 122 to 10 with 24 abstentions on 24 December 2017. The resolution called for an end to the military campaign against Rohingya militants and for the appointment of a UN special envoy.

As a result of the crisis in Rakhine state, Aung San Suu Kyi's reputation as a champion of human rights and an icon of democracy has been substantially diminished. In addition, her political support in the west has seen an about-turn and she is now facing serious challenges in maintaining a progressive foreign policy agenda. In the midst of the Rohingya crisis, China proposed a three-phase plan—ceasefire, bilateral dialogue between Myanmar and Bangladesh, and reconstruction of Rakhine state—for resolving the crisis, inviting both Min Aung Hlaing and Aung San Suu Kyi to Beijing, in November 2017, to demonstrate their diplomatic support.

Meanwhile, the Tatmadaw has engaged in defence diplomacy. Due to the existence of several EAOs along bilateral borders, the military has maintained bilateral military-to-military relations with neighbouring countries, especially with China, Thailand, and India. In this way, Myanmar's China policy and Thailand policy are partially influenced by the Tatmadaw as it has an extensive network of contacts between the two militaries, which are equally influential in their respective countries. Moreover, through its arms procurement program, it has also played a leading role in shaping Myanmar's external relations. To illustrate this point, one could indicate the Tatmadaw's procurement of *Yak-130* advanced training aircraft from Russia, *K-8 and Y-8/12* aircraft from China, *Super Dvora Mk 3 FAC* warships from Israel, and *JF-17 Thunder* multi-role fighters from Pakistan. These activities can easily distract or undermine the NLD government's foreign policy objectives. Having said that, the Tatmadaw is also cooperative with the NLD leadership on matters of foreign policy. For instance, up until the Rohingya crisis, the Tatmadaw has

been cooperating with military institutions from the UK— Royal Military
Academy Sandhurst (RMAS), the US—Daniel K. Inouye Asia-Pacific Center
for Security Studies (DKI-APCSS) and Japan—National Defence Academy
(NDA) for training its officers, in addition to training programs in China
and India.[47] It has also refrained from going beyond the normal diplomatic
relations or deepening military ties with North Korea and has suspended
the procurement of North Korean military equipment.

## CONCLUSION

The NLD's electoral victory in November 2015 has transformed the party
from an opposition of almost three decades into a ruling party with a
clear mandate. However, the party has little experience in governing a
country and running a bureaucracy. In addition, it seems that the party
lacks sufficient resources and preparation for the execution of any major
policy reforms. There is growing criticism of the NLD government both
internally and externally for their failure to deliver campaign promises
and their increasingly authoritarian tendencies. At one point, just weeks
before the NLD took the office, Nicholas Farrelly remarked:

> The irony is that even at the best of times the NLD is far from a model of
> transparency or democratic management. The authoritarian instinct starts at
> the top, with Aung San Suu Kyi's iron grip on decision-making... What has
> not changed is her requirement for intense personal loyalty and her need to
> remain the final authority. The NLD is her vehicle and, as its revolutionary
> leader, she makes no apologies for taking charge (Farrelly 2016).[48]

In many ways, this assessment remains relevant and correct. There is
no denying that Aung San Suu Kyi perceives herself to be the embodiment
of national will, a perception which could have significant implications for
democratization in Myanmar. What we are witnessing now in Myanmar
with the initial period of NLD administration is that the NLD and its
leadership have increasingly marginalized the role of mediating institutions
in governance. Whilst political freedom and freedom of expression have
improved under the NLD administration, rule of law and access to justice
is still very weak. Despite their strong mandate and political legitimacy,
the NLD government has been cautious and seems reluctant to take major
steps in transforming Myanmar's polity and political structure.

In terms of civil-military relations, the Tatmadaw, though it may not
necessarily be satisfied with the present situation, has so far managed to

retain its influence over civilian affairs in defence and national security. It is not yet prepared to tolerate any structural changes that would undermine its national political role in the Constitution, the basic principles it has laid down for national unity, or its institutional autonomy. Yet there is room for cooperation and for making the current pattern of civil-military relations work for their mutual benefit.

On the one hand, the NLD has suspended its attempts to alter the current framework of civil-military relations through constitutional amendments. On the other hand, it has sought to minimize the Tatmadaw's "image of influence" by circumventing the latter's control over parliament and policy making. However, there is no visible signs of transformation in civil-military relations. In the meantime, the Tatmadaw has tried public relations exercises to improve its image, which includes, among others, disaster relief operations, mobile medical teams for local people, and disciplinary actions against military personnel for violations of ethical codes and humanitarian law. For example, Min Aung Hlaing's attendance of the Martyr's Day ceremony, as Commander-in-Chief, on 19 July 2016 was the first time in almost five decades. The Tatmadaw's security operations in Northern Rakhine state since August 2017 has also drawn considerable support from local population and many Myanmar people in the name of counter-terrorism. Despite the Tatmadaw's effort to improve its public image, the heavy-handed nature of security operations in the country's north and some other ethnic minority areas as well as its business activities remain sources of public discontent and thus major obstacles to improving its public image.

In the case of the ongoing peace process and national reconciliation, the NLD government has more or less decided to adopt the Tatmadaw's position as its own default policy. Since they came to power, Aung San Suu Kyi has followed the path laid out by the predecessor government, even at the expense of its own initial skepticism towards the NCA process. There is little change in form and substance of the peace negotiation process and the NLD government continues to follow the NCA framework and its procedural commitments, such as the Union Peace Conference, political dialogue and so on. In this area too, as the most important stakeholder, the Tatmadaw has exercised substantial influence over the policy and process, whilst the NLD government has fine-tuned the process.

Foreign relations is one of the key areas where the NLD government has been relatively confident in making changes due to the international popularity of Aung San Suu Kyi. The NLD's foreign policy statements reflect a neoliberal worldview with a greater reliance on "international institutions". If this assumption is correct, it suggests that there is a considerable shift in worldview, from a realist to a neoliberal orientation in international affairs. However, in terms of actual conduct of external relations, contrary to public expectations of pro-US and anti-China policy, the NLD government maintains pragmatic and balanced relations with all major powers, especially with the US, China and Russia. However, the NLD government's stance on Rakhine State and other human rights accusations has attracted growing pressure from the international community and caused considerable strain in relations with western countries and UN bodies. The crisis in Rakhine state is likely to continue to complicate Myanmar's delicate foreign policy and push them further towards powers such as Russia and China. This is further complicated by the role of the military in influencing foreign affairs, defence diplomacy and border security.

Overall, there are concerns that there may be longer-term implications for the NLD government's apparent unwillingness to follow through on campaign promises. Indeed, the public's support for the NLD and Aung San Suu Kyi may continue to erode in the coming years if they do not see significant changes in their lives. Moreover, the Tatmadaw's lead in certain policy areas, such as the peace process and foreign relations, could also cast doubt on the NLD's commitment to building a genuine democratic government.

There is very little evidence to suggest that the NLD government has brought about any major transformations in the political structure of the country or to its democratic consolidation. Therefore, to take a cautious view, Myanmar has remained a defective democracy with a powerful military occupying reserved political domains and prerogatives. In spite of its strong mandate and political legitimacy, the NLD's lack of expertise, political will and centralized decision making means that the government has merely survived on the political capital generated by decades of public support and sympathy for its charismatic leader, Aung San Suu Kyi. Without seriously nurturing and strengthening institutions indispensable for democratic governance, many fear that it will be difficult for Myanmar's democracy to survive.

## Notes

1   The NLD party overwhelmingly controls both houses of *Pyidaungsu Hluttaw* (Union Assembly) and was thus entitled to nominate two vice-presidential candidates. In the meantime, the Tatmadaw (Myanmar Armed Forces) sent 110 officers and 56 officers to *Pyithu Hluttaw* and *Amyotha Hluttaw*. One of the three vice-presidential candidates, Htin Kyaw, was then elected by the electoral college of all members of Pyidaungsu Hluttaw, in full strength of 664 (440 for Pyithu Hluttaw and 224 for Amyotha Hluttaw), as President of the Republic of the Union of Myanmar.

2   *Global New Light of Myanmar* Newspaper (31 March 2016)

3   Deputy Minister for Agriculture was dismissed in November 2016 and replaced with another appointment. On 1 August 2017, Union Minister for Electricity and Energy was permitted to resign and Union Minister for Construction concurrently holds the position.

4   On that day, Win Myint was elected as speaker and T. Khun Myat as deputy speaker. Two days later, the first regular session of the second Amyotha Hluttaw was convened and elected Mahn Win Khaing Than as Speaker. On 8 February 2016, the first session of Pyidaungsu Hluttaw was convened and it was presided over by Mahn Win Khaing Than as its speaker, and he will remain in that position for 30 months before turning it over to the Speaker of Pyithu Hluttaw.

5   Shoon Naing, "Demonstrators take aim at section 66(d)", *Myanmar Times* – online edition (23 January 2017). <https://www.mmtimes.com/national-news/yangon/24644-demonstrators-take-aim-at-section-66-d.html> [accessed on 2 February 2017].

6   Thomas Fuller, "Aung San Suu Kyi and Myanmar General Meet, Taking Steps Toward Sharing Power", *The New York Times*, 2 December 2015 <http://www.nytimes.com/2015/12/03/world/asia/myanmar-aung-san-suu-kyi-meets-president-army.html?mwrsm=Facebook&_r=1>.

7   Ei Ei Toe Lwin, "General and NLD Leader Talk Transition", *Myanmar Times*, 26 January 2016<http://www.mmtimes.com/index.php/national-news/18648-general-and-nld-leader-talk-transition.html> [accessed 1 February 2018]; Ei Ei Toe Lwin & Htoo Thant, "Military Chief, NLD Leader Begin Third Meeting", *Myanmar Times*, 17 February 2016 <http://www.mmtimes.com/index.php/national-news/19038-military-chief-nld-leader-begin-third-meeting.html> [accessed 1 February 2018].

8   This message was repeatedly mentioned by the Commander-in-Chef on 20 October 2015, 28 February 2016, and 9 March 2016.

9   *Myawaddy* Newspaper, 24 February 2016.

10  On 10 March 2016, the NLD, which dominated and controlled both houses of Pyidaungsu Hluttaw, nominated two Vice-Presidential candidates. While the Pyithu Hluttaw's nominee, U Htin Kyaw, who is not a member of Hluttaw, did not have any issue, there were some issues about the Amyotha Hluttaw's nominee and member Henry Van Thio's background. During the screening process by the seven-member committee for eligibility, Tatmadaw representative, Major General Than Soe, although neutral, suggested that Htin Kyaw's background should be reviewed thoroughly in accordance with the law. But he opposed the nomination of Henry Van Thio as the nominee had lived in a foreign county for six years and it was necessary to refer this case to constitutional tribunal to define what it was meant by "the state's permission" as prescribed in the constitution. This was because the constitution requires a [vice-]presidential candidate to continuously stay in the country for 20 years except when [s]he is staying overseas with the permission of the state. In both cases, the other six members of the committee voted in favour and the candidacies were approved. On 15 March 2016, 360 out of 652 members of Pyidaungsu Hluttaw voted for Htin Kyaw as the President, and Ex-General Myint Swe and Henry Van Thio as Vice-Presidents. Although the latter's case could have been brought to the constitutional tribunal, the military delegates did not pursue it.

11  Tatmadaw representatives were against the appointment of two individuals, Khin Htay Kywe and Twar Kyin Paung, nominated respectively by the speakers of Pyithu Hluttaw and Amyotha Hluttaw, on the grounds of "insufficient information on the profiles" to ascertain the eligibility for the posts and asked the nominees to resubmit fuller CVs; but they said that they would support them if they met the criteria after reviewing the full CVs. The Speaker of Pyithu Hluttaw strongly intervened in this case and the military's proposals to discuss whether the nominees were eligible for the post were voted down (195 for, 435 against and 4 abstention for Daw Khin Htay Kywe and 196 for, 432 against and 5 abstention for U Twar Kyin Paung).

12  On 30 March 2016, the draft of "State Counsellor Bill" was circulated among Hluttaw members for parliamentary debate and approval. On 1 April, the bill was debated in Amyotha Hluttaw where three Tatmadaw representatives, along with four other members of the house, strongly argued against it and asked for revisions. Nevertheless, the bill was immediately approved in the NLD dominated house (135 for, 70 against and 2 abstention). Then, on 5 April 2016, in Pyithu Hluttaw, three Tatmadaw representatives and one member from the USDP proposed 13 amendments to the bill; all were rejected by vote. Brigadier General Maung Maung proposed that the title of the bill and the position itself should be changed from "state counsellor" to "presidential counsellor", because the use of the term "state" is the embodiment of all three branches of power

and the Constitution encouraged the separation of power as much as possible. He also said that the term "democratic federal Union" in the preamble of the bill was contrary to a basic principle of the Constitution that holds that "the Union practises genuine, disciplined multi-party democratic system"; therefore, it should be changed accordingly. In addition, he proposed that the holder of the office should answer only to the President and not to the Hluttaw as stated in the bill. Then, he told the house that the bill violated constitutional provisions and if the house pushed it through without revision of the draft, the military representatives would boycott the voting. Despite the boycott by the military delegates by standing up in protest, the bill was approved by the house by 262 votes in favour, 22 against and 9 abstentions, out of a total of 406 eligible voters.

13  Colonel Khin Maung Tun told the house that the Rakhine issue was a domestic one and an investigation commission with local experts had thoroughly studied and submitted a report on the issue. If another commission was necessary, it should be formed in consultation with Pyidaungsu Hluttaw, "As seeking opinions and advice from a foreigner-led commission for a domestic affair or nationalities affair, because of international pressure or for better international image, is inappropriate and could undermine the interests of the local people; thus it is necessary to reconsider the formation of an advisory commission", the Colonel said. Despite the support from the military delegates, the motion was defeated as it secured only 148 votes, with 250 against and one abstention.

14  Mary Callahan. "Fears of Military coup in Myanmar are exaggerated", *Nikkei Asian Review*, 14 December 2016 < https://asia.nikkei.com/Viewpoints/ Mary-Callahan2/Fears-of-military-coup-in-Myanmar-are-exaggerated?n_ cid=NARAN012> [accessed 17 December 2016].

15  With regard to the "Provisions on State of Emergency", Articles 410 – subsequently 411 (in accordance with 410), Article 412 – subsequently 413 (in accordance with 412), and Article 417 - subsequently 418 (in accordance with 427), require the President to consult with NDSC. Articles 410 and 412 are for subnational administrative units and Article 417 is for the whole country. Articles 410 and 411 are to deal with the failure of administrative functions in local subnational administrative units and they do not provide specific individual or institution to implement the "state of emergency". The president may form an appropriate body or a suitable person and entrust such body or individual with the executive power. (No mention of transfer of power or authority to the Tatmadaw.) But in accordance with Article 410, consultation with NDSC is necessary. Articles 412 and 413 are to deal with situation endangering the lives, shelter and property of the public in local subnational administrative units. Article 412(A) requires consultation with NDSC. But Article 412(B) includes an "exceptional clause": If all members are unable to attend

the NDSC meeting, then the president may declare state of emergency after coordinating with C-in-C, Deputy C-in-C, Minister for Defence and Minister for Home Affairs – four persons. Later, the declaration will be submitted to the NDSC for approval as soon as possible. Article 413(A) indicates the "aid to civil power" while Article 413(B) says that the president may declare "Military Administration" and transfer of [local administrative] power to the C-in-C, who, in turn, may empower a suitable "military authority". Therefore, article 412 and article 413 encompass "state of emergency", "aid to civil power", and "military administration".

16  NDSC members are the president, two vice-presidents, two speakers of the Pyidaungsu Hluttaw, Commander-in-Chief, Deputy Commander-in-Chief, and ministers for defence, home affairs, border affairs, and foreign affairs. Since either president or one of vice-presidents is a nominee from the Tatmadaw, together with three ministers for defence, home affairs, and border affairs who are from the military, the Tatmadaw secures six out of 11 members.

17  Mizzima. "Political parties call for Intervention by NDSC", *Mizzima*, 30 November 2016 <http://www.mizzima.com/news-domestic/political-parties-call-intervention-ndsc> (accessed 2 December 2016); Kyaw Thu, Win Naung Toe and Win Ko Ko Latt. "Political Parties Seek Myanmar Security Council's Intervention in Rakhine Crisis", *Radio Free Asia*, 29 November 2016 <https://www.rfa.org/english/news/myanmar/political-parties-seek-myanmar-security-councils-intervention-in-rakhine-crisis-11292016154247.html> [accessed 2 December 2016].

18  Two Vice Presidents, two speakers of Hluttaw and the Minister for Border Affairs were absent while Minister for State Counsellor Office was present.

19  The Irrawaddy. "The Unpublicized Summit in Naypyidaw", *The Irrawaddy*, 5 February 2017 <http://www.irrawaddy.com/news/burma/the-unpublicized-summit-in-naypyidaw.html> [accessed 11 February 2017].

20  Whtut. "Suu Kyi warns ethnic armed organisations not to quickly sign NCA", Eleven, 26 August 2015 <http://www.elevenmyanmar.com/local/suu-kyi-warns-ethnic-armed-organisations-not-quickly-sign-nca> [accessed 30 August 2015]; Mizzima. "Suu Kyi warns ethnic organisations over signing NCA", *Mizzima*, 27 August 2015 <http://www.mizzima.com/news-domestic/suu-kyi-warns-ethnic-organisations-over-signing-nca> [accessed 30 August 2015].

21  Nay Thar. "Why Aung San Suu Kyi did not sign the NCA", *Mizzima*, 8 December 2015 <http://www.mizzima.com/news-domestic/why-aung-san-suu-kyi-did-not-sign-nca#sthash.VFgbVZJe.dpuf> [accessed 10 December 2015].

22  *Kyemon* Newspaper (28 April 2016), p. 1.

23  *Kyemon* Newspaper (17 May 2016), p. 1.

24  *Kyemon* Newspaper (17 May 2016), p. 3.

25  The UWSA and other three EAOs did not participate in the Mai Ja Yang conference.

26  David Mathieson, "Self-Defeating Approach to Peace in Myanmar", *Asia Times Online*, 28 July 2017, <http://www.atimes.com/article/self-defeating-approach-peace-myanmar/> [accessed 6 September 2017].

27  Lun Min Mang. "Ethnic unity urged as summit kicks off in KIA-held Mai Ja Yang", *Myanmar Times*, 27 July 2016 < https://www.mmtimes.com/national-news/21583-ethnic-unity-urged-as-summit-kicks-off-in-kia-held-mai-ja-yang.html> [accessed 3 December 2016)].

28  Details will be discussed later.

29  For example, UWSA asked for "Wa State". Likewise, Shan (red) also ask for creation of a federating state.

30  Paper presented at the 21st Century Panglong Conference.

31  *The Global New Light of Myanmar*, 27 March 2015 < http://www.globalnewlightofmyanmar.com/speech-delivered-by-commander-in-chief-of-defence-services-senior-general-thayaysithu-min-aung-hlaing-at-the-parade-of-the-70th-armed-forces-day-held-on-27th-march-2015/> [accessed 28 March 2015].

32  The National League for Democracy (NLD). *National League for Democracy 2015 Election Manifesto* - official translation, (Yangon: the NLD, 2015), p. 8.

33  Lally Weymouth, "Aung San Suu Kyi: 'I'm going to be the one who is managing the government'", *The Washington Post*, 19 November 2015 <https://www.washingtonpost.com/opinions/aung-san-suu-kyi-im-going-to-be-the-one-who-is-managing-the-government/2015/11/19/bbe57e38-8e64-11e5-ae1f-af46b7df8483_story.html> [accessed 20 November 2015].

34  *Myanma Alin* Newspaper, 7 April 2016

35  Ibid.

36  *Kyemon* Newspaper, 18 April 2016.

37  This statement comes from Foreign Minister Daw Aung San Suu Kyi's briefing for foreign diplomat at the Ministry of Foreign Affairs in Naypyitaw on 22 April 2016. The video clip is downloaded by the author.

38  It is from the same source.

39  *Kyemon* Newspaper, 23 April 2016.

40  This statement comes from Foreign Ministry Spokesperson Lu Kang's Regular Press Conference in Beijing on 6 April 2016. It could be accessed at http://www.fmprc.gov.cn/mfa_eng/xwfw_665399/s2510_665401/t1353604.shtml

41  Xinhua. "Chinese FM meets with Myanmar's Suu Kyi", *Xinhua News*, 6 April 2016 <http://news.xinhuanet.com/english/2016-04/06/c_135252904.htm> [accessed 7 April 2016].

42  Ibid.

43  Ibid.

44  This information comes from the homepage of the Rakhine Commission, particularly in its statement about the commission. It could be accessed at <http://www.rakhinecommission.org> [accessed 1 February 2018].
45  For detail, please consult with the reported entitled "Myanmar: A New Muslim Insurgency in Rakhine State" published by the International Crisis Group, Myanmar. The report was released on 15 December 2016 and it can be accessed and downloaded at <https://www.crisisgroup.org/asia/south-east-asia/myanmar/283-myanmar-new-muslim-insurgency-rakhine-state> [accessed 1 February 2018].
46  *Kyemon* Newspaper, 26 August 2017.
47  In the wake of Rohingya crisis since August 2017, the UK sent Myanmar military trainees back home. The Tatmadaw also issued a statement that it will never send trainees to the UK.
48  Nicholas Farrelly. "The NLD's iron-fisted gerontocracy", *Myanmar Times*, 1 February 2016, <https://www.mmtimes.com/opinion/18759-the-nld-s-iron-fisted-gerontocracy.html> [accessed 5 February 2016].

## References

Callahan, Mary. "Fears of Military Coup in Myanmar are Exaggerated", *Nikkei Asian Review*, 14 December 2016 < https://asia.nikkei.com/Viewpoints/Mary-Callahan2/Fears-of-military-coup-in-Myanmar-are-exaggerated?n_cid=NARAN012> [accessed 17 December 2016].

Ei Ei Toe Lwin & Htoo Thant, "Military Chief, NLD Leader Begin Third Meeting", *Myanmar Times*, 17 February 2016 <http://www.mmtimes.com/index.php/national-news/19038-military-chief-nld-leader-begin-third-meeting.html> [accessed 18 February 2016].

Ei Ei Toe Lwin, "General and NLD Leader Talk Transition", *Myanmar Times*, 26 January 2016 <http://www.mmtimes.com/index.php/national-news/18648-general-and-nld-leader-talk-transition.html> [accessed 5 February 2016].

Farrelly, Nicholas. "The NLD's Iron-Fisted Gerontocracy", *Myanmar Times*, 1 February 2016, <https://www.mmtimes.com/opinion/18759-the-nld-s-iron-fisted-gerontocracy.html> [accessed 5 February 2016].

Fuller, Thomas. "Aung San Suu Kyi and Myanmar General Meet, Taking Steps Toward Sharing Power", *The New York Times*, 2 December 2015 <http://www.nytimes.com/2015/12/03/world/asia/myanmar-aung-san-suu-kyi-meets-president-army.html?mwrsm=Facebook&_r=1> [accessed 5 December 2015].

Kyaw Thu, Win Naung Toe and Win Ko Ko Latt. "Political Parties Seek Myanmar Security Council's Intervention in Rakhine Crisis", *Radio Free Asia*, 29 November 2016 <https://www.rfa.org/english/news/myanmar/political-parties-seek-myanmar-security-councils-intervention-in-rakhine-crisis-11292016154247.html> [accessed 2 December 2016].

Lun Min Mang. "Ethnic Unity Urged as Summit Kicks off in KIA-held Mai Ja Yang", *Myanmar Times*, 27 July 2016 < https://www.mmtimes.com/national-news/21583-ethnic-unity-urged-as-summit-kicks-off-in-kia-held-mai-ja-yang.html> [accessed 3 December 2016].

Mathieson, David. "Self-Defeating Approach to Peace in Myanmar", *Asia Times Online*, 28 July 2017 <http://www.atimes.com/article/self-defeating-approach-peace-myanmar/> [accessed 6 September 2017].

Mizzima. "Political Parties Call for Intervention by NDSC", *Mizzima*, 30 November 2016 <http://www.mizzima.com/news-domestic/political-parties-call-intervention-ndsc> [accessed 2 December 2016].

_____. "Suu Kyi Warns Ethnic Organisations Over Signing NCA", *Mizzima*, 27 August 2015 <http://www.mizzima.com/news-domestic/suu-kyi-warns-ethnic-organisations-over-signing-nca> [accessed 30 August 2015].

Nay Thar. "Why Aung San Suu Kyi did not Sign the NCA", *Mizzima*, 8 December 2015 <http://www.mizzima.com/news-domestic/why-aung-san-suu-kyi-did-not-sign-nca#sthash.VFgbVZJe.dpuf> [accessed 10 December 2015].

Shoon Naing, "Demonstrators Take Aim at Section 66(d)", *Myanmar Times*, 23 January 2017 <https://www.mmtimes.com/national-news/yangon/24644-demonstrators-take-aim-at-section-66-d.html> [accessed 2 February 2017].

The Irrawaddy. "The Unpublicized Summit in Naypyidaw", *The Irrawaddy*, 5 February 2017 <http://www.irrawaddy.com/news/burma/the-unpublicized-summit-in-naypyidaw.html> [accessed 11 February 2017].

The National League for Democracy (NLD). *National League for Democracy 2015 Election Manifesto* - official translation. Yangon: the NLD, 2015.

Weymouth, Lally. "Aung San Suu Kyi: 'I'm Going to be the One who is Managing the Government'", *The Washington Post*, 19 November 2015 <https://www.washingtonpost.com/opinions/aung-san-suu-kyi-im-going-to-be-the-one-who-is-managing-the-government/2015/11/19/bbe57e38-8e64-11e5-ae1f-af46b7df8483_story.html> [accessed 20 November 2015].

Whtut. "Suu Kyi Warns Ethnic Armed Organisations not to quickly sign NCA", *Eleven*, 26 August 2015 <http://www.elevenmyanmar.com/local/suu-kyi-warns-ethnic-armed-organisations-not-quickly-sign-nca> [accessed 30 August 2015].

Xinhua. "Chinese FM meets with Myanmar's Suu Kyi", *Xinhua News*, 6 April 2016 <http://news.xinhuanet.com/english/2016-04/06/c_135252904.htm> [accessed 7 April 2016].

*The Global New Light of Myanmar* (GLNM) Newspaper – 28 March 2015.
*The Global New Light of Myanmar* (GNLM) Newspaper – 31 March 2016.
*Myawaddy* Newspaper (2016) – 24 February 2016.
*Kyemon* Newspaper (2015) – 28 March 2015.
*Kyemon* Newspaper (2016a) – 18 April 2016.

*Kyemon* Newspaper (2016b) – 23 April 2016.
*Kyemon* Newspaper (2016c) – 28 April 2016.
*Kyemon* Newspaper (2016d) – 17 May 2016.
*Kyemon* Newspaper (2017) – 26 August 2017.
*Myanma Alin* Newspaper (2016) – 7 April 2016.

# 10

## FROM CEASEFIRE TO DIALOGUE: THE PROBLEM OF "ALL-INCLUSIVENESS" IN MYANMAR'S STALLED PEACE PROCESS

Lwin Cho Latt, Ben Hillman, Marlar Aung and Khin Sanda Myint

A key principle underpinning Myanmar's peace process has been the principle of "all-inclusiveness." Initially, this principle represented a commitment to the inclusion of all ethnic armed organizations (EAOs) in a nation-wide ceasefire agreement (NCA) that would serve as a basis for reconciliation, political dialogue and negotiation over constitutional reform. When President Thein Sein's transition government (2011–16) began making peace overtures, the principle was widely embraced by EAOs and the military, and ultimately enshrined in the text of the NCA. When Aung San Suu Kyi's National League for Democracy (NLD) came to power in 2016 and made the peace process its top priority it, too, championed the principle of "all-inclusiveness." However, as the NLD and the military struggle to convince more EAOs to sign the NCA, it has become apparent that, for all its good intentions, the principle of "all-inclusiveness" has become an obstacle to the peace process. This chapter reviews the peace process to date to examine the problems that have emerged around the concept of "all-inclusiveness." Drawing on interviews with signatories of the NCA and other key stakeholders,[1] the chapter highlights a central challenge confronting the government in its efforts to advance Myanmar's stalled peace process.

## THE ORIGINS OF INCLUSIVENESS

When the NLD was elected in 2015 as Myanmar's first civilian government in more than half a century, NLD leader Aung San Suu Kyi declared that reconciliation with the country's fractured and warring ethnic groups would be her government's top priority. The NLD assumed leadership of a peace process initiated under Thein Sein's Union Solidarity and Development Party (USDP)-led transition government (2011–16). As part of wider efforts to end six decades of conflict and to build a new political culture based on compromise and consensus, President Thein Sein made peace overtures to the country's multiple ethnic armed organizations (EAOs). The USDP government acknowledged that peace could not be achieved if the central government refused to negotiate political settlements with EAOs or provide stability and development opportunities for the frontier regions. From 2011 the government initiated a series of talks and confidence-building measures designed to eventually lead to peace agreements and political integration into a reformed federal democratic system of government. Thein Sein's breakthrough overtures with EAOs were based on the following principles: "no surrender of arms, equality in negotiation, political dialogue, all-inclusiveness, constitutional amendment, and democratic federal union" (see Maung Aung Myoe, Chapter 9 this volume).

Among the principles underpinning peace negotiations, "all-inclusiveness" quickly assumed prominence. The USDP government and EAOs agreed that a lasting peace needed to be comprehensive—that all warring parties needed to reach agreement with the government about their future in the union. It was thereby determined that a nationwide ceasefire agreement (NCA) would be the first step in working towards a comprehensive peace. Although the NCA did not address many of the more challenging issues such as the future status of armed groups, and the precise nature of power and revenue sharing under a restructured federal system, the NCA was nevertheless seen as a breakthrough when the government and negotiating teams tentatively agreed on the draft text of the NCA on 31 March 2015.

Over the following months the USDP government went to great lengths to win support for the NCA, inviting the "all-inclusive" participation of fifteen EAOs, among which fourteen had previously signed bilateral ceasefire agreements with the government. Despite the government's efforts over the following months, only eight armed groups signed the NCA before the 2015 elections were held and political power was transferred to the NLD.[2] Groups refusing to sign defended their position on the principle of all-inclusiveness, arguing that all ethnic armed groups should be invited to participate, and not only those which had signed ceasefires. Groups that signed the NCA hailed from the Thailand border region where there had been limited or no fighting in recent years. Non-signatories largely hailed from the China border region and included EAOs such as the Kachin Independence Organization (KIO), which had been engaged in intense fighting with the Tatmadaw through its armed wing the Kachin Independence Army (KIA) since the breakdown of a seventeen-year ceasefire agreement in 2011 (see Sadan 2016). Another key player was the United Wa State Party/Army (UWSP/A) which, although not engaged in hostilities with the Tatmadaw since a 1989 ceasefire, governs two de facto independent enclaves with the backing of its own 30,000 well-trained and well-armed troops.

Signatories to the NCA saw advantages in signing on as a means of advancing to the next stage of the peace process. According to an interviewee from a signatory organization, "[t]he main objective of the NCA is to hold political dialogues while both sides are under ceasefire... The NCA is the preliminary step for next political goals to be achieved." According to many interviewees, because there was no major disagreement of the text of the NCA, it was inevitable that all EAOs would eventually come to sign it. However, some respondents also pointed to different motivations for signatories compared to non-signatories. Signatories were keen to proceed in the expectation that it would lead to greater opportunities for political participation via the formation of political parties. As a reward for their stated commitment to sign the NCA, the Karen National Union (KNU), All Burma Students' Democratic Front (ABSDF) and Restoration Council for Shan State/Shan State Army-South (RCSS/SSA-S) were de-listed as Unlawful Associations. The government also removed the ABSDF and RCSS/SSA-S from the List of Terrorist Organizations.

Some signatory organizations highlighted the potential of the NCA to allow for the legalization and expansion of group-controlled businesses. And because signatories had not been involved in recent fighting, joining the NCA involved less complications and risks. By contrast, many non-signatories had been involved in recent fighting and were faced with a potentially more precarious post-NCA situation, especially regarding disarmament, demobilization and reintegration (DDR) arrangements (see also Jones 2016). As one respondent explained, some EAOs became concerned that the NCA would lead to a "negotiated surrender" rather than a politically "negotiated settlement." Several powerful EAOs controlled large swathes of territory and needed firm political guarantees about what they would receive in return for bringing these territories into the fold. Respondents highlighted EAOs' concerns with future mechanisms for political participation including the registration of political parties, since many rejected the 2008 Constitution in accordance with which political parties would need to be formed and registered.

Among signatories and within government circles it was widely believed that another reason for non-signatory hesitation was the potential impact of the NCA on EAO-operated businesses such as jade mining and (illegal) logging, the revenues of which had funded the insurgencies (Jones 2016; Woods 2016). As one interviewee suggested, several EAOs have freely run lucrative businesses across wide territories. Following the NCA, it is likely that their spheres of operations would be significantly reduced. These differing, even opposing, concerns highlighted the wide gap between the interests of NCA signatories and non-signatories, and the challenge of the "all-inclusiveness" principle, which continued to serve as the basis of the peace process. The government and military continued to insist that all EAOs must sign the NCA before political negotiations could commence. Non-signatories also embraced the "all-inclusiveness" principle, but argued that the principle should be taken to mean that all EAOs be invited to join the NCA and not just those that had previously signed bilateral ceasefires with the government.[3]

Despite the government and military's firm position on the status of the NCA, they did not seek to exclude recognized non-signatories in the first post-NCA political dialogue—that is, EAOs originally invited to sign the NCA. The government and military did not recognize three EAOs that had taken up arms since the commencement of the peace process in 2011, namely the Arakan Army (AA), Ta'ang National Liberation Army

(TNLA), and the Myanmar National Democratic Alliance Army (MNDAA). However, as will be discussed later in the chapter, these groups and some other non-signatories argued that the exclusion of these groups contradicted the "all-inclusiveness" principle to which the government and military maintained firm commitment. The first dialogue—the Union Peace Conference—was subsequently held in January 2016 during the lame duck period between the 2015 elections and the transition of power to the NLD. In holding the conference, the transition government sought to advance the process in accordance with the roadmap outlined in the NCA and to secure a major political achievement before handing over the reins of government to the NLD. However, in a repudiation of Thein Sein's transition government, nearly all of the invited non-signatories declined the invitation.

## ALL-INCLUSIVENESS UNDER THE NLD

When the NLD came to power Aung San Suu Kyi declared the peace process to be a top priority. She upheld the principle of all-inclusiveness as understood by the previous government and the military that all groups must sign the NCA as a first step to political negotiations. Promising to lead the peace process personally, Aung San Suu Kyi reorganized the institutional architecture, and rebadged the Union Peace Conferences as the 21st Century Panglong. This was in reference to the 1947 Panglong Conference convened by Aung San Suu Kyi's father, General Aung San, in which several ethnic groups agreed to join an independent Burma in return for full autonomy over local affairs. Aung San Suu Kyi chaired the first Panglong 21 Peace Conference in Naypyitaw at the beginning of September 2016. In what was seen as a very positive development, nearly all armed groups attended. However, it was clear that non-signatories were able to attend because the conference was considered more of a symbolic launch of the NLD's renamed and reorganized peace process rather than a substantive political dialogue (International Crisis Group 2017).

Following the conference, the NLD made it a priority to bring non-signatories into the NCA. The government focused on the United Nationalities Federal Council (UNFC), a coalition of several non-signatory groups founded in 2011.[4] The UNFC embraces the principle of all-inclusiveness, but in contrast to the definition of all-inclusiveness emphasized by the government and military, the coalition of non-signatories interpreted the principle to mean that the government should work to create the conditions under which all groups would be able to sign the NCA.[5] The UNFC thus proposed nine conditions for signing the NCA including "the declaration by the military of a nationwide ceasefire within twenty-four hours of agreement on the nine points; commitment to the establishment of a federal union with full guarantees for equality and self-determination; international participation in ceasefire monitoring; and an independent and partly international commission to mediate disputes" (International Crisis Group 2017).

Government and UNFC negotiators had made little headway when the UWSP stormed into the process, asserting leadership of non-signatory groups, including many combat-active EAOs, by convening a summit at its Pangkham headquarters in February 2017. A ceasefire between the USWP/A and the Tatmadaw had successfully held since 1989, and the group had since largely stayed out of the fray. The UWSP-led summit resulted in the creation of a new coalition, subsequently named the Federal Political Negotiation and Consultative Committee (FPNCC), which signed on several UNPC members, and advocated for a new NCA or comprehensive revision to the current document. The FPNCC, also known as the "Wa alliance", produced a "principles document" outlining its understanding of the "Panglong Spirit" as the basis for political negotiations as well as its members' expectations for those negotiations including major constitutional and political reforms. The FPNCC proposed a draft text of a new nationwide ceasefire agreement, which required the Tatmadaw to cease military operations and voluntarily withdraw from "conflict areas of national minorities" seven days prior to signing, delimit a ceasefire boundary between "the National Defense Force and all revolutionary armed powers", and agree not to trespass or interfere with local affairs beyond the demilitarized ceasefire boundary.[6]

Citing the principle of "all-inclusiveness", the FPNCC also insisted upon the participation of all armed groups in the peace process, including the AA, TNLA and MNDAA. The FPNCC's invocation of "all-inclusiveness", reflected a different interpretation of the principle, and was in stark contrast to the government and Tatmadaw's position that groups taking up arms since the commencement of the peace process in 2011 should not be recognized. Naypyitaw claimed that AA was an offshoot of KIO/KIA and should be represented by the larger Kachin group. The government suggested that TNLA and MNDAA could be admitted to the NCA regime, but only if they first surrendered their weapons. According to one of our respondents, a government official, Naypyitaw wanted to avoid the moral hazard of bestowing official recognition on new groups taking up arms against the Union. However, the government later suggested, as a compromise, that the three excluded groups could participate in talks if they temporarily surrendered their arms to a third-party EAO, and issued a public announcement of their disarmament.

Most NCA signatories appeared to support the government's position on the three excluded EAOs, highlighting the divide between the signatory and non-signatory blocs. Noting that AA had no political ideology or program and was but a follower of the KIA, one signatory representative told us "[w]e fifteen EAOs are the major ones; if we take into consideration new small armed groups our problems will not be solved." For NCA signatories that we spoke with, including the KNU and Democratic Karen Buddhist Army (DKBA), the "all-inclusiveness" principle meant that all groups would eventually be included in a political bargain, but it did not mean that all groups had to be included in the NCA or initial talks.

Another reason that some NCA signatories were motivated to push ahead with the process was the fact that many represented sub-state territorial units, and were thus content with government proposals to grant greater autonomy to localities rather than to the states. This lay in contrast to the expectation of many non-signatories that full autonomy (self-determination) be granted to the states, including the right to have state-level constitutions. Some smaller signatory groups appeared satisfied with the benefits, including local organizational autonomy and business opportunities, afforded them as an apparent result of joining the NCA regime.[7] An example is the Pa-O National Liberation Organization (PNLO), which signed a ceasefire with the military in 2012, and has since used its organization to build a wide portfolio of business interests in the southern Shan state, including tourism assets around Inlay Lake. The experience of the PNLO and other similar small organizations highlights the differences between the interests and concerns of the NCA signatory group and the non-signatory group.

The Wa alliance, by contrast, made it clear that its members were not ready to move forward with political negotiations until a new or substantially revised NCA could be negotiated—a position the government considered to be a major setback for the peace process. The UNFC coalition of non-signatories, which the government recognizes, had at least accepted the NCA text and was seeking to negotiate conditions under which their members could sign. The main reason for the UWSP's late-stage intervention in the wider peace process appeared to be a lack of trust in the military's intentions.[8] Since the signing of the NCA by Thai border-area groups, the Tatmadaw has intensified offensive operations against non-signatories in the north, creating the prospect that the hitherto secure Wa enclaves might become encircled by Tatmadaw troops. This threat appears to have provided the impetus for military cooperation among non-signatory EAOs in the China border regions in the form of a northern alliance, and motivation for the formation of a new negotiating bloc in the form of the FPNCC (Wa alliance).

Trust was further undermined by missteps in earlier talks with UWSP, which only became publicly known in May 2017 during the second Panglong 21 conference. At the conference, which Wa alliance members were invited to attend as "special guests" due to last-minute diplomatic intervention by China, the Wa alliance presented the government with three position papers. One of these position papers—*Process of Wa State's Consultation and Negotiation with the Government of Myanmar on Modification of Nationwide Ceasefire Agreement* (Central Committee of United Wa State Party, 30 April 2017), documented a series of secret talks between UWSP, the military and government in March and April 2017 that were previously unknown. Despite the military's public insistence that the NCA not be subjected to further revision, the Wa alliance document suggests that the military expressed openness to some minimal changes to the NCA. However, the Wa alliance insisted on more profound changes that would retain "the original content of NCA to maximum extent", but that would also "take care of the interests of all parties involved" (cited in International Crisis Group 2017). The document then cited examples of the government and military acting in bad faith following the secret talks, "humiliating" Wa alliance members with public statements such as a 21 April 2017 announcement by one of Aung San Suu Kyi's senior bureaucrats, Zaw Htay, insisting that the nationwide ceasefire text must be signed without modification, and a 24 April 2017 statement by Deputy Commander-in-Chief General Soe Win that "not one word of the NCA can be changed" (cited in International Crisis Group 2017).

Trust has been further undermined by major military operations against EAOs, including the Wa alliance member Kachin Independence Army (see

Jones 2016). The trust deficit is manifest in the Wa alliance and military's expectations for the DDR process, which is a critical component of the ceasefire agreement. The Tatmadaw insists that DDR commence during the ceasefire period to lay groundwork for reconciliation through political means, which is in line with provisions in the 2008 Constitution. However, the Wa alliance rejects the notion that the 2008 Constitution be strictly observed since major changes to the constitution are a key EAO demand and that constitutional reform has been agreed to in principle by the government, and, implicitly, by the military in its recent references to a future "federal" Myanmar. The Tatmadaw insists that DDR is sine qua non of any ceasefire deal. One of our respondents, a military officer, expressed concern that EAOs might take advantage of the ceasefire "to mobilize new armed personnel and to rearm in order to become larger armed organizations." The officer argued that, to prevent such a development, "[it] is compulsory for EAOs to transform their combatants into Border Guard Forces (BGF) or People's Militia Forces (PMF) as part of DDR." In fact, it has been Tatmadaw policy since the beginning of the current peace process that ceasefire participants be transformed into BGFs, which are treated as integrated Tatmadaw battalions, and PMFs, which are responsible for supporting the Tatmadaw by gathering information about other armed groups and providing navigational support during combat operations (see Buchanan 2016). The former combatants of several ceasefire groups have already transformed into such units. However, pressure to form a BGF was one of the reasons why the Kachin ceasefire broke down in 2011, with hostilities continuing to the present (Jones 2016, p. 109). Wa alliance members thus reject the Tatmadaw's BGF/PMF proposal, and advocated instead to transform their forces into State/Region-level armies modeled on China's People's Armed Police. The Wa alliance has suggested that these armies could then be incorporated into a future federal army. The government and Tatmadaw insist that the Tatmadaw already serves as a federal (union) armed force and that EAO combatants must integrate into it. When we asked a military officer in what sense the Tatmadaw could be considered a federal army, he cited the fact that the Tatmadaw already counted members of various ethnic groups among its ranks. The differences of opinion on such fundamental issues highlight the wide gap between NCA signatories and non-signatories and present a major challenge for an "all-inclusive" peace process.

Another military officer we interviewed suggested that rehabilitation and development programmes could also commence during the ceasefire period, and that the Tatmadaw could use such programs to help EAO combatants integrate into communities after the deactivation of their forces. However, the suggestion that the Tatmadaw would be involved in the reintegration of ex-EAO combatants lies in stark contrast to the proposals recently put forward by the Wa alliance (FPNCC) that demand the Tatmadaw remain outside the boundary of any agreed ceasefire line. In fact, a major difference between the Wa alliance's proposed ceasefire agreement and the NCA are the provisions on the ceasefire arrangements. The Wa alliance proposal seeks to establish more detailed ceasefire arrangements, including territory demarcation and force separation, going beyond the provisions of the NCA.

In another major departure from the government and Tatmadaw's position, Wa alliance members have argued that security sector reform (SSR) should take place before DDR. As one of our respondents observed, many northern EAOs believe it would be impossible to achieve equality in negotiations in the absence of arms. And Wa alliance EAOs have expressed concerns that the Tatmadaw will repeat past practices and use the ceasefire period to weaken them militarily. Concerns about the Tatmadaw's intentions have been further undermined by recent military operations in the China border areas, including intensive clashes in Kachin state. Accordingly, in contrast to the government and military's position on the ceasefire and dialogue process, EAOs engaged in combat such as the KIA propose political dialogue in advance of a ceasefire agreement (see Gabusi, Chapter 6 this volume).

The government and Tatmadaw reject the idea that SSR should take place before DDR. One of our military respondents argued that SSR only needs to be undertaken in advance in the case of failed states that have limited resources and are unable to protect citizens. The respondent argued that Myanmar has good state capacity and is already gradually becoming a peaceful and developed nation. However, although our respondent insisted that DDR must come first, he suggested that the scope of DDR was negotiable: "We need to discuss the definition of DDR; it may be that it is not necessary to surrender weapons, but only to stop using weapons for armed struggle against the government and Tatmadaw." Despite expressing the possibility of such a compromise, the government and Tatmadaw continue to insist that groups must sign the NCA before political dialogue can begin in earnest, reflecting the Tatmadaw's unyielding interpretation of the "all-inclusiveness" principle.

## STANDING FIRM ON ALL-INCLUSIVENESS

The government and Tatmadaw continued to emphasize their version of "all-inclusiveness" at the second Panglong 21 conference held in late May 2017. At the conference Tatmadaw Commander-in-Chief Senior General Min Aung Hlaing declared "the standpoint of Tatmadaw on peace process is to stand firmly on the NCA path, which is the peace strategy of our country." The Commander-in-Chief noted that NCA signatory regions were already benefiting from development as a direct result of the NCA, and refused to offer benefits to non-signatories. He further admonished non-signatories, warning that the pursuit of alternatives to the current NCA signified rejection of "the establishment of a Union based on peace, democracy and federalism. As such, we have to assume that the attempt is tantamount to grabbing power and splitting from the Union through armed struggle" (Global New Light of Myanmar 2017). The senior general's comments were an explicit rejection of the Wa alliance proposals, which the group had presented to the government before departing from the conference two days before it concluded.

However, the second Panglong 21 conference showed signs that some NCA signatories were sympathetic to a more accommodating approach to non-signatories, lending the principle of "all-inclusiveness" its widest possible meaning. According to our respondents, some groups were concerned that the military would exert physical pressure on groups and regions not covered by the NCA, and that conflict would continue, or get worse, undermining prospects for a comprehensive peace. In his opening remarks at the conference General Mutu Say Poe, Chairman of the KNU, the largest of the signatory organizations, declared it "essential that we leave no one behind in this peace process" (cited in International Crisis Group 2017).

However, despite entreaties from the UNFC and the Wa alliance for a more generous interpretation of "inclusiveness", the Tatmadaw continued to reject the inclusion in the NCA regime of several ethnic-based organizations, namely the AA, TNLA, MNDAA, Arakan National Congress (ANC), Wa National Organization (WNO), and Lahu Democratic Union (LDU). These groups were initially not invited to sign the NCA in October 2015 because they did not previously sign bilateral ceasefires, and only groups with bilateral ceasefires could participate in the NCA. Since then the Tatmadaw have raised further reason for excluding these ethnic-based organizations. According to the Tatmadaw, the ANC, the WNO, and the

LDU are not eligible to join the NCA because they do not have active military operations nor do they have well-defined territories, although these groups have separate agreements allowing them to attend political dialogues. In the case of the MNDAA, TNLA and AA, the Tatmadaw rejects their participation on the grounds that they were affiliates of larger EAOs and that they continue to be involved in clashes with the military. The Tatmadaw has held firm to the rejection of these EAOs, which have, since November 2016, begun to fight alongside the KIA in a new military alliance. In keeping with earlier USDP government policy, the Tatmadaw and government refuse to engage with these EAOs until they surrender their arms. However, even some NCA signatories have expressed concern that the exclusion of these groups could derail the quest for nationwide peace. One of our respondents noted that guerilla groups could wage war against the military no matter their size, and suggested that "[b]oth government and Tatmadaw should make room for them in the peace process." In Kayin State, we spoke with a senior Buddhist monk who had been a leading voice in the local peace process. He expressed the view that "all-inclusiveness" should be a political instrument for those who decline to participate in the NCA regime. He explained that the KNU had good reasons to leave the UNFC and sign the NCA and that this was a positive development for the Karen people, but he also recognized that not all groups were in the same situation.

Perhaps recognizing the Tatmadaw and government's narrow interpretation of "all-inclusiveness" as an obstacle to the peace process, some staff at the National Reconciliation and Peace Centre (NRPC), the official organization tasked with administering the peace process under Aung San Suu Kyi's direct leadership, have touted the possibility of a compromise. One NRPC officer told us "[w]e might accept the participation of the ANC, LDU, and WNO[9] in the first category of groups to sign the NCA. The other three groups (AA, TNLA, and MNDAA) could perhaps join as a second category and be allowed to discuss the peace process, together with the KIA, as they have requested. However, the NLD government must also take into consideration the Tatmadaw's strong views on these three groups." The comments highlight a further divergence of views between the government and Tatmadaw on the scope of inclusiveness.

Indeed, while the government has generally followed the previous USDP government and the Tatmadaw in adopting a narrow interpretation of "all-inclusiveness" in the context of the NCA, the government has adopted an expanded interpretation of the term in relation to the wider peace process. Since the first Panglong 21 conference State Counselor Daw Aung San Suu Kyi and her NLD government have used the term "all-inclusiveness" to embrace wider public participation in political dialogue, including by non-EAO civic organizations representing women, youth and other interests. The government has also established forums and state-level dialogues in parallel to the political dialogue with EAOs that are intended to facilitate civil society and wider public engagement in the process. Several youth and women's organizations and networks have sought to secure a place within these formal structures. Although such steps are hailed as a positive development for Myanmar's peace process, they also highlight the myriad ways in which the "all-inclusiveness" principle is understood and invoked as part of the peace process.[10]

## CONCLUDING REMARKS

The government, military, NCA signatories and non-signatories all agree on an "all-inclusive" peace process. However, each party imbues the principle with different meaning, which has created a stumbling block for the peace process. The military uses "all-inclusiveness" in the narrowest sense, insisting that it covers the participation of recognized groups in the NCA as a mandatory first step to dialogue. For NCA signatories, the principle refers to the gradual inclusion of all EAOs in the peace process, even without signing the NCA. For some non-signatories represented by the UNFC, "all-inclusiveness" requires compromises by the government and military to make signing the NCA possible. For other non-signatories, including members of the increasingly powerful Wa alliance, "all-inclusiveness" means further negotiation about and revision to the text of the NCA. For the government, the principle of "all-inclusiveness" is deployed in two ways—on the one hand the government adheres to the Tatmadaw position on the NCA; on the other hand, the government invokes "all-inclusiveness" to embrace the participation of non-EAO actors in political dialogue, thus merging the peace and reconciliation process with broader constitutional and political reform. This is a promising development given the challenge of forging an inclusive national identity on the basis of which a new federal state can be imagined (see Medail, Chapter 12 this volume).

However, despite the different ways in which the "all-inclusiveness" principle is understood and invoked in Myanmar's peace process, the government and Tatmadaw's application of the term to the sequencing of ceasefire and dialogue is what matters most. The government and Tatmadaw maintain that all eligible groups must sign the nationwide ceasefire agreement before political negotiations can commence in earnest. The government and military's position on "all-inclusiveness" contains two further restrictions: (i) only groups with bilateral ceasefires previously in place can be admitted to the NCA regime, and (ii) the NCA text cannot be renegotiated. The government and Tatmadaw's position is at odds with the UNFC and the FPNCC coalitions representing non-signatories, and increasingly at odds with the interests and stated preferences of several NCA signatory organizations that are determined to move ahead with political dialogue and not wait indefinitely for non-signatories to join the NCA.

The government and military's steadfast adherence to its version of "all-inclusiveness" risks slowing the momentum of the peace process and could possibly derail it. Only a handful of EAOs have signed on to the NCA since it was launched in 2015 and signatories are mostly groups from the Thai border area where hostilities had already ceased. The major combat active EAOs are not signatories, challenging the very notion of a "nationwide" ceasefire. The UNFC continues to demand that certain conditions be met before its members sign. As negotiations with the UNFC dragged on, a new coalition of non-signatories emerged in the form of the FPNCC, demanding wholesale revision of the document. The FPNCC represents Myanmar's most powerful EAOs as well as those engaged in some of the most intense fighting with the Tatmadaw, but the government and Tatmadaw refuse to recognize the coalition.

The Myanmar government and military now face a conundrum. If they insist on "all-inclusiveness" in the current NCA regime before proceeding to substantive political negotiations, and continue to fail in bringing more groups into the NCA, current signatories might lose patience with the process. The KNU, the most influential signatory group, has already expressed a desire to move forward with political negotiations, and other signatories expressed a similar preference by suggesting that "all-inclusiveness" can be understood to mean that all EAOs will join the process eventually if not right now. The government cannot afford to take NCA signatories for granted. A former commander of the DKBA, an NCA signatory, told us that if his group encountered "problems in its dealings with the NLD" they would return to their original position of fighting for self-determination. If the government were to lose one of the signatories, especially a powerful one such as the KNU, the peace process would derail (see also Thawnghmung 2017).

At the same time, although the government and military have had discussions with the UNFC about the conditions under which the group's members might sign, the emergence of the Wa-led FPNCC and its demands for a comprehensive revision of the NCA present the government and Tatmadaw with a conundrum. The Wa alliance represents major EAOs, the participation of which is essential for the success of the peace process. However, responding to the demands of the UNFC and the FPNCC could open potentially interminable talks. But the conundrum does highlight the fact that the NCA was an imperfect document that left many details of the ceasefire arrangement unspecified, and this is something the government and Tatmadaw will have to deal with, either within the parameters of the NCA through a process of negotiated revision or through separate agreements.

Regardless of the next steps, it has become clear that the government and military's understanding of an "all-inclusive" peace process is increasingly at odds with the preferences and demands of EAOs—NCA signatories and non-signatories alike. Given the difficulties of accommodating various demands for changes to the NCA, the government and military should consider de-linking the NCA from political dialogue, while continuing to seek maximum participation in both. This would be a bold step given the military and government's firm statements on the matter. Nevertheless, Myanmar urgently needs to begin serious dialogue on constitutional reform and the design of a federal system, which all parties now embrace. Indeed, a federal solution for Myanmar's divisions has emerged as one item everyone agrees upon. Perhaps it is time to bring all of the country's EAOs into political dialogue to discuss the details of the federal solution; and to invite all EAOs to the table as full participants and not just as "special guests," as NCA non-signatories have been treated in previous peace conferences. Such a move would constitute a significant confidence-building measure. Further, learning from its experience in previous peace conferences, if the government can successfully manage constructive and inclusive dialogue about Myanmar's future political architecture, EAOs might come to realize that they have more to gain from investing in such a future than they do in perpetuating the status quo. This will require further compromise on the part of the government and military, and both will need to tread carefully so as not to create a moral hazard for future disruptions. However, given the lack of trust and the recent escalation of hostilities, Myanmar's government and military have little choice but to compromise on their version of "all-inclusiveness" if they are to secure a sustainable peace.

**Table 10.1 Members and Non-members of the Nationwide Ceasefire Agreement**
*Source: Myanmar Peace Center (MPC), NCA Lat Mhat Htoe Htar Thaw Taing-Yin-Thar Lat Net Kaing Ah Phwet Myar and NCA Lat Mhat Ma Htoe Hhar Thaw Taing-Yin-Thar Lat Net Kaing Ah Phwet Myar Sar Yin [List of NCA-EAOs and Non-NCA EAOs] (Yangon: MPC, 2016).*

| NCA Regime (Major Invited Armed Groups) | | | | Non-NCA Regime | |
|---|---|---|---|---|---|
| NCA Members | | Non-NCA Members | | First Category (UNFC/ NCCT) | Second Category (UNFC/ NCCT) |
| Non-NCCT | UNFC/NCCT | Non-NCCT | UNFC/ NCCT | | |
| 1.ABSDF[1]<br>2. RCSS[2] | 3. ALP<br>4. CNF[5]<br>5. KNU[4]<br>6. PNLO[5]<br><br>NCCT[3]<br>7. KNU/ KNLA-PC<br>8. DKBA | 9. NDAA<br>10. NSCN-K<br>11. UWSA | 12. KIO<br>13. KNPP<br>14. NMSP<br>15. SSPP | 16. ANC<br>17. LDU<br>18. WNO | 19. MNDAA<br>20. TNLA<br><br>NCCT3<br>21. AA |

1 ABSDF is semi-aligned with the UNFC, and represented in SD.
2 RCSS is not a member of UNFC or NCCT.
3 KNU/KNLA-PC, DKBA, and AA are non-UNFC members, but joined the NCCT.
4 KNU withdrew from the UNFC in September 2014.
5 CNF and PNLO were expelled from UNFC for their willingness to ignore the UNFC's understanding of "all-inclusiveness" by separately seeking to sign the NCA.

## Table 10.2 Peace Plans

Source: Burma News International (BNI). "Deciphering Myanmar's Peace Process: A Reference Guide 2015". Burma News International (BNI).First Edition: August 2015, 43.

| | 2011 | 2012 | 2013 | 2014 |
|---|---|---|---|---|
| **Govt** | 1. Enter the legal fold (disarm and transform into BGF/PMF, i.e. submit to Myanmar Army control)<br><br>2. Set up political parties to contest elections<br><br>3. Set up business | Three-Phase Plan<br><br>1. State Level Ceasefire (5 pts)<br><br>2. Union Level Ceasefire (8 pts)<br><br>3. Create political parties to amend the constitution | 1. NCA<br><br>2. Negotiations to agree framework for political dialogue<br><br>3. Political dialogue | 1. NCA signing<br><br>2. Drafting pol'l framework<br><br>3. Pol'l dialogue (DDR/SSR)<br><br>4. Union Convention<br><br>5. Signing Union accord<br><br>6. Interim Arrangement<br><br>7. Implementation of the union accord |
| **EAOs** | 1. Political talks (amend the Constitution to ensure ethnic self-determination)<br><br>2. Agreement on Federal Union<br><br>3. Approval and ratification by parliament | Six-point Plan (UNFC)<br><br>1. Host a meeting with CBOs and EAOs<br><br>2. A meeting (govt and EAOs) representatives monitored by int'l community<br><br>3. Referenda in each ethnic state to ratify the agreement<br><br>4. A meeting with all ethnic people to talk about peace<br><br>5. Tripartite dialogue (govt, EAOs & democratic groups)<br><br>6. Implementation of agreement reached within a set time-frame | 1. Drafting the political framework<br><br>2. NCA<br><br>3. Political dialogue<br><br>4. National accord | 1. NCA signing<br><br>2. Drafting political framework<br><br>3. Pol'l dialogue (SSR/DDR)<br><br>4. Union Convention<br><br>5. Signing Union accord<br><br>6. Interim Arrangement<br><br>7. Implementation of the union accord |

## Notes

1    Interviews were conducted with government officials, military officers, representatives of EAOs, and United Nations advisors engaged in the peace process. Interviews were conducted in Hpa-an township, Kayin State and Naypyitaw in April and June 2016 respectively, in Shan state in July 2017, and again in Naypyitaw in August and September 2017.

2    NCA signatories: 1) All Burma Students' Democratic Front (ABSDF), 2) Restoration Council for Shan State (RCSS), 3) Arakan Liberation Party (ALP), 4) Chin National Front (CNF), 5) Karen National Union (KNU), 6) PaO National Liberation Organization (PNLO), 7) KNU/KNLA Peace Council (KNU/KNLA-PC), and 8) Democratic Karen Benevolent Army (DKBA). Groups invited to join the NCA, but that have thus far declined to sign are: 1) National Democratic Alliance Army (NDAA), 2) National Socialist Council of Nagaland-Khaplang (NSCN-K), 3) United Wa State Army (UWSA), 4) Kachin Independence Organization (KIO), 5) Karenni National Progressive Party (KNPP), 6) New Mon State Party (NMSP), and 7) Shan State Progressive Party (SSPP).

3    According to the USDP government, three non-signatory organizations—Arakan National Congress (ANC), Lahu Democratic Union (LDU), and Wa National Organization (WNO) were not invited to join the NCA, because they had been militarily inactive for a long period of time and because they do not control or seek to control territory. However, these groups were invited to participate in political dialogue, including the Union Peace Conferences. The Myanmar National Democratic Alliance Army (MNDAA), Ta'ang National Liberation Army (TNLA) and Arakan Army (AA) comprise a second category of non-signatories. The government and military insist that these three groups must lay down their arms as a precondition to joining the NCA.

4    The UNFC boasted twelve members at its peak, but the number of members has since decreased to five: Karenni National Progressive Party (KNPP), New Mon State Party (NMSP), Shan State Progress Party/Shan State Army (SSPP/SSA), Arakan National Council (ANC), and Lahu Democratic Union (LDU). Among departed members, the NMSP and SSPP-SSA withdrew with the apparent intention of joining the NCA, although the groups' plans remain unclear at the time of publication. The KNU withdrew in 2015 over disagreements about proposed revisions to the NCA. In November 2015, the UNFC suspended the Chin National Front-CNF and Pa-O National Liberation Organization-PNLO for failing to adhere to the UNFC's all-inclusiveness principle and for separately seeking a ceasefire with the government. In May 2017, in a final major blow to the umbrella organization, the Kachin Independence Organization (KIO), Wa National Organization (WNO), Ta'ang National Liberation Army (TNLA), and Myanmar National Democratic Alliance Army (MNDAA) withdrew from the

UNFC to join the UWSA-led Federal Political Negotiation and Consultative Committee (FPNCC).

5   Interview with United Nations liaison to the Myanmar Peace Process, September 2017.
6   The full text of the document is available at: fpncc.org/FederalPeaceAgreement.pdf (accessed 21 October 2017).
7   Interview with United Nations liaison to the Myanmar Peace Process, September 2017.
8   Interview with representative of Wa United Party, July 2017.
9   The WNO has since merged with the UWSP.
10  Some observers have called for the direct inclusion of civic groups in formal committees and processes. See Vanessa Johanson. 2017. "Creating an Inclusive Burmese Peace Process." Center for Security Studies and United States Institute of Peace (May).

## References

Buchanan, John. "Militias in Myanmar." The Asia Foundation (July), 2016. <http://asiafoundation.org/wp-content/uploads/2016/07/Militias-in-Myanmar.pdf> [accessed 30 October 2017].

Burma News International. "Deciphering Myanmar's Peace Process: A Reference Guide 2015". *Burma News International (BNI)*. First Edition (August), 2015.

*Constitution of the Republic of the Union of Myanmar (2008)*. Naypyitaw: Printing and Publishing Enterprise, Ministry of Information, Union of Myanmar. <http://www.burmalibrary.org/docs5/Myanmar_Constitution-2008-en.pdf>. Accessed 12 July 2016.

Institute for Security and Development Policy. Myanmar's Nationwide Ceasefire Agreement (October), 2015.

International Crisis Group. "Building Critical Mass for Peace in Myanmar". Asia Report No. 287 (29 June 2017). <https://www.crisisgroup.org/asia/south-east-asia/myanmar/287-building-critical-mass-peace-myanmar> [accessed 10 September, 2017].

Johansen, Vanessa. "Creating an Inclusive Burmese Peace Process". United States Institute for Peace and Centre for Security Studies (May), 2017. <http://www.css.ethz.ch/en/services/digital-library/articles/article.html/cc29da43-3b91-43b8-a9fb-087fa3f03468/pdf> [accessed 30 October 2017].

Jones, Lee. "Understanding Myanmar's Ceasefires Geopolitics, Political Economy and State-Building". In *War and Peace in the Borderlands of Myanmar: The Kachin Ceasefire, 1994–2011*, edited by Mandy Sadan. Copenhagen: NIAS Press, 2016.

KNU-DOI and Research Institute for Social and Ecology (RISE). Nationwide Ceasefire Agreement: Implementation archives. *KNU-DOI and RISE*, second edition (11 September), 2016.

Mizzima News. "Suu Kyi Warns Ethnic Organisations Over Signing NCA". *Mizzima News* (27 August 2015). <http://www.mizzima.com/news-domestic/suu-kyi-warns-ethnic-organisations-over-signing-nca> [accessed 5 October 2016].

New Light of Myanmar. "The Government of the Republic of the Union of Myanmar today issued Announcement No. 1/2011 dated 18 August 2011". *New Light of Myanmar* (19 August), 2011.

———. "The Republic of the Union of Myanmar, Ministry of Defence: Press Release". *New Light of Myanmar* (29 January), 2013.

San Pwint, (Col.) (Retd.). *Ah Myo Thar Pyan Lal Si Lone Nyi Nyut Yae (or) Hnint Nyein Chan Yae Mhyat Taing Myar* (1988-2004) [National reconciliation (or) peace milestones (1988-2014)]. Myanmar: La-win-pyar, first edition (April), 2016.

Maung Maung Soe. *Nyein Chan Yae Hnint Taing Yin Thar Lat Net Kaing Tat Phawt Myar Ee Pya-tha-nar Saung Par Myar* [Articles on peace and ethnic armed troops' problem]. Myanmar: Thein Min, first edition (August), 2016.

Sadan, Mandy, ed. *War and Peace in the Borderlands of Myanmar*. Copenhagen: NIAS Press, 2016.

Sakhong, Lian H. and Paul Keenan. *Ending Ethnic Armed Conflict in Burma: A Complicated Peace Process (A collection of BCES Analysis and Briefing Papers)*. Burma Centre for Ethnic Studies: Wanida Press, 2014.

Sakhong, Lian H. *Taing Yin Thar Lu Myo Myar Lo Lar Thaw Nyein Chan Yawe Phit Sin* [A search for peace process by ethnic peoples]. Myanmar: Pan-wai-wai, first edition (September), 2013.

Thawnghmung, Ardeth M. "Signs of life in Myanmar's Nationwide Ceasefire Agreement? Finding a Way Forward." *Critical Asian Studies* 49, no. 3 (2017): 379–95.

The Global New Light of Myanmar. "The Government of the Republic of the Union of Myanmar today issued Announcement No. 2/2015 and 3/2015 dated 12 October 2015". *The Global New Light of Myanmar* (13 October), 2015.

The Global New Light of Myanmar. "The greetings extended by Commander-in-Chief of Defence Services Senior General Min Aung Hlaing."(May), 2017. <www.globalnewlightofmyanmar.com/the-greetings-extended-by-commander-in-chief-of-defence-services-senior-general-min-aung-hlaing/> [accessed 11 September 2017].

Woods, Kevin. "The Commercialisation of Counterinsurgency: Battlefield Enemies, Business Bedfellows in Kachin State, Burma". In *War and Peace in the Borderlands of Myanmar*, edited by M. Sadan. Copenhagen: NIAS Press, 2016.

Zaw Oo (Lt. Col.). "Tatmadaw's Policy." Paper presented by a military representative at the 21st Century Peace Conference on 2 September 2016.

# 11

## SECURITIZATION OF THE ROHINGYA IN MYANMAR

Kyaw Zeyar Win

In the last five years the Rohingya community has been subject to renewed waves of anti-Muslim propaganda and accompanying violence, killings and systematic marginalization that aim both to permanently disenfranchise and to displace them from their native land. The relaxation of media restrictions alongside the ongoing political liberalization in Myanmar has exacerbated this situation. The brutal "clearance operations" inflicted upon the Rohingya community in 2017 saw more than 750,000 people flee across the border to Bangladesh amidst reports of extrajudicial killings, sexual violence and arson by Myanmar's state military Tatmadaw. While the United Nations has declared this to be a "textbook example of ethnic cleansing" (UNOHCHR 2017a), the attacks on government targets have validated many Myanmar citizens' long held belief that the Rohingya pose a threat to their nation and an existential threat to Buddhism, the majority religion.

As a result of the attacks on border police posts by the Aarakan Rohingya Salvation Army (ARSA) in October 2016 and August 2017, widespread misinformation and propaganda has inflated the threat of "terrorism", fuelling Myanmar people's sense of insecurity and mistrust towards the Rohingya people. Part of this attitude is embedded in the colonial experience (1824–1948), and the view that Rohingya people came to Rakhine State under the British from neighbouring Bangladesh to address labour shortages on agricultural plantations. In line with global events, people in Myanmar also see the latest string of attacks from ARSA as part of a wider phenomenon of global terrorism taking root in many parts of the world. However, the situation now facing the Rohingya is located in a much more complex history of violence and the ongoing securitization of their community by Myanmar's successive military dictators.

So why has the Rohingya problem become so intractable? This paper explores how people's attitudes to recent events in Rakhine State builds off decades of systemic persecution and institutionalized discrimination of the Rohingya on the pretext of threats to national sovereignty. This article draws on recent literature which describes the way Muslims, and the Rohingya in particular, have been constructed as "other" in Myanmar (Gravers 2015; Nyi Nyi Kyaw 2016; Schissler et al. 2017). In this article I advance this argument, demonstrating how over time successive governments in Myanmar have securitized the Rohingya community based on a narrative of the Rohingya as a foreign "enemy other" and an existential threat to state and society. I then go on to demonstrate how these narratives are reproduced and reinforced by horizontal and bottom-up securitization processes.

This paper is structured into three main sections. Firstly, I provide the relevant historical outline of the Rohingya crisis in Myanmar. Secondly, I explain the underlying social context as a necessary predisposing factor for the socialized securitization of the Rohingya. Finally, I examine various patterns of securitization as a result of different actors and audiences as well as analyse the patterns of securitization on Rohingya communities at top-down, horizontal and bottom-up levels. I argue that although we can observe unidirectional top-down (that is, elite-driven) patterns of securitization inside Myanmar, bottom-up and horizontal patterns of securitization also add to the complexity of solving this issue. As I demonstrate, this also helps to explain why we see this crisis taking on a new scale in the contemporary period despite the change in government and more open democratic environment.

# HISTORICAL BACKGROUND

In examining the securitization of the Rohingya it is important to consider some of the historical dimensions of the current crisis. The people who call themselves Rohingya namely identify with the Mayu frontier area of northern Rakhine State in present day Buthidaung and Maungdaw Townships near the border with Bangladesh. The most common explanation in contemporary Myanmar for the persecution of the Rohingya is related to their national identity and the widespread perception that they are illegal immigrants from Bangladesh. This is bounded in static categories of ethnicity or *taingyintha,* which defines indigenous races as those who have resided in Myanmar prior to 1823 or before British colonialism (Nyi Nyi Kyaw 2015; Cheesman 2017a). Indeed, at the core of the current tensions that we see unfolding today between Muslim and Buddhist communities in Rakhine State is the experience of British colonialism (1824–1948) and the post-colonial fixation with borders and the nation state.

Many Myanmar people believe the Rohingya are descendants of Chittagonian coolies who arrived in Arakan State under the British colonial empire. In the contemporary period, much of this view continues to rest on the notion that the Rohingya have foreign origins and that by claiming indigeneity in the area they pose a threat to the majority Buddhist Rakhine population. Ruled from Calcutta by the British as a province of India,[1] hundreds of thousands of people from across the sub-continent took the opportunity to migrate eastwards to Myanmar during colonial rule (Webb 1912; Thant Myint-U 2006). However, the majority of these people moved to urban centres such as Yangon and Moulmein to take advantage of the increase in trade and business opportunities there. While some Muslims also entered contemporary western Rakhine State during this period, this was based on centuries-old networks of seasonal labour (Webb 1912). Indeed, such bounded conceptions of nationhood ignore the complex history of this region and the shifting geographical lines of Rakhine State as a frontier zone between South and South-east Asia.

Claims by Rakhine nationalists and others in Myanmar that the Arakan Muslim population arrived under the British colonial era are unconvincing. Contrary to present-day conceptualizations of the state, which emphasise stability and continuity, prior to colonial rule the western border region of Myanmar did not exist as one country, but rather as various city-states and kingdoms in which central authority was only gradually asserted.

Archival research suggests, for example, that from the fifteenth to the eighteenth centuries contemporary Rakhine State was caught up in a struggle for territory between Muslim empires expanding west and the Buddhist Arakan kingdom of Mrauk U (Harvey 1925; Charney 1999). This area of modern-day Myanmar was also part of the well-traversed network of overland and sea routes used by Muslim traders, warriors and slaves. Early evidence of Muslim settlement in northern Rakhine State during the time of King Narameikhla (1430–34), for example, includes the adoption of Islamic titles by Arakan kings and the employment of Muslims in the royal administration.[2] There is also evidence that under the Buddhist kingdom of Mrauk U Bengal Muslims were deported to contemporary Rakhine State as slaves (Van Galen 2008).

Further to this, Charles Paton, civil administrator and sub-commissioner of Arakan, wrote an inclusive report on the geography, history, administration, population, culture and traditions, production and military aspects of the region submitted to the British Government prior to colonial rule (Paton 1826). This report revealed that a substantial Muslim population (approximately thirty per cent of the population) had permanently settled in today's Rakhine State before the British invasion in 1823 (ibid., p. 36). Paton also notes the existence of many local Muslim district heads, including notable figures under the Arakan kingdom including former police officers, landlords, judges and a defence minister (ibid.).

The earliest record of the name "Rohingya" is seen in Francis Buchanan's (1798) book, in which he stated: "I shall now add three dialects, spoken in the Burma Empire, but evidently derived from the language of the Hindu nation. The first is that spoken by the Mohammedans, who have long settled in Arakan, and who call themselves Rooinga, or natives of Arakan" (2003 [1798]), p. 55). Historian Michael Charney also suggests that the term Rohingya has been adopted by both Hindu and Muslim people living in Rakhaing since the sixteenth century (2005, p. 23). He also adds: "Rohingya and Rakhaing were not mutually exclusive ethnonyms. Rakhaing's topography may have led to Rohingya and Rakhaing emerging as separate versions of the same term in different geographical contexts that came, in the eighteenth century to be associated closely with the predominant religious makeup of the local area concerned" (2005, p. 31). Indeed, there is much evidence to show that a sizeable Muslim population has resided in Rakhine State for many hundreds of years. However, the experience of colonialism has had a deep impact on the positioning of

Muslims in Rakhine as "other". This is also enhanced by the experience of World War II and the problematic process of decolonization.

The first major sectarian violence between Muslim and Buddhist communities in Rakhine State was during the political and social tumult of the 1940s when the Japanese entered western Myanmar with the support of Burmese and Rakhine soldiers. Communal violence broke out during this time, resulting in the burning of many Rohingya and Rakhine villages and the death of thousands of people in both communities (Leider 2017, p. 196). As a result, Muslims were forcibly driven from the central regions of Myebon and Minbya townships while the northern areas of Buthidaung and Maungdaw were cleared of Rakhine Buddhists (Irwin 1945; Yegar 2002). These incidents appear to have played a significant role in inflaming tensions between Rakhine and Rohingya communities at the time and in coalescing divisions between the northern and central geographic regions.

As a result of the communal violence, at the end of World War II a small group of middle-class, educated Muslims who had fought alongside the British against the Japanese, sought autonomy for the predominantly Muslim community in northern Rakhine State. Like other ethnic nationality projects such as the Karen National Union, political autonomy was believed to be a realistic political project during the decolonization period.[3] Due to little public support and pressure from the new government, the remnants of the Mujahidin surrendered in 1961, but the Rohingya continued to be positioned as a security threat. This argument has also been amplified by the work of various scholars of Rakhine State who position the plight of the Rohingya as a political project of the elite.

Another historical lens through which to delegitimize the Rohingya's claims to citizenship in Myanmar is the view that they constitute a political rather than ethnic identity. Archival research by historian Jacques Leider (2013), in particular, has been used to justify this argument and dismiss the notion of Rohingya as an indigenous ethnic group. Rakhine historians and others, including the former diplomat Derek Tonkin, have used Leider's work to deny legitimacy to the claims of the Rohingya as citizens, claiming that the term "Rohingya" only came into use in the 1950s (e.g. Aye Chan 2005; Chia 2016). However, the widespread conception in Myanmar of ethnicity as static, bounded and stable over time ignores the fluidity and constructed nature of ethnic labels all over the world (Anderson 1991; Baumann 1996; Kymlicka 1995). This is especially prescient in Myanmar, where the protracted nature of ethno-nationalist conflicts in the borderlands has stoked the creation of strong political exile identities (Smith 1991; Cheesman 2002; Harriden 2002). Indeed, Rakhine as an ethnic identity has also changed over time and become more politicized in the last five decades. However, whilst it is important to appreciate that ethnic labels are not created or used in a social vacuum, it is also essential to recognize their purchase amongst everyday ordinary people.

Many Muslims in Rakhine State identify as "Rohingya" and it is important to recognize their claims as an ethnic group native to the country of Myanmar. They refer to Arakan as Rohang and the inhabitants of Rohang are thus called Rohingya in their local language. Despite some contemporary scholars denying the veracity of Rohingya as an ethnic group native to this region, many Arakanese Muslims have internalized this identity and it is now enshrined in their popular discourse. As Kymlicka's important work on minority rights argues, people's bond to their own identity "lies deep in the human condition, tied up with the way humans as cultural creatures need to make sense of their world" (1995, p. 90). And yet, as I will demonstrate throughout the rest of this article, Rohingya people's claims to belonging to Myanmar have been marginalized over successive decades, positioned instead as a foreign "enemy other" and a threat to the nation-state.

## UNDERLYING SOCIAL CONTEXT FOR SECURITIZATION

Since independence was gained from Britain in 1948, ethnicity and religion have played an influential role in state building in Myanmar (Smith 1991). As a result of the successive groups that migrated to Myanmar under British colonial rule from India and Bangladesh, Burmese nationalism in the lead-up to independence had a distinctly racial tone, which was partly directed against Indians who "became the symbol of colonialism and foreign exploitation" (Tinker 1990, p. 40). As a result of the 1930s economic crisis, many Burmese people became indebted to the burgeoning class of Indian money lenders (Chakravarti 1971), leading to significant tensions between the two communities, which saw anti-Muslim riots in 1926 and 1938 concentrated in urban centres across the country.[4] In the early independence period, this resulted in a public discourse which sought to "other" people of South Asian heritage.

"Othering" is the process of perceiving or portraying someone or something as fundamentally different or alien (Holslag 2015). The "foreign other" refers not only to different nationalities, but also to any group in terms of their ethnic identity, religion, political alignment, class or caste, or gender. The process of "othering" is always linked with "reverse mirroring" as whenever we attach a connotation to the "other", we are in essence creating an imaginary "self" (ibid.). Policies introduced in the early independence era thus disenfranchised the remaining Indian landlord class by nationalizing land and banning private lending to farmers. During this period, the Prime Minister U Nu also sought to implement policies to restore Buddhism as the national religion of Myanmar (Egreteau 2011). Integrated as part of the Burmese nationalist movement, ethnic and religious minorities were also progressively "othered", provoking some of the ethnic-nationalist conflicts which still plague the country today (Smith 1991).

In Myanmar, these policies of othering were further enhanced under General Ne Win following the 1962 coup, where xenophobic economic nationalist policies prompted some 125,000 to 300,000 ethnic Indians to flee the country (Taylor 2009, p. 342). During this time, the army also expelled Muslims from its ranks and the Rohingya community was gradually degraded from holders of indigenous ethnic minority status to illegal immigrants from former East Pakistan and later Bangladesh. As a precursor to this shift, the Rohingya language radio program, broadcast from the state as part of the national minorities' language program, was abruptly ceased on 1 October 1964. As a result of these state policies of "othering", Myanmar's majority Buddhists increasingly came to categorize Rohingya people as "Bengali" foreigners. This view was exploited by the state in their campaigns against Rohingya people in the notorious "Nagamin" (Dragon King) Operation of 1978.

On 6 February 1978, General Ne Win launched the Nagamin (Dragon King) Operation targeting Rohingya Muslims in northern Rakhine State. Justified as a counter-insurgency operation against Mujahid fighters and under the supposed "threat" that "Bengalis" from the subcontinent had taken advantage of the state's weak border controls, the military launched a clearance operation displacing more than 200,000 Muslims into Bangladesh (Smith 1991, p. 241). When their return was negotiated by the UNHCR, they were offered "Foreigner Registration Certificates", effectively rendering much of the community stateless (Yegar 2002). The government's view towards the Rohingya during this time is encapsulated by Anand (1978, p. 1100):

The so-called refugees, it is contended, are Bangladesh nationals, who had illegally settled along the border inside Burma. According to the official Burma News Agency (NAB) the "Bengalis" had fled because they lacked proper entry registration papers and also because of instigation by "unscrupulous persons". They wanted to escape the scrutinisation drive, code-named "Nagamani", launched in the region commencing on March 17 to classify the status of residents – bonafide citizens and foreigners; and they preferred to flee rather face detection and prosecution.

The above passage demonstrates the securitization narratives that Myanmar's military government used to justify violence against Rohingya communities over time. This culminated in the removal of Rohingya citizenship in the 1982 Citizenship Act. In his speech on 8 October 1982, General Ne Win argued that anybody in Myanmar with a foreign bloodline was not trustworthy and so they did not deserve to be granted full-fledged citizenship status and full rights, because of the security of the country (The Working People's Daily 1982). According to this definition, only those ethnic groups which were already in Myanmar prior to 1823 could qualify as "national races" (B. *taiyinthar*). Openly using the term *kalar*, a derogatory term used to refer to dark-skinned people from the Indian subcontinent, this was the first concrete legal measure of state policy which came to institutionalize the othering and securitization of select minorities (see also Nyi Nyi Kyaw 2015). Furthermore, this securitizing speech-act came to serve as a justification for successive securitization policies emplaced on the Rohingya community conducted over the subsequent years of the authoritarian military dictatorship (1962–2010).

The 1982 citizenship law left many Rohingya people stateless, leaving them extremely vulnerable to repeated waves of persecution and forced displacement (Cheung 2011; HRW 1996, 2012). By portraying the Rohingya community as the source of a national security threat, a number of military leaders used the state apparatus to reposition the Rohingya issue as part of the militarized security agenda, resulting in the introduction of draconian policies including a birth control order, restrictions on movement, denial of healthcare services and the right to higher education, allegedly for the sake of state security (HRW 1996). In addition, the Border Area Immigration Control Headquarters (*Nel-Sat-Kut-Kel-Ye* or *Na Sa Ka*)[5] was set up in 1992 on the border with Bangladesh to enforce the use of these extraordinary measures in Muslim-dominated regions of northern Rakhine State. As a result, Rohingya people were increasingly cut off from other parts of the country and forced to live in designated areas with severe restrictions on their freedom of movement.

During the 1990s, more intense and systematic securitization of the Rohingya community became the *modus operandi* of the state. During this time government-owned media and newspapers actively positioned Rohingya people as "illegal Bengalis"[6] and a threat to the territorial security and sovereignty of the Myanmar state, playing down their longstanding residence in Rakhine and amicable relations with Buddhists. The deep sense of antagonism between the two communities is reflected on by Alexandra de Mersan, who notes that at the beginning of her research in the 1990s "there was a tendency to deny and even erase any Indian presence and influence in Rakhine culture, and for the Rakhine to throw all Muslims together into one basket" (2016, p. 127). This also involved linking Muslims concentrated in northern Rakhine State to the past Mujahidin rebellion of 1947, as a people who had always been secessionists and sought to separate Rakhine State from its motherland, Myanmar. In line with this view, the slogan "No race faces extinction from being swallowed up by the earth, but by human beings", was posted as a reminder in every immigration office across the country.

By the early 2000s this rhetoric became even more incendiary, as the state media drew from the international war against terrorism to frame the broader Islamic community in Myanmar as part of a global security threat. This included presenting regular news updates of terrorist attacks across the world and reinforcing a prejudiced message throughout the country that: "Not all Muslims are terrorists, but all terrorists are Muslims". While military leaders did not directly link this to the Rohingya community the majority Buddhist population began to perceive Islam as linked to terrorism and their existence in the country as an existential threat to their national religion.

These views were also cultivated internally in the military. For example, Muslims were prohibited from joining the army and other government institutions, and the regime designed refresher courses for public servants to strengthen the abovementioned securitization process. Any public servants seeking promotion were required to attend refresher courses at the PhaungGyi training camp, where intelligence and top military officials provided lectures on national security, highlighting the existential threat of Muslims to the majority Buddhist nation and the Rohingya in particular as a threat to the security of the state and its borders.

Consistent with these ideas, the Burmese consul in Hong Kong, Ye Myint Aung, in February 2009 asserted that the Rohingya could not be considered genuine citizens of Myanmar because they did not resemble any of the officially designated ethnic groups. Describing their appearance as "ugly as an ogre" (BBC 2009), according to Ye Myint Aung, their position as "outsiders" was immediately evident because of their dark skin colour. Examples such as this are widespread throughout Myanmar and have only served to further marginalize the Rohingya and reinforce a message that they are "other" and therefore a threat to Myanmar's national security. Indeed, prejudice against the Rohingya has become ingrained within the majority Buddhist population in Myanmar, including among many ethnic minority groups and pro-democracy campaigners who have adopted the military's labelling of the entire Rohingya population as "Bengali terrorists". This view has come to the fore of public discussions and statements since communal violence in 2012.

The aforementioned social context which resulted in the perception of Rohingyas as "enemy-other" has provided the necessary pre-condition for the socialization of top-down securitization processes. The next section explores how these processes have played out since the political and social reform processes initiated by Thein Sein administration as well as the communal violence which broke out between Muslim and Buddhist communities in 2012. I demonstrate that despite the important steps away from repressive military rule, there are significant hurdles to overcome the securitization processes that have been directed against the Rohingya over the past half century.

## HYPER-SECURITIZATION OF THE ROHINGYA SINCE 2012

The communal violence that broke out in June 2012 was ignited by the reported rape and murder of a 28 year-old Rakhine woman by three Muslim men in Ramree Township, Rakhine State and the subsequent killing of ten Muslim males on a bus. Immediately after the crime, graphic photos of the woman were spread online and shared by thousands of people on social media, provoking a strong backlash from the majority Rakhine Buddhist population. Many netizens perceived this act of violence as part of an existential threat from the majority-Muslim population of northern

Rakhine State and what they saw as the teachings of "evil" Islamic doctrine. This was also instantiated by government propaganda and the influence of hardline Buddhist monks who spread rumours about uncontrolled Muslim births and fears of a renewed separatist insurgency (van Klinken and Su Mon Thazin Aung 2017).

As a result, a wave of deadly communal violence erupted in Rakhine State, which saw many Rohingya people flee into neighbouring Bangladesh amidst reports of rape, extra-judicial killings, the confiscation of land and property, physical torture and other grave human rights abuses (HRW 2012). Over the next fifteen months, Myanmar saw hundreds of civilians killed in communal violence that spread across the country, in attacks which mainly targeted Muslim homes, businesses and mosques (Cheesman 2017b). These events led to a nationwide campaign led by political leaders and hardline Buddhist monks calling for anti-Muslim legislation and popular calls from the Rakhine community to rid the country of what they saw as illegal "Bengali *Kalar*". As I will demonstrate below, these views were only further entrenched as a result of the response from the political elite and a popular Buddhist movement directed against Muslims.

Not only did the government fail to prevent the violent attacks against Muslim communities in 2012, they also played a role in spreading rumours and misinformation. Three main myths in particular were used to justify violence against the Rohingya community. First, hardline nationalist and military elites claimed that the Buddhist Rakhine population, especially in Northern Rakhine State, has the potential to be overrun by large numbers of Bengali immigrants (Rohingya) through illegal migration and uncontrolled population growth in what Nyi Nyi Kyaw (2016) calls a "myth of deracination". This, they argue, would jeopardize the existence of the Rakhine ethnicity that makes up only a minority of the population in the area. Second, prominent public figures claimed that the Rohingya community do not adhere to local cultural traditions and beliefs and that they cannot speak the local Rakhine or Burmese national language. This was presented and perceived by the Rakhine community as evidence of their threat to the ethnic and cultural identity of Rakhine State and as evidence that they are not citizens of Myanmar.[7] Finally, elites also argued that the Rohingya community are trying to increase the Muslim population in Rakhine State through a deliberate process of inter-marriage with non-Muslim women (see also McCarthy and Menager 2017). This rumour added to the perception of the Rohingya community as posing an existential threat to the Buddhist religious identity of Rakhine and Myanmar society as a whole.

These incendiary allegations were frequently repeated in Myanmar's mass media and in the public speeches of many politicians (van Klinken and Su Mon Thazin Aung 2017). The most popular rhetorical term at the time was the portrayal of the Maungdaw District border area as "the Western Door of the Country", in which the word "door" connotes its helpless nature, suggesting that the area is vulnerable to the influx of trespassers and could potentially lead to loss of the country's territory and consequently loss of their religion (that is, Buddhism) and racial identities. For example, on 8 June 2012, when conflict erupted in Maungdaw Township, the director of President Thein Sein's office Zaw Htay posted inflammatory information on his Facebook page, describing Rohingya people as "terrorists" who had come across the border from Bangladesh (see HRW 2013, p. 29). Defending the role of the military "against the Rohingya invaders onslaught" he noted, "since our Military has got the news in advance, we will eradicate them until the end" (cited in Ibid.). His securitizing speech-acts were distributed within hours on social media and widely cited in domestic media. In saying this, he demanded that the international community tolerate any exceptional measures used during the military operation without any outcry of human rights abuses.

Unsurprisingly, the nationalist leaders of the Rakhine National Development party (RNDP) also publicly articulated these perceived security threats in public forums and social media. The RNDP chairman Aye Maung said in an interview with *Venus News* weekly journal (2012) that Myanmar should behave like "Israel", calling on the government to put in place oppressive controls against the Rohingya community within Rakhine State in a systematic and strategic way. He also urged the local Rakhine people to protect the region against illegal immigrant Muslims, citing the 1942 violent attacks between the two communities. Likewise, on 28 June 2012, the secretary general of RNDP, U Oo Hla Saw, argued during a radio interview with the BBC that the Rakhine Buddhist community faced the threat of Islamization. By linking the source of threats to religious identity, the securitizing speech acts galvanized government officials as well as the general public.

On 12 July 2012, President Thein Sein told the UNHCR Chief Antonio Guterres that the government would take responsibility for its own ethnic nationalities, but it was not at all possible to recognize the illegal immigrant Rohingya who are not citizens of Myanmar. He also added that the Rohingya posed a threat to national security and that "the only solution is to hand those illegal Rohingyas to the UNHCR or to send them to any third country that would accept them" (cited in Saw Yan Naing 2012). This view was also echoed by the Minister for Border Affairs, Lieutenant General Thein Htay, who in a response to claims of "genocide" from an Al Jazeera documentary said, "In Rakhine, there were only 250,000 Rohingya in 1980 and now there are one million. Think for yourselves. Is this genocide?" (cited in Ei Ei Toe Lwin 2012).

Just how entrenched this discourse became is exemplified during the refresher courses (Batch-81) of school teachers on 17 July 2012 and 7 August 2012, when Colonel Myint Oo, dean of Ye Mon military academy, gave a lecture on Myanmar's national security. In response to the 2012 inter-communal violence in Rakhine State his lecture highlighted the threat of Islam and Rohingya people to the state and the Buddhist religion. He noted the following:

> Myanmar is a Buddhist country and there were no Kalar in its history except the descendants of lower-class Kalars who were brought into the country by the British colonial government. The current bloodshed violence occurring in Rakhine State is mainly due to the illegal immigrant Kalars who have bullied the native people. Those Kalars are also followers of the Al Qaeda terrorist group; and therefore, they threaten Buddhist society, national security and the sovereignty of our country.[8]

Similarly, in October 2012, the training program for the military officers at the No. (13) Combatants Organizing School of Naypyitaw's regional headquarters delivered the indoctrinatory course titled "Fear of the Extinction of Myanmar's Races (B. *taing yin tha)*" as part of a training module. The PowerPoint lecture for the course stated that "Bengali (Rohingya) Muslims" have plans to overrun Myanmar through a deliberate mission of population growth and mass illegal immigration. It also noted that their population is increasing in Yangon, Mandalay and other cities in Myanmar and that Myanmar faced an existential threat of being "devoured" by "Bengali Kalars" (Al Jazeera 2015).

Likewise, when the Union Parliament speaker and USDP Chairman Thura Shwe Mann met with members of the Rakhine community in Yangon in September 2013, he noted "It's not an easy task to take care of national sovereignty, territorial integrity, culture, traditions, customs, and religion, so I appreciate the attempts of the Rakhine people to protect Myanmar, despite the difficulties" (cited in Ei Ei Toe Lwin 2013). Furthermore, the government never lifted the curfew and the "state of emergency" order remained enforced in Muslim-dominated Maungdaw and Buthidaung Townships.

Such securitizing speech-acts and restrictions on Rohingya peoples' lives served to reinforce the view of the Rohingya as "enemy others" within the wider population, helping to justify acts of violence committed against them. Moreover, this environment led people to publicly support the use of extraordinary measures against the Rohingya community through horizontal and bottom-up securitization acts, entrenching their position in the community as "enemy-other".

## HORIZONTAL AND BOTTOM-UP PATTERNS OF SECURITIZATION

As the discourse of an existential threat was propagated with higher frequency from Myanmar's political elite, the prevailing security discourses targeting the Rohingya community were further reinforced through horizontal peer-to-peer narratives. While the political liberalization of Myanmar and the opening up of the media in 2012 allowed people and civil-society groups a platform to challenge the government, it has played a significant role in spreading misinformation about the Rohingya and reinforcing the perception of them as illegal immigrants from Bangladesh (see also McCarthy and Menager 2017). Indeed, the long-lasting securitization policies of the Myanmar military government (1962–2010) already described have cultivated an internalized perception of the Rohingya as "enemy others" and a zero-sum mentality among the Buddhist majority population and Rakhine people in particular. Over time, these processes have served to entrench the elite-driven securitization of the Rohingya community through horizontal and peer-to-peer securitization processes.

According to Adamides (2012), securitization processes that take place within the community on a horizontal level influence both the top-down (that is, mainstream) and bottom-up securitization processes. Moreover, top-down securitization processes are likely to be more successful as people become more willing to accept securitization acts and exceptional measures placed on particular groups, and also to "fight" to convince other people of their views. These horizontal processes of securitization also help to explain why the Rohingya continue to be securitized under the National

League for Democracy (NLD) government and why we have seen very little compassion shown by the broader Myanmar community towards their plight since the enactment of "clearance operations" in August 2017. This situation is also reinforced by bottom-up securitization processes which have resulted in zero-sum positions that have become both irreconcilable and extremely polarized.

Adamides (2012) argues that "bottom-up securitization" processes occur when parts of the public engage in securitizing acts aiming at influencing elites and authorities. This pattern of securitization can also be observed in Myanmar, where everyday people have also come to play a strong role in influencing politics around the Rohingya. Processes of bottom-up securitization have been particularly evident in the last five years in Myanmar since the transition to democracy. While anti-Muslim sentiment can be traced back to the colonial era in Rakhine State, since 2012 hate speech directed at the Rohingya community has dominated public discourse in Myanmar (Schissler et al. 2017). Much of the analysis exploring these attitudes has focused on top-down processes; however, ordinary people have also played a significant role in framing these debates.

In Myanmar, the emergence of a hardline Buddhist nationalist movement has played a particularly prominent role since 2012 in further securitizing the Rohingya community as a threat to Myanmar's "race and religion" (Schissler et al. 2017). After communal violence broke out in Rakhine State in 2012, Ashin Wirathu, the firebrand monk dubbed by *Time Magazine* as the "Buddhist Face of Terror", posted on his Facebook page comments promulgating violence against Rakhine Muslim communities. Further to this, he stated that northern Rakhine State including Maungdaw, Buthidaung, and Radaedaung Townships were approaching a critical threat of Islamic terrorism because the illegal immigrant Rohingya were threatening to wage a jihad against all Buddhist Rakhine people in that area (Maung Zarni 2015). U Wirathu and his networks also disseminated pamphlets and CDs across the country suggesting that through the practice of polygamy and illegal migration from Bangladesh, Myanmar was under threat from Islamization.

Following this, a group of Rakhine ultra-nationalist monks held a meeting entitled the "All Rakhine Monks' Solidarity Conference" at a local monastery in Sittwe Town. Afterwards, they released a "Ten-points Document" whereby they called on the local Rakhine people to seek out and expose photos of sympathizers of "Bengali Kalar" who appeared to be supporting or selling goods to the Rohingya (Hindstrom 2012). In Rakhine State, they spoke out openly against selling food and trading with Rohingya people in their villages and with people living in IDP camps. They claimed that Muslims are not human beings and so they do not deserve to be considered under the norms of human rights norms. Vilifying the Rohingya as subhuman, they explicitly expressed their willingness for Muslims to die of starvation.[9]

This led to a series of incidents in towns and villages across the state where people were publicly shamed and led through the streets as national traitors (Hindstrom 2012; Wade 2012). Illustrating the extent of this movement, two photos spread on social media showing two Rakhine men experiencing humiliating punishment from their own community. In one picture, a Rakhine man from Myaybon Township wore a placard saying, "I am a traitor and slave of Kalar". A caption beneath the photo read, "A man who buys/sells groceries to *Kalars* in Myaybon Township on public display (a lesson for all Rakhine people to take)" (Wade 2012). A second photo showed another Rakhine man, from Kyauk Taw Township, with a sign saying, "I am a traitor" while wearing a woman's longyi on his head (Wade 2012). According to local cultural idioms in Myanmar, men consider the wearing of female garments on the head as a symbolic fall from power and a loss of dignity, making this act especially denigrating. Indeed, the communal violence of 2012 only served to further deepen the securitized narratives of the Rohingya community, marginalizing them as "enemy-other". In addition, the horizontal peer-to-peer securitization processes enacted against the Rohingya community demonstrate the ability of both religious leaders and everyday people to position the Rohingya as a security threat and as "enemy-other".

Between 2012 and 2017 a number of prominent Buddhist monks and Rakhine nationalist leaders used horizontal securitization processes to reinforce the narrative of Islam and Rohingya people in particular as an existential threat to Myanmar's national races and the majority Buddhist religion. The "969" organization, for example, used public sermons and mass rallies across the country to express their active endorsement of the Thein Sein government's extra-judicial measures imposed on the Rohingya community in the wake of the 2012 violence. Later, the movement was supplanted by the more strategic and powerful group, the Organization for the Protection of Race and Religion (MaBaTha), which was highly successful in lobbying the government to implement a series of laws aimed at restricting interfaith marriage (Frydenlund 2017). In their campaign to introduce the four "race and religion protection laws" MaBaTha emphasized the perceived threat of the "Islamization" of Myanmar (Frydenlund 2017). In addition, Buddhists around the country organized local MaBaTha units in towns and cities, reinforcing and reiterating the established security discourses of the Rohingya as an existential threat to the majority Buddhist population. As Frydenlund (2017, p. 6) explains, "through preaching, rituals in sacred sites, signature campaigns, and communication through both print and social media, the monks managed to convince broad sections of the public about the threat of Islam and the necessity of the laws." Indeed, it is evident that Myanmar people have become securitization actors themselves, envoys of the mainstream militarized securitization actors.

As demonstrated by the introduction of the race and religion protection laws Myanmar citizens have also clearly played a role in influencing public policy. This was also evident in the lead-up to the nationwide census conducted in 2014. For several months before the census was conducted, the United Nations Population Fund (UNFPA), which was assisting the government, explicitly announced that anybody in the country who did not belong to the 135 recognized ethnic groups could self-identify as "other" in sub-code (914) and verbally answer their desired ethnic affiliation to the enumerator. However, this policy of "all-inclusiveness" resulted in a strong backlash from the Rakhine community who publicly protested this decision. Linking their concerns to the 1982 Myanmar Citizenship Law, Rakhine people argued that the recognition of the Rohingya population in Rakhine State would cause a loss of political power and cultural identity for the Rakhine people.

In addition to their public protests, many Rakhine people in all townships displayed the Buddhist flag on their homes and vehicles as a symbol of their boycott of the international community's interference in national politics. A new surge of violent attacks against international organizations erupted in February 2014 after staff from Malteser International removed the Buddhist flag from the building that the organization rented. During these attacks, Rakhine mobs destroyed many INGO office rooms and houses in Sittwe Town. In response, the Myanmar government agreed to support the Rakhine community's wishes by excluding the Rohingya Muslim population in Rakhine State in the 2014 census (The Guardian 2014). The government response and the reports around these events served to reinforce the ultra-nationalist Buddhist agenda across the country and further positioned the Rohingya people as "enemy-other" in the national domain.

The influence of the public over policy decisions was also highlighted in the lead-up to the November 2015 national parliamentary elections when a number of Rakhine and other nationalist hardliners insisted that the government exclude the Rohingya community from voting, all the while citing reasons of national security and sovereignty. As a result of their protests, the Union Parliament voted to prevent those with temporary identification papers (also known as "white cards") from voting and competing in the elections. It is estimated that 500,000 Rohingya voters were eliminated from voter registration lists, despite many having participated in previous polls (Mizzima 2015). Moreover, the Rakhine Election Commission decided not to allow a number of Rohingya candidates to run in the 2015 election. Shwe Maung, a sitting Rohingya MP from Buthidaung constituency with the ruling Union Solidarity and Development Party (USDP), for example, was declared ineligible to run in the 2015 elections under the new rules because he was not considered a full-fledged citizen on the basis that his parents were not citizens of Myanmar at the time of his birth. That was not the instant decision of the ruling Thein Sein regime but was prepared nine months before, after a number of public protests insisted that the government exclude the Rohingya community from running and voting in the upcoming election, citing the protection of national security and sovereignty.

The main opposition party at that time, the National League for Democracy (NLD), also did not confront these problematic views to help shore up their influence in the national political arena. In line with the ruling Thein Sein government and in fear of a potential public backlash, the NLD also chose not to put up any Muslim candidates to run in the election. Illustrating this idea, Win Htein, one of the leaders and Central Executive Committee (CEC) members of the NLD, when interviewed by the media in October 2015, explicitly said that in order to secure victory, his party was unable to select Muslim candidates for "political" reasons (Hardh and Parmar 2015).

The influence of the public in Myanmar has also been felt in discussions around changing the 1982 Law on Citizenship. Consistent with top-down and horizontal securitization narratives, Rakhine and other nationalists claim that the 1982 Myanmar citizenship law is like "the Great Wall of Myanmar", designed to prevent the influx of "virus-like" Bengalis (Rohingya) who have sought to eliminate the Rakhine Buddhist religion, culture, identity and control over territory. This securitized enunciation has positioned the 1982 Law as sacrosanct and makes it very difficult to amend it in accordance with international norms. Indeed, while the discourse of ethnic indigeneity, *taing yin tha*, is a "term of the state" as Nick Cheesman (2017a) argues, it has also become a marker of national belonging in a discourse which is largely controlled by the public domain.

The aforementioned episodes demonstrate that while securitization processes have been driven by elite actors for many years, everyday people have also played an important role in reinforcing these messages from below. This has become particularly evident in recent years as a result of the more open information environment. As a result of the now internalized perception of the Rohingya as "enemy-other", ordinary Myanmar citizens have become powerful actors in the securitization of the Rohingya. As new political elites under the more democratic environment attempt to cater to these views, the Rohingya problem has become a self-sustaining issue.

## CONCLUSION: THE VICIOUS CYCLE OF SECURITIZATION

Over the last six decades, the Rohingya community has been systematically securitized as a national threat in Myanmar resulting in an entrenched view of their community as "enemy-other". As this paper has discussed, the securitization processes socialized under the military regime have also led to horizontal and bottom-up securitization patterns which have become more powerful in the more open political environment. In this environment, the change of leadership from the military-backed President U Thein Sein to the pro-democracy icon Aung San Suu Kyi has had little impact on the chronic securitizing environment in which the Rohingya community now lives. As has been demonstrated in their response to the plight of Rohingya civilians, despite calls for the protection of human rights and "rule of law", even Aung San Suu Kyi and the ruling National League for Democracy (NLD) party continue this process of securitization.

While many analysts and observers rightfully argue that that the amendment of the 1982 Citizenship Law to allow a pathway to citizenship for Rohingya people would help to achieve a political solution (Kipgen 2014), a much more holistic solution should be sought. Indeed, the securitization of the Rohingya community over the last six decades has become socialized across many sectors and attempts at de-securitization are now much more complex. More specifically, there are difficulties because the source of threats (that is, Rohingya) cannot easily be de-linked from all referent objects such as religious and ethnic identities, territory, society and the economy. This has been especially difficult to overcome in Rakhine State where little development has occurred and unemployment remains a significant issue. This problem creates an "all or nothing" environment (Adamides 2012) where unless the source of the threat is completely eliminated from all sectors, actors will be unwilling to attempt de-securitization because it is too costly or risky for them due to bottom-up and horizontal pressures.

In late 2017 Aung San Suu Kyi and her government oversaw what has been confirmed by the United Nations and the United States as "ethnic cleansing" (UNOHCHR 2017a). Rohingya refugees in Bangladesh speak of summary executions and other forms of torture in their villages (UNOHCHR 2017b). Rape and sexual violence as a means of inflicting shame and fear on Rohingya women and their communities has also been well documented (UNOHCHR 2017b). However, the majority of Myanmar's people have been unwilling to question the use of severe security-related measures inflicted against the Rohingya community. In this environment, where the perception of the Rohingya as an existential security threat is already internalized, the public has willingly accepted exceptional security measures and systematic forms of violence as a response. Instead, political, media, online and offline public discussions of these events have been dominated by the view of the Rohingya as "enemy-other" "terrorist Bengalis".

The public support for Aung San Suu Kyi and the military operations in Rakhine State deeply reflects the securitization processes as described above. Where securitization takes place in various modes by multiple sectors of society, there is little incentive for actors to challenge the security threat discourses, a vicious cycle conceptualized in Figure 11.1.

As a result, the securitization of the Rohingya community is self-perpetuating and de-securitization is highly unlikely without societal change and strong elite leadership. Despite high expectations of Aung San Suu Kyi's NLD government elected in November 2015, prospects

Figure 11.1 The Vicious Cycle or Obstacles to Resolving the Rohingya Problem

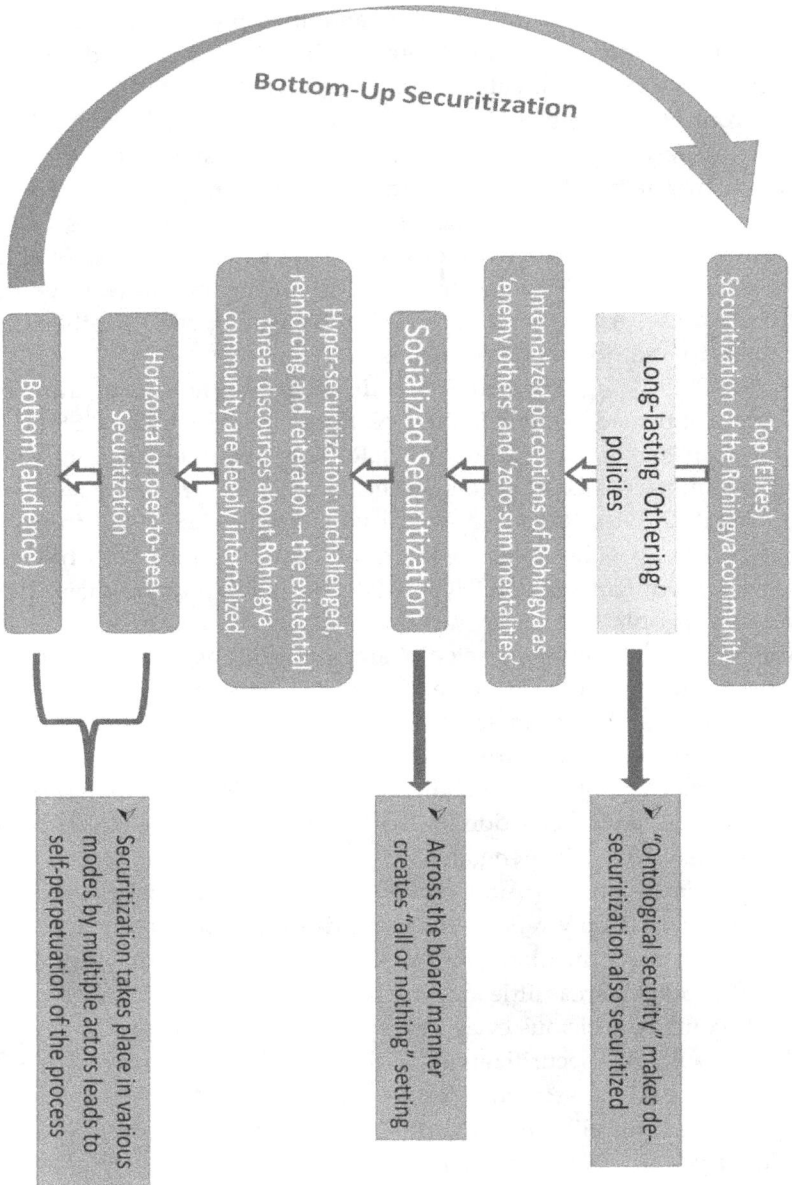

Bottom-Up Securitization

Top (Elites)
Securitization of the Rohingya community

Long-lasting 'Othering' policies

Internalized perceptions of Rohingya as 'enemy others' and 'zero-sum mentalities'

Socialized Securitization

Hyper-securitization: unchallenged, reinforcing and reiteration – the existential threat discourses about Rohingya community are deeply internalized

Horizontal or peer-to-peer Securitization

Bottom (audience)

➤ "Ontological security" makes de-securitization also securitized

➤ Across the board manner creates "all or nothing" setting

➤ Securitization takes place in various modes by multiple actors leads to self-perpetuation of the process for reform on the Rohingya remain low. Indeed, the securitization of the Rohingya community has become the rational option for Myanmar's political leaders and there is a long road ahead to change this. Every effort to de-securitize their situation is highly unlikely to succeed as long as the Buddhist majority's negative perceptions of them as "enemy-other" remains unchanged.

## Notes

1   Myanmar was part of British India as a province until 1937, when it was separated through the introduction of home-rule under the Government of Burma Act 1935.

2   Portuguese Priest Sabestein Manrique who was based in Arakan from 1629–43 records the presence of Muslim merchant settlements in the capital and the arrival of Muslim captives from Bengal for the coronation ceremony of the Arakan king (see Manrique 1927). In his detailed descriptions of the coronation he notes that that the predecessor of the King was a Muslim who had performed the Haj twice. He also notes that the head of the army was a Muslim who was leading the coronation procession and a whole contingent of Muslim soldiers participated in the ceremony.

3   See Smith (1991) for more detail on these ethnic nationality projects.

4   It's important to note that these did not spread to Rakhine State, where a significant Muslim population had resided for hundreds of years.

5   The 'Na Sa Ka' or Nel-Sat-Kut-Kel-Ye (the Border Area Immigration Control Headquarters) was a unique organization that brought together officials from the departments of immigration and customs, as well as members of the military and police academy.

6   In this paper, I try to reflect the Rakhine and Burmese population's negative perceptions of the Rohingya community, therefore I occasionally use the terms "Bengali" and "Kalar" that are used by Rakhine and Burmese people to identify the Rohingya as foreigners.

7   This is despite the fact that many ethnic nationalities, such as the Kachin, Shan and Karen, also have different language groups and cultural and religious practices.

8   Interview with an attendee of the Phaung Gyi Refresher Courses training, 4 December 2012.

9   This is based on my own social media discourse analysis during the 2012–13 anti-Muslim violence.

# References

Adamides, C. *Institutionalized, Horizontal and Bottom-up Securitization in Ethnic Conflict Environments: The Case of Cyprus*. PhD dissertation, University of Birmingham, 2012.

Al Jazeera. "Exclusive: 'Strong Evidence' of Genocide in Myanmar", 28 October 2015. Available at: <http://www.aljazeera.com/news/2015/10/exclusive-strong-evidence-genocide-myanmar-151024190547465.html> [accessed 4 January 2018].

Anand, J. P. "Refugees from Burma". *Economic and Political Weekly* 13(27) 1978: 1100–1101.

Anderson, B. *Imagined Communities: Reflections on the Origin and Spread of Nationalism*. London: Verso, 1991.

Aye Chan. "The Development of a Muslim Enclave in Arakan (Rakhine) State of Burma (Myanmar)". *SOAS Bulletin of Burma Research* 3(2) 2005: 396–420.

Baumann, G. *Contesting Culture: Discourses of Identity in Multi-Ethnic London*. Cambridge: Cambridge University Press, 1996.

Buchanan, F. "A Comparative Vocabulary of the Languages Spoken in the Burma Empire". *SOAS Bulletin of Burma Research*, 1(1) (2003 [1798]): 40–57.

Chakravarti, N. R. *The Indian Minority in Burma: The Rise and Decline of an Immigrant Community*. London: Institute of Race Relations, 1971.

Charney, M. *Religious Change and the Emergence of Buddhist Communalism in Early Modern Arakan*. PhD dissertation, University of Michigan, 1999.

Charney, M. "Theories and Historiography of the Religious Basis of Ethnonyms in Rakhaing (Arakan), Myanmar (Burma)", presented at The Forgotten Kingdom of Arakan, 23 November 2005, Bangkok, Thailand.

Cheesman, N. "Seeing 'Karen' in the Union of Myanmar". *Asian Ethnicity* 3(2) 2002: 199–220.

Cheesman, N. "How in Myanmar 'National Races' Came to Surpass Citizenship and Exclude Rohingya". *Journal of Contemporary Asia* 47(3) (2017a): 461–83.

Cheesman, N. "Introduction: Interpreting Communal Violence in Myanmar". *Journal of Contemporary Asia* 47(3) (2017b): 335–52.

Cheung, S. "Migration Control and the Solutions Impasse in South and Southeast Asia: Implications from the Rohingya Experience". *Journal of Refugee Studies* 25(1) 2011: 50–70.

Chia, J. "The Truth About Myanmar's Rohingya Issue". *The Diplomat*, 5 March 2016. Available at: <https://thediplomat.com/2016/03/the-truth-about-myanmars-rohingya-issue/> [accessed 4 January 2018].

CNN. "Fareed interviews Myanmar's leader Aung San Suu Kyi", 23 September 2016. Available at: <http://edition.cnn.com/videos/tv/2016/09/26/exp-gps-0925-aung-san-suu-kyi.cnn> [accessed 4 January 2018].

de Mersan, A. "Ritual and Other in Rakhine Spirit Cults". *Myanmar's Mountain and Maritime Borderscapes: Local Practices, Boundary Making and Figured Worlds*, ed. Su-Ann Oh. Singapore: ISEAS, 2016, pp.121–45.

Egreteau, R. "Burmese Indians in Contemporary Burma: Heritage, Influence, and Perceptions Since 1988". *Asian Ethnicity* 12(1) 2001: 33–54.

Ei Ei Toe Lwin. "Government slams Al Jazeera documentary on Rakhine State 'genocide'," *Myanmar Times*, 14 December 2012. Available at: <https://www.mmtimes.com/national-news/3560-government-slams-al-jazeera-documentary-on-rakhine-state-genocide.html> [accessed 4 January 2018].

Ei Ei Toe Lwin. "Speaker Pledges 'Support' for Rakhine People", *Myanmar Times*, 4 October 2013. Available at: <http://www.mmtimes.com/index.php/national-news/8350-speaker-pledges-support-for-rakhine-people.html> [accessed 4 January 2018].

Fuller, T. "Charity Says Threats Foil Medical Aid in Myanmar", *New York Times*, 5 November 2012. Available at: <http://www.nytimes.com/2012/11/06/world/asia/aid-for-refugees-in-myanmar-threatened-by-violence.html> [accessed 4 January 2018].

Gravers, M. "Anti-Muslim Buddhist Nationalism in Burma and Sri Lanka: Religious Violence and Globalized Imaginaries of Endangered Identities". *Contemporary Buddhism: An Interdisciplinary Journal* 16(1) 2015: 1–27.

Hardh, R. and Parmar, S. "How the Rohingya Have Been Excluded from Myanmar's Landmark Elections," *The Nation*, 3 November 2015. <https://www.thenation.com/article/how-the-rohingya-have-been-excluded-from-myanmars-landmark-elections/> [accessed 4 January 2018].

Harriden, J. "Making a Name for Themselves: Karen Identity and the Politicization of Ethnicity in Burma". *The Journal of Burma Studies* 7 (2002): 84–144.

Harvey, G. E. *History of Burma*. London: Longmans Green, 1925.

Head, J. "Burma Offers Rohingya Return Deal", *BBC News*, 28 February 2009. Available at: <http://news.bbc.co.uk/2/hi/7916254.stm> [accessed 4 January 2018].

Hindstrom, H. "Monk Group calls on Locals to Target Rohingya Sympathizers," *Democratic Voice of Burma*, 23 October 2012. Available at: <http://www.dvb.no/news/monk-group-calls-on-locals-to-target-%E2%80%98rohingya-sympathisers%E2%80%99/24389> [accessed 4 January 2018].

Holslag, A. "The Process of Othering from the 'Social Imaginaire' to Physical Acts: An Anthropological Approach". *Genocide Studies and Prevention: An International Journal* 9(1) 2015: 96–113.

Human Rights Watch (HRW). *Burma: The Rohingya; Ending a Cycle of Exodus?* New York: Human Rights Watch, 1996.

_____. *'The Government Could Have Stopped This': Sectarian Violence and Ensuing Abuses in Burma's Arakan State*. New York: Human Rights Watch, 2012.

_____. 'All You Can Do is Pray': Crimes Against Humanity and Ethnic Cleansing of Rohingya Muslims in Burma's Arakan State. New York: Human Rights Watch, 2013.

Irwin, A. Burmese Outpost (Memoirs of a British Officer who fought in Arakan with the Arakanese V Forces during the Second World War). London: Collins, 1945.

Kipgen, N. "Addressing the Rohingya Problem". Journal of Asian and African Studies, 49(2) 2014: 234–47.

Kymlicka, W. Multicultural Citizenship. Oxford: Oxford University Press, 1995.

Leider, J. P. "Rohingya: The Name, the Movement, the Quest for Identity". Nation Building in Myanmar. Yangon: Myanmar Egress and Myanmar Peace Center, 2013.

Leider, J. P. "Transmutations of the Rohingya Movement in the Post-2012 Rakhine State Crisis", in Ethnic and Religious Identities and Integration in Southeast Asia, edited by Ooi Keat Gin and V. Grabowsky. Chiang Mai: Silkworm Books, 2017, pp. 191–239.

Manrique, S. Travels of Fray Sebastien Manrique 1629-1643. Oxford: Hakluyt Society, 1927.

Maung Zarni. "Is Norway - Royal Family, Government, Corporations & the Gov-funded NGO – Collaborating with Myanmar's Genocidal Regime?" 3 June 2015. Available at: <http://www.maungzarni.net/2015/06/is-norway-royal-family government.html#sthash.1mCQZC4a.dpuf> [accessed 4 January 2018].

McCarthy, G. and Menager, J. "Gendered Rumours and the Muslim Scapegoat in Myanmar's Transition". Journal of Contemporary Asia 47(3) 2017: 396–412.

Mizzima. "Muslim Politicians Excluded from Election", 9 September 2015. Available at: <http://www.mizzima.com/news-election-2015-election-news/muslim-politicians-excluded-election> [accessed 4 January 2018].

Nyi Nyi Kyaw. "Alienation, Discrimination, and Securitization: Legal Personhood and Cultural Personhood of Muslims in Myanmar". The Review of Faith & International Affairs 13(4) 2015: 50–59.

_____. "Islamophobia in Buddhist Myanmar: The 969 Movement and Anti Muslim Violence", in Islam and the State in Myanmar: Muslim-Buddhist Relations and the Politics of Belonging, edited by M. Crouch. Oxford, Oxford University Press, 2016, pp. 183–210.

Paton, C. A Short Report on Arakan. London: Colonial Office, 1826.

Saw Yan Naing. "UNHCR Rejects Rohingya Resettlement Suggestion," The Irrawaddy, 13 July 2012. Available at: <https://www.irrawaddy.com/news/burma/unhcr-rejects-rohingya-resettlement-suggestion.html> [accessed 4 January 2018].

Schissler, M., Walton, M. and Phyu Phyu Thi. "Reconciling Contradictions: Buddhist-Muslim Violence, Narrative Making and Memory in Myanmar". Journal of Contemporary Asia 47(3) 2017: 376–95.

Smith, M. Burma: Insurgency and the Politics of Ethnicity. London: Zed Books, 1991.

Taylor, R. The State in Myanmar. Honolulu: University of Hawaii Press, 2009.

Thant Myint-U. *The River of Lost Footsteps: Histories of Burma*. New York: Farrar, Straus and Giroux, 2006.

The Guardian. "Burma Census is not Counting Rohingya Muslims, says UN Agency," 2 April 2014. Available at <https://www.theguardian.com/world/2014/apr/02/burma-census-rohingya-muslims-un-agency> [accessed 4 January 2018].

The Working People's Daily. "The Speech by General Ne Win Provided in the Meeting Held in the Central Meeting Hall, President House, Ahlone Road". 9 October 1982.

Tinker, H. (1990) "Indians in Southeast Asia: Imperial Auxilaries", in *Southeast Asians Overseas: Migration and Ethnicity*, edited by C. Clarke, C. Peach, and S. Vertovec. Cambridge: Cambridge University Press, 1990, pp. 39–56.

United Nations Human Rights Office of the High Commissioner (UNOHCHR) . "Darker and More Dangerous: High Commissioner Updates the Human Rights Council on Human Rights Issues in 40 countries," 11 September 2017 (2017a). Available at: <http://www.ohchr.org/EN/NewsEvents/Pages/DisplayNews.aspx?NewsID=22041> [accessed 4 January 2018].

United Nations Human Rights Office of the High Commissioner (UNOHCHR). *"Mission Report of OHCHR Rapid Response Mission to Cox's Bazar, Bangladesh, Sep 13-24*. Available at: <http://www.ohchr.org/Documents/Countries/MM/CXBMissionSummaryFindingsOctober2017.pdf> [accessed 4 January 2018] (2017b).

Van Galen, S. "Arakan and Bengal: The Rise and Decline of the Mrauk U Kingdom (Burma) from the Fifteenth to the Seventeenth Century AD". PhD dissertation, Leiden University, 2008.

Van Klinken, G. and Su Mon Thazin Aung. "The Contentious Politics of Anti-Muslim Scapegoating in Myanmar". *Journal of Contemporary Asia* 47(3) 2017: 353–75.

Venus News. "Interview with Dr. Aye Maung, Chairman of Rakhine Nationalities Development Party (RNDP)". *Venus News*, 3(47) 2012.

Wade, F. "Photos Emerge of Anti-Muslim Witch Hunt in Burma". *Asian Correspondent*, 4 December 2012. Available at: <https://asiancorrespondent.com/2012/12/photos-emerge-of-anti-muslim-witch-hunt-in-burma/> [accessed 4 January 2018].

Webb, M. C. *Census of India 1911 Vol. IX Burma Part I*. Rangoon: Office of the Superintendent, Government Printing, Burma, 1912.

Yegar, M. *Between Integration and Secession: The Muslim Communities of the Southern Philippines, Southern Thailand, and Western Burma/Myanmar*. Lanham: Lexington Books, 2002.

# 12

## FORMING AN INCLUSIVE NATIONAL IDENTITY IN MYANMAR: VOICES OF MON PEOPLE

### Cecile Medail

In Myanmar, the failure to fulfil the needs and aspirations of the country's ethnic minorities in the wake of independence caused the outbreak of some of the world's longest-running civil wars. The process of democratization in plural societies is often fragile because different political actors who influence the transition may articulate potentially incompatible conceptualizations of national identity (Linz and Stepan 1996, p. 16). This can be particularly challenging when a majority group dominates the political landscape and attempts to impose its vision of the nation on other minority groups. This is the case in Myanmar where since independence ethnic people have aspired to the recognition of their cultural identities and the implementation of self-rule. This view has often clashed with the vision of the Tatmadaw, the military group that took power in 1962. Indeed, the Tatmadaw, which is predominantly comprised of members of the dominant "Bamar"[1] ethnicity, imagines the country as a centralized state with a unified Bamar national identity, as opposed to the Bamar as one ethnic group among many.

The military government's resolve to strengthen the Burmanization or "Myanmafication" of culture and history as described by Gustaaf Houtman (1999, p.142–8) is a main cause of the gradual suppression of Myanmar's distinct cultural identities. The case of the Mon, one of Myanmar's main ethnic groups, illustrates this situation well. The 2017 decision of the NLD-dominated parliament to rename a major bridge in Mon State after General Aung San despite strong local opposition is representative of the many ongoing challenges ethnic nationality groups still face (Htet Naing Zaw 2017). The renaming of this major infrastructure link after the "father of independence" was indeed strongly criticized for celebrating a Bamar hero rather than local identity. This controversy illustrates the incompatibility of ethnic aspirations with a particular notion of national identity promoted by the Bamar militarized elite, which is one of the reasons why civil war has been raging for more than half a century. In this light, building an inclusive national identity that respects the multinational character of Myanmar instead of presenting the nation as an expression of the Bamar alone would positively support peace.

The purpose of this paper is therefore to shed light on Mon people's attitudes towards ethnicity and aspirations in order to provide indicators as to the scope for new policies supporting the development of an inclusive national identity. In other words: do current Mon attitudes indicate whether and how an inclusive national identity might be built? The first section introduces Mikesell and Murphy's (1991) framework for minority aspirations from which the analysis is drawn. The second section then examines Mon people's perceptions of Mon ethnicity and Myanmar citizenship in order to identify various voices and determine degrees of nationalism. The third section presents what Mon people see as policies creating insecurities and the corresponding aspirations that Mon people consider as essential to support the development of an inclusive national identity. Lastly, the conclusion discusses whether the current peace process is addressing these demands in any genuine and meaningful way.

The findings are based on interviews and focus group discussions conducted in English, Burmese and Mon[2] over five months in 2016 and 2017, in seven townships of Mon State as well as in a Mon village in Karen State, with Mon people across various social groups.[3] For the purpose of this analysis, informants have been categorized into two main groups, which are divided into the following sub-groups: the elite (E), including armed group affiliated members (E1) and urban intellectuals (E2); and community members (C), including ordinary people living in government-controlled areas (C1) and those living under armed group control (C2).

## THEORETICAL FRAMEWORK

The development of an inclusive national identity could positively support peace in Myanmar. As a Mon scholar noted: "We need a consensual vision of national identity, which provides equal rights for all. Democracy won't work without this and civil war will break out again" (Interview 18, 2015). Indeed, Kymlicka (1995, p. 13) highlights that in stable multinational democracies, citizens usually have a strong sense of loyalty to the larger community in addition to their ethnic allegiances because the state could not survive without recognizing and protecting the existence and particularity of distinct ethnic groups. According to Brown (1994, p. xix), the development of ethnicity as an identity marker and the escalation of ethnic minority nationalism and aspirations are greatly influenced by the state which plays a significant role in adopting policies that create insecurity for its citizens. The adoption of policies that would positively respond to ethnic aspirations therefore has the potential to reverse the process of ethnic identification and allow for the development of a common, inclusive identity.

Mikesell and Murphy (1991, p. 588) propose to examine the aspirations of minority groups by using a framework that links these aspirations with policy demands and the request for particular cultural and political arrangements. According to this framework, we can classify minority group demands into categories, of which five are relevant to the current situation in Myanmar: claims for cultural recognition, access to economic opportunities, participation in decision-making, cultural autonomy, and territorial autonomy or self-rule. These categories are part of a continuum, which reflects varying degrees of a "desire to benefit from or withdraw from a larger national society" (Mikesell and Murphy 1991, p. 588).

This framework is applicable to Myanmar, where oppressive state policies have created human, economic, social and cultural forms of insecurity. These insecurities have in turn inspired ethnic nationalism and insurrections since the early stages of independence up until today in the north of the country. This ethnic nationalist struggle includes to varying degrees claims that cover the whole spectrum of Mikesell and Murphy's framework for minority aspirations. Using their framework, this paper will look at Mon people's aspirations in order to identify policies that could create a sense of inclusion. Since the aspirations of minority groups such as the Mon are influenced by their particular sense of identity, the following section will attempt to characterize this identity and evaluate how strongly it is felt by Mon people.

## THE STRENGTH OF MON IDENTITY: RELATIONSHIP BETWEEN MON ETHNICITY AND MYANMAR CITIZENSHIP

### Distinctive characteristics of Mon identity in contrast to the Bamar majority

According to Nai Hongsar (2014), Vice Chairman of the Mon ethnic armed organisation (EAO), the New Mon State Party (NMSP), the Mon struggle for recognition and equality started immediately after independence, as demands for recognition as a distinct ethnic group were ignored by the Bamar-dominated government on the pretext that the Mon and the Bamar are alike and that therefore the Mon do not need to have a separate identity or rights.[4] However, Mon people identify themselves through the six distinct attributes that commonly define an ethnic community: a name, a shared culture, a distinct language and literature, a common descent, a common history, an association with a specific homeland and a sense of pride and solidarity (Smith 1987, pp. 22–31).

The Mon, who are identified as one of Myanmar's eight main ethnic groups and are mostly located in Mon State, historically use the name *Raman* to refer to themselves and *Ramanya* to refer to their territory instead of Mon State.[5] On the surface, Mon culture is easily differentiable from the Bamar culture through distinctive clothing, food, musical instruments, traditional dances, religious festivals and national symbols such as the Brahminy duck or *Hinta* that is represented on the Mon flag. But above all, language and literature appear as an essential defining aspect of Mon identity. Mon language is different from the Burmese language as it comes from the Mon-Khmer ethno-linguistic group while Burmese derives from the Tibeto-Burman group. For many, the long history of Mon script is a source of pride. Indeed, with a written language that can be traced back to the sixth century, the Mon are the most ancient literate living culture in

Myanmar from which the Burmese and other scripts are derived (Bauer 1990, pp. 16–17).

Since the last official census conducted in 2014 did not release information on ethnic populations,[6] it is difficult to provide accurate numbers. While the Bamar majority is commonly said to represent between sixty and seventy per cent of the fifty-one million-plus people living in Myanmar today, Ashley South roughly estimates that there are between one and one and a half million Mon-speaking people, a figure which excludes many people of Mon descent who do not speak the language (South 2003, p. 18). Indeed, although some people with Mon ancestry still identify themselves as Mon despite not being familiar with the language, government restrictions on teaching Mon language seem to have had a significant impact on the decision to self-identify as Mon. As one young person noted, "many Mon people who did not have an opportunity to learn the language are more likely to register as Bamar" (Focus group 1, 2016).

Mon people have not always represented a minority. As illustrated by G.H. Luce and B. Shin (1969, p. 3): "The pioneers in civilization, both in old Burma and old Siam, were the Mons." With its literature, art and introduction of Theravada Buddhism to the region, Mon civilization was one of the earliest and most significant in pre-colonial Southeast Asia. Evidence suggests that groups that arrived later such as the Bamar actually appropriated these contributions (Coedés 1966, p. 113; McCormick 2010, p. 1; Guillon 1999, p. 53). For more than a thousand years, until the Bama king Alaungphaya defeated the Mon in 1757, the Mon homeland stretched over central and lower Myanmar (South 2007, p. 3). Most Mon people are now located in Mon State although they hardly represent a majority with only 38.8 per cent of the total population against 37.2 per cent Bamar and 15.7 Karen, according to the last available census in Mon State (Immigration and Manpower Department 1987). However, this figure is likely an underestimation: many civil society members report that a high number of people of Mon descent are likely to have been registered as Bamar by government officers, sometimes as a result of an automatic assumption and sometimes as a result of their own will.

## The strength of Mon nationalist spirit

The strength of ethnic identity and therefore the nationalist spirit that characterizes an ethnic group can vary greatly depending on the extent of mobilization and politicization of the communities. In his well-known essay "Origin of Nations", Anthony Smith notes the dual dimension of the process of identity formation (Smith 1987, p. 13). While ethnic identity is based on powerful ancient attachments such as social distinctions and common experiences, ethnic belonging also appears as a constructed reality using these social distinctions and common experiences as the foundation for political identity and claims (Gurr 2000, pp. 4–5; Brown 1994, p. xix; Ghai 2000, p. 4; Gravers 1999, p. 153). Although ethnicity initially appears as a fluid identity marker, the politicization of ethnic consciousness has the potential to crystallize into a more rigid identity marker, with the consequence that once mobilized, "it is almost impossible for ethnic communities to extricate themselves from the political arena" (Smith 1987, p. 156).

Some scholars attempt to downplay the importance of ethnicity in Myanmar, which as Aung-Thwin (1998, p. 147) would argue, could be reduced to a mere creation of historians, politicians or other scholars. Others claim that ethnic categories, while deeply rooted in ancient common historical experience, have developed into strengthened cultural identities for defensive purposes (Walton 2013, p. 14). The case of the Mon clearly illustrates such a development. Contrary to Robert Taylor (1987, p. 24), who claims that Mon identity was already disappearing in the pre-colonial era, Ashley South (2003, p. 31) demonstrates that a strong Mon identity undoubtedly existed during this time. Although the Mon did not have their own laws and government while they were under the domination of the Bamar kings and later the British colonial power, Halliday and Bauer (2000, p. 25) argue that they maintained "a sense of separate nationality and pride of race". South (2003, p. 40) therefore concludes that there is nowadays a "strong Mon nationalist spirit".

This sense of a separate Mon identity developed after independence into a symbol of resistance against the government (South 2007, p. 3). The Mon nationalist movement started with the establishment of the first nationalist organization in 1945, the United Mon Association, and started to express separatist claims at a Mon national conference in 1947 (South 2003, p. 105). The NMSP and its armed wing the Mon National Liberation Army (MNLA) now lead this struggle for autonomy and self-determination.[7] In 1972, Nai Shwe Kyin stated that the NMSP aimed "to establish an independent sovereign state unless the Burmese government is willing to permit a full confederation of free nationalities exercising the full right of self-determination inclusive of right of secession" (South 2003,

p. 171). The NMSP signed a ceasefire agreement with the Tatmadaw in 1995 but the agreement was invalidated when they refused to transform into a border guard force in 2010. A state-level ceasefire was adopted under President Thein Sein's government and the NMSP participated in the National Ceasefire Agreement (NCA) negotiations which involved eighteen EAOs.[8] While the NMSP is among the ten EAOs that initially refused to sign the agreement, it recently reversed this decision in order to participate in the current peace process (Nyein Zaw Lin and Lun Min mang 2018)[9] which will be discussed further in the concluding section.

The existence of the NMSP as a parallel authority, with a government-like structure, control over some parts of the territory,[10] its own education system (as developed below) as well as its own laws (Harrisson and Kyed Von Sponek 2017) illustrates well the persistence of a "strong Mon nationalist spirit". This nationalist spirit is also reflected in the common view that the NMSP is representative of Mon people's aspirations. Opinions of the NMSP are unsurprisingly high in villages under their control (Focus groups 9 and 13, 2017). Similarly, in Mawlamyine, a large majority of urban educated people view the NMSP very positively. While some villagers in Chaung Zon Township denied having any connection with the NMSP (Focus groups 8 and 11, 2017), other villagers in Mudon Township highly regard the group as representative of their interests: "We have our Mon literature because our monks maintain it; in the same way, we exist because the NMSP is here" (Focus group 10, 2017).

## Variety of voices and degree of nationalism

While the Mon nationalist movement suggests that there is a "strong Mon nationalist spirit", the assumption that ethno-nationalist leaders and the urban elite would be more likely to have rigid positions on ethnicity than rural people who may have more flexible attitudes cannot be verified.

Since a number of common traits or important distinctions characterise the research participants, two main categories, with two sub-groups each, can be identified. The elite (category E) characterized by its involvement in the nationalist movement and higher level of education includes NMSP-affiliated members (E1) and urban intellectuals who are politically or socially engaged people working with civil society organizations, political parties, as journalists or through Buddhism (E2). Community members (category C), mostly located in rural areas and characterized by their limited access to economic opportunities and lower levels of education, include those living under government control (C1) and those living in conflict-affected areas under NMSP control (C2). Since fluid attitudes would provide scope for a national government to reach out to the population with a more inclusive vision of nationhood, this paper will now evaluate the degree of nationalism expressed in each category by considering the question of belonging and whether one identifies more as Mon ethnic or as Myanmar citizen.

The elite, who are involved in promoting Mon identity in various ways, do not always have strong ethno-nationalist views that reflect the armed struggle for more autonomy and decentralization. One would expect that people affiliated to the Mon armed group (E1) would have strong nationalist standpoints. However, voices are not necessarily homogeneous. In the words of one NMSP officer, claims for recognition of ethnic identity and self-rule do not exclude potential identification to the state: "Only if people can feel that their identity is recognized can they start to feel that they belong to the country" (Interview 3, 2016). Surprisingly perhaps, one teacher working for the NMSP's Mon National Schools expressed a rather moderate view: "I am equally proud to be a Mon national and a Myanmar citizen because Mon State is a part of Myanmar, where different ethnic people with similar cultures live" (Interview 10, 2016).

Interestingly, not all urban intellectuals (E2) who have strong ties with the NMSP or have previously worked with the organization express strong nationalist views. Some civil society members, for instance, strongly refuse to acknowledge their Myanmar citizenship even when going abroad, preferring to present themselves as Mon (Interview 8, 16, 2016). However, others have a more nuanced perception of their allegiance, arguing for instance that people would be happy to identify as Myanmar citizens if federalism was institutionalized or the country's name was changed (Interviews 4, 8, 2016). Some emphasize a possible decrease in the significance of ethnic identification: "People will feel less about their identity if they can act according to their will and their rights" (Interview 1, 2016). Others are very practical, suggesting that identification depends on the situation as Mon nationality can be used inside the country while Myanmar citizenship can be used outside the country (Interview 17, 2016). For a Mon National Party (MNP) member, identification as a citizen of Myanmar is essential as "it creates a responsibility to work to change the country" (Interview 11, 2016). Interestingly, some regard ethnicity as a fluid identity marker, which can vary depending on political allegiances, therefore excluding those who work for the NLD while theoretically including those without Mon descent but working for Mon people (Interview 7, 2016).

Since for community members (C) income is generally a main concern, one could assume that their ethnic consciousness would be quite limited. Again, viewpoints are not homogeneous. In rural areas under government control (C1) where Mon people live alongside the Bamar majority, ordinary villagers are more likely to be vulnerable to assimilation and be oblivious of their identity. A group of men from Chaung Zon Township shared their indifference, while not hiding a feeling of unfairness: "We cannot think whether we are proud to be Myanmar citizens or not. We just know that it is difficult to survive in this country. But even though we are Myanmar citizens, we are Mon and we have no chance to study Mon as an official subject even at university" (Focus group 11, 2017). A stronger sense of dissatisfaction was generally expressed. Women from the same village clearly identify more as Mon nationals. "We are not satisfied to be citizens of this country because there are no job opportunities and incomes are not good" (Focus group 8, 2017). One of them shared how she experienced discrimination when mentioning her Myanmar citizenship abroad: "When I worked in Thailand, I said I was a Myanmar citizen. Because Thai people understand that Myanmar citizen equals Bamar ethnicity, they did not give me a job easily. After I explained I was Mon, I could get a job easily. Even I cannot understand this well, I feel it is different." Similarly in Mudon Township, a group of villagers consider themselves primarily as Mon. "In former times, we were not Myanmar citizens. We were Mon, because we had our own palace, culture, traditions and literature. We are Mon ethnic and should be Mon citizens" (Focus group 10, 2017).

In conflict-affected areas (C2), since villagers had to endure abuses committed by the Myanmar army and relied on the NMSP for their basic needs, strong nationalist standpoints are more likely to be found. Unsurprisingly, villagers living in remote NMSP-controlled areas tend to reject Myanmar citizenship. Mon villagers in Kyarinn Seik Gyi Township in Karen State don't talk about the "government office" but about the "Bamar office" (Focus group 7, 2016). This reference to the majority ethnic group clearly demonstrates that they do not feel included by government institutions. Villagers in Ye Township similarly shared negative feelings towards Myanmar citizenship, pointing at the impacts of civil war: "I am really disappointed to be a Myanmar citizen. Since it was difficult to travel and find income, many people under 40 are not educated. Currently it is very similar: many states and townships are developed except here" (Focus group 9, 2017). A youth group in Kyaikmayaw Township equally rejects Myanmar citizenship: "We don't want to be Myanmar citizens because we never get support from the government. Whenever I see 'Myanmar citizen' on my ID card, it is really painful [...] actually we should be Mon citizens" (Focus group 13, 2017).

Although more research could be conducted to expand the sample, the assumption that the elite would have stronger nationalist views than community members cannot be verified: NMSP members (E1) and urban intellectuals (E2) expressed hard-line as well as moderate views while attitudes of villagers in government-controlled areas (C1) were sometimes quite strong and views in NMSP-controlled areas (C2) were rather radical. While people's attitudes demonstrate the existence of a "strong Mon nationalist spirit", the fact that they are not homogenous suggests that there is still space for the development of an inclusive national identity. The paper will now look at Mon people's aspirations in order to identify policies that would make people feel more included.

## MON PEOPLE'S ASPIRATIONS: SUPPORTING AN INCLUSIVE NATIONAL IDENTITY

Five insecurities in particular tend to institutionalize differential treatment between Bamar and non-Bamar. These have generated five corresponding "minority aspirations" that will be examined in this section. These five insecurities are: cultural assimilation, exploitation and discrimination, structural inequalities, government restrictions and a lack of self-determination. These insecurities reflect and reinforce the existence of "Bamar privilege" which represents an obstacle to the development of an inclusive national identity. Matthew Walton (2013, pp. 2–3) demonstrates that the supremacy of the Bamar as an institutionalized dominance functions as a privileged identity because their position as the majority group enables them to experience some benefits merely because of their ethnicity. Decades of conflict between the Bamar-led military and ethnic rebellions have indeed generated practices institutionalizing differential treatment between Bamar and non-Bamar people, especially evident in the military and bureaucracy. However, the Bamar have a perception of themselves as equal victims of oppression by the military and this prevents them from recognizing their privilege. Yet, according to Walton, without acknowledging this privilege and actively working against it, ethnic unity will be difficult to achieve. It is therefore important to understand these five insecurities and their corresponding aspirations in order to work towards reconciliation. Using Mikesell and Murphy's framework, this paper will now briefly introduce each insecurity and present Mon people's aspirations and the corresponding policies that should be prioritized to address these insecurities and therefore promote inclusiveness.

## Claims for recognition

When the military was in power between 1962 and 2010, the pressure of assimilation through "burmanization campaigns" was harshly felt as all manifestations of non-Bamar identity were repressed (South 2003, p. 33). As a result, many elements of Mon history and Mon symbolic representations were absorbed by the Bamar culture. The Mon origin of a number of significant symbols of Myanmar national identity, for instance the Shwedagon pagoda, is often forgotten (Hall 1974, p. 35; South 2003, p. 54). In Mon State, the military regime removed the *Hinta* (a Brahminy duck, symbolic of the Mon) at the entrance to Mawlamyine and replaced it with an alms bowl. According to a civil society member (E2), this was seen as a replacement with a Bamar cultural symbol (Interview 8).[11] In NMSP-controlled areas (C2), villagers in Ye Township remember that, "when Burmese soldiers came to our village […], they asked for money and food and if we could not give what they wanted, they destroyed houses and Mon symbols" (Focus group 9, 2017). Mon villagers in Karen State also recalled that throughout the civil war up until 1995, most Mon names on pagodas and in villages were changed to Bamar names (Focus group 6, 2016).

As Salem-Gervais and Metro (2012, p. 30) demonstrate, educational curricula have also been used as a tool to build a national identity based on "an ancient and glorious 'Myanmar' essence". Textbooks have indeed conveyed for decades ideological messages stressing traditions of nationalism and militarism that are essentially linked to a Bamar identity, reflecting an attempt to assimilate ethnic minorities (Lall and Hla Win 2013, p. 87). In a government-controlled village (C1), a resident of Mudon township noted that: "My mum told me that the history I learnt at school was wrong, so we know that the government is trying to brainwash us" (Focus group 10, 2017). For instance, some political party members suggested that the appropriation of Mon heroes such as Tamainbarang, Logooneain or Byatsa, who were depicted in middle school history textbooks as Bamar heroes, has contributed to downplaying the Mon's historical significance (Focus group 2, 2016). The celebration of Burmese identity is also reinforced in and outside school by cultural competitions where only Bamar costumes and dances are represented (Interview 10, 2016).

The 2017 controversy around the naming of the bridge connecting the entire Chaung Zon Township[12] to Mawlamyine is also perceived as an inappropriate imposition of Bamar identity. The decision of the national parliament to name the bridge after General Aung San triggered protests attracting over 20,000 people, expressing their discontent for a name that does not reflect local identity. Among the Mon elite (E2), a monk from Chaung Zon sees this decision as "one strategy of Burmanization". He noted: "They chose a Bamar hero name even though the bridge is situated in a Mon area. Later, they will change more things. This way is the scariest: now all our Mon village names have changed to Burmese names" (Interview 21, 2017). Some villagers from Paung Township (C1) also think that the bridge should have a geographic name or refer to a Mon leader: "The bridge was not built by Aung San, he never came here, he is not from here, therefore, this is not his business" (Focus group 12, 2017). Even in conflict-affected villages (C2) far away from Chaung Zon Township, people make references to the bridge: "Now we have peace but the government does not care about ethnic people, they do not recognize that Mon and Burmese people are different" (Focus group 9, 2017).

Measures promoting recognition could effectively address insecurities caused by such assimilation policies. According to Mikesell and Murphy (1991, p. 588) "recognition claims" refer to demands for the acknowledgment of group identity and the respect of its specific attributes such as religious, linguistic and cultural distinctiveness.

During my fieldwork, I witnessed the replacement of the alms bowl at the entrance of Mawlamyine by the Mon *Hinta*: its inauguration was well attended and celebrated and widely perceived in the community as a symbolic step towards recognizing the unique cultural heritage of the Mon people. This is a start but there are many other things that people would like to see happen. Most importantly, the recognition of Mon as an official language is considered as essential across all social groups. In order to address a feeling of exclusion, a number of symbolic measures that would further reduce perceptions of Bamar privilege could also be implemented. Some teachers (E1) and community activists (E2) advocate for the adoption of a multicultural curriculum emphasizing historical plurality and peaceful coexistence instead of the current centralized curriculum, which does not reflect ethnic identities and causes people to perceive the Bamar majority as an occupant (Interviews 2, 9, 2016).

Likewise, names have the potential to reduce such a perception and create a symbolic sense of inclusion. The bridge controversy captures well the potential impact of symbolic measures. As Matthew Walton (2017) deplores, while the re-writing of Myanmar's history is "a basic component of national reconciliation (…) the much simpler step of just recognizing local agency in naming a landmark is even too difficult for the current government." The symbolic decision of renaming the bridge according to local desire would indeed be positively perceived as an effort to contribute to national reconciliation and therefore reduce perceptions of Bamar privilege. As a group of women from Chaung Zon Township put it: "The Bamar are trying to control us by imposing names. If the government respected local people, we could have many places with Mon names" (Focus group 8, 2017).

The country's name itself is also an issue. The former military government decided to rename the country Myanmar in 1988, without consulting its people, claiming that it represented all ethnic groups. Most of the informants argue that despite the government's claim, there is no clear distinction between Burma/Bamar and Myanmar. As a Mon teacher (E1) explained, "Myanmar" is not inclusive because it can also be used to refer to the majority group's language and culture (Interview 2, 2016). A monk (E2) added that "Myanmar" is not representative because Myanmar people originally come from the Bagan area only (Interview 20, 2017). Villagers in government-controlled areas (C1) are also not satisfied with the name, "because we are Mon, not Myanmar" (Focus group 10, 2017). Unsurprisingly, villagers in NMSP-controlled areas (C2) actively support the change of name: "I would like to change it so much, even since before I was born. Others feel the same" (Focus group 9, 2017). While most people interviewed supported changing the country's name, some had reservations. For Dr Aung Naing Oo, Deputy Speaker of the Mon State

Parliament who is strongly opposed to the bridge naming decision, the country's name is not as important as local names (Interview 23, 2017). For the NMSP, it is a sensitive issue that should not be discussed yet (Interview 2, 2016).

## Claims for access to economic opportunities

The institutionalization of differential treatment between Bamar and Mon people is most obvious in the economic sector. This is especially evident in the exploitation of natural resources in ethnic nationality states (see Gabusi, Chapter 6 in this volume). Pointing to the economic dominance of the Bamar, many Mon people feel like they are "second class citizens" (Focus groups 1–4, 2016). A common grievance among Mon intellectuals (E2) is the exploitation of natural resources by the central government without sharing the benefits with ethnic people living in the area where the resources came from. As a CSO member put it: "We cannot feel that we are part of a nation if we are exploited" (Interview 15, 2016). In addition, discrimination makes access to job opportunities or higher positions more difficult for an ethnic person (Interview 5, 2016). For people in government-controlled areas (C1) economic hardship is a major concern. A Chaung Zon woman voiced that: "Livelihood is the main challenge as for us it is hard to get money so it is hard to eat" (Focus group 8, 2017). Farmers in Chaung Zon Township also complain that they find it difficult to make any profit because of high labour costs and low rice prices (Focus group 11, 2017). In NMSP-controlled areas (C2), villagers said that "during the civil war, it was very difficult to find income for our survival. Now, it has only changed a little bit" (Focus group 9, 2017).

Policies that promote equal access to economic opportunities can effectively address insecurities caused by exploitation and discrimination. According to Mikesell and Murphy (1991, p. 588) "access claims" include demands for policies aimed at tackling discrimination through employment, advancement opportunities and subsidies. Access to social welfare programs can be a concrete way to build trust and sustain political legitimacy (see Yaw Bawm and Griffiths, Chapter 3 in this volume). Reflecting this, many urban intellectuals suggest the adoption of a number of policies that would make ethnic people feel that they benefit from being part of the state-wide community.

Firstly, the products of natural resource exploitation should benefit local people, with a priority towards local development. For instance, community activists (E2) would like to see that companies also contribute to the development of the local area and employ local people. In government-controlled areas (C1), young women in Thanbyuzat argue that the government should use money from natural resources to support ethnic people, especially the youth (Focus group 14, 2017). Villagers in Kyaikmayaw Township (C2) would simply like the nearby coalmine operation to stop as it has negative health and environmental impacts (Focus group 13, 2017).

In the agricultural sector, farmers (C1) would like the government to help maintain stable market prices and create loans to help farmers buy machines, and therefore save time, money and make more of a profit (Focus group 11, 2017). This in turn, notes a monk (E1), would also have a positive impact on Mon identity, as Mon farmers would keep working on their farms rather than migrating to foreign countries (Interview 10). Access to land that was previously confiscated by the military would also not only improve ethnic people's economic situation but it would also help reduce feelings of unfairness and insecurity. For example a villager from Ye Township (C2) said: "The government school was built on my land. I would like to get my land back but I don't dare to do anything" (Focus group 9, 2017).

The creation of job opportunities is another major priority. In rural areas under government control (C1), people perceive employment as essential to help families stay together instead of sending family members to work abroad (Focus group 12, 2017). For a group of women in Chaung Zon Township, it is important that people can work according to their education level. "Only people familiar with the government can get good opportunities even if they are university graduates" (Focus group 8, 2017). In an NMSP-controlled village (C2), a shopkeeper said that "good jobs and good salaries would be enough to make us proud of our country" (Focus group 9, 2017). Youth in Kyaikmayaw Township would like to get vocational training to increase their family's income (Focus group 13, 2017). A village leader in Chaung Zon Township (E2) also highlighted that affirmative actions supporting the inclusion of people from all ethnic backgrounds in the administration with a majority of Mon in the local government departments would effectively promote a sense of inclusion (Interview 14, 2016).

In other rural areas, particularly in NMSP-controlled Ye and

Kyaikmayaw Townships (C2), but also in Paung and Mudon Townships (C1), villagers have also requested the improvement of road infrastructure and health facilities. "If we do not have education, we can survive but without health we cannot survive" (Focus groups 9, 2017).

## Claims for participation

Whether explicitly or implicitly, all social groups referred to the existence of deeply entrenched structural inequalities as an obvious factor of non-inclusion. Among the elite, NMSP officers (E1) condemn the very centralized 2008 Constitution, which gives most powers to the central government (Interview 3, 2016). Among the urban elite (E2), a monk highlighted that "after independence, the country was divided into seven states and seven divisions; it is not fair because for each ethnic state the Bamar took one division" (Interview 20, 2017). If we look at the legislative power, Min Soe Lin, Mon representative at the national parliament, notes that with only five per cent of ethnic representatives the electoral system does not support ethnic representation. This obstacle is reinforced by the impossiblity to ask any question without the agreement of the Chairman speaker (Interview 22, 2017). If we look at the executive power, the Bamar dominate the Union government ministries. In addition, special representation with the new Ministry of Ethnic Affairs at the Union level is not effective because it is a new, not-well-established department (Interview 22, 2017). A monk commented that the Bamar also dominate the state governments with only a few Mon ministers in the Mon state government (interview 21, 2017). Moreover, chief ministers of ethnic states are appointed by the central government, leaving no chance for ethnic states to have a say on the designation of their head of states.[13] Likewise, Bamar officers dominate the General Administrative Department and the civil service in general. Villagers from Mudon Township point out the following problem: "Here ninety per cent of the people are Mon, but the elite is Bamar, appointed by the government" (Focus group 10, 2017). Other villagers in Paung Township deplore that although the village is Mon, the Mon Chairman has no power (Focus group 12, 2017). Lastly, the inefficiency of the judicial power, also dominated by Bamar people, is even worse for ethnic people as a result of language issues: "When we have a court case, Mon people are not able to speak Mon in courts so it is a problem when people do not understand the Burmese language" (Focus group 12, 2017).

Measures promoting equal participation could effectively address insecurities caused by structural inequalities. Mikesell and Murphy (1991, p. 588) associate "participation claims" with demands for power sharing and input in decision-making, which can be achieved through proportional representation, quotas in government and special legislative majorities or vetoes.

The Mon elite usually considered that meaningful equality should be achieved through participation. Among the urban elite (E2), an MNP member noted that people would like to hear more statements such as Aung San Suu Kyi's declaration, "our Bamar group is an ethnic group" .According to him, this kind of statement is very positive for nation building because it implies a sense of equality with other ethnic groups (Interview 6, 2016).[14] More radically, many consider that such equality could only be achieved through changing the borders, so that the Bamar would have only one state instead of seven regions. This, argues a village leader, would ensure that the Amyotha Hluttaw (Upper House) would represent ethnicity rather than population (Interview 14, 2016).[15] However, since all states are ethnically very mixed, many doubt the feasibility of redefining borders.

For the NMSP (E1), power sharing could be achieved through different means that do not involve dealing with the sensitive question of borders. For instance, representatives of Mon people should be able to elect Mon State's chief minister instead of the current presidential appointment. In addition, special representation through reserved seats could be granted to ethnic groups who are minorities within ethnic states (Interview 3, 2016).

## Claims for separation or cultural autonomy

For decades, a number of restrictive policies implemented by the military government have put Mon identity under threat of extinction. Although things have changed since the ceasefire was signed in 1995, the restriction on teaching Mon language in government schools since the 1960s and to a lesser extent the non-recognition of Mon national day[16] are still perceived as significant obstacles to the preservation of Mon identity.

For many years, children who attended government schools could only learn Mon language in Mon monasteries during summer literacy programs run by the Mon Literature and Culture Committee (South and Lall 2016, p. 137). Teaching Mon literature in government schools has been possible since 2014 (Lawi Weng 2014) but there is a lack of supportive measures from the government: it is not compulsory, there are no exams and classes mostly take place before or after school time (Interview 8, 2016). This language restriction is reinforced at home where Mon parents often speak in Burmese because they are worried that their children will face difficulties at school if they are not fluent (Interview 4, 2016). As a result, many Mon people who have been living alongside Bamar people cannot speak the Mon language at all (Interview 2, 2016).[17] This reality is often reflected in government-controlled areas (C1). For instance, in Kahnwa village, Chaungzon Township, although Mon is the mother tongue, villagers tend to use Burmese even when they communicate amongst each other because it is the common language used for everyday transactions (Focus group 8, 2017). However, the situation is different in places under NMSP control where the armed group established an independent education system in 1972, the Mon National Schools.[18] Unlike in government-controlled areas, villagers in Ye Township (C2) do not feel that there is any threat to Mon identity: "We can protect our Mon language, this is not a problem for us because our area is under NMSP control" (Focus group 9, 2017). [19]

Cultural autonomy could positively address insecurities caused by government restrictions on language and culture. According to Mikesell and Murphy (1991, p. 588), "cultural autonomy claims" refer to demands for a non-territorial form of autonomy in order to address a group's desire to be exempted from certain social norms. It usually involves the formation of public institutions representing members of a certain group, which typically have the power to make binding regulations and collect taxes in relation to cultural matters (McGarry and O'Leary 2010, p. 255).[20]

It is a general request that teaching Mon literature in government primary schools should always happen during school time and should be extended until high school. For the Mon armed group (E1) institutional arrangements, which move towards decentralization, especially through language and education are the first priorities of ethnic aspirations (Interview 3, 2016). The urban elite (E2) also shared this view. According to a monk, real freedom to maintain culture, literature and traditions would not only imply teaching Mon literature in all government schools in all Mon areas, but also valuing the ethnic literature subject for instance by creating university diplomas (Interview 21, 2017). For farmers in Chaung Zon Township (C1), "if we had real democracy, the government should listen to people, give ethnic rights and give a chance to teach our language fully" (Focus group 11, 2017). Across these groups, the adoption of a mother tongue based multilingual education system is a necessary step.[21]

A number of measures supporting Mon culture were also suggested. Many urban intellectuals (E2) noted the importance of protecting history: "This is the first step towards maintaining identity" (Focus group 2, 2016). Research on Mon history by Mon experts in Mon State and other areas where Mon people live should therefore be conducted (Focus group 3, 2016).[22] In order to promote Mon culture more widely, a monk suggested the establishment of a Mon TV channel, coupled with support to develop the capacity of Mon people to make movies and TV shows in Mon language (Interview 12, 2016). A group of villagers (C1) suggested that Mon history should be reflected in the curriculum so that the younger generation could learn about Mon history not only after school time or during summer schools (Focus group 4, 2016).[23] Mon youths in Karen State (C2) also proposed the promotion of the Mon naming system in order to encourage people to request it in their ID cards instead of the Bamar particles (Focus group 7, 2016).

## Claims for autonomy

The lack of self-determination is perceived as the root cause of all the above-mentioned insecurities (that is, assimilation, exploitation and discrimination, structural inequalities and government restrictions). There is a common sentiment that these insecurities will be perpetuated unless the majority group creates space for ethnic nationality groups to manage their own affairs. The Chaung Zon bridge controversy illustrates this grievance well. Denying the state government the right to choose a local name and using the NLD-dominated national parliament to impose the bridge name led many to feel that nothing has changed although there is a civilian government in power. Member of Parliament Min Soe Lin expressed this view: "The change of name by the national parliament made people feel a lot of pain in their heart. This is totally against the will of our ethnic people. This happened during the peace conference, but in spirit it means that the Bamar occupies the Mon" (Interview 22, 2017). Some villagers (C1) even think that the situation is worse than under the previous military-backed Thein Sein government (Focus groups 10 and 12, 2017). Villagers from Ye township (C2) expressed their frustration that "Myanmar people act as if they own the country" (Focus group 9, 2017).

Territorial autonomy is a central claim as it is the only arrangement that could satisfy demands for self-determination. According to Mikesell and Murphy (1991, p. 588), "autonomy claims" involve demands for territorial control and devolution of powers, which can translate into confederalism, federalism or regional decentralization.

The Mon elite strongly supports autonomy as the only way out of the conflict. For the NMSP (E1), changing the 2008 Constitution to establish a federal system is a top priority (Interview 3, 2016). The 1994 NMSP constitution recommends the creation of a Mon National Democratic Republic within a larger Union of National Democratic Republics (that is, a federal union).[24] The urban elite (E2) perceives decentralization as essential to exercise the right to self-determination provided it is guaranteed by a constitutional arrangement listing the devolution of powers between the central government and the states. This would allow Mon people to choose their own representatives for a Mon State government that would have control over the economy, education, health, and social welfare as well as the capacity to make laws based on the cultural context (Interview 12, 2016). For instance, the Ministry of Natural Resources and Environmental Conservation at the State level should have the power to control the companies that operate in Mon State instead of just being able to receive complaints and wait for the Union government's decision (Interview 13, 2016). Min Soe Lin suggests that Myanmar should adopt several administrative levels of autonomy to address ethnic concerns. For instance, in Shan State, there could be an autonomous state for the Wa, an autonomous region for the Pa-O and a national area for the Lisu (Interview 22, 2017). The urban elite therefore sees federalism as the best way to guarantee control over education, shared ownership of land and natural resources as well as to ensure sufficient budget for development based on local needs (Interview 19, 2016).

Surprisingly, perhaps, many community members also share this view although it is less elaborated. In rural areas under government control (C1), villagers mention that they would like to get equal rights for all people and "create a Union country, not a Myanmar country" (Focus group 11, 2017), where each state could manage themselves instead of being controlled by the Bamar (Focus groups 10 and 12, 2017). In NMSP-controlled areas (C2), people strongly support more autonomy. For young villagers in Kyaikmayaw Township, "the Bamar government should not interfere in

Mon State" (Focus group 13, 2017). Villagers from Ye Township added that if the country changed to federalism, they would want to be governed by the NMSP (Focus group 9, 2017).

## CONCLUDING REMARKS: MON ASPIRATIONS AND THE CURRENT PEACE PROCESS

While showing some elements of progress, the present peace process does not yet address Mon aspirations in a meaningful way. Following the adoption of the NCA, the goal of the current "political dialogue" phase, which takes place within the bi-annual 21st Century Panglong Conferences (Panglong 21),[25] is yet to reach a more comprehensive peace agreement. This agreement, which is meant to pave the way for amending the 2008 Constitution, will deal with the most challenging issues: the type of federalist arrangement, revenue sharing and the question of the integration of EAOs in the military. The NSMP has finally decided to sign the NCA so that it is no longer a simple "observer" and can participate in this process in order to "obtain the right to amend the 2008 constitution" (Shwe Yoe 2018).

In preparation for the second Panglong 21 conference, a series of sub-national consultations were held to discuss proposals to be adopted in the conference. This resulted in a set of forty-one principles covering four sectors: political, economic, social and land/environment. However, these consultations, which only involved NCA signatories—therefore excluding Mon State at the time—were criticized for not being representative (International Crisis Group 2017). The conference was held in May 2017 and reached consensus on the adoption of thirty-seven "principles",[26] which are yet to address the issues identified in this paper.

Some of the political and economic principles adopted at Panglong 21 appear as a positive development towards the satisfaction of "autonomy claims", especially the commitment to the concept of "federal democracy", the sharing of economic management rights and the potential for a land policy that reduces central control. However, progress has been limited so far as there was a staunch disagreement over the Tatmadaw's pre-requisite that EAOs must explicitly discard any prospect of secession and agree to be integrated into a federal army (International Crisis Group 2017). Indeed, these two requirements go directly against the federal state imagined by the EAOs (Kipgen 2017) and as a result the principles of self-determination and state constitutions could not be adopted at the conference. While not asking expressly for a secession clause any more, the NMSP as well as other ethnic armed groups remain opposed to the inclusion of the non-secession clause requested by the Tatmadaw.

The political sector's fourth principle of equality is relevant to "cultural autonomy claims", as it recognizes the right to maintain and promote ethnic languages, traditions and cultures. However, it remains vague and far from the demands for mother tongue-based education. None of the social sector principles further address these issues.

In the economic and social sectors some principles address "access claims" seeking to raise living standards, protect vulnerable people without discrimination, provide equal development opportunities between states and regions and discourage economic monopolization. However, land sector principles do not address clearly the issue of land confiscation.

The national dialogue that is taking place through the Panglong 21 conference process is unprecedented and the agreement on the federal nature of the state undeniably denotes that progress is being made. However, the fact that no meaningful agreement could be reached in the political sector demonstrates the lack of trust between ethnic minorities and the military. This mistrust is reinforced outside the peace talks as illustrated by the decision of the NLD to push for a bridge name that does not recognize Mon identity despite local opposition.

In Myanmar, there is still a "strong Mon nationalist spirit" among the elite as well as among community members. Many do not feel comfortable identifying as Myanmar citizens because this identity is associated with the oppression of the Bamar military and the perpetuation of Bamar privilege. However, this situation is not irreversible as Mon people's attitudes toward ethnicity do provide indicators on how an inclusive national identity can be built. The examination of Mon people's aspirations through Mikesell & Murphy's framework suggests what policies should be prioritized to address insecurities that are causing a feeling of exclusion from the national community.

Structural inequalities and the lack of self-determination appear as the root causes of other insecurities such as assimilation, economic exploitation and government restrictions. Power sharing and territorial autonomy are therefore perceived as the core institutional arrangements that would enable and guarantee the effective implementation of measures promoting a sense of inclusiveness. However, they do not need to be in place for other less sensitive measures to be adopted.

On the contrary, a sequencing of policies that addresses the other insecurities would create a positive space for further political reform. First, the political dialogue should focus on developing policies recognizing and promoting Mon identity. "Symbolic recognition" and "cultural autonomy" would make people feel more secure, which is fundamental to create a sense of belonging (Stepan, Linz, and Yadav 2010, pp. 52–4). Second, since the denial of an equal share in economic life is one of the main grievances, particularly among community members, the political dialogue should prioritize measures ensuring access to economic opportunities to cultivate a feeling of inclusion.

In conclusion, my findings highlight that it is essential to prioritize policies promoting multi-ethnic identity as well as equal access to economic opportunities. Such policies are essential to the peace process. Indeed, they would not challenge the Tatmadaw militarily, but would allow ethnic nationality people to feel more secure about the protection of their unique cultural heritage whilst also supporting a feeling of inclusiveness and trust. These measures would help Myanmar to re-create itself as a multi-national state, building an inclusive national identity that generates loyalty from all of its citizens whilst simultaneously protecting and celebrating ethnic diversity.

## Notes

1   In this paper, "Bamar" and sometimes its English equivalent "Burman" are used interchangeably to refer to members of the Bamar ethnic group or "bamar luu-myo", which represents the majority in the country. "Burmese" refers to the language of this group, "bamar zaga", which is used as a lingua franca throughout the country. While commonly used especially amongst English-speakers "Burmese" will not be used to refer to all citizens of the country because for most non-Bamar, "Burman", "Burmese" and "Bamar" mean the same thing. To complicate the picture, "Myanmar", which replaced "Burma" as a country name in 1988, is often used interchangeably to refer to the Bamar group as in "myanmar luu-myo" as well as to the Burmese language as in "myanmar zaga", which is why, as will be discussed later, Myanmar as a country name is often controversial among non-Bamar people.

2   Interviews were conducted in English when possible or in Mon/Burmese, with an interpreter. While discussions in armed group-controlled areas were always in Mon, conversations in urban and rural areas under government control often defaulted to Burmese or fluctuated between the two languages. This meant

that while conducted with the help of a Mon interpreter, I was able to partly understand interviews that had this dual language feature. While relying partially on translation can alter the data-gathering process, the extensive time spent living with the interpreter, who is also a friend, ensured that she had an in-depth understanding of the research topic and of the questions asked. Further, this provided multiple opportunities to engage in reflective conversations after the interviews.

3    The research participants include 145 Mon people from a range of social groups, such as farmers, villagers, women, youth, teachers, village leaders, monks, civil society members, journalists, political party members, government officials, civil servants and armed group officers. The research is based on 23 interviews with 24 people and 14 focus group discussions including 121 people. The first seven focus group discussions were conducted with the help of three Mon researchers, who are grassroots activists and were selected with the support of the interpreter. The researchers attended a two-day preparation workshop prior to conducting focus group discussions on their own. The workshops introduced the concepts studied and gave an opportunity for the researchers to be involved in the design of the questions and activities. Upon completion of the focus group discussions, the researchers met again to present and analyse the data gathered, again with support from the interpreter. While such a method enables reaching out to a wider number of people from different townships and walks of life, it is not devoid of possible bias. As a result the researcher conducted the following focus group discussions in person.

4    General Ne Win in 1962 as well as General Saw Maung in 1991 made statements denying the need for a separate Mon identity (South 2003, p. 33).

5    Raman and Ramanya can also be spelt as Yaman or Yamanya since it is sometimes pronounced differently.

6    Although it is anticipated that the census data on ethnicity will be released in the near future, the methodology used was deeply flawed, mostly because it was based around the 135 groups that are officially recognized—an out-dated colonial legacy—that it is unlikely to provide accurate data when it comes to questions of ethnic identity (Transnational Institute 2014).

7    Several nationalist movements preceded the NMSP and its armed wing, the MNLA. The first Mon political organization, United Mon Association (UMA), was established in 1945. The Mon Freedom League was the first Mon political party established in 1947, followed by the creation of several Mon nationalist movements, conceived as umbrella groups, the Mon Affairs Organization (MAO) and the Mon United Front (MUF). The first Mon armed organization, the Mon National Defence Organization, was established in 1948 as the military wing of the MFL-MUF. Mon People's Solidarity Group was established in 1952 to reunite the Mon insurgent forces and was reorganized as Mon People's Front

in 1955. The NMSP was initially formed as an underground organization in 1958 after the MPF signed a ceasefire with the U Nu government. For detailed information see South 2003, Chapter 7, Burma and the Mon: 1945–1962, pp. 99–124.

8   For a list of the main EAOs and their ceasefire status, see International Crisis Group (2017).

9   Out of twenty-one active EAOs, only eight groups initially signed the NCA in October 2015. The NMSP was among the ten groups that refused to sign the NCA, mainly because three EAOs, which haven't signed a bilateral ceasefire with the Tatmadaw yet, have been excluded from the negotiations. However, since only NCA signatories can participate in the political dialogue, the NMSP expressed in May 2017 its intention to join the NCA (Hintharnee 2017), which was officially confirmed in January 2018.

10  NMSP-controlled areas include the southern part of Ye Township and some villages in Kyeikmayaw Township, Mon State as well as some villages in Kyarinn Seik Gyi Township, Karen State.

11  However, a monk (interview 27, 2017) claims that the alms bowl itself used to be a Mon symbol that was appropriated by the Bamar, highlighting the ancient character of the Mon civilization, of which the Bamar have taken numerous elements.

12  The entire Chaung Zon Township is situated on an island known as "Bilugyun", which literally means "Ogre Island".

13  Some chief ministers are of ethnic background though, such as current Mon Chief Minister Aye Zan.

14  However, one should note the way in which such a statement is only selectively employed by the Bamar to emphasize solidarity when it is politically expedient and how rarely their language includes themselves in words like *"taingyintha"* that is commonly used to designate only *minority* ethnic groups.

15  Although Nicholas Farrelly (2016, p. 56)'s research demonstrates that the present system of parliamentary constituencies is actually skewed towards representation of ethnic nationalities in the *Pyithu Hluttaw* (lower house), some interviewees also claim that the redefinition of the borders to align geography with the majority group in a given area would help promote representation of the majority group at the *Pyi Ne Hluttaw* (state parliament) as well as in the lower house (Interview 18, 2016).

16  The non-recognition of Mon national days is yet another example of government restrictions that has accelerated the destruction of Mon culture. Mon National Day is the most popular celebration for Mon people as it offers an opportunity to exhibit Mon strength and unity and encourage cultural and linguistic resurgence (South 2003, p. 38). While large-scale cultural celebrations with traditional dances, music and food are now allowed, villagers from Chaung Zon Township

(C1) still complain that "it is not easy to get a permit from government offices to organize our Mon activities, so we don't feel equal" (Focus group 8, 2017). Further, many complain that only a few people can enjoy this cultural event because it is not recognized as a public holiday. Unsurprisingly, villagers living in NMSP-controlled areas (L2) have a different perspective: "We have no problem to hold our national day celebrations. This year, we did not set up the Union flag and Burmese soldiers did not say anything" (Focus group 9, 2017).

17  Some only learned the Mon language as adults, often when attending training run by exile groups in Thailand (Interview 19, 2016).

18  The Mon National Schools now include 121 primary schools, 12 middle schools and 3 high schools (Interview 9, 2016) with 20,000 pupils according to Min Soe Lin (Interview 22, 2017). With the open goal of maintaining ethnic identity, all subjects are taught in Mon and have a focus on Mon history while preserving the existence of linkages to the government school system (South and Lall 2016, pp. 137–9).

19  However, the parallel Mon education system has a number of limitations. A group of youths from Kyarinn Seik Gyi Township, Karen State are concerned that not being able to speak Burmese properly is a major challenge for children attending Mon Schools particularly if they try to enrol in government schools (Focus group 7, 2016). Furthermore, many cast doubts on the capacity of Mon schools to effectively maintain Mon literature in the long term. Mon teachers in Karen State as well as villagers in Ye Township complain that since teacher salaries are very low, many qualified teachers seek better paying positions in government schools, which therefore more students are tempted to join (Focus group 5, 2016; Focus group 9, 2017).

20  This form of autonomy may be granted to all members of a certain group within the state, usually ethnic, cultural, linguistic or religious minorities, regardless of their location in the state. It consists mainly of the right to protect and promote the cultural, linguistic and religious identity of a minority through institutions created by the minority itself and which are actually binding only to people who voluntarily choose to identify with the groups for which it was established (Lapidoth 1997, p. 38). While this system is more likely to be accepted as a temporary step for groups that are geographically concentrated such as the Mon in Mon State, it is particularly suitable for groups that are spread out, and therefore beneficial to minorities within Mon State as well as Mon people living outside of Mon State.

21  Such a system, which was accepted in principle by the government in the Incheon Declaration (UNESCO 2015)dNote>, aims at bridging mother tongue and Burmese language, which acts as a lingua franca to communicate with other ethnic groups. It implies that at the primary school level, teaching is in

the mother tongue and Burmese is a subject; at the middle school level, teaching is in Burmese, and the mother tongue is a subject; at the high school level, teaching is in English while Burmese and mother tongue are subjects. While started in some government schools, this system has yet to be implemented beyond kindergarten in rural areas (Interview 9, 2016).

22  However, research conducted by non-Mon people does not appear as important although this could positively counterbalance the tendency to potentially adopt a lower threshold of verification for factual histories of her or his own group as described by Patrick McCormick (2010).

23  New textbooks designed for Mon communities were however developed with the support of UNICEF in 2016. See (Mon Htaw 2016).

24  This Union would be "based on equal rights of self-determination for all ethnic people, including the Mon National Democratic Republic", an arrangement that would ensure "a fully democratic system" and "multi-nationality unity" (South 2003, p. 171).

25  This "political dialogue" phase was envisaged by the previous government as a series of "Union Peace Conferences", which were later rebranded by Aung San Suu Kyi as "21st Century Panglong Conferences" (Panglong 21) in reference to the pre-independence Panglong conference, summoned by Aung San, the independence hero and her father. The first "Panglong 21 conference" held in August 2016 launched the NLD-led political dialogue. Its main achievement was rather symbolic: "This was the first time in more than fifty years that [representatives of almost all armed groups were] able to express their desires and pent up aspirations to a national audience without fear of being arrested and put in prison" (Euro-Burma Office 2016).

26  For a detailed list of the thirty-seven principles, see Ministry of information 2017.


## Interviews and focus group discussions:

Semi-structured interviews:
Interview 1: Mon Women Network, Mawlamyine, July 2016
Interview 2: Mon National School teacher, Mawlamyine, July 2016
Interview 3: New Mon State party, Vice Chairman Nai Hongsar, and another officer, Mawlamyine, July 2016
Interview 4: Mon Women Organization, Mawlamyine, July 2016
Interview 5: Nai Shwe Kyin Foundation, Mawlamyine, July 2016
Interview 6: Mon National Party member, Yangon and Mawlamyine, June 2016
Interview 7: Elected member of Municipality Council, Thanbyuzayat Township, July 2016

Interview 8: Mon Women Organization, Mawlamyine June 2016
Teacher 9: Mon National School teacher, Mawlamyine, June 2016
Interview 10: Monk, Mawlamyine, August 2016
Interview 11: Mon National Party member, Yangon, June 2016
Interview 12: Senior Mon National Party member, Mawlamyine, August 2016
Interview 13: Ministry of Natural Resources Department, Mawlamyine, August 2016
Interview 14: Village Development Committee Board member, Kahnyaw village,
    Chaungzon Township, August 2016
Interview 15: Mon Youth Progressive organization, member, Mawlamyine, July 2016
Interview 16: Human Rights Foundation of Monland (HURFOM), Mawlamyine,
    July 2016
Interview 17: Thanlwin Times, Mawlamyine, August 2016
Interview 18: Postgraduate student, Australia, November 2015
Interview 19: Youth Initiative Human Rights (YIHR), Mawlamyine, June 2016
Interview 20: Monk, Chaung Zon Township, June 2017
Interview 21: Monk, Chaung Zon Township, June 2017
Interview 22: Min Soe Lin, Member of Parliament, representative of Ye Township,
    June 2017.
Interview 23: Dr Aung Naing Oo, Deputy Speaker at the Mon State Parliament

Focus Group Discussions:
FGD1: Youths, Paung and Chaungzon Townships, August 2016
FGD 2: Political parties, Paung and Chaung Zon Townships, August 2016
FGD 3: Civil servants, Paung and Chaung Zon Townships, August 2016
FGD 4: Villagers, Paung and Chaung Zon Townships, August 2016
FGD 5: Mon School teachers, Weangsapaw Village, Kyarinn Seik Gyi Township,
    Karen State, August 2016
FGD 6: Villagers, Weangsapaw Village, Kyarinn Seik Gyi Township, Karen State,
    August 2016
FGD 7: Youths, Weangsapaw Village, Kyarinn Seik Gyi Township, Karen State,
    August 2016
FGD 8: Women villagers, Kahnwa village, Chaung Zon Township, June 2017
FGD 9: Villagers, Kabyarwa village, Ye Township, June 2017
FGD10: Villagers in Mudon Township, July 2017
FGD 11: Men villagers, Kahnwa village, Chaung Zon Township
FGD 12: Villagers, Paung Township, July 2017
FGD 13: Villagers, Kyaikmayaw Township, July 2017
FGD 14: Women villagers, Thanbyuzayat Township, July 2017

# References

Aung-Thwin, Michael. *Myth and History in the Historiography of Early Burma : Paradigms, Primary Sources, and Prejudices.* Singapore: Institute of Southeast Asian Studies, 1998.

Bauer, Christian. "Language and Ethnicity: The Mon in Burmma and Thailand." In *Ethnic Groups Across National Boundaries in Mainland Southeast Asia,* edited by Gehan Wijeyewardene. Singapore: Institute of Southeast Asian Studies, 1990.

Brown. *The State and Ethnic Politics in Southeast Asia.* London: Routledge, 1994.

Coedés, George. *The Making of South East Asia.* Berkeley: University of California Press, 1966.

Euro-Burma Office. Political monitor No 20, 2016.

Farrelly, Nicholas. "Electoral Sovereignty in Myanmar's Borderlands." In *Myanmar's Mountain and Maritime Borderscapes: Local Practices, Boundary-making and Figured Worlds,* edited by Su-Ann Oh. Singapore: ISEAS-Yusof Ishak Institute, 2016.

Ghai, Yash P. "Ethnicity and Autonomy: A Framework for Analysis." In *Autonomy and Ethnicity: Negotiating Competing Claims in Multi-ethnic States,* edited by Yash P. Ghai. Cambridge: Cambridge University Press, 2000.

Gravers, Mikael. *Nationalism as Political Paranoia in Burma : An Essay on the Historical Practice of Power.* 2nd ed. Richmond: Routledge Curzon, 1999.

Guillon, Emmanuel. *The Mons: A Civilization of Southeast Asia.* Edited by James V. Di Crocco. Bangkok: Siam Society under Royal Patronage, 1999.

Gurr, Ted Robert. *Peoples Versus States: Minorities at Risk in the New Century.* Washington, D.C.: United States Institute of Peace Press, 2000.

Hall, D.G.E. *Burma.* New York: Hutchinson's University Library, 1974.

Halliday, Robert, and Christian Bauer. *The Mons of Burma and Thailand.* Vol. 1. Bangkok: White Lotus Press, 2000.

Harrisson, A.P. and H.M. Kyed Von Sponek. "Ceasefire State-Makings: Justice Provision in Karen and Mon Controlled Areas." Myanmar Update Conference, Canberra, 2017.

Hintharnee. "New Mon State Party to Sign Nationwide Ceasefire Agreement." *The Irrawaddy,* 2017.http://www.irrawaddy.com/news/burma/128581.html. Accessed 12/05/2017

Houtman, Gustaaf. *Mental Culture in Burmese Crisis Politics : Aung San Suu Kyi and the National League for Democracy.* Tokyo: Tokyo University of Foreign Studies, Institute for the Study of Languages and Cultures of Asia and Africa, 1999.

Htet Naing Zaw. "Lower House Names Mon State Bridge after Gen Aung San Despite Protest." *The Irrawaddy,* 2017. Accessed 27/03/2017. https://http://www.irrawaddy.com/news/mon-state-bridge-renamed-controversy.html.

Immigration and Manpower Department. Mon State 1983 Population Census. Rangoon: Government of the Union of Myanmar, Ministry of Home and Religious Affairs, 1987.

International Crisis Group. *Building Critical Mass for Peace in Myanmar.* 2017.

Kipgen, Nehginpao. "The Continuing Challenges of Myanmar's Peace Process." *The Diplomat,* 2017. https://thediplomat.com/2017/06/the-continuing-challenges-of-myanmars-peace-process/. Accessed 01/10/2017.

Kymlicka, Will. *Multicultural Citizenship : A Liberal Theory of Minority Rights.* Oxford: Oxford University Press, 1995.

Lall, Marie and Hla Win. "Perceptions of the State and Citizenship in Light of the 2010 Myanmar Elections." In *Myanmar's Transition: Openings, Obstacles and Opportunities,* edited by Monique Skidmore and Trevor Wilson. Singapore: ISEAS, 2013.

Lapidoth, Ruth Eschelbacher. *Autonomy: Flexible Solutions to Ethnic Conflicts.* Washington, D.C: United States Institute of Peace Press, 1997.

Lawi Weng. "Mon State to Allow Ethnic Language Classes in Government Schools." *The Irrawaddy,* 2014. https://http://www.irrawaddy.com/news/burma/mon-state-allow-ethnic-language-classes-govt-schools.html. Accessed 01/03/2017.

Linz, Juan J. and Alfred C. Stepan. 1996. *Problems of Democratic Transition and Consolidation : Southern Europe, South America, and Post-Communist Europe.* Baltimore: Johns Hopkins University Press, 1996.

Luce, Gordon H. and Bo-Hmu Ba Shin. "Old Burma: Early Pagán." *Artibus Asiae. Supplementum* 25 (1969):iii–422.

McCormick, Patrick. "Mon Histories: Between Translation and Retelling." ProQuest, UMI Dissertations Publishing, 2010.

McGarry, John, and Brendan O'Leary. "Territorial Approaches to Ethnic Conflict Settlement." In *Routledge Handbook of Ethnic Conflict,* edited by Karl Cordell and Stefan Wolff. Abingdon: Routledge, 2010.

Mikesell, Marvin and Alexander Murphy. "A Framework for Comparative Study of Minority-Group Aspirations." *Annals of the Association of American Geographers* 81 (4) 1991:581.

Ministry of Information. 37 Points Signed as Part of Pyidaungsu Accord. 2017.

Nai Hongsar. "Nai Hong Sar message, Part 1." 2014. http://www.burmaenac.org/?p=131. Accessed 28/02/2017.

Salem-Gervais, Nicolas, and Rosalie Metro. "A Textbook Case of Nation-Building: The Evolution of History Curricula in Myanmar." *Journal of Burma Studies* 16 (1) 2012: 27–78.

Smith, Anthony D. *The Ethnic Origins of Nations.* Oxford: B. Blackwell, 1987.

South, Ashley. *Mon Nationalism and Civil War in Burma : The Golden Sheldrake.* London: Routledge Curzon, 2003.

South, Ashley. "Ceasefires and Civil Society: The Case of the Mon." In *Exploring Ethnic Diversity in Burma,* edited by Mikael Gravers. Copenhagen: NIAS Press, 2007.

South, Ashley. *Ethnic Politics in Burma States of Conflict.* New York: Routledge, 2008.

South, Ashley and Marie Lall. "Language, Education and the Peace Process in Myanmar." *Contemporary Southeast Asia* 38 (1) 2016:128–53.

Stepan, Alfred, Juan Linz and Yogendra Yadav. "The Rise of 'State-Nations'." *Journal of Democracy* 21 (3) 2010: 50–68.

Taylor, Robert H. *The State in Burma.* Honolulu: University of Hawaii Press, 1987.

Transnational Institute. "Ethnicity without meaning, data without context." 2014.

UNESCO. Incheon Declaration, 2015. *Education 2030: Towards Inclusive and Equitable Quality Education and Lifelong Learning for All.*

Walton, Matthew. "The 'Wages of Burman-ness': Ethnicity and Burman Privilege in Contemporary Myanmar." *Journal of Contemporary Asia* 43 (1) 2013:1–27.

Walton, Matthew J. "Has the NLD Learned Nothing About Ethnic Concerns?" *Tea Circle,* 2017. https://teacircleoxford.com/2017/03/29/has-the-nld-learned-nothing-about-ethnic-concerns/. Accessed 29/03/17.

# V
## Epilogue

# 13

## REFLECTIONS ON MYANMAR UNDER THE NLD SO FAR

Matthew Walton

2016 was supposed to be the time for change in Myanmar. Swept to power on the strength of that slogan, the National League for Democracy would finally get to form a government and realize a democratic transition decades in the making. Even the most cynical Myanmar observer could find reasons to be excited about this crucial step in the process of transferring power from the military to civilian leaders. Yes, the 2008 Constitution still institutionalized military rule in a variety of ways. Yes, a host of seemingly intractable problems remained, including a lagging peace process with ethnic armed groups and persistent anti-Muslim sentiment—especially toward the Rohingya. And yes, it was worrying that the party that was about to take over governing had virtually no experience in doing so, and hadn't really demonstrated much expertise (or interest) in policy development throughout its single-minded campaign. Even with all of these concerns, to see Daw Aung San Suu Kyi and her colleagues achieve the victory that had been deferred since 1990 gave reason to hope that her widespread support could translate into progress in national reconciliation, economic development, political reform, and a host of other areas.

This political update was originally presented in February 2017, weeks away from the NLD government's first anniversary. At that time, I noted that it was not easy to find the success stories. Indeed, having now passed the second anniversary, in most respects, the situation looks frustratingly not only bleaker than it was a year in, but worse than it did under the previous USDP government. With the international outcry against Myanmar's actions against the Rohingya showing no signs of abating, and the long-term effects of that conflict being added to an already-long list of challenges, the country's prospects for further political or economic development are dimming.

## ETHNIC CONFLICT AND THE PEACE PROCESS

Eager to show its commitment to national reconciliation, the NLD sought to prioritize the peace process. When Daw Aung San Suu Kyi re-branded the national political dialogue as the "21st Century Panglong Conference," it was a chance to establish her government's ownership over the process and inject a new spirit by linking it to the famous conference convened by her father in 1947. Despite worries that the NLD might move too quickly, the August 2016 conference proceeded more like a listening convention than a negotiating session, with various groups having an open platform to share their perspectives and plans. It was, although not a triumph, generally thought to be a success, if only because it avoided any catastrophic blunders.

But since that time, only two smaller groups have signed the Nationwide Ceasefire Agreement (NCA) and in fact, the situation on the ground has deteriorated. Sporadic fighting continued and in some places, intensified, throughout 2016 and 2017 between the military and ethnic armed groups in Kachin and Shan States, exacerbating an already-intolerable IDP crisis. Indeed, one of the tragedies of Myanmar's politics is that there are so many tragedies spread throughout the country that inevitably serious and unacceptable human suffering gets virtually ignored in favour of more compelling stories. The situation of IDPs in Kachin and Shan States, who have been regularly cut off from most sources of aid for a number of years, is one of those stories that has been shamefully under-reported by the media and remains inexplicably unaddressed by the Myanmar government.

In a risky but understandable move, a coalition of EAGs called the "Northern Alliance"—which includes the Kachin Independence Army

(KIA), Myanmar National Democratic Alliance Army (MNDAA), Ta'ang National Liberation Army (TNLA) and Arakan Army (AA)—attacked Tatmadaw positions in November 2016, effectively upping the stakes, but concluding that, without sympathy from the NLD government for their negotiating positions, they must protect their territory and demonstrate to their constituencies that they continue to fight for ethnic rights. With the gradual unravelling of the United Nationalities Federal Council, the umbrella group that had been leading in negotiations up to the signing of the NCA, a new coalition emerged in 2017 that included the members of the Northern Alliance along with the powerful United Wa State Army (UWSA), and other groups. This body, called the Federal Political Negotiation and Consultative Committee (FPNCC), has been increasingly assertive in participating in the peace process and in negotiating directly with the Myanmar government. Yet it is unclear whether the pattern of regularly shifting alliances and allegiances among ethnic armed groups benefits anyone but the Tatmadaw, which seems perfectly capable of waiting out the confusion to continue the status quo.

In addition to the strong military response to the Northern Alliance's offensive, the government's negotiating team also dug in its heels and adopted the military's long-standing position that the only way to dialogue is by signing the NCA. This stance was repeatedly reinforced by both government and military spokespeople throughout 2017, including during the lead-up to the second anniversary of the signing of the NCA in October. The military rhetoric during the May 2017 session of the 21st Century Panglong Conference saw hardened stances on language related to secession and self-determination, some of the most contentious yet essential topics of discussion, for which there appears to be limited prospect for agreement. This represents a dangerous situation for the ethnic armed groups and for non-Burman populations more generally, since the ethnic Burman majority public has been fickle in its support for ethnic armed movements and their longstanding demands for federalism and devolution of power.

Given all of this, it is hard to see what productive outcomes might emerge from the 21st Century Panglong process. The May 2017 meeting took place after more than a month of delays and subsequent meetings have been postponed as well. The ability of the government to facilitate agreement on challenging issues (and more importantly, to implement meaningful and effective reforms to fix them) seems more limited than ever, as much of its attention is now taken up with the crisis in Rakhine State. Additionally, we shouldn't forget that these concerns regarding the peace process and continued fighting run parallel to persistent complaints that the dialogue process itself isn't sufficiently or meaningfully inclusive and participatory. Myanmar's vibrant, influential, and sometimes progressive civil society organizations have largely been allowed to participate only as observers, with at most, indirect input into the process. Granted, it has been an important development to witness dynamic meetings and consultations at local and state levels, as different groups prepare for the next national meeting. But in the absence of clear processes and mechanisms for incorporating these diverse citizen concerns into nationwide deliberations, this is likely to remain an elite-driven process.

## RELIGIOUS CONFLICT AND THE ROHINGYA CRISIS

Turning to the other major area of conflict in the country, the attack on security forces on the Rakhine State border with Bangladesh, carried out by militants in October 2016, not only reignited active conflict but fundamentally changed the political dynamics of this persistent dispute. The initial result was a brutal clampdown by security forces that continued into 2017, accompanied by regular and credible reports of extrajudicial killing, rape, and the burning of Rohingya villages.

The stakes were raised even higher when the insurgent group, which changed its name from Harakah al-Yaqin ("Faith Movement") to the Arakan Rohingya Salvation Army (ARSA) in March 2017, conducted coordinated attacks on police posts in late August 2017. Although still only crudely equipped and loosely organized, this second wave provoked an even more vicious response from the Myanmar military. In the six weeks following the ARSA attacks, more than half a million Rohingya had fled northern Rakhine State, mostly to overcrowded camps inside the Bangladesh border. Few would dispute Myanmar's right to respond to the attacks, but the heavy-handed retaliation, which also included the burning of countless Rohingya villages, touched off uncharacteristically strong criticism from Muslim-majority ASEAN nations and near-universal global condemnation of the country.

Somewhat remarkably, given Myanmar's divided political dynamics—but not surprisingly to anyone aware of the level of vitriol directed toward the Rohingya from inside the country—Myanmar's population appears to be almost completely unified on this issue. Domestic sentiment has strongly supported not just Daw Aung San Suu Kyi and the NLD government, but also the Tatmadaw, against the criticisms of the world. "Fake news" has become a rallying cry on Myanmar social media, but the moral standing of the former Nobel Laureate has been tarnished, probably irreparably.

And in fact, while the blame for the absolutely unjustified violence must be put squarely at the feet of the security forces (over which the NLD government has no control), what is at issue is how the government has responded to the crisis. In the face of calls for more transparency and restraint, the government instead forcefully denied the allegations and put public pressure on journalists seeking to cover the story. The arrest and continued detention of two Burmese Reuters journalists in late 2017, having been set up by security forces, has marked the nadir of a rapidly-deteriorating respect for freedom of the press. In a preposterous move, the Ministry of Religion and Cultural Affairs announced that it would be conducting a definitive study of the true history of Myanmar that would demonstrate that the Rohingya were not an ethnicity in the country's history. A spokesperson for the State Counsellor's Office shared a video on social media that allegedly depicted "Bengalis" (as Rohingya are commonly referred to in Myanmar) burning their own homes. After it was quickly debunked, he issued a disingenuous statement warning people not to spread unproven claims that could further inflame the crisis.

Although many of those that study this conflict have, in the past, cautioned against making the argument that continued repression of the Rohingya could generate an armed resistance—not wanting to give the government or military ammunition for pre-emptive action—it is somewhat remarkable that it has taken this long for armed resistance to emerge. And even though it has, it is very important to keep in perspective the scope of this potential threat. In an interview at the start of 2017, one of the alleged leaders of ARSA said that the attackers didn't even have firearms until they stole them from a depot they targeted. The further problem, beyond the overwhelmingly imbalanced security response, has been the tendency of not just military spokespeople, but government representatives, journalists and activists to label the entire Rohingya population as terrorists, based on the actions of a group that, even at the beginning of 2018, appears to have no more than a few thousand fighters.

The creation of an Advisory Commission on Rakhine State, headed by former UN Secretary-General Kofi Annan, was supposed to represent a way forward, to find a middle ground between domestic interests and international concerns. However, the Commission might have been hamstrung at its conception, as it was greeted with protests and boycotts from its very first visit in September 2016. ARSA's leadership clearly sought to undermine the initiative further, launching its August attacks the day after the Commission issued its findings and recommendations. A parallel domestic commission was predictable in its denials and delays and yet another parallel international advisory body was subjected to harsh criticism with the frustrated public resignation of US politician (and former close ally of Daw Aung San Suu Kyi) Bill Richardson. All of these advisory groups face a nearly impossible task, as early on in its tenure, the NLD government unwisely pursued a course of confrontation with Rakhine political groups, exacerbating the current oppositional attitude. This hostility was further entrenched after police shot and killed eight Rakhine people after a public event turned violent in January 2018. Any hope for the re-establishment of peace in Rakhine State depends on the willingness of political leaders to adopt a compromise attitude. But even then, the prospects of reconciliation and reintegration remain bleak.

Looking more broadly, anti-Muslim sentiment is still a matter for concern. While there have been visible cracks in the movement led by Ma Ba Tha—the Organization for the Protection of Race and Religion—Buddhist activism in the country has not dissipated. Other nationalist groups have taken over some of the more high-profile protest roles as Ma Ba Tha has refocused on grassroots organizing and the promotion of Buddhist education. There were some highly visible setbacks and public criticism of the group early in the NLD's tenure. This was ramped up in May 2017 with a statement from the State Sangha Maha Nayaka Committee (the highest Buddhist authority in the country) that officially banned the use of the Ma Ba Tha name. While many of the organization's monastic leaders acquiesced, some chapters resisted, and lay supporting groups multiplied, to continue its work and publications.

Frustratingly, there has been limited concerted attention paid by the government to the persistent problems of hate speech (especially online) or everyday discrimination suffered by religious minorities in Myanmar. We do not yet know for certain whether the tragic and stunning assassination of U Ko Ni, the prominent Muslim lawyer and political activist, in January 2017 was due to his religion, but it seems highly likely (and there has been shockingly little progress on further revealing the network behind his killing). While this was reasonably taken as a chilling warning to all political figures and activists, its effects were felt most strongly by those vulnerable minorities who have primarily experienced the repressive hand of the Burmese state, rather than its protection.

## CIVIL SOCIETY AND COMMUNITY ACTIVISM

In a positive and unsurprising trend, community activism has continued to grow and develop, with groups and networks becoming more vocal and effective in their advocacy efforts. Despite the fact that the armed conflicts in Rakhine, Kachin and Shan States continue to attract most of the attention, land remains the key issue that animates so much discontent in Myanmar and has the power to mobilize people nationwide. The government must tread carefully in its efforts to standardize regulatory practices and make the country a more appealing destination for investment; without robust consumer and citizen protections—including a system of land titling that recognizes the history of largely informal claims—increased economic growth could simply be the catalyst for more civil conflict and opposition.

The disappointing part of this increased activism is that many observers had expected the same vibrancy from an NLD-dominated Parliament that included dozens of former political prisoners and grassroots activists. Unfortunately, this has been actively stymied by party leadership, which restricted its MPs' freedom to talk with the media and closed off opportunities for constructive debate in the legislature by demanding that MPs not ask tough questions that might make the government look bad.

While the NLD still enjoys popular support, there is increasing chatter regarding new opposition parties. The USDP is staking its reputation on national security issues, including the protection of race and religion. This will win it some support, but probably not broad enough to challenge the NLD, although the security-oriented elements of the Rakhine State crisis may have created an opening for the former ruling party to rebuild popularity. Unless the ruling party begins to listen more to popular demands, it could be vulnerable to a new challenger on its left, made up of students, farmers, workers, and disgruntled activists shunned by the NLD leadership in 2015. This could be a powerful oppositional coalition, especially if it was able to create alliances with ethnic parties that did not perform well in the 2015 elections but could benefit from dissatisfaction with the way the NLD is handling the peace process and political dialogue.

Above all, progress will be elusive as long as Myanmar's governance remains a one-woman show. Multiple reports since the NLD took power have described the bottleneck at the top of the government, where most decisions need to be approved by Daw Aung San Suu Kyi. Simply put, a country like Myanmar, which must deal with a multitude of priority issues in a timely fashion, cannot afford to be governed in such a centralized, restrictive fashion. The argument for patience due to lack of capacity was a smokescreen when it was made by the USDP and it is the same under the NLD. The amount of expertise and energy present in Myanmar's impressive array of community-based organizations is staggering and a constant source of inspiration for those interested in the country's political development. The NLD government must fulfil its promises and embrace the power and skill of all of its citizens who have been waiting for this opportunity for decades, if it wants to generate inclusive, just political reforms that will secure the country's still-tentative democratic transition.

# ABBREVIATIONS AND KEY TERMS

| | |
|---|---|
| 969 | Buddhist ethno-nationalist movement |
| AA | Arakan Army |
| ABSDF | All Burma Students' Democratic Front |
| ALD | Arakan League for Democracy |
| ALP | Arakan Liberation Party |
| Amyotha Hluttaw | Upper House, Pyidaungsu Hluttaw |
| ANC | Arakan National Congress |
| ANP | *See* RNP |
| Arakan | *See* Rakhine |
| ARSA | Arakan Rohingya Salvation Army |
| ASEAN | Association of Southeast Asian Nations |
| Bamar | *See* Burman |
| Burman | Majority ethnic group (or its language); also known as Bamar |
| CBO | Community-based organization |
| CNF | Chin National Front |
| CPB | Communist Party of Burma |
| CRPP | Committee Representing the People's Parliament |
| CSO | Civil society organization |
| Dhamma | Buddhist conception of natural law |
| DKBA | Democratic Karen Benevolent Army |
| DDR | Disarmament, demobilization and reintegration |
| EAG | Ethnic armed group |
| EAO | Ethnic armed organization |

| | |
|---|---|
| EHO | Ethnic health organization |
| EITI | Extractive Industries Transparency Initiative |
| GAD | General Administration Department |
| FPNCC | Federal Political Negotiation and Consultative Committee |
| FSER | Framework of Social and Economic Reform |
| HCCG | Health Convergence Core Group |
| Hluttaw | *See* Pyidaungsu Hluttaw |
| IA | Interim arrangement |
| IDEA | Institute for Democracy and Electoral Assistance |
| IDP | Internally displaced person |
| IFES | International Foundation for Electoral Systems |
| IOM | International Organization for Migration |
| INGO | International non-government organisation |
| IRC | International Rescue Committee |
| JICA | Japan International Cooperation Agency |
| JMC | Joint Monitoring Committee |
| Kachin | Ethnic group, language or administrative area in northern Myanmar |
| Karen | *See* Kayin |
| Kayin | Ethnic group, language, or administrative area in eastern Myanmar; also known as Karen |
| KDHW | Karen Department of Health and Welfare |
| KIA | Kachin Independence Army |
| KIO | Kachin Independence Organization |
| KNLA | Karen National Liberation Army |
| KNU | Karen National Union |
| KSDP | Kachin State Democracy Party |
| Kyat | Myanmar currency |
| LNDP | Lisu National Development Party |
| LDU | Lahu Democratic Union |
| MaBaTha | Committee for the Protection of Race and Religion |
| MADB | Myanmar Agricultural Development Bank |
| MEC | Myanmar Economic Corporation |
| MOGE | Myanmar Oil and Gas Enterprises |
| MNDAA | Myanmar National Democratic Alliance Army |

| | |
|---|---|
| MNLA | Mon National Liberation Army |
| MNP | Mon National Party |
| MPC | Myanmar Peace Center |
| Naypyitaw | Myanmar national capital; also Naypyidaw or Nay Pyi Taw |
| NCA | Nationwide Ceasefire Agreement |
| NCCT | Nationwide Ceasefire Coordination Team |
| NDAA | National Democratic Alliance Army |
| NDSC | National Defence and Security Council |
| NGO | Non-governmental organisation |
| NHN | National Health Network |
| NHP | National Health Plan 2017-2021 |
| NLD | National League for Democracy |
| NMSP | New Mon State Party |
| NRPC | National Reconciliation and Peace Centre |
| NUP | National Unity Party |
| Panglong 21 | 21st Century Panglong Conferences |
| PNO | Pa-O National Organisation |
| Pyithu Hluttaw | Lower House of Myanmar's Union Parliament |
| QSEM | Qualitative Social and Economic Monitoring (World Bank) |
| Rakhine | Ethnic group, language, or administrative area in coastal western Myanmar; also known as Arakan |
| RCSS | Restoration Council of Shan State |
| RNP | Rakhine National Party (also known as Arakan National Party) |
| Rohingya | Ethnic group (or language) on coastal border of Bangladesh |
| SAD | Self-Administered Division |
| SAZ | Self-Administered Zone |
| SEZ | Special Economic Zone |
| Shan | Ethnic group, language, or administrative area in hilly northeast Myanmar |
| SLORC | State Law and Order Restoration Council |
| SP | Social Protection |
| SPDC | State Peace and Development Council |
| SSR | Security sector reform |

| | |
|---|---|
| Tatmadaw | Myanmar armed forces |
| TNLA | Ta'ang National Liberation Army |
| TSDG | Thilawa Social Development Group |
| UEC | Union Election Commission |
| UHC | Universal health coverage |
| UMEHL | Union of Myanmar Economic Holdings Ltd. |
| UNFC | United Nationalities Federal Council |
| UNFPA | United Nations Population Fund |
| UNHCR | United Nations High Commissioner for Refugees |
| UPCC | Union Peacemaking Central Committee |
| UPDJC | Union Peace Dialogue Joint Committee |
| UPWC | Union Peacemaking Working Committee |
| USDA | Union Solidarity and Development Association |
| USDP | Union Solidarity and Development Party |
| UWSA | United Wa State Army |
| VTA | Village tract administrator |
| WNO | Wa National Organization |

# INDEX

Notes are indicated by page and note number, for example, "44n6" means note 6 on page 44.

## A

centralization of power, 139
elections 2015 in Kachin State, 146
ethnic parties' views, 147
foreign policy, 214–216
foreign visits, 216–217
and Nationwide Ceasefire
    Agreement, 208–209
in peace process, 235
portfolios, 202
reputational damage from
    Rohingya issue, 219
as source of national legitimacy, 59

# B

Backpack Health Worker Team, 93
    midwife training, 96
Border Area Immigration Control
    Headquarters, Rakhine State, 258
Border Guard Forces, 239
Buddhism, 14, 192, 257, 262, 281
    as tool for legitimacy, 58
Buddhist activism, 265–266, 316
Buddhist flag, 267
Buddhist nationalists, 193 see also
    Committee for the Protection of
    Race and Religion
Burma Medical Association, 93
Burmanization, 7, 278, 286, 287
Burmese Way to Socialism, 57, 64

# C

ceasefire capitalism, 11
    in Kachin State, 144, 145
    and social protection, 69
ceasefire provisions, 239, 240
census, 2014, 113, 267, 281
centralization of power, 139–140
Charles Paton, 254

Chaung Zon Bridge controversy, 7,
    288
    names, 289
    self-determination for minority
        groups, 295
Chin State, village administrators, 28
China, Kachin trade with, 144, 145
Citizenship Act, 1982, 258, 269
civil society networks, 36–37 see also
    advocacy groups
civil-military relations, 8, 203, 212,
    220–221
    post-2016, 205
    under NLD government, 207
"clearance operations", by Tatmadaw,
    4, 14, 218, 251, 257, 265
climate change, 63
colonial rule, legitimacy challenges,
    56
Community Partners International, 95
community-based primary health
    care services, 86 see also Ethnic
    Health Organizations
conflict and economic activity, 140,
    141
Constitution, 1947, 57
Constitution, 2008, 7, 26, 57, 70, 147,
    311
    Article 40(c) , 206–207
    Article 436, 207
    civil-military relations, 203
    emergency provisions, 206
    inequalities in, 292, 296, 297
    legitimacy by consent, 58–59
    and peace process, 239
    referendum, 187
    role of military, 201–202, 212
Constitutional Tribunal 2016, 205
convergence, health, 94–95
and MoHS, 94
corruption, 73

# T

T Khun Myat, 11
Ta'ang National Liberation Army
(TNLA), 213, 234
Tatmadaw, 4, 219, 85
and Burmanization, 277
business interests, 139, 152, 162
ceasefire with New Mon State
Party, 282–283
"clearance operations" in Rakhine
State, 218, 219, 251
Defence White Paper 2016, 204–205
in Kachin State, 144
and NLD government, 202, 203–204
and non-signatory EAOs at second
Panglong 21 conference, 242
in peace process, 212–213
on DDR in Nationwide Ceasefire
Agreement, 212, 221, 236, 239
role post-2016, 206
taxation, 6, 9, 60
Telecommunication Law, 203
telecommunications, 25, 36, 37
and village governance, 39
Ten Duties (Mhin Kyint Thayah Say
Bah), 56, 74n2
terrorism, and Rohingya problem,
252, 259
Than Shwe, 57, 162
Thaung Tun, 208
tha-yè-nah-yè, 64
Thein Sein, 57, 189, 232
new government 2011, 188
Thilawa Special Economic Zone, 164,
165
compensation for land, 166, 169
role of intermediary NGOs, 172
Thilawa Social Development Group,
165, 166–167
three national causes, 57

Thura Shwe Mann, 188, 263–264
purge of, 191
Tin Myo Win, 97
tourism, post-2011, 190
Township Health Working Groups,
101
trust deficit, 59
21st Century Panglong Conference,
138, 235, 312
advocacy groups in, 175
civil society orgs, 314
DDR and SSR, 212
ethnic armed organization
positions, 211–212
ethnic armed organizations at, 210
secession and self-determination,
313
Tatmadaw position, 212–213
Tatmadaw's secession clause,
297–298

# U

U Htin Kyaw, 3
U Ko Ni, 4, 316
U Nu, 257
Union of Myanmar Economic
Holdings Ltd, 139, 162
Union Solidarity and Development
Party government, 57
and advocacy groups, 175
in 2010 elections, 188
and Nationwide Ceasefire
Agreement, 233
and peace process, 211, 232
as opposition party, 317
United Mon Association, 282
United Nationalities Federal Council,
210, 313
"all-inclusiveness" principle, 236
members, 248 n4
and Nationwide Ceasefire
Agreement, 235

www.ingramcontent.com/pod-product-compliance
Lightning Source LLC
Chambersburg PA
CBHW060142280326
41932CB00012B/1600